Jonathan Miller:
One Thing and Another

Selected Writings 1954–2016

One Thing and Another

Selected Writings 1954–2016

Jonathan Miller

Edited by
Ian Greaves

First published in paperback in 2017 by Oberon Books Ltd

521 Caledonian Road, London N7 9RH
Tel: +44 (0) 20 7607 3637 / Fax: +44 (0) 20 7607 3629
e-mail: info@oberonbooks.com
www.oberonbooks.com

A catalogue record for this book is available from the British Library.

PB ISBN: 9781783197453
E ISBN: 9781783197460

Printed and bound by Replika Press Pvt Ltd, India.

Visit www.oberonbooks.com to read more about all our books and to buy them. You will also find features, author interviews and news of any author events, and you can sign up for e-newsletters so that you're always first to hear about our new releases.

CONTENTS

CONTENTS

CONTENTS

Foreword

As I get older, my memory has faded. Looking through this collection it isn't that I'm indifferent to it – quite proud, in fact, and delighted that it has been assembled. But these pieces are distant to me. Nor, it must be said, do I sit with the audience or stand in the wings on my own first nights in the theatre. It is the doing which interests me, not the seeing.

Many of the things that I wrote are associated with the time when I was just getting out of medicine. It was a time when I was being offered unsolicited invitations to do things which I'd never done in my life before: to write, to direct, to present. This all began when George Devine of the Royal Court invited me to direct a play, and consequently for the first ten years of my life in the theatre I kept on being invited to 'do things' without my actually being on the look-out for the possibility of doing things. I always thought I was going to go back to medicine. There was one invitation after another, which in fact had not been promoted by my wanting to do things at all. It was just that people thought there was something interesting about my attitude which would make interesting works for the theatre and even for opera.

It was simply whichever opportunities I found appealing. The things which interested me in medicine were many, many aspects of what interested me about doing things in theatre. I wanted to reproduce human behaviour, and the capacity to observe the negligible details – which are actually the interesting details of human behaviour – is what in fact leads you as a doctor to a diagnosis. And the audience suddenly realize that you've done something which has never been done in the theatre before, which is getting the commonplace back onto the stage, rather than what they regard as the dramatic. I enjoyed the action of interacting with performers

ix

and reminding them of the trivial details which most of my more highly qualified colleagues never addressed them to.

If you look at these apparently trivial details when you're doing medicine, there are certain things you notice which 'give the game away' – and that's everything I've ever done in the theatre. It's noticing the things people *actually* do. The study of gesture in public places goes right back to a man called Marcus Fabius Quintilianus (35–100 A.D.), and there is a huge literature which has been going on consistently since then and has become enormously highly developed in the last 40 years. It has had a great influence on me.

Whenever I addressed myself to a script, I saw that they were written down texts where very little corresponds to people actually talking. If you read the texts of classical works, you get person A talking for four rows and then person B talking for four rows. They never interrupt one another. But then I became aware of the fact that a large number of people, when talking, interrupt one another all the time. With that in mind, I took nearly 40 minutes off the running time of *Long Day's Journey into Night* by having this family all talk at the same time. I just put all of that back in.

Living in New York in the early Sixties had a profound effect on me. In England, people were only interested in what was their subject, but in America my friends at the *New York Review of Books* were an amazing liberation. I am pleased to see the inclusion in this book of my interview with Susan Sontag for *Monitor*. For this, back home, I was pilloried: 'How could you possibly broadcast something as trivial as that?' And yet, 25 years later, people realised that her talk was addressing aspects of human behaviour which the Americans took seriously and no one in England did. Here, it always had to be art of the 'highest order.' On *Monitor* I tried to break that apart.

The transcript also reminded me that all conversations are filled with the punctuation of hesitations, or expressions of assent and dissent – hmm, erm, ah, and so on. If you look at classical texts there is a completely grammatical sequence, but it wasn't until the start of recordings that we suddenly realised that when you hear people talking there are all these extraordinary things which are characteristic of *all* talk. People also perform to a notion of what is expected of them; what is verbally disclosed and not disclosed. I talk about this in my foreword to *Voices of Victorian London* (pp. 332–339) and it is hinted at in the dialogue which opens this collection, from my film of M. R. James's *Whistle and I'll Come to You*: the Professor's non-verbal communication is a vessel for his intellectual arrogance.

I hope that you find much to interest you in this collection – an assortment of life-long obsessions and passing fancies. In the end 'one thing and another' is all I've ever been interested in.

Jonathan Miller
London, July 2016

A Note on the text

Editing a collection of 'occasional writing' can be a complex process. In the case of Jonathan Miller, his work cuts across print, radio, television and the podium, and survives in the form of transcripts, recordings and versions edited for print, subject to myriad house styles and the use of either UK or US English. The mission with *One Thing and Another* was to select the most representative and entertaining range of material and to provide the reader with a consistent text. This has prompted many minor adjustments and occasional amendments to source material, none of which infringe on Miller's original intentions. Any significant corrections are acknowledged in the Notes, where full credits for source material – including quotations – can also be found.

Acknowledgements

I am grateful to the following for permission to reproduce material: the British Broadcasting Corporation, California Institute of Technology, Dick Cavett, Condé Nast, Richard Holloway, Immediate Media Company, Sue Lawley, Norman Lebrecht, Ralph Montagu, the National Portrait Gallery, *New Statesman*, *New York Review of Books*, *Opera*, Ann Pasternak Slater, *Spectator*, the Taylor and Frances Group and Kirsty Wark.

Several great institutions helped in the gathering of material. My thanks go to the staff at BBC Written Archives Centre (especially Louise North), the BFI Reuben Library, the British Library (not least Steven Dryden) and King's College London Foyle Special Collections.

I wish to thank the following people for advice, information and friendship during the preparation of *One Thing and Another*: Mark Aldridge, Alan Andres, Steve Arnold, John Bassett, Kate Bassett, Andrew Billen, Lez Cooke, Michael Coveney, Caroline Cowie, Paul Ebbs, Dick Fiddy, Bob Franklin, Gavin Stewart Gaughan, Peter Gilman, Peter Gordon, Jason Hazeley, John Hill, Remy Hunter, Emily Jenkins, Mark Lewisohn, Andrew Martin, David Miller, Joel Morris, Marcus Prince, Rosy Rickett, David Rolinson, Karl Sabbagh, Billy Smart, Vicky Thomas, Simon Usher, Anthony Wall, John Williams and Zoë Wilcox. Simon Scott, always. Thanks also to Michael Brooke, Mark Duguid, Andrew McGibbon and David Quantick for granting earlier opportunities to research the career of Jonathan Miller, and to Simon Farquhar and W. Stephen Gilbert for their collegiate support and wisdom during the editing process.

I am grateful too to all at Oberon Books for another opportunity to follow my nose, especially my editor George Spender. Thanks also to Caroline Waldron and Martin Hargreaves for typesetting and indexing, and Justin Lewis for his careful proofreading. Any remaining errors are my responsibility.

Finally, I am indebted to those most important to the project: Jonathan and Rachel Miller, for their blessing, support and generosity. I am grateful to them for permitting me such a free hand to select from and evaluate a remarkable career.

Ian Greaves
London, July 2016

Chronology

Jonathan Miller's career presents a challenge to those who seek to summarise it with economy. The following timeline is therefore heavily abbreviated, taking in key works but with an emphasis on activities – particularly in prose and broadcasting – which are of greater relevance to *One Thing and Another*. For a definitive Life, I commend to you Kate Bassett's carefully researched and highly entertaining *In Two Minds: A Biography of Jonathan Miller* (London: Oberon Books, 2012). This also furnishes the reader with a comprehensive Chronology (pp. 421–436). In addition, I am indebted to Ronald Bergan and the editor of Miller's *Subsequent Performances* for earlier efforts to put such a diverse career into perspective.

1934   Jonathan Wolfe Miller is born in London on 21 July.

1937   Birth of sister, Sarah.

1939–53   Attends various schools during the war, then Arnold House prep school in London (1945–47) and St Paul's School for Boys, London (1947–53).

1953–56   Studies natural sciences at St John's College, Cambridge.
Stage: *Out of the Blue, Between the Lines*.
Radio: *The Cambridge University Footlights 'Take the Mike'* (BBC Home), *The Man from Paranoia: A Thing for Radio* (BBC Home), *Under Twenty Parade* (BBC Light).
TV: *Sunday Night at the London Palladium* (ATV).
Journalism: *Gadfly, Granta, Varsity*.

1956   Marries Rachel Collet.

1956–59   Studies at University College Hospital, London. Qualifies as a doctor.
Radio: *Monday Night at Home* (BBC Home), *Saturday Night on the Light* (BBC Light).

_TV_:	_Tonight_ (BBC TV).
Stage:	_Bright Periods._
Journalism:	_Spectator, UCH Magazine._

1960   Addenbrooke's Hospital, Cambridge.

Stage:	_Beyond the Fringe_ (Edinburgh).
Radio:	_Monday Night at Home_ (BBC Home).
Journalism:	_Queen, Spectator, Twentieth Century, UCH Magazine._

1961   Resigns position at Addenbrooke's. Takes up part time work at Royal Marsden in Chelsea and London Hospital in Whitechapel.

Stage:	_Beyond the Fringe_ (London).
Radio:	_Monday Night at Home_ (BBC Home).
_TV_:	_Tempo_ (ABC/ITV).
Journalism:	_Lancet, New Statesman, Observer, Sight and Sound, Spectator, Twentieth Century._

1962   Birth of first son, Tom.

Stage:	_Beyond the Fringe_ (New York), _Under Plain Cover_ (Royal Court).
Radio:	_The Alberts_ (BBC Third), _The Art Trade Runner_ (BBC Third).
Journalism:	_Daily Herald, New Statesman, Observer, Private Eye, Punch, Sunday Times, Times._

1963

Radio:	_East-Side Taxi Driver_ (BBC Third).
_TV_:	_What's Going On Here?_ (NBC).
Journalism:	_Commentary, New Society, New Statesman, New Yorker, New York Review of Books, Partisan Review, Sunday Times._

1964   Birth of second son, William.

_TV_:	_Monitor_ (editor; BBC1), _A Trip to the Moon_ (CBS).
Film:	_One Way Pendulum_ (Woodfall).
Stage:	_The Old Glory_ (New York).
Journalism:	_New Statesman, New York Review of Books, New York Times, Observer, Partisan Review, Radio Times, Times Literary Supplement._

1965

_TV_:	_Monitor_ (editor; BBC1), _BBC-3_ (BBC1), _Profiles in Courage: The Anne Hutchinson Story_ (NBC), _The Drinking Party_ (BBC1).
Journalism:	_New Statesman, New York Times, Observer._

1966

_TV_: *Alice in Wonderland* (BBC1), *On the Margin* (BBC2), *Mr Sludge, the Medium* (BBC1), *The Death of Socrates* (BBC1).

Journalism: *Listener, New York Review of Books, Punch, Radio Times, Sunday Times Magazine, Vogue.*

Books: Designs jacket for *The Kandy-Kolored Tangerine-Flake Streamline Baby* by Tom Wolfe.

1967   Birth of third child, Kate.
Member of Royal Society study group.

Stage: *Prometheus Bound* (Yale).

Journalism: *Guardian, Listener, New York Times, Punch, Times Literary Supplement, Vogue.*

1968

_TV_: *Whistle and I'll Come To You* (BBC1), *From Chekhov with Love* (Rediffusion).

Stage: *The School for Scandal* (Nottingham), *The Seagull* (Nottingham).

Film: *Scotch.*

Journalism: *Architectural Design, Listener, Observer, Sunday Times, Vogue.*

Books: *Harvey and the Circulation of the Blood.*

1969

_TV_: *The Zoo in Winter* (BBC2).

Film: *Take A Girl Like You* (Columbia; released 1970).

Stage: *Twelfth Night* (Oxford and Cambridge Shakespeare Company), *King Lear* (Nottingham).

Journalism: *Radio Times, Vogue.*

1970   Develops work on mesmerism via an honorary research fellowship at University College London.

Stage: *The Merchant of Venice* (National Theatre), *The Tempest* (Mermaid), *Hamlet* (OCSC).

_TV_: *Canvas: Illumination* (BBC2).

Radio: *Dickens* (BBC Radio 3).

Journalism: *Punch.*

1971

Stage: *Julius Caesar* (OCSC), *Danton's Death* (NT).

_TV_: *West Side Stories* (BBC2).

Radio: *Prometheus Bound* (BBC Radio 3), *Jonathan Miller on the Television Picture* (BBC Radio 3).

Lectures: Thank-Offering to Britain Fund Lecture ("Censorship and the limits of permission"), Royal Institution ("Alternative worlds").

Journalism: *Vogue*.

1972

Stage: *Richard II* (Los Angeles), *The Taming of the Shrew* (Chichester), *Noye's Fludde* (first opera; Roundhouse).

Radio: *Man: the Double Animal* (BBC Radio 3).

Books: *Freud: The Man, His World, His Influence* (editor).

Lectures: Institute of Contemporary Arts.

1973   Appointed associate director of the National Theatre.

Stage: *The Malcontent* (Nottingham), *Measure for Measure* (NT).

_TV_: *Charles Darwin Lived Here* (BBC2), *Clay* (BBC2).

Radio: *Mesmerism in Nineteenth-Century England* (BBC Radio 3).

Lectures: Conway Memorial Lecture ("The uses of pain").

Books: *The Uses of Pain*.

Journalism: *Times*.

1974

Stage: *Family Romances* (Greenwich), *The Marriage of Figaro* (NT), *The Freeway* (NT), *Arden Must Die* (Sadler's Wells), *Così fan Tutte* (Kent Opera).

_TV_: *The Merchant of Venice* (ATV).

1975   Resigns from National Theatre.

Stage: *The Importance of Being Earnest* (Greenwich), *Bed Tricks* (Greenwich), *The Cunning Little Vixen* (Glyndebourne), *Rigoletto* (Kent Opera).

_TV_: *King Lear* (BBC1).

Radio: *The Strongest Influence in My Life* (BBC Radio 4).

Journalism: *Sunday Times*.

1976

Stage: *Three Sisters* (Guildford), *Orfeo* (Kent Opera), *A Poke in the Eye with a Sharp Stick* (Amnesty).

Lectures: Marsden Lecture.

Journalism: *New York Review of Books*.

1977

Stage: *Eugene Onegin* (Kent Opera), *An Evening Without Bernard Miles* (Amnesty).

Lectures: T. S. Eliot Memorial Lecture.

1978

TV: *The Body in Question* (BBC2).

Stage: *The Marriage of Figaro* (ENO debut).

Books: *The Body in Question*.

1979   Appointed associate director of ENO (until 1988).

TV: *The Body in Question* (BBC2), *Cities* (ITV; transmitted 1981), *Orfeo* (BBC2).

Stage: *She Would if She Could* (Greenwich), *The Flying Dutchman* (Frankfurt), *La Traviata* (Kent Opera), *The Turn of the Screw* (ENO), *The Secret Policeman's Ball* (Amnesty).

1980

TV: *Television Shakespeare* (producer; BBC2).

Stage: *Arabella* (ENO), *Falstaff* (Kent Opera).

1981

TV: *Television Shakespeare* (producer; BBC2).

Stage: *Otello* (ENO).

Radio: *Transformations* (BBC Radio 4).

1982   Made honorary fellow of St John's College, Cambridge.

Stage: *Hamlet* (Donmar Warehouse), *Così fan Tutte* (St Louis), *Fidelio* (Kent Opera), *Rigoletto* (ENO).

TV: *Television Shakespeare* (producer; BBC2), *King Lear* (BBC2).

Lectures: Samuel Gee Lecture ("A Gower Street Scandal").

1983   Awarded CBE.
Joins University of Sussex on a three-year research placement, which is ultimately aborted.

TV: *The Beggar's Opera* (BBC2), *States of Mind* (BBC2).

Stage: *The Magic Flute* (Glasgow).

Radio: *Transformations* (BBC Radio 4).

Lectures: MacTaggart Lecture ("Valete"), Ernest Jones Lecture, Happiness Lecture.

Journalism:	_The Journal of the Royal College of Physicians of London._
Books:	_States of Mind: Conversations with Psychological Investigators_, _The Human Body._

1984 Appointed chairman of Edinburgh Fringe Festival.

_TV_:	_Ivan_ (BBC2).
Books:	_The Facts of Life._
Lectures:	Clark Lectures.

1985

Stage:	_Don Giovanni_ (ENO).
Books:	_Steps and Stairs._
Lectures:	US tour.

1986

Stage:	_Long Day's Journey into Night_ (Broadway), _The Mikado_ (ENO), _Tosca_ (Maggio Musicale).
_TV_:	_Virtuoso_ (Channel 4), _Origins_ (BBC2), _Così fan Tutte_ (BBC2), _Prisoners of Consciousness_ (Channel 4).
Lectures:	Royal Society (_Images and Understanding_ symposium), FT Arts Lecture.
Books:	_Subsequent Performances._

1987

Stage:	_The Emperor_ (Royal Court), _The Barber of Seville_ (ENO), _Tristan und Isolde_ (LA Opera).
_TV_:	_Long Day's Journey into Night_ (Showtime), _Acting_ (BBC2).
Radio:	_Helen Lessore: A Life Among Paintings_ (BBC Radio 3).
Journalism:	_Cortex._

1988 Appointed artistic director of Old Vic.

Stage:	_Andromache_ (Old Vic), _One Way Pendulum_ (Old Vic), _Bussy D'Ambois_ (Old Vic), _The Tempest_ (Old Vic), _Candide_ (Old Vic), _The Taming of the Shrew_ (RSC debut).
_TV_:	_My God_ (Channel 4), _The Emperor_ (BBC2), _Four Virtuosos_ (Channel 4).
Books:	_Laughing Matters: A Serious Look at Humour_ (co-editor).
Journalism:	_Granta._

1989

Stage:	_The Liar_ (Old Vic), _King Lear_ (Old Vic), _La Traviata_ (Glimmerglass), _Rise and Fall of the City of Mahagonny_ (LA Opera).

_TV_: Who Cares? (BBC2), _Dialogue in the Dark_ (BBC2), _Moving Pictures_ (Channel 4).

Lectures: Darwin College Lecture ("Communication without words"), Squiggle Foundation ("_King Lear_ in rehearsal"), Kennedy Lecture.

Journalism: _Independent_.

1990

Stage: Don Giovanni (Maggio Musicale).

_TV_: What's So Funny About That? (BBC1), _Born Talking_ (BBC2).

Books: _The Don Giovanni Book: Myths of Seduction and Betrayal_ (editor).

1991

Stage: _La Fanciulla del West_ (La Scala), _Katya Kabanova_ (New York Met), _Turn of the Screw_ (LA), _The Marriage of Figaro_ (Vienna), _Così fan Tutte_ (Maggio Musicale), _The Magic Flute_ (Tel Aviv), _Fidelio_ (Glimmerglass).

_TV_: _Who Cares Now?_ (BBC2), _Madness_ (BBC2).

1992

Stage: _The Double Dealer_ (Gate), _Roberto Devereux_ (Monte Carlo), _Manon Lescaut_ (La Scala), _The Marriage of Figaro_ (Maggio Musicale), _Il Matrimonio Segreto_ (Glimmerglass), _Ermione_ (Omaha), _Die Gezeichneten_ (Zürich).

Books: _The Afterlife of Plays_.

Journalism: _Scientific American_.

1993

Stage: _The St Matthew Passion_ (London), _Maria Stuarda_ (Monte Carlo), _Capriccio_ (Berlin), _Maria Stuarda_ (Buxton Festival), _Fedora_ (Bregenz Festival), _Ariadne auf Naxos_ (Broomhill), _Falstaff_ (Zürich).

1994

Stage: _Der Rosenkavalier_ (ENO), _Anna Bolena_ (Monte Carlo), _L'Incoronazione di Poppea_ (Glimmerglass), _La Bohème_ (Maggio Musicale).

_TV_: _The St Matthew Passion_ (BBC2).

Lectures: New York ("Going unconscious"), National Gallery (_From the Look of Things_ series), Royal Exchange.

Journalism: _Observer Magazine_.

1995

Stage: _Così fan Tutte_ (Royal Opera House debut), _She Stoops to Conquer_ (Gate), _Pelléas et Mélisande_ (New York Met), _Tamerlano_ (Glimmerglass), _Carmen_

(ENO), *Anna Bolena* (Munich).

Journalism: *Guardian.*

Lectures: *Sunday Times* Lecture ("On apologizing").

1996

Stage: *Idomeneo* (Maggio Musicale), *Il Matrimonio Segreto* (Zürich), *A Midsummer Night's Dream* (Almeida), *The Bear* (Ischia), *Rodelinda* (Broomhill), *La Traviata* (ENO), *Ariadne auf Naxos* (Maggio Musicale).

TV: *Voices of Victorian London* (BBC2).

Journalism: *Sight and Sound.*

1997   Made honorary doctor of literature by Cambridge University, as well as honorary fellow of the Royal College of Physicians.

Stage: *Mitridate, re di Ponto* (Salzburg Festival), *The Rake's Progress* (New York Met), *La Traviata* (Paris).

TV: *Jonathan Miller's Opera Works* (BBC2).

Lectures: Rivers Lecture.

1998

Stage: *The Marriage of Figaro* (New York Met), *Nabucco* (Zürich), *The Magic Flute* (Santa Fe Opera).

TV: *Dr Miller and the Islanders* (BBC2), *Jonathan Miller on Reflection* (BBC2).

Exhibitions: *Mirror Image: Jonathan Miller on Reflection* (curated; National Gallery).

Books: *On Reflection.*

1999

Books: *Nowhere in Particular.*

Stage: *The Beggar's Opera* (Broomhill).

Lectures: The Michelin Distinguished Visiting Lecture.

2000

Stage: *As You Like It* (Gate), *Ermione* (Santa Fe Opera), *I Puritani* (Munich).

2001

Stage: *Don Pasquale* (Maggio Musicale), *Die schweigsame Frau* (Zürich).

Exhibitions: *Jonathan Miller: Paper and Metal Works* (Flowers East).

Journalism: *Social Research.*

2002   OBE for services to music and arts.

Stage:	_Camera Obscura_ (Almeida), _King Lear_ (Ontario), _Eugene Onegin_ (Santa Fe Opera), _Così fan Tutte_ (Bornholm), _Capriccio_ (Turin).
Radio:	_The Nation's Health_ (BBC Radio 4).
Lectures:	Los Angeles ("The gaze: looking as it appears in pictures").

2003
Stage:	_Die Entführung aus dem Serail_ (Zürich), _Cleopatra_ (Graz Opera), _Oedipus Rex_ (Graz Opera), _The Elixir of Love_ (Stockholm).
Exhibitions:	_Jonathan Miller_ (Boundary Gallery).

2004
Stage:	_Falstaff_ (Tokyo), _Don Pasquale_ (ROH), _La Traviata_ (Bornholm).
_TV_:	_Atheism: A Rough History of Disbelief_ (BBC4), _The Atheism Tapes_ (BBC4).
Radio:	_Flu – A Medical Mystery_ (BBC Radio 4).

2005
Stage:	_La Clemenza di Tito_ (Zürich).
Radio:	_Self-Made Things_ (BBC Radio 4).
_TV_:	_Sensitive Skin_ (BBC2).
Exhibitions:	_Jonathan Miller: Wood Work_ (Daniel Katz Gallery).

2006
Stage:	_Jenůfa_ (Glimmerglass), _Don Giovanni_ (Valencia).

2007
Stage:	_The Cherry Orchard_ (Crucible), _La Traviata_ (Vilnius), _Der Rosenkavalier_ (Tokyo), _Fidelio_ (Aarhus).
Exhibitions:	_Camouflage_ (adviser; Imperial War Museum).

2008
Stage:	_Hamlet_ (Bristol), _Dido and Aeneas_ (Chelsea Festival).

2009
Stage:	_La Traviata_ (Glimmerglass), _Dido and Aeneas_ (Glimmerglass), _La Bohème_ (ENO).
Radio:	_Dear Darwin_ (BBC Radio 4), _The Line Between Life and Death_ (BBC Radio 4).

2010
Stage:	_The Elixir of Love_ (ENO).

Exhibitions: *On the Move* (curator and catalogue; Estorick Collection), *One Thing and Another* (NT).

2011

Stage: *The St Matthew Passion* (NT).

2012

Stage: *Don Pasquale* (La Scala).

Lectures: Penny Lectures.

2013

Stage: *Rutherford and Son* (Northern Broadsides).

2014

Stage: *Carmen* (Mid Wales Opera).

Books: *On Further Reflection*.

2015

Stage: *King Lear* (Northern Broadsides).

Exhibitions: *Jonathan Miller* (Cross Street Gallery).

2016

Books: *One Thing and Another*.

Death and destruction

COLONEL: Do you believe in ghosts, Professor?

PROFESSOR: Ghosts? Well, that's a sticky one, isn't it? I'm not quite certain what you mean. I mean, I don't quite know what I'm being invited to believe when anyone asks me a question like that. I'm not even quite certain what I'm being invited to disbelieve, if it comes to that.

COLONEL: Not quite with you, old chap.

PROFESSOR: No. Well, I mean, when you ask me do I believe, say, in Australia, I know perfectly well what sort of thing I'm being asked to judge. We all agree what we mean by Australia. Large continent... Southern Hemisphere...discovered by Captain Cook...four or five main cities...kangaroos. So on and so on. Given *that*, one can perfectly well imagine the procedure one might put in motion to confirm, or on the other hand *dis*confirm, its existence. Now, it's not the same thing with ghosts. Is it? I mean, there's no broad consensus about what a ghost is... Is there? There's no common agreement as to what a ghost is, or even might be. Which makes it hard to imagine the procedures that one might put in hand to confirm or to disconfirm their existence. So that given this ambiguity about initial definitions, it makes it very hard for me to answer your question, at least phrased as it is. 'Do you believe in ghosts?' It's rather like saying, 'Do you believe in bandersnatches?' It makes no sense to say that I do or I don't.

COLONEL: You've bowled me a bit of a Chinaman there. Ghosts. Well, all right – spirits of the dead, the survival of the human personality.

PROFESSOR: Aha. Survival of the human personality. Well now, that's a

1

different question again, really. And once again, it's got the grammatical *appearance* of a real question. But I wonder…I mean, does it really mean anything either? I mean, does it? Well, let's see. We say, for the sake of argument at least, that the human personality survives death. All right?

COLONEL: Right.

PROFESSOR: Very well, then. Now would we want to say it in the same way that we might say, for example, that someone survived a train crash?

COLONEL: Yes…

PROFESSOR: Ah, but would we? Would we, you see? I mean we say, don't we, that Pausanias survived the train crash but was very badly injured by it. Now we wouldn't want to say Pausanias survived death but was very badly injured…by it. We wouldn't want to say that, would we?

COLONEL: No, I suppose not.

PROFESSOR: Well, quite. So we've clearly got a logical difference in usage here, haven't we? In the sense that death is not quite like other physical catastrophes; in that survival from it need not, and indeed cannot, entail severe injury. Or at least, not injury due to it. Directly. We don't talk about anyone being very badly hurt by death. The relatives of the deceased, possibly, but not the victim himself – excluding, of course, the special interpretation in which one might say that he had been injured *fatally* by death. Or for that matter that she had.

COLONEL: True, true. But there are more things in heaven and earth than are dreamed of in your philosophy.

PROFESSOR: I prefer to put it another way. There are more things in philosophy than are dreamed of in heaven and earth.

Whistle and I'll Come to You, BBC1, 7 May 1968[1]

My day

Vogue, 1 October 1971[2]

In the house that I bought ten years ago, I inherited and was foolish enough to retain a huge whitewashed wardrobe with a long mirror set into the doors. Not having had the initiative to shift it in the first place or the energy to move it since, I now have to suffer its blistered reminders of my own mortality each morning. Set at right angles to the long axis of my waking body, this mirror throws back a foreshortened memento of my own accelerating senescence. I have only to raise myself from the waist to confront a ghastly grey face topped by a pile of dry, red chicken-feathers. Me as I might be when dead. Far from refreshing it, sleep seems to unravel my physique and it is only through the good fortune of waking each day at eight that my complete decomposition is delayed for another day. Reversed and even repaired to some extent by a further 12 hours of regenerating activity. It's as if we are out of depth in the flood-tide of our own mortality and must tread water each day simply to prevent ourselves from sinking into death. Each day we wallow a little deeper in the waterline and it is only by the frenzied enterprises of the day that we can undo the damage done by the night. The difficulty is to improvise an activity that will convince one that the initiative is worth taking in the first place. Wouldn't it be easier after all to languish all day in this one man *Radeau de la Méduse*, and drift off into some merciful Sargasso of delirious oblivion? Today I am lucky, however. A pressing obligation provides the motive for getting up. There's a play to be rehearsed. Actors await my arrival and the immediate necessity of solving the problems of a scene left unfinished from the day before prompts me to repair myself with a bath and breakfast. The days that I dread are the ones when a long-term literary task waits on the cluttered desk in the room below. The days, that is, when I am thrown back upon my own resources of creative motive; when there is nothing but an improvised goal towards which I can drive the day's work.

For some two years now, I have been struggling with a history of mesmerism in the nineteenth century. The implications of this study stretch away into many different areas. Which one to tackle today? The influence of Newton's theory of the ether on Anton Mesmer? No. Best to leave that till later. Dickens and mesmerism? That seems like a manageable topic for this month. It's compact and well defined and the material is easy to root out of the London University Library. But what about that interesting stuff to do with Coleridge that I bumped up against last week? Surely that would be a more profitable line to pursue today? Coleridge, after all, was going to write a whole book on mesmerism before he too was waylaid by the glittering eye of some other topic. All right. Let's have a look at what Hazlitt has to say about Coleridge before brushing my teeth. Hello, what's this? I seem to be in the same boat as Coleridge!

> It is hard to concentrate all our attention and efforts on one pursuit, except from ignorance of others; and without this concentration of our faculties, no great progress can be made in any one thing [...] Action is one; but thought is manifold. He whose restless eye glances through the wide compass of nature and art, will not consent to have "his own nothings monstered:" but he must do this, before he can give his whole soul to them.[3]

Better leave Coleridge on one side for fear of lending vicarious respectability to my own vice of drifting into the consideration of everything. Anyway, the decision is neatly postponed by the need to get down to the theatre and rehearse that damned scene. Kill two birds with one stone at least: pocket a copy of the *Biographia Literaria* and read it on the bus, and with a bit of luck I could have researched half a topic before I get off at Waterloo. Already the day seems a bit more promising. Up and wash! Shave off the grave-mould and sluice out the rotting mouth. My God, another two hours sleep and I'd have been a goner! Nine o'clock. Time for a quick nip down to the junk stall in the local market to rummage for old group photographs. No doubt some cynical trendspotter would identify this as yet another example of fashionable camp but the collection of the last five years already justifies its own existence. Group after group face posterity with the same vulnerable confidence. Masons in their jingling aprons; young subalterns of the Warwickshire Regiment squinting into the summer sun of 1916; city diners, half-turned in their chairs, distracted for a moment by the unseen photographer's request to smile. Celebrations of the easily extinguished human capacity for getting on with one another.

4

Perhaps someone will snap our rehearsal group before the play closes and gets forgotten.[4]

Down at the rehearsal room, we artfully postpone the moment when we have to come to grips with the scene that was proving so troublesome the night before. Plastic cups of coffee circulate and while we gossip about the notices of another play that has opened the previous evening, Carl Davis kills time by taking one of the actors through a song routine. Twenty minutes pass like this and it is only when someone arrives to rehearse the next scene on the schedule that we stir ourselves and begin to do what we came for in the first place. What exactly *is* that though? What are we all doing here? Eleven o'clock on a midweek morning. All over London the world is at its work. Surgeons are clipping off arteries at St Thomas's. Truck drivers are easing their enormous trailers into tight alleys on the river and, across the roofs at Shell House, self-evidently important business has already been underway these two hours. And what are we up to meanwhile? Standing around with open texts, trying to think of a way to recreate a scene that has already been played one way or another a hundred times before. How did they do it at the Lyric in 1959? Someone remembers having seen that production and although he knows he was impressed by what he saw, he cannot quite recall the details. Of course, no-one suggests that we should try and imitate another successful production, but one cannot help feeling a sense of impotent envy in the knowledge that someone has previously come up with an impressive solution to the problem that is taxing us this morning. How *do* you guillotine someone on the stage and make it look significantly different from what was done before? The next sequence cannot be rehearsed until this problem has been dealt with. How about doing it in silhouette? 'That's just because you can't think how to do it better than they did at the Lyric,' says Lord Olivier, entering with a cup of coffee from the canteen, obviously taking a malicious delight in the fact that we have reached an impasse on this technical point. Six weeks before the rehearsals began, he was already telling me to find out how Caspar Wrede managed to do that damned execution. 'It was very convincing, dear boy! You'll have to be very smart if you're going to come up with anything as good as that.' 'For Christ's sake, I'm a director, not a public hangman. I'll think of something when the time comes.' 'All right. But meanwhile find out how they did it at the Lyric, there's a good chap.'

5

Lord Olivier drifts back to his office and I decide that it's time for more coffee and another think.[5] The actor who has arrived for the next scene is meanwhile sitting quite happily on a 'prop' bed on the far side of the room reading Irving Wardle's notice of last night's production. Two years ago and I'd have been in a blind panic to find myself at a loss like this, but now I recognize the doldrums come and go and that actually one *gains* prestige with the actors by acknowledging these periods of becalmed impotence. And in some curious way, conscious efforts to arrive at solutions only delay them – one learns to remember that the imagination is always at work even when it seems that nothing is happening. So we get back on our feet and block in a provisional version of the execution of Danton, knowing quite well that it's no more than a row of theatrical hyphens indicating that this space remains to be filled. 'Look, I've got no idea how this scene is going to turn out, so just walk across the stage in a group and assume that some time or other you'll land up guillotined.' In some joint recess of the cerebral imagination the issue is being turned over and before long – or perhaps only at the final run-through itself – a tableau will suggest itself either in its entirety to one person alone, or else, more often than not, in bits and pieces, to several people, variously. Quite frequently, the solution arrives in the shape of an almost irrelevant suggestion made by an actor who has no part in the scene itself but who has been watching from the sidelines and who can therefore see it with a detached eye.

How can one retain one's self esteem as a director in the face of such haphazard sources of inspiration? Is the credit for the final product really to be distributed amongst the participants like this? If so, where does the director fit in? Everywhere and nowhere, as it turns out. One is merely the president of a republic of dreamers, assuming priority simply by virtue of having created the first overarching idea. If this first notion is compelling enough, one can be perfectly certain that whatever ideas suggest themselves to the cast, they will all somehow conform to and feed off the original inspiration. One creates, as it were, a magnetic field of the imagination and although the actors feel themselves free to invent, they always do so in terms that are defined by the original suggestion that one makes on the first day of rehearsals. It is vital, therefore, that this notion should be one that readily fertilizes the imagination of everyone concerned. It must be general enough to leave the actors free to manoeuvre within their own imagination and at the same time decorated with the sort of concrete images that make dreams so invigorating.

It would be nice to report that the solution to the problem of Danton's execution emerged on the day in question. For emerge it did, as I knew in my heart of hearts it had to; but it came much later, and in dribs and drabs, so that I cannot properly say who was responsible for it. It certainly wasn't done in silhouette, nor by topping the gruesome realism of the 1959 production; but, figuratively speaking, by moving two squares to the left and one back. By not letting the audience see it at all – but by presenting the doomed quintet of victims the moment after the execution had happened, in some posthumous limbo where the pain of the slicing blade has already been forgotten. So far as I can remember, the answers came in separate bits from several members of the cast, one after another. As if some master-plan had been sliced up and distributed in sealed envelopes. When these partial solutions were all put together the result seemed quite inevitable, as if we had somehow known it all along and had simply been too stupid to see it right in front of our noses. But by 5.30 on that particular day, we were still in a state of irritating deadlock. Just before taking leave of each other, though, someone says that it would be nice to make use of the museum cases which Pat Robertson's set has provided. A vague panorama flickers seductively in front of the mind's eye. Bloodless torsos standing fixed for eternity in a cosmic museum. Why not? But how to get them there exactly? There's an image to work on at least. Let's sleep on it and give the esemplastic power of the imagination its head. Good old Coleridge! Let's hope that the Person from Porlock doesn't intervene meanwhile.

Anyway, I've got an appointment with the designer of my next production at 6.15 p.m. Problem. How to set *Julius Caesar*?[6] How to avoid the deadening picturesque familiarity of ancient Rome on the stage? There's no point doing it modern. Everyone's seen that already and besides, the modern parallels are too pat. Why not set it in some dream annex, to the left of real history. Somewhere that will put one *in mind* of ancient Rome but which will still leave enough room to associate the action with subsequent tyrannies. It would be nice to have something that suggested Mussolini's Rome. But how can one do that indirectly without stretching Shakespeare's text to cover events that he knew nothing about? By finding *some* intermediate condition that is congruent with both; some abstract generality, which glistens at the same time with concrete visual individuality. I can only think of harsh afternoon sunlight and of black shadows lying aslant deserted piazzas. Of course! De Chirico. Those disquieting Ferrara canvases of 1920. Painted within a few years of the March on Rome and yet at the same time glowing with the mysterious melancholy of departed classical antiquity. The idea appeals to the designer, Bernard Culshaw, and with an enviable deftness he begins to sketch out a ground plan which includes a ramp inscribed with a false perspective – an aquamarine sky-cloth against which we can stand a cut-out red-brick factory chimney.[7] Or if *that* seems too modern, it could always be a scarlet palazzo. The hours have passed and the two of us have been successfully visited by Ted Hughes' thought-fox. The production is as good as set and we have already gone some way towards establishing the magnetic field within which the actor's imagination will need to work. The substantive problems of the play are still unforeseen and six weeks from now, with the knots of Danton all unravelled, a new set of actors will be heart-searching the difficulties of bumping off Julius Caesar in a Chirico piazza.

With Culshaw gone for the night, I feel I need a break from the stage and it seems like a good moment to get back to mesmerism. The privacy of a book. Robert Schofield's new essay on the fate of Newtonian ideas in the eighteenth century. I can begin to see quite clearly that mesmerism would have never emerged if it hadn't been for Newton's proposals for the existence of an ether.[8] And, of course, Coleridge was fascinated by Newton. I wonder if Coleridge ever knew Danton. Or better still, how Coleridge would have staged Danton's execution. It would be nice to pick up a group photo that included Coleridge, Danton, de Chirico and Mesmer. But that sort of thing only happens in dreams.

Communication without words
Lady Mitchell Hall, Cambridge, 17 February 1989[9]

Wittgenstein once asked what was left over after one subtracted from the sentence 'I raise my arm' the sentence 'My arm goes up.' A comparable question about communication might go something like this: 'If I were to set aside all those communications which are expressed or expressible in words – written, spoken or signed – what would be left over?'

For anyone who regards *language* as the canonical form of human communication, the answer would probably be 'Not much is left over' and the residue, such as it is, is either a redundant supplement to words – something which the telephone shows we can do without – or else a sadly impoverished alternative which we are sometimes compelled to use when circumstances make the ordinary use of words awkward or impossible.

On the other hand, for those who regard language with suspicion – especially written or printed language – on the grounds that it misleads and confuses as much as it informs and expresses, eliminating words and sentences exposes a level of communication of unsuspected richness, one in which human beings express their true meanings. The idea is that articulate language is a barrier to, rather than a medium of, communication; and that if only this barrier could be removed, human beings would revert to a golden age of wordless, heartfelt communication. This attitude to non-verbal communication has been encouraged by the popularization of right-brain/left-brain studies and, amongst those who sponsor the soft primitivism that I have just referred to, it is widely assumed that the verbal capabilities of the left cerebral hemisphere have been over-developed by a culture which puts too much emphasis on linguistic finesse, and that the expressive repertoire of the supposedly holistic right hemisphere has been dangerously neglected as a consequence. In fact there are those who go even further, insisting that favouring the verbal capacities of the left hemisphere not only conceals but actually deforms and disables right-sided accomplishments. The most widely publicized example of this claim is to be found in Betty Edwards' bestselling *Drawing on the Right Side of the Brain* (1979). In this astoundingly popular and not altogether unpersuasive book, Miss Edwards sponsors a pedagogical programme designed to diminish the influence of linguistically determined ways of seeing the world. Her argument is that by learning to overlook those parts of the world which are easily nameable we can revert to a mode of perception more favourable to successful drawing. Here is one of her recommendations.

The left hemisphere is not well equipped to deal with empty spaces. It can't name them, recognise them, match them with stored categories, or produce ready-made symbols for them. In fact, the left brain seems to be bored with spaces [...] Therefore, they are passed over to the right hemisphere [...] To the right brain, spaces, objects, the known and the unknown, the nameable or unnameable, are all the same. It's all interesting[10]

And so on. There are some other interesting strategies recommended in the book and as someone who has always been frustrated by his inability to draw nicely I am bound to admit that the exercises suggested by Miss Edwards have brought about an unexpected improvement in my performance as a draughtsman. Now, whether this has anything to do with a conflict between right and left halves of the brain is not really the issue here. In any case I don't intend to discuss the visual arts as an example of non-verbal communication and I only introduce the topic of drawing to illustrate the extent to which antagonism to language has infiltrated itself into at least one important department of educational theory. There are other examples, though. Although the advertising industry is almost promiscuous in its use of verbal slogans, the creative emphasis falls more and more upon the persuasive power of imagery – slow-motion shots demonstrating the lustrous lightness of newly washed hair, or the soft resilience of freshly laundered towels. In fact it would be tiresome to list the repertoire of non-verbal devices deliberately designed to bypass a critical vigilance based upon language.

A comparable tendency is to be found in the theatre. Inaugurated in the 1960s with the rediscovery of Artaud's manifestos in favour of the so-called Theatre of Cruelty, drama in the last quarter of the twentieth-century displays a noticeable interest in bizarre expressionistic décor, extended pantomimic gestures and sometimes a cacophony of non-verbal sounds. In the increasingly popular idiom of so-called 'performance arts,' actors and audiences revel in non-verbal excesses in the belief that such behaviour addresses itself directly to the human soul and that all other forms of traditional theatre are disgustingly 'literary.' This repudiation of language is often associated with the more romantic forms of political radicalism, the idea being that language is one of several devices by which the ruling elite manipulates cognitive structures to its own advantage, and that it is only by storming the Bastille of linguistic tradition that human beings have any hope of being restored to a state of primeval egalitarian fellowship. This attitude is one of the things that has given non-verbal communication such a bad name, and since it already has a somewhat shaky reputation due to the fact that it has no powerful theory associated with it, its academic credibility suffers in comparison to that of formal linguistics. In fact, even if one succeeds in dissociating oneself from some of the more romantic claims that are made on its behalf, it's easy to get the discouraging impression that communication without words is after all a residual topic and that once orthodox language has been subtracted all that is left is a rubbish heap of nudges, shrugs, pouts, sighs, winks and glances – or, to put it another way, that non-verbal communication is simply the behavioural exhaust thrown out of the rear-end of an extremely high-tech linguistic machine.

And yet…*is* it all that easy to subtract language in the first place? Can one really strip away the lexical component, leaving behind a non-verbal residue which has nothing to do with communication in words? The fact that one can commit words to paper without any apparent loss of intelligibility suggests that there is, in fact, a clean division between the lexical and the non-verbal component of human communication, and that the so-called kinesic variables such as facial expression, posture, and hand movements are just optional extras. But this conclusion overlooks the fundamental distinction between the meaning of an utterance and the meaning which the utterer wishes to convey by means of that utterance. Because, although it could be argued that what an *utterance* means is readily recoverable by anyone who can read printed English, it is important to understand that what the speaker wishes to express is more often than not defined by the factors which get lost in the process of transcription. The problem is that writing was not developed in the first place to preserve the meanings of talk or conversation. It was developed originally to promulgate priestly or legislative initiatives, and since these were collective and in some sense impersonal productions, what the writer meant was to all intents and purposes recoverable from what he wrote down. If there was any ambiguity, that is to say implications which might escape the first or indeed many subsequent readings, they were not the ones which would have made themselves more readily apparent if some form of graphic representation had preserved the tone of voice, the facial expressions or the hand movements of their author. So that there was no incentive to develop a notation designed to represent the non-lexical parts of an utterance. In

11

fact, the notational shortcomings of writing only became apparent when authors tried to reproduce the talk of individuals. Then, and perhaps only then, the difficulty of identifying speech acts becomes apparent.

The notion of speech acts was introduced by the Oxford philosopher J. L. Austin, who pointed out that in uttering this or that well-formed sentence a speaker is doing something over and above expressing its literal meaning. He or she may be stating, describing, warning, commanding, apologizing, requesting or beseeching. In fact, according to Austin there are more than a thousand of these acts which are performable in English, and unless the hearer or reader recognizes which of these is being expressed by the utterances in question, he or she has missed the point.

Of course, the identity of a speech act, its illocutionary force as Austin calls it, is often made apparent by an explicit lexical indicator: 'I *warn* you that I will take steps to prevent you' or 'I *promise* that I will be there on time.' And in such cases, the non-lexical cues – finger-waggings, handshakes and so forth – are indeed superfluous, and the printed text preserves everything that the utterer intended to convey. But for each of the thousand or so explicitly identifiable speech acts there are just as many for which there is neither a name nor a lexical indicator. And in that case the only way of identifying them with any accuracy is to hear them spoken and to witness the non-verbal behaviour with which they are preceded, accompanied or followed. A playwright will often do his best to supply this non-lexical information by telling the reader that the character shrugs, winks, or looks heavenwards as this or that phrase is uttered. A novelist can be even more helpful by saying that the phrase in question was spoken waggishly, or grimly, or that it was snapped out as the character turned angrily on his heel. However, the grain of this behavioural notation is unbelievably coarse and one is often surprised by the extent to which two performances of the same written utterance can differ – even when the actors in question are apparently following the same instruction with respect to intonation, facial expression or manual gesture. The result is that instead of trying to recover the often indeterminable illocutionary force intended by the author for this or that character, the actor finds himself inventing someone who might have wished to express this or that speech act by means of the speeches assigned to him in the text. In which case the non-verbal concomitants of the various utterances are improvised as if for the first time, and in the best of all possible productions an unforeseeable Lear, Macbeth or Rosalind emerges in performance, and the speeches come across expressing meanings which would have been hard to foresee from reading the bare text.

The point I am labouring at such length is that there is a large and complicated repertoire of non-verbal behaviour without which it is impossible to communicate meanings through the medium of spoken words, and, although it is tempting to regard this non-lexical repertoire as something which can be painlessly removed without any significant loss of meaning, the experience of reconstructing talk from a medium in which the representation of this aspect of speech is so poor is a salutary reminder of its importance.

Up to this point I have concentrated on the way in which non-verbal behaviour helps us, as Austin would say, 'to *do* things with words.'[11] I would now like to turn my attention to something which is in a sense a mirror image of what we have been considering. How can we 'say things with deeds'?

There is, of course, a sense in which all our actions or deeds speak louder than words, and that everything we do – or fail to do, for that matter – is open to interpretation and therefore counts as a communication. In fact, it doesn't have to be anything properly identifiable as a deed to communicate interpretable evidence. A blush, a hangdog posture or a limp handshake can all convey information, and experts in so-called body language – horrid phrase – have compiled long lists of postures and gestures from which an observant onlooker can glean some information about the attitudes or intentions of others. Mere 'presence' can speak volumes. Someone who turns up at an occasion which is known to be an ordeal for him communicates information whether he wishes to or not. His unexpected presence may be interpreted, rightly or wrongly, as a deed deliberately intended to express his courage or defiance. A well-known alcoholic who unexpectedly turns up at a cocktail party may inadvertently communicate the fact that his sessions with AA have given him newfound confidence in his self-control. But his turning up at such an occasion may be an explicit act of communication – a way of saying without words that he can now resist the blandishments of the bar and that his friends and colleagues are to regard him as a reformed character. It is important to distinguish, as far as one can, between behaviour which wordlessly *betrays* information – behaviour, that is, from which an onlooker may *glean* something – and non-verbal behaviour which is performed with the express purpose of *communicating* this or that information. Here is another example: someone who manages to read in a noisy, crowded room may inadvertently communicate evidence as to his enviable powers of concentration, but since the act of reading monopolizes his attention, he is by definition 'dead to the world' and therefore unaware of that fact which his behaviour communicates. In contrast, I have chosen the following passage from *Barnaby Rudge* (1841):

'How do you find yourself now, my dear?' said the locksmith, taking a chair near his wife (who had resumed her book), and rubbing his knees hard as he made the inquiry.

'You're very anxious to know, an't you?' returned Mrs Varden, with her eyes upon the print. 'You, that have not been near me all day, and wouldn't have been if I was dying!'

'My dear Martha –' said Gabriel.

Mrs Varden turned over to the next page; then went back again to the bottom line over leaf to be quite sure of the last words; and then went on reading with an appearance of the deepest interest and study.

'My dear Martha,' said the locksmith, 'how can you say such things, when you know you don't mean them? If you were dying! Why, if there was anything serious the matter with you, Martha, shouldn't I be in constant attendance upon you?'

'Yes!' cried Mrs Varden, bursting into tears, 'yes, you would. I don't doubt it, Varden. Certainly you would. That's as much as to tell me that you would be hovering round me like a vulture, waiting till the breath was out of my body, that you might go and marry somebody else.'[12]

Unlike a person whose *actual* reading betrays his powers of concentration, Mrs Varden's *pretended* reading prevents her from actually reading, because in order to monitor and enjoy its communicative effect it would be impossible for Mrs Varden to accomplish the deed of reading in earnest. But not all pretended deeds have to fall short of their normal function in order to accomplish their communicative purpose. Take the example of the burglar in Austin's famous essay on pretending – surely a classic example of saying something with deeds as opposed to doing something with words.[13] A burglar is inspecting a window with a view to breaking and entering, but in order to make his interest look innocent he pretends to be cleaning the windows. As it happens, the most convincing way of pretending to clean a window is to actually do so.

The most observant reporter of saying things by means of deeds was the late Erving Goffman, and it is to his work that I would like to dedicate the rest of this lecture. I do so as a grateful tribute to someone who has liberated the study of non-verbal communication from the dead hand of ethological reductionism.

A central feature of Goffman's approach to non-verbal behaviour is his assumption that it is to be visualized against the background of institutional norms which create the salient facts of social life.[14] Without an appreciation of these norms it is almost impossible to make sense, let alone describe, much of the conduct which characterizes our mutual involvements. According to Goffman, what lends credibility to our concepts of personal self is the recognition of certain rules or conventions which limit the claims we can expect to be acknowledged with respect to freedom from untoward threat, interference and so forth. We venture into public life protected not so much by the sanctions of formal law but by an unwritten charter of civil rights which assigns us both access *to* and independence *from* others with whom we come into contact.

Those who lay claim to these rights and expect to have violations recognized and remedied, know that they undertake reciprocal obligations and will be expected to provide appropriate remedies if they are guilty of infraction, even if innocently. In our transit across public places we rely on others recognizing the rules which assign us the right to proceed without being inconvenienced by impudent stares or unsolicited conversational openings. On the other hand, we also proceed on the assumption that we have some measure of personal access to others if the occasion unexpectedly requires it, and vice versa; and that if such openings ensue, that there are supportive rituals which allow us to engage in them without offence and terminate them without insult. In return for such a privilege we implicitly acknowledge that there are reciprocal obligations incumbent upon us.

What this means is that the individual in public feels obliged to broadcast an unceasing stream of non-verbal signs, intended to inform others – whether they be acquaintances or more often otherwise – of the place which he or she expects to have in the undertakings which follow. By means of such conduct, we inform one another about the legitimacy of our presence, the innocence of our motives and our readiness to grant access or cooperation if the situation arises. And at times or places where our actions are likely to be misinterpreted, the intensity of this indicative behaviour increases.

As Goffman points out, these signs have been neglected or disparaged as trivial items. Or even worse they may be misdescribed as vestigial bequests from our primate ancestry – yet another example of the naive reductionism which sometimes passes as orthodox science. Where Goffman scores is by allocating scientific importance to the *moral* representation of self in everyday life.

Consider for a moment the question of legitimate presence. In places where anything short of purposeful warning might be misinterpreted as either suspicious loitering or aberrant vacancy, the normal person feels obliged to put on a show, which tells anyone who might be watching that orderly motives are in hand. He or she will glance ostentatiously at his watch, as if to indicate that an expected arrival is late for an appointment and if he happens to meet the glance of a passer-by, he will more often than not look once again at his watch and cast a long-suffering glance at heaven; as if by recruiting sympathy for a *familiar* predicament he will pre-empt any suspicion of more suspect motives. Such behaviour will perhaps be even more pronounced if the innocent loiterer happens to have stationed himself at places where his presence might be misinterpreted. Washrooms and lavatories are classical locations for such conduct. In men's rooms, which are the only ones from which I can report personal experiences, there are elaborate rituals for avoiding the impression of suspect motives. A concentrated stare at the white tile immediately ahead of one usually takes place when someone unknown unexpectedly occupies the stall alongside, sometimes accompanied by the onset of a tuneless and preoccupied whistle; anything to avoid creating the impression that one might be showing an untoward interest in the UG equipment of one's neighbour. Of course such behaviour won't wash, and I use the word advisedly, if the neighbour happens to be a colleague. For in *that* case, the elaborate precautions to avoid eye contact could be read as a suspicion of *his* motives and thereby create a second order of virtual offence.

For obvious reasons, the situation is less fraught with risk in the purposeful *va* and *vient* of open corridors. Nevertheless even here an unremitting etiquette prevails. It is an etiquette in which the participants tacitly assume that there are reciprocal obligations with respect to right of way, freedom from inquisitive glances and capricious encroachments upon privacy. All the same the management of eye movements leaves room for the possibility of accesses which can and often do develop into what Goffman describes as focussed encounters; episodes which are themselves introduced and terminated by rituals of greeting and farewell. Such episodes may, of course, be confused as passing acknowledgements, but the readiness to exchange such signals is *one* of the ways in which we register the normality of the passing scene and it is when we encounter consistent anomalies in the broadcast that we begin to suspect and perhaps report something odd.

In institutions such as hospitals or the BBC, where colleagues and acquaintances run the risk of passing one another many times in the same morning, the ritual resources for handling brief encounters are often over-stretched. First and second encounters can be managed by conventional openness; a third meeting may necessitate a humorously resigned grin; a fourth can be handled by pretending to be wrapped in thought; a fifth may require some dramatized horseplay such as play-acting a Western duel. And you've all seen and probably participated in the scene where a sequence of such meetings is brought to its climax by one partner coming right out with the movie cliché 'We can't go on meeting like this,' or, less effectively, 'Long time no see!'

All this, as Goffman points out, presupposes three levels of normal functioning:

a. The recognition of the fact that an individual is a potential source of alarm, inconvenience, offence and encroachment.

b. Recognition of the fact that each individual has both the obligation to minimize these aspects of himself *and* the capacity to do so.

c. Recognition of the need to perform remedial work if one recognisably infringes any of the norms which one intuitively regards as binding.

The point is that almost any configuration of events with which an individual is likely to be associated in public carries the risk of a *worst* possible meaning which might reflect unfavourably upon him, and it is a sign of intact mental functioning that one recognizes this risk, without of course being incapacitated by the thought, and at the same time that one is equipped to perform repair work if and when infractions occur.

It is, I think, in the analysis of this so-called remedial work that Goffman is at his most imaginative and productive. One of the things that makes his account so useful – so much more than the anecdotal triviality of which he is so carelessly accused – is his ability to compare and contrast this *informal* repair work with the formal structures of explicit legal process. As in law there is an orderly sequence of offence, arrest, remedy and reconciliation. But what distinguishes these *interchanges* is the fact that the offender is so often the first to recognize that an infraction has occurred and usually initiates the appropriate repair work without being asked to do so.

An even more important distinction is the fact that the remedial work is expressive rather than productive. In other words the remedial performance is designed to restore a favourable image of the offender as opposed to offering substantial compensation to the offended.

Taking his cue from yet another of Austin's philosophical essays, the famous and often reprinted "A plea for excuses" (1956), Goffman distinguishes various forms of remedial ritual, of which the first is the so-called *account*.[15] In this, the offender redescribes his or her act so that its offensiveness may be overlooked or discounted. It may take the form of an explicit explanation. Someone, for example, who finds himself in the embarrassing situation of seeming to have winked at an unknown passer-by may offer the account that he has some grit in his eye – this often accompanied by a flurry of overacted eyelid-rubbing and nose-blowing. In this way he re-establishes his image as an altogether innocent victim. Of course, one has to be careful in this context to recognize that many of the infractions I'm referring to are not necessarily offences *against* others, but represent errors of performance – imperfections which reflect badly on the offender, so that one undertakes remedial work, *not* for the purpose of making amends but to re-draw the picture of oneself so that it corresponds more closely to the one which one would *like* to project to the world at large. So important is this consideration – and it would be perfunctory to regard it as *mere* vanity – that it may motivate performances to anonymous and usually unconcerned strangers. You only have to think of the otherwise incomprehensible behaviour of someone who hails a cab with a flailing gesture of the outstretched arm and who, having failed, then feels it necessary to provide an *account* of what happened by using the same hand to smooth down their hair. Or in Goffman's own example of the man who trips in the street, to his own and no one else's inconvenience, who then feels it necessary to retrace his steps and conscientiously examine the sidewalk – as if to establish the impression that the fault lies in the pavement and not, as might otherwise be suspected, in the nervous system of the person concerned. The point is that whether it's addressed personally or all round to anyone who might be watching, whether it's verbal or mimetic, the function of an *account* is to correct a potentially unfavourable impression of oneself which an infraction of the unwritten rules might produce.

And the same principle applies to *apology*, although as Austin pointed out in his essay, the *logic* of apology is not the same as that of accounts. In making an apology one accepts blame for what has happened, but at the same time one tries to convince the injured party, if there happens to be one, or the world at large if not, that the error is not to be taken as representative of the *real* self.

Apology, in other words, is aimed at convincing anyone interested that the miscreant recognizes his fault, and by *that* token alone, is to be regarded as someone whose *typical* tendency is to observe the conventions. Such a performance may be verbal or non-verbal. In circumstances when words are inappropriate or impractical, the apology may take the form of an elaborate pantomime of contrition. On entering a small seminar room, where a meeting is already underway, the show may take the following complex form: a self-uglifying expression of humility, plus an elaborate show of stealthiness – which is as good as saying 'Yes, I am late, and please pay attention to my performance of humbly *not* wishing to be paid attention to', i.e. 'Here's me entering as unostentatiously as I know how, so you can see how much I regret my rudeness!'

A comparable version of this is the face made by someone who barges into a room unannounced, expecting to speak to a friend, only to find that this friend is engaged in an intimate professional consultation with another colleague. Although a verbal apology would probably fit the bill, the offender may feel constrained to act the fool he expects to be accused of being. Hence an otherwise unintelligible grimace. Or the actor who stumbles over his words for the *second* time at a rehearsal. He will often apologize by overplaying the spastic idiot everyone around must suspect him of being.

There are also, I think, concealed apologies included in the otherwise straightforward rituals of farewell. As Goffman points out, the *end* of conversational encounters carry an increased risk of creating offence – in the sense that careless or perfunctory termination may convey the misleading impression that one couldn't wait for the session to end and that as far as *one* was concerned the whole episode was a waste of time. On occasions where this is felt to be a risk, preventive apologies may be issued in the form of prolonged negotiations to meet again soon, or anything to avoid the potentially offensive gesture of actually *leaving*!

This of course raises the question of the apologies and/or accounts which accompany failed farewells. The situation I'm thinking of is this. One's been talking with a small group of colleagues. Because of an appointment or whatever, one has to leave before the group as a whole breaks up. Having successfully manoeuvred an inoffensive farewell, one discovers that one has left a book in the room. Now, try and visualize the risks of re-entry. First, the offence to oneself. This is usually surmounted by merely explaining 'Left my book,' but since one may suspect that one'll be thought a fool for having done so, it may be necessary to overact being a fool and murmur 'Forget my own head next!' Perhaps this show is reinforced by miming a stumble or a mindless struggle with the door on leaving yet again, but the situation is complicated by the knowledge that – in one's all too brief absence – the space left by one's departure is already in process of closing over; new topics are in hand and one might create offence to the members of the reconstituted group by seeming to reinsert oneself. Once again, the tip-toe manoeuvre – but this time it's not quite an apology so much as an unsuccessful account. An account which tries to convey the impression that you're not there at all. And so forth.

Now, in my enthusiasm for *anecdotal* aspect of all this, I have neglected to mention the other half of Goffman's analysis of remedial procedure. I am referring of course to the process of *closure* – that is to say the ritualized responses, whereby the injured party acknowledges and accepts the accounts or apologies, thus allowing social activity to resume its productive course. If this so-called round is left incomplete, the offender – virtual or actual – is left hanging in the air, uncertain as to his moral status in the undertakings that will follow. These replies may seem too trivial to mention – a nod, a murmur, 'that's OK,' or whatever – but if these signs are not provided, the offender is left with the uneasy sense that his or her offence, trivial or not, is permanently entered in the criminal record.

It is, I think, one of Erving Goffman's most lasting achievements to have made these interchanges both visible and intelligible. And what makes his analysis so attractive is the fact that he has resolutely turned his back on the temptations to reduce what he has seen to some supposedly more fundamental principle of animal behaviour. As far as he was concerned, what we are witnessing in these exchanges is the expression of the distinctly *moral* part of human nature. In his own words:

> If we examine what it is one participant is ready to see that other participants might read into a situation and what it is that will cause him to provide ritual remedies of various sorts (followed by relief for these efforts), then we find ourselves directed back again to the core moral traditions of Western culture.[16]

Evacuee
The Evacuees, 1968[17]

It's a bit of cheek for me to talk about evacuation. I never went through the real thing and people who did always make me feel ashamed of mentioning my own comfy dislocations during the Second World War. I endured none of those really bitter separations which give such painful double meaning to the bland official term.

I was not suddenly taken away from my parents and I did not have to live through the horror of bedwetting in strange houses. Nothing like that. But I *was* evacuated. I was moved out of London, away from a settled home; and for reasons which I was too young to understand, travelled here and there in the depths of rural England without staying long enough in any one place to feel that I ever put down roots. Nothing ever seemed quite certain in those peculiar wartime years. We were together as a family but comfortably homeless at the same time. I don't think we stayed longer than six months in any one place and I must have been to at least eight schools between Dunkirk and D-Day. Existence seemed quite provisional and, although I never knew any real danger or discomfort, the restless inconstancy of those four nomad years have left traces which can never be rubbed out.

My father was practising as a psychiatrist in London when the war broke out. I can remember nothing of the occasion itself or at least not more than a very general sense of atmospheric alteration spread rather vaguely over a period of six months or perhaps even a year. It's all associated with a sense of diffuse novelty. We had moved into a new house anyway – perhaps a year before the war itself broke out – and there was a smell of new paint; bare ringing rooms still to be furnished and the thrill of a large new space waiting to be taken over and occupied. And then my father seemed to vanish. Not with any painful suddenness. But here, there and everywhere, he casually disappeared and the smell of turps and house-paint appeared in his place. And then he reappeared in uniform, mysteriously renovated by his absence, spruced up in a new coat of khaki trimmed with a Sam Browne belt.

He seemed younger, neater and altogether more bushy and vivid. And even my mother seemed to have been born again by courtesy of this strange political Easter. She sparkled now as an officer's wife; her suit had a chic military cut and in her lapel she sported an RAMC badge, tricked up into a piece of costume jewellery with diamonds, seed pearls and a flash of deep crimson enamel. And there were soldier suits for me and my sister – flimsy, sand-coloured denim with little glengarry hats. I still have the snapshot of this renovated family group – taken at some spare moment before the war got properly going – posed against a summer house (where?) with me and my sister caught in a priggish spasm of newly learned salutes.

And then everything seemed to fly apart and the travelling began. At first to escape the bombs – the ones that never came in that first six months. It seemed like an extended erratic holiday and not much more. My father had gone off to Aldershot for basic training and didn't join us again until the summer of 1940. Now it turns out, however, many years later, that there had been anxious journeys to and from London as my father and mother, panicked by the prospect of the German invasion, had used up his occasional weekend leaves to house-hunt for a safe haven somewhere in the West Country. But I can recall none of that. Not even my mother's absences. We were staying, I think, near Monmouth, right on the Wye, a short distance from Tintern; and the only thing which does come back from that hot dark summer is a sense of drugged rural heat, hay, and the hallucinatory memory of my father, heroically uniformed, standing among the harvest sheaves, taking a glass of cider with the local farmer. I don't think I can remember a single specific reference to the war. Or at least not as such. But there must have been something which got through to me, since the memory of that delicious corn-coloured heat is poisoned with suggestions of danger too. Perhaps it's something which I read into it backwards, now, after everything I've heard about the period as an adult. But I don't think so. The sweating stillness of that Wye Valley, almost 30 years ago, still frightens me much more than it pleases. There *was* an air of dreadful pregnancy and I can still hear the cool unhurried morse of a cuckoo hidden in those distant woods spelling out the orders for some horrible but as yet unrealized enactment. But then came the autumn and we were on the move again.

So was everyone else, though. There was a huge convection current and nothing seemed to be anchored any more, but drifted instead in slow perpetual motion. The trains were crowded with troops who seemed to have been *en route* for ever. They snoozed in the corners of our compartment and the corridors were jammed with their helmeted kitbags. Whenever the trains pulled into grimy midland junctions, they'd be waiting there too, propped up against each other, assembling for some obscure connection but without any real prospects of a final destination. It was called total mobilization. And that's just what it was. The cutting of everyone's local attachments so that everything and everyone became chronically mobile – as if the whole of English society had turned into plankton. It wasn't until much later that I associated all this movement with the war, or had any idea that these tired young men in uniform might be bound for anywhere except other railway stations. I knew nothing about the war itself anyway. I saw no wreckage, no ruins and no bloodshed. The only direct intrusion from the war itself happened quite early on, when a siren went off very loud right in the middle of the night for a raid which never materialized anyway. It happened in the first of our strange temporary homes, so the memory of it is perhaps more vivid than it might have been if the surrounding circumstances had been more ordinary. As it is, the raucous unclassifiable ululation burst into the blackness in such a way that the whole universe seemed to be on the point of breaking up and closing down forever. There was a blackout too and, as we had not been in the house long enough to have put up really effective blinds, we couldn't turn the lights on, so I was quite unable to place myself in the middle of this chaos. Added to which the room was totally unfamiliar – as so many rooms were to be in the next few years – so that, in the deafening silence which followed the last groan of the siren, I seemed to be as lonely and as disoriented as if I were hanging in the dark somewhere between Saturn and Betelgeuse. I can't remember where all that happened – somewhere in Britain, I suppose, like they used to say on the wireless about some factory or airfield. That was what evacuation meant in my first two years of the war: we moved, diffusely and at large, somewhere in Britain – so that my only firm memory is one of generalized and almost entirely abstract mobility.

I became very familiar with railways as a result, but with sidings and junctions in particular. I can't ever recall any rapid movement and nothing clearly recognized as a departure; certainly nothing so decisive as an arrival. No…*shunting* is what I remember most. Slow creaking advances along stationary lines of empty coaches and then coming to a halt while other trains, out of sight behind rows of tarpaulined trucks, passed on and away.

And there was always the fear of being split up during one of these slow uncertain moves in or out of a station. After a long hot afternoon in the clanking silence of some midsummer siding near Yeovil – or Swindon, it often was – one of my parents would sometimes get out and disappear along the crowded platform to try and obtain something for us to drink. And then the train would start to move, very slowly, back along the track we had come in on. And then suddenly (oh, unspeakable horrors) more swiftly, off at an angle, on to another line altogether: coming to rest at last alongside carriages of a completely alien colour…not GWR at all! Then silence, except for someone coughing and talking very quietly three compartments down. What tears! What irreparable desolation! Then there would be a sudden jerk in the opposite direction and slowly, with long soprano squeals from the metal bogies, the whole shooting match would creak back again into the station where the vanished parent would be waiting to laugh at one's blubbering face pressed to the filthy window.

I had no idea what all this *va-et-vient* was for. It certainly wasn't like ordinary evacuation, where you left home once and that was that – pending the duration, as they used to say. Most of our moves were made in the effort to try and keep the family together. My father had volunteered for the RAMC at the start of the war and since he was just too old to be sent abroad he moved around the south west of England, from one hospital to another. Wherever he went the family followed, and this generally meant packing up and leaving without much notice and after a brief stay. We covered an area only 70 miles in radius, in and around Hereford. It seemed to take in a landscape of infinite vastness and it seemed to go on forever. The official secrecy of the period just helped to confirm the gathering vagueness. The names had been taken off the railway stations so that all our travel took place in limbo. You couldn't ask anyone either – careless talk cost lives. Even proper names were in jeopardy, what with all that panic about identity cards. Everything seemed to be fading out as if it had once been written in invisible ink.

Things got cleared up in 1943. I was old enough by then to make out the sightlines, and the sense of general whirl seemed to subside. I also began to see what the war was about and knew something about the danger we had once been in. I had also begun to meet real evacuees and saw how their predicament differed from mine. In fact, these children, displaced like me yet mysteriously different, took a peculiar place in my imagination and assumed a baleful and tragic role. I had no reason to think that my own situation was at all unusual. I can only see that it was now. I certainly didn't think of myself as an evacuee and whenever the word was used at that time it only signified the situation of these other little city waifs who were billeted so oddly, without parents and without possessions of their own, in other people's houses. It seemed to us, knowing nothing about the violence of war, to represent the absolute of misfortune and loss. They were all rather like those horrible figures in M. R. James's story called "Lost Hearts" (1904) – grieving little phantoms with a long dark gash over their heart.[18] There were at least two or three of these lost hearts in each of the towns or villages we visited, and I can still remember their shrunken Fair Isle jumpers handed down from one of the children of the families in which they were staying. And they always seemed to have special evacuee colds, as well, with a thick jade dribble coming from one nostril. They were also stronger and much more aggressive than we were, despite their pallor and weakness and their grief. Possibly because of it. To comfortable middle-class children like myself these displaced infants were rather like werewolves. That is to say they were strong *because* of their weakness and dangerous *because* they were sick. They also represented a living embodiment of the condition which nannies threaten one with. They were, after all, the protagonists of banishment, so that looking at them in all their lost wolfishness one could see an image of oneself, turned out of the house and sent away for naughtiness.

By the time the war was drawing to a close our own travels were slowing down as well. In the last 18 months, by the time my own puberty was at least in sight, we had been long enough in one house for me to think of it as home, even though it was rented from an absent landlord who was fighting for his life in some corner of a foreign field. The social landscape stretched out to the horizon on each side and I knew perfectly well by then where I was both in space and time. I knew that the war must end, and would within the conceivable future, and that London was where we really lived and must finally return to.

My own childhood and my real sense of evacuation finished quite suddenly one morning in the summer of 1944. For half an hour I had been awake to the noise of a sky filled with aircraft. Not passing one way in huge formations as they had done for the past year – *en route* for raids over Germany – but backwards and forwards, with hundreds of aircraft going both ways in the same sky. It was the morning of D-Day. The prospects were crystal clear and I knew that my own homecoming was not far off. A year or so later, still in the same village, we watched with a rather drained sense of anti-climax as a large effigy of Hitler slumped on to a bonfire built in the backyard of the pub on the corner. A few months later my father's uniform had vanished and we were back in the house which had been newly painted when I left it, but which was now riddled with damp and rotten with mildew. Everyone seemed tired, ill and grey, and home life got going again.

Views
Listener, 19 December 1968[19]

It's coming round again: another godless Christmas – my twenty-eighth to be precise. Not that I actually lost my belief at the age of seven; I never had it to lose, but in that year I first became conscious of the fact that there was dispute on the subject, and insofar as I understood the issue I sided without much enthusiasm with the people who said that God didn't exist. My eldest son is now at the same age and although he differs from me in that he once did believe in God – a vague, somewhat Sumerian God – he has lapsed this year into a glum apostasy of his own. He has accepted this divine deliquescence with decent resignation and is even prepared to lend his secular presence, as a shepherd, to the school nativity play. I wonder how long it will be before he will first begin to feel those pangs of loss which I am only just beginning to feel now. For each Christmas I find myself thinking, against what I know to be unshakable conviction, that it would be nice if I could lend myself to the belief that on the evening of 24 December the world actually was trembling on the edge of some large redemptive fulfilment. No matter how much of a sceptic one may be, the imagination must be very inert indeed if it is not stirred by rootless feelings of piety in that hushed hour just before midnight on Christmas Eve. None of the other Christian festivals moves me quite like this: in fact, I am physically repelled by Easter, with all its trappings of the romantic agony. For this reason, I find myself – a godless Jew – gravitating at this time of the year to the back of Advent services, and although the words make no sense to my depraved understanding, the atmosphere of collective pious expectancy mysteriously quickens whatever sense of the holy still survives inside my pagan conscience. Not that I am ever likely to be converted by such skulking, vicarious epiphanies, but – like the poet Larkin – I find, without being able to help myself, that at Christmas time I recognize the church for what it is: 'A serious house on serious earth,'

> In whose blent air all our compulsions meet,
> Are recognised, and robed as destinies.[20]

Whatever seriousness is brewed in the churches this Christmas, it will all be dispersed and debauched by the time Boxing Day comes round. Just think of the profane utility of the gifts we exchange nowadays. The piles of presents under the tree look more like a bundle of contraband in the customs shed at Dover than anything which might commemorate the anniversary of human salvation. Odd, too, that it should be the Chancellor of the Exchequer rather than the Archbishop of Canterbury who should seasonally bemoan the 'flight into things.' There was a time when the presents exchanged at Christmas had some sort of sacramental significance; simple trinkets through the agency of which we expressed our mutual obligations in the sight of God. The very uselessness of such baubles somehow ensured a spiritual value which might otherwise be lost if the objects concerned had some practical function, over and above their role as gifts handed ceremonially from one person to another. In fact, presents of this sort become profane in direct proportion to their practical usefulness – just as the Host would become profane if it gave immediate physical nourishment.

What I am complaining about here is something much larger than the downright commercial vulgarity of Christmas. It's something to do with the way in which the poetical part of the public soul is progressively becoming replaced by prose. By the way in which we are less and less able to understand what is said or done to us unless we can readily translate it all into the Esperanto of common pragmatism. It is the awareness of this tendency, I am sure, which is responsible for the renewed interest in restoring ritual to the modern theatre. And yet, the process has gone too far for someone like Peter Brook, for example, to be able – by a conscious effort of will, or even imagination – to graft the heart back into the corporate imagination. The whole point about ritual, with its use of formal ceremony, is that the potency of symbols, or indeed of any hierophany, is dispersed immediately once the congregation knows that it is in the presence of something being used as such.

Two weeks ago I stood in the wings of a large provincial repertory theatre, gossiping to one of the actors, when he cut off in mid-sentence, took a deep breath, hung an artificial smile on his face, and plunged on stage, into the brightness of a scene we had rehearsed together a few days before. At one moment we were whispering our casual unfinished commonplaces and at the next we were separated from each other by a gulf that seemed wider than the one which lies between the living and the dead. Out there, only a few steps away, my friend was vivid and alien; his features and gestures brought into absurd clarity by the glare of a collective scrutiny which was quite invisible to me from where I was standing. After a minute or two he finished his assigned 'bit,' delivered his exit line with dazzling finality and climbed back into the natural shadows where I was waiting to carry on our conversation. Seeing me, he giggled at the transition and then turned to watch the colleagues he had left out there, acting to each other in the electric daylight of a limbo afternoon 'a few days later.' How odd to do a job where one gets paid for dressing up and speaking lines that have already been chosen for you long before you decide to utter them! How long can we survive like this? From what I have seen at the Nottingham Playhouse in the last few months, I suspect that the obituary of the live theatre has been written too soon.[21] Paradoxically, television, which seemed such a threat when it began, has gradually served to highlight the public appetite for live performance. It has something to do with the rough conviviality of the theatre and with the thrill that comes from knowing that both the audience and the actors occupy the same precious square of space and time. I remember talking about this with Stanley Kubrick, who expressed his impatience with the primitive rusticity of the theatre. I could see what he meant, but I felt that he had missed the point. The stage can never capture the dizzy vistas of the cinema, and even when the filmmaker sticks to small indoor scenes there is a wonderful narrative fluency about the camera. But the stage doesn't compete on this level of communication. Its stilted limits define its virtues – for something shocking happens when you confine dramatic mimicry to a small wooden rostrum. The action, even when it's trivial and vulgar, seems much more stark and exemplary, and the unrepeatability of each performance insists upon attention in a way that the celluloid never does.

It's not just that actors and stage hands might make mistakes – although the vague subliminal fear of that in itself creates a tension all of its own – it's because of the by now well-established cliché that every performance lives as something in its own right, over and above the text which provides the frame for what is done. In other words each performance is a unique incident in the history of the world, and although there is a superficial similarity between one matinee and the next, the audience turns up partly for the pleasure of seeing what is different. At one and the same time they are watching a scene and the accomplishment of a job. They are seeing what is depicted and at the identical moment they are watching the act of depiction. That act, that job, is totally new each time the curtain goes up on a fresh performance. Cinema has obliterated the job element from the drama. For no matter how hard the cast try to repeat what they did the previous evening, they confront the written text with personalities that have moved on in time since the last occasion. The very process of making up one's mind to try to repeat exactly what one did the night before abolishes the conditions for being able to do so. This fact is only too well known to actors, who stumble one night on a successful bit of business and try to repeat it at the next performance. It is in the theatre more than anywhere else that one discovers the truth of Heraclitus's proposition that you cannot step twice in the same river. For everything about the stage would make it seem that one ought to be able to do just that. The text is fixed, the moves have been worked out in rehearsal, and the lights, scenery and costumes are just as they were the night before. And yet, when the curtain comes down, you can always hear the actors talking about the peculiarities of what had happened that particular evening. The very immutability of all that surrounds the performance helps to throw into high relief the precious uniqueness of what was in fact done on the night, let's say, of 24 December.

Dickens
BBC Radio 3, 31 May 1970[22]

I was struck on reading Dickens for the first time by his pessimism, his sense of the inexorable process of history which drags human beings to their destinies, in spite of any action which they may take on their own behalf. I've often thought about the similarity between him and Darwin, about the strange parallel between the theory of natural selection and Dickens's great images of destruction in which only a few people survive, except that in Dickens's case it's not necessarily the fittest who survive. You get a feeling that the public Dickens would like to think that virtue is rewarded and that right prevails; and if one were to trace out the elementary lines of the plot, one would imagine that Dickens was an elementary moralist. But the events finally are so enormous that the individuals do become dwarfed, and you feel that underneath Dickens is secretly – perhaps unconsciously to himself – acknowledging the violent and destructive indifference of both nature and history.

It would be facile to say that he was simply a pessimist. It's just that underneath that jocular exterior, underneath that love of human foible, there is something much more secret, something much more passionate and peculiar and mad than people are publicly willing to acknowledge in him. Because to see Dickens as a purveyor of darkness would be to take him out of the area of BBC serials, the area of Christmas cards and of the jolly plum-pudding and Toby-jug world which makes him so popular. The Victorians had a very complex sense of depression and the part which depression played in the Victorian literary imagination has been underestimated. They were very torn between their sense of seriousness and duty and moral responsibility on the one hand, and their romantic sense of the imaginative power and virtue which were resident in the child on the other. This presumably was why they were so outraged by the Darwinian suggestion that we had descended from the apes: the apes are a sort of hairy children, and the idea that these frivolous coconut-throwing monsters should be our ancestors appalled them, since to be a heavily-suited, responsible, industrial creature making the wealth of England must have appeared to the Victorians to be the prize achievement. To have to acknowledge within themselves either the ape or the child, and to see in some cases that there was value in such an acknowledgment and value in such an ancestry, produced a sense of conflict which may have been one of the origins of this melancholy and despair which run through Victorian literature, particularly among the men.

It's clear when you read Dickens that to be a child at that period was a wretched business. Yet even in the most depressed of all the Dickensian childhoods – in Copperfield's, for example – there is a sense of some mysterious imaginative power which is going to be extinguished by the passage through the blacking factory into adult life. I will always remember, for instance, the minute perception that the child has in *Copperfield* of Peggotty's fingers or thumbs being like nutmeg graters: that sudden, almost hallucinatory vividness with which the child sees a tiny detail of the adult world.[23] One feels that as Copperfield grows up and becomes expedient he loses this minute sense of the visual world. What is so interesting about Dickens is that he himself came out intact from his passage through the blacking factory, in the sense that his visual imagination was still monstrously overdeveloped. Perhaps this is what being a successful artist is: it's being able to survive the process of growing up and to drag a certain element of that primeval vision of childhood with you.

I often wonder how important fear and repression and darkness and unexpectedness and gloom are to the creative imagination. One hesitates, for example, to take children to frightening films or plays and I don't just mean violent plays where they're going to see sadism: I'm thinking simply of gloomy or pessimistic plays. One always thinks that children shouldn't be exposed to this sort of thing, that they should have a bright, pleasant, interesting and creative childhood. But looking back on experiences which frightened me a great deal when I was a child, I can say quite clearly that they are, in fact, very important elements of what elements of imagination I now have in adult life. That the experience of fear, as long as it's not overwhelming and damaging and really mutilating, is an absolutely essential part of the imagination. One of the things which I feel about modern life – and in a sense I share this feeling with Malcolm Muggeridge – is that there's now an orthodoxy which insists that happiness is so much to be desired that every single institution, every single occasion, every single incident of our lives, should be bent in order to achieve this for ourselves and for our offspring. There is a feeling today that death perhaps is a postponable accident and that the doctors will have it licked before long, that we can transplant organs ad infinitum if not ad nauseam, and that human life can survive and human happiness be perpetuated for ever; a feeling that there are no glooms, no dark areas and no inexplicable patches. Now, in removing all these things we have gone some way to removing perhaps the essential features of the creative imagination which in fact rests ultimately on the sense of dread, the sense of mystery, the sense of the uncanny.

One gets a feeling, with Dickens, of one of those town-hall clocks in Nuremberg which display a series of very simplified, very grotesque allegorical figures who come racketing past us as the chimes occur, but who nevertheless seem somehow to project and summarize the human condition in a very effective way. The interaction of all these strange, monstrous, embossed, warty creatures who run through a Dickens novel is like a medieval allegory. The characters have vast hook-noses and monstrous gleaming blue eyes and very gaudy clothes, but in their total collaboration they communicate something essential about human life.

Dickens's sexuality often took the form, as it did with a lot of Victorians, of a sort of paedophilia. A tiny, chubby, rounded knee, seen through the childish petticoat, attracts the child molester in Dickens; and the only female characters in Dickens who seem to have any sort of sexual glow about them are in fact these young, discontented, sad, downtrodden girls – Little Dorrit and Little Nell, of course. It's like a Pre-Raphaelite innocence. The Victorians would have thought of this as the illustration of all that was sweet and just; after all, the child in Victorian iconography occurs again and again as the very symbol of innocence and of affection and of moral spotlessness. Therefore it's a very crafty manoeuvre of the imagination to desire the very thing which in fact is a representation of the denial of desire. The little angels that hover over the Victorian tombs, the child's hands that come in Victorian séances bearing flowers, the whole underworld of sentimental literature dealing with the death of children, and the little angels that come back – all show the place that the child played in the Victorian imagination as a representative of virtue. Perhaps it was because of this that they came to stand also as a paradigm of sexual desirability. In this way, Dickens is the victim of his times.

One of the interesting things is to ask why it's possible for someone like George Eliot to have written so intelligently about sexual relationships, thereby contrasting herself with Dickens, who seems so incapable of dealing with this subject. I wonder sometimes whether it isn't to do with the position of women; whether it isn't precisely because the woman was so functionless in public life that it was much easier for her to acknowledge these deeper streams of feeling and to deal with them honestly: she would not jeopardize her reputation by doing this. George Eliot had the advantage of being a true intellectual who finds every detail of human life a matter for discussion and examination. Dickens is not like this. There's a sense of the lapsed Methodist about him. Also, Dickens was a man, determined to make his way in the world and be a public success. And for a person of this sort it would have been very difficult to write with honesty about sexual affairs.

Dickens's sense of the destructive effects of the city is one of his most significant achievements. There's a marvellous description of the devouring ferocity of the city seen from afar in *Dombey*, when he looks towards it from some brick-filled desert about five miles outside London. Dickens describes the character going on towards this awful machine, which was going to engulf him and turn him into one of a number of impersonal particles jostling with each other in a giant process.[24] In this sense he's the creator of one of the most potent metaphors of human society that I know of.

I think, too, of that wonderful description of the morning after the suicide of Merdle in *Dorrit*: of the rumour spreading through the great city and of the sense that everyone – no matter who – in London is somehow going to be brought crashing to their ruin by the ruin of this single man. Dickens has an extraordinary capacity for building these doom-laden metaphors in conjunction with a whole series of subsidiary images. It's not just the giant Merdle collapse: it's also the minor metaphor of the dark house which gives way beneath the weight of its own brooding evil.[25] It's similar in some ways to the death by spontaneous combustion of Mr Krook in *Bleak House*. After Krook dies, the young lawyers upstairs become aware of the catastrophe in an extremely peculiar and surrealistic way: by the fact that grease starts to run down the window panes and a sort of greasy smoke starts to fill the room.[26] This is a completely impossible circumstance but Dickens is using it with such power and such control that he's somehow capable of making us believe that it has reality – which is the ultimate mastery of the imagination.

A bit of a giggle
Twentieth Century, July 1961[27]

Some years ago I woke in the middle of the night and found to my astonishment that I was shaking with laughter. I had had no dream to account for this immoderate mirth and as I lay there in the darkness giggling foolishly I experienced a curious sense of guilt. For in broad daylight, in the usual run of things, laughter comes attached to circumstances, soldered to a situation. It is, as it were, a rare commodity, pure and strange, issued by quota to sweeten the rigours of reality. In this way, lying in my bed at night, laughing for no reason, I had raided the psychic larder and was illicitly enjoying the primal honeycomb itself.

Humour, even when legitimate, fastened to a joke, has something of the naughty to it. Like fire, elusive and spirituous, it seems quite foreign to the ordinary world and must have been stolen, like fire, by Prometheus from the gods.

If it was, then cataplexy is surely the punishment. This is a strange disease in which the patients, fortunately a rare few, suddenly become paralyzed when confronted by a humorous situation. As they are about to laugh, they are seized by a total paralysis and they slither helpless to the floor. They remain quite conscious throughout but are unable to move a limb until the sense of mirth evaporates. Everyone is familiar with the feeling of being weak with actual laughter. Cataplexy is not to be confused with this. In this condition the paralysis precedes the laughter. It is provoked by the mental act of seeing the joke, by the first tremor of silent mirth which rocks the mind before it shakes the body.

The Victoria Palace, tattily decorated in fading Sickert tones, twice-nightly houses a revealing paradox of English theatrical humour. Enclosed in a triangle whose points are Victoria Station, Buckingham Palace and St George's Hospital, the ritual to be seen here each night somehow conveniently exemplifies the spirit of these utterly British institutions. The palace housing imperial tradition, the hospital professional respectability and student bumptiousness, and then the station, escape-hatch to a supposedly sexy continent. The Crazy Gang are licensed jesters of this rickety Establishment, performing an act which neatly symbolizes all the arrogance and evasiveness of the Englishman at his worst.[28]

This is not to say that I dislike the act. I love it; but every time I see this smutty rollick, I have an uneasy feeling that under the camouflage of outrageous irreverence these ageing gentlemen are bolstering up some of the more unpleasant aspects of our national character. Thinly disguised and often blatantly apparent, the performance deals with sex. I say 'deals' advisedly, since the method involved does exactly this: it deals with sex; disposes of it; and renders it apparently harmless. Though bawdy in the extreme, sex as such is actually eliminated as effectively as if it had in fact been bowdlerized from the text.

The routine consists of a series of sparsely constructed sketches which allows free reign to elaborate jokes in which bottoms, breasts and urinals receive obsessional attention. Also high on the list of topics are trousers, pants, trusses and hernias. Bed-pots, farts and contraceptives are not ignored. Few opportunities are lost for these knobbly old gaffers to get themselves up in 'drag,' which leads us neatly back into the bottoms, breasts and knickers routine. The audience, needless to say, shrieks its delight, indicating by its enthusiasm the power of the psychic tension which these performers seem so kindly to release. I believe that in fact the sense of release is entirely false and that this performance simply discharges neurotic transformations of much deeper tensions which are themselves studiously left untapped. It is a psychological decoy which gives a false impression of relief so that the more dangerous issues can fester undisturbed. For when it comes down to it the items mentioned above – the urinals, the breasts, the brassieres and bed-pots – are no more than the second XI of sexuality. The first XI, the central sexual issues, are never allowed to get out to the wicket.

The effect, I am sure, is unintentional. I cannot believe that the cast set out deliberately to lay a false scent. Nevertheless it falls in quite happily with the intentions of the Lord Chamberlain, who will blithely license this routine at the same time that he bars an honest treatment of the crucial themes. In this way the Chamberlain is exploiting the immaturity of English humour in order to preserve that very immaturity.[29] The very fact that jokes about farts and bed-pans *can* give a sense of release is a sign of this naivety. It is a sign of an infantile confusion; one which Freud points out to be a natural phase in normal development – the confusion between excretion and eroticism, the blurred elision between dung and love. It is significant that so much English humour rests on this confusion; witness "The Miller's Tale".[30] The Crazy Gang routine only serves to emphasize and confirm this confusion in the public mind. And as long as the confusion exists it will always be possible for Lord Chamberlains to exploit it to obscure the explosive issue of adult sexuality.

Many people have said that the Goons are the English Marx Brothers. How can anyone be so insensitive? For a start *The Goon Show* is probably the least American of any. It is crucially and quintessentially English; a delicious compound of Carrollian fantasy and imperial nostalgia. The whole series reeks of G. A. Henty and Rider Haggard, and the most successful episodes are centred on the outposts of a far-flung romantic Victorian Empire. Rickety forts in the Khyber Pass are endlessly besieged by frontier tribes. Ned Seagoon sets out on futile safaris into the heart of Africa. Major Bloodnok erupts with fearful dysentery in some tatty Sudanese latrine. The pleasure of this wonderful show is contained in the garbled memories of childhood reading which it excites, sauced with a sly scepticism of all the values of these nursery tales. Bloodnok's cowardice reaches heroic proportions. Grytpype-Thynne is utterly commendable in his suave and devious malevolence. And then, on the other hand, there is the purely *Alice* whimsy. The snotty, pubescent Bluebottle; Henry Crun, inarticulate with senility, White-Knightish and benign. The narrative abounds in lovable eccentrics: March Hares, Dormice and the like. American, indeed!

There is one curious thing about the Goons: some of the accents have been taken over and used by a very distinct group of the British population. These are the sub-technocrats. No other description really fits them. They usually work in television as cameramen or electricians. They are often lab technicians and many of them work in firms which make computers. They wear Government-surplus Lovat-green trousers with very wide bottoms. They have Fair Isle jumpers and sports coats with four different colours of ball-pen tucked in the top pocket. They are relentlessly up in hi-fi and belong to scooter clubs which go on weekend rallies to Burnham Beeches. There is no other way to describe these people. They belong to no distinctive social class but they are horribly at home with machines of all sorts. They are almost a genetic group and the spontaneous adoption of Goon accents seems to support this. They share a vague resentment of the Establishment and they exploit the cheeky accents of the show as a cabalistic language of protest. They are, to borrow a Goon term, the crutty Herberts of this world.

English humour leans heavily on accent. I can think of few successful shows which do not depend for their success on a parade of vocal grotesques.

ITMA was an uninterrupted stream of such figures.[31] The English seem, in some strange way, unable to be funny in their own voices. It is almost Shakespearian, this device. The humorous is co-extensive with the ludicrous and the ludicrous synonymous with the bucolic. Speak in your own voice here and you automatically speak seriously; the personal voice is sober and exalted. Dickens's comic figures are all contorted in one way or another. I personally flee into the sanctuary of an accent whenever I can – anything to escape the flaccid ineffectiveness of normal English with its toneless pallor and extended syntax.

For years I have envied the compact directness of American and when I first heard Mort Sahl my dissatisfaction with normal English reached its climax. Here at last was a man who could speak for himself without the protection of an accent and still be funny. In fact, as a purely verbal comedian I am sure that there is no one to touch him. He relies on no special effects but simply fires off a breathless sequence of laconic comments on the world as he finds it. His technique is associative, leading him from topic to topic in an eruptive pattern of breaks and improvisations which lead him back, sometimes only after 20 minutes or so, to the original theme. He is heavily indebted to the cannibalism of American speech. Nowhere else does a language build up from so many sources so that the final product is a rich agglomerate allowing the raconteur the widest range of allusion and suggestion. All sorts of dialects and group vocabularies are kidnapped for general use. Yiddish, German, professional jazz talk, psycho-analytic and sociological terms all combine and allow Sahl's often mumbled and unfinished sentences to set up vibrations of Empsonian complexity. It is quite impossible to reproduce these nuances in print.

Sahl himself stands head and shoulders above all the others of the American *Nouvelle Vague*. He deals with force and effect with issues that matter: from desegregation in the South to the wilder excesses of John Foster Dulles.[32] None of the others have this headlong relevance. Shelley Berman, a more conventional American nightclub entertainer, depends on fantasy. (A woman hanging from a flagpole of a department store becomes the subject of a frantic phone call from a man who lives in the opposite office block: '...There is a woman hanging from the flag pole of your third floor window... Yeah... Look! She has been there a *very* long time; her knuckles are *very* white.') Lenny Bruce, sometimes and unreliably, is excruciatingly funny but depends for much of his act on impossible sick jokes (cancer as a status symbol).[33] All betray the same disenchanted cynicism. Mort Sahl is alone in the intelligent curiosity which he brings to this yawning, adult *Weltschmerz*.[34] But, my God! What a relief to hear *Weltschmerz* voiced, clearly and succinctly: a humour that reflects a sophisticated pessimism, now entirely proof against shock or disappointment.

I think that I admire pessimism in humour above everything else. It really is the gold standard of laughter and that is why American-Jewish humour has such an attractive lustre. Groucho is the Archduke of this estate – dilapidated, disgruntled and irascible; an arsenal of withering wisecracks which puncture the romantic delusions of the American dream. He is surrounded by an entourage of deluded optimists: sweet young couples drugged with a sentimental narcissism, set to music in sugary duets which Groucho interrupts with caustic, leering innuendos. Margaret Dumont, flatulent figurehead of propertied American womanhood, is systematically insulted ('I'm Rufus T. Firefly. I cover a lot of ground.' 'Say, you cover a lot of ground. When are they going to tear you down and put up office buildings where you stand?')

Sexual schemes are set at nought. Groucho is caught necking with Margaret Dumont; Harpo is breaking in downstairs with thunderous sound effect. 'What's that?' flutes Miss Dumont. 'Sounds like mice,' cracks Groucho and abandons the already ludicrous love-making. Groucho embarks on all his projects equipped with a paranoid conviction that the whole thing will go awry, so that the enterprise is conducted as a joking relationship where the rancid humour protects him from inevitable disappointment.

This, at root, is a Jewish mechanism. Conditioned to expect that everything will turn out for the worst and that there's a bad time coming be it never so far away, the Jew feels sceptical hesitancy to every enterprise, sexual or financial. In the final reduction one's own opinions suffer the same introspective decay. My favourite Jewish joke – indeed my favourite joke – is the primal *Ur*-jest of this philosophy. Two men are talking:

'What is it hangs on a wall, is green and whistles?'

'I don't know. So, what is it?'

'A herring!'

'But a herring doesn't hang on a wall.'

'So? You can hang it on a wall, can't you?'

'Sure! But a herring isn't green.'

'Well you can paint it green, can't you?'

'Sure! But see here! A herring doesn't whistle.'

'Okay. Okay. So it doesn't whistle.'

Many English people mistake the point of the Marx Brothers and enthuse over the zany antics: the cabin scene in *A Night at the Opera* (1935), the mirror scene in *Duck Soup* (1933). These are brilliant, to be sure, but they are standard vaudeville routines: any good team of clowns could have done them. No, the crucial Marxist thesis is the mocking doubt, the weary scepticism and the cheerful conviction that everything under the sun – sexual, financial and political – will, nay *must* turn out about as badly as anything could.

Intestinal ethics
Spectator, 20 January 1961[35]

Whatever else happens to him, when a patient goes into hospital he can be sure that his bowels will receive passionately close attention. As often as not his induction into the ward community starts with a ritual purge and, if he resists it, he is often regarded with beady suspicion by the nursing staff throughout his stay. And this is only the initial baptism. While he remains in the ward he is closely watched for signs of backsliding. Each day a fresh-faced junior nurse will mince prettily around the ward with a clipboard conducting a sort of inverted consumer-research poll. At the first sign of irregularity the missionaries pounce again with alarming instruments of forcible conversion. The actual phraseology of the daily poll is significant. The patients are rarely asked point blank whether they have had their bowels open. 'Have you been good?' is a favourite usage. It is interesting how few patients take this for anything else but a question about their bowels.

This elaborate programme goes on quite independently of the actual medical treatment and is sometimes even at cross-purposes with it. It is the older ward sisters who get most wrapped up in their Augean business, and will even slip in a crafty suppository when the doctor has ruled out such measures only a moment before.

And as for the poor incontinents – these unfortunate people, often the victims of advanced neurological disease, become damned in an unrelenting system of intestinal ethics. This is not to say that the nurses are actually cruel to such patients, though I have seen this. Indeed they are usually kind and forbearing, but there is without doubt an insidious sense of moral indignation in addition to mere physical repulsion.

Nurses are not alone in this preoccupation with the bowels. Doctors themselves may suddenly go quite gaga over this very issue. It is not so long ago that the great Arbuthnot Lane was shouting for the removal of the large bowel with just a bit more heat than scientific conviction alone would have provoked.[36] The large bowel, he thought, was a great cistern of toxic evil left inside the abdomen by a sanitary oversight. Deep colonic irrigations, laxatives and special breakfast foods all cater for the same irrational anxiety where regularity and ethical purity are so painfully confused. The patients themselves are often very grateful for these personal attentions, since lying in a hospital bed will often disturb their personal rhythms. Some of them become quite upset and agitated if they do not revert quickly to their old habits. I remember several women who went in for unaccountable fits of weeping until the sister restored their composure with a well-timed enema. I remember asking another patient why he was looking so fretful. He glanced conspiratorially around the ward, whispered darkly that he had not 'been' for three days and leaned back to enjoy the look of shocked amazement which he expected to flood across my face. I flickered not a muscle. I bent towards his ear instead and hissed triumphantly that I had often not 'been' for ten days. He recoiled in horror and would not be persuaded that I had suffered no ill-effects from the stoppage. Perhaps group confessions of this sort would help to dispel this silly guilt – a sort of Constipateds Anonymous. There is nothing to suggest a physical basis for such a disturbance, but it is true to say that the patients who exhibit this petulant, listless behaviour seem to share the same fastidious personality, along with a strong sense of thrift and duty. Many psychologists have felt tempted to attribute such personality traits to features in the patient's early bowel training. Of course, it is very hard to establish such hypotheses on a firm footing: the variables are so enormous. However, on first principles alone it would be hard to believe that the elaborate business of Western toilet-training would act on the bowels alone. The whole set-up is too fraught with love, aggression, bribery, threats and seduction. It would be very strange indeed if continence were the only result of the experience. In fact one could say that continence emerged as a trivial by-product of the whole noisy transaction.

The small child voids himself automatically and derives considerable pleasure from the relieving sense of evacuation. Later on he learns to turn around and look on the product of this pleasurable activity with pride. Then, quite suddenly, as one psychologist has pointed out, he must learn, under pain of losing love, to attach anxiety to excretory materials. He gets involved in a sort of cash nexus in which he learns to barter faeces for affection. He gets acquainted with what must seem to him to be strangely changeable values of bowel produce: here is an object which has high value when deposited in one place only, disgusting when put on the floor. It is not surprising that the child develops a somewhat ambivalent attitude toward this function of his body. In households which focus obsessional attention on the bowels, the child is taught to feel ill if he does not eliminate regularly. The normal muscular sensations come to be thought of in terms of terrible toxins seeping into the bloodstream. Eventually the child is brainwashed into a feeling of guilty lassitude if he does not empty his bowels each day at the right time. Nannies are specially given to this sort of bogus physiology and the child who spends any time in her care will carry her dotty ideas to the grave. At the same time the rest of his emotional apparatus will be geared to this first encounter. This, after all, is his first engagement with the adult world, so that by analogy all later situations involving order and restraint will be underpinned by the system of values which he has learnt with so much noise and shouting in the control of his bodily functions. So that it is hardly surprising that thrift, tidiness and other forms of moral continence have a scatological undertow. In this way adult disturbance of bowel action will quite naturally engender the obsessional fretting which the makers of patent medicines must find so profitable.

Reflections
California Institute of Technology, April 1999[37]

I feel overawed at the idea of coming to Caltech, particularly as I'm a guilty fugitive from science.

I descended into the disreputable morass of the theatre and constantly feel remorse at having lost what I believe to be, and what my teachers thought was, a more serious subject. There are still one or two ageing professors of mine whom I always cross the street to avoid for fear of meeting their disapproval.

I'll start by talking about a question which I'm often asked: how is it possible for someone who had an interest in the biological sciences, and then in medicine, and then in neurology, to go into the theatre? Aren't they completely incompatible? Aren't they incommensurable disciplines? In fact, in some mysterious way there is a curious and almost inevitable connection between the work that I was trying to do in neurology and the work that I continue to try to do in the theatre. It has to do with the fact that my interest in neurology and my interest in the brain was never specifically neurophysiological. I was never a good enough mathematician or a good enough biophysicist to be in traditional, hard, cutting-edge neurophysiology, though at Cambridge I was taught by some of the greatest men in the field: the late Alan Hodgkin, Andrew Huxley and E. D. Adrian. So I was, as it were, brought up in the purple of the subject, but embarrassingly recognized at a very early stage that I really wasn't up to the maths and physics required to do important neurophysiological research. But in any case I think that my interest in the brain was almost entirely connected with what I would call 'higher orders' of human action; I was really interested in what went wrong with the brain and what went wrong with conduct, with movement, with speech and with perception. And I recognized that I could probably make a perfectly interesting career for myself in the qualitative observation of patients' behaviour, competences and performance as a result of brain damage.

I undertook to take a medical degree, not because I was interested in helping anyone; I didn't really want to go into medicine to do good. I didn't want to do *harm*, but I knew that a medical degree assured you a ringside seat closer to the action than you could have if you were merely qualified as a neurophysiologist. You were allowed to ask ruder questions and poke your hands into ruder parts than you could if you didn't have a medical degree. I was interested in seeing what happened when the brain was damaged, what it was that people couldn't do, and I hoped that would give me some sort of insight into what went into being able to do the things that we seem not to have to think about.

One of the extremely striking things about human behaviour is the peculiar transparency, and indeed inaccessibility, of the apparatus which mediates our performances and our competences. If mine were the only brain in the world, and I didn't have access to other people's brains – which I could see by opening their skulls – then I wouldn't know that I had one, nor would I have any information from my competence or from my experience or from my performances or from my sensations. I would not actually be aware of the fact that all of these things were mediated in some way by some material substance or some material apparatus.

In a sense I'm reminded of this rather more acutely by having recently curated an exhibition on reflection at the National Gallery in London.[38] I was struck by the fact that the mirror has been so frequently invoked as a metaphor for the mind, for the reason I think that there is nothing to be seen in a mirror except what the mirror reflects – that the mirror only gives you an image of a world elsewhere; it gives you an image of the world of which it is a reflection. And looking into a mirror, try as you can, unless the mirror is flawed or damaged in some way, you are absolutely unaware of the medium which supports the reflection of which you are conscious. The only thing that can be seen in a mirror is what it reflects. You don't see the mirror itself at all, though of course you get these rather peculiar and paradoxical experiences in which, when you are aware of the fact that it is a mirror – if you have circumstantial evidence to the effect that what you are looking at is not a window, for example, but is in fact a mirror and is reflecting something – in addition to seeing what it reflects, in some mysterious way you are also aware of its objectively non-existent surface.

I was first struck by this about ten years ago when my wife and I were driving back from Switzerland and stopped off for a rest at a lakeside on the Swiss-French border.[39] And I immediately noticed the peculiar sheen, a shine on the surface of the lake. I found myself asking my wife what to her was an extremely tedious question, and that was, 'Why does it look so glassy?' And she said, 'Well, because it *is* glassy.' And I said, 'But there's nothing to be seen on the surface of the lake except a perfect upside-down replica of what's to be seen on the other side of the lake. If you look very carefully, there is no debris floating on the surface, there is no ripple on the surface, there is no deformation of the surface. All that is to be seen is a perfect upside-down reflection.' Why, in addition to seeing what was reflected in the lake, did I also see the surface which supported the reflection?

And I then started to bore her even further by conducting a series of informal experiments. I brought up a piece of paper from the foreground, which blocked off the view of the near shore, and I then brought down a piece of paper from on top which blocked off the vision of the distant shore, of which we could see the reflection in the lake, so that now all that could be seen was a sort of letterbox view of the reflective surface. Now, once I had deprived myself of the information that it was a reflection I saw, I suddenly became aware of the fact that all that I could see was an upside-down image, a paradoxically upside-down image of mountains and trees. But in the absence of the circumstantial evidence to the effect that it was a reflection, the only evidence to that effect was that it was upside-down.

Deprived of its context, it was also, I found, deprived of its glitter. Now the sheen of the lake was no longer there, all that was to be seen was what was represented in the lake. I then became very interested in this presence of what I would describe as an illusory surface. It's the counterpart of something which has been pointed out by experimental psychologists for a long time – started by the great Italian Gestalt psychologist Gaetano Kanizsa, who introduced something which has become the logo now for the Exploratorium in San Francisco. You know, the three black discs arranged in a triangular format, in which there are bites taken out so it looks like three Pac-Men (p. 46). Now, in addition to seeing three black discs with wedges taken out of them, you see – as a result of their configuration – something which objectively is not present, which is a white triangle overlying the three black discs, to the point that you can actually see or seem to see subjectively a contour between the edge of this non-existent triangle and the white background upon which it lies. Here you have an illusory contour.

Now, I believe that something similar is going on when you look at a reflection in a lake and when you look at a shiny surface in which you see an absolutely perfect reflection. When you are allowed to see the entire composition from which you can infer that you are in the presence of something reflected in an invisible surface, you credit that invisible surface with a presence which it otherwise doesn't have, objectively. And this seemed to me to be a perfect metaphor for the mind. Looking at you, there, in front of me, looking up into the lights, all that I can see is what my senses deliver to me. I cannot, by inspecting my own experiences, see the grain or the substance, which actually supports this in exactly the same way as my not seeing anything in a mirror except what the mirror reflects.

I was puzzled at a very early stage, long before I sat on that lakeside, by the strange invisibility and impalpability of the apparatus I was told I had inside my head, which afforded me these experiences and competences I could undertake without having to think about them. I found myself doing sort of Wittgensteinian things: I lifted my arm without thinking what I had to do in order to lift my arm. I knew when I became a medical student that, in order to clench my fist, a necessary condition of my clenching my fist was the contraction of the muscles in my forearm. But in no way could I actually bring about the contraction of the muscles in my forearm as a prior condition of my clenching my fist. In fact, paradoxically, it seemed to be the other way around. The only way in which I could get access to the forearm muscles and make them contract was by clenching my fist. I don't really know what I have to do in order to contract my biceps, but I know that the best way of contracting my biceps is to bend my arm against resistance. So, in other words, all of this apparatus which affords me my motor competences, all of this apparatus through which I experience the world, is in fact totally transparent to me. It is totally without physical, visible, palpable properties. And I was puzzled by this gap that lay between experience and the third-person knowledge that I had a brain inside my head which afforded me all these experiences.

So I went into neurology in order to get myself into the best third-person seat in the house, from which to see what the connection might be between having a brain and having experiences. I am still puzzled, in a way that some philosophers in Southern California seem not to be puzzled, by the fact that one of the consequences of having a brain is that one sees red and tastes coffee. Now, it seems to me that there is no problem about what David Chalmers, for example, has called the 'psychological properties' of having a brain: the competences that come from perceptual distinctions, memory and the sorts of things we can easily reproduce with computers.[40] But there does seem to me to be an absolutely insoluble problem, and I believe it to be radically insoluble, about how it is that this stuff can actually taste coffee and see redness.

Now, I know that there's no mystery involved. I don't think something magical gets snuck into the system and confers experience upon an otherwise totally material setup. But I think it is probably impossible in the foreseeable future that we will solve the problem of how it is that having this rather unpromising porridge inside the skull can actually yield redness to its owner. There seems to me to be no problem about how it is that having this porridge inside the skull can yield all sorts of abilities to distinguish and press buttons when different hues of redness are exposed to the owner. That's not a problem at all. You haven't got to have an experience in order to do it; you can actually set up a machine which can make such discriminations. But, to quote Thomas Nagel, there is a mystery in the fact that there is something it is like to be us. As he points out, there must be something 'it is like to be a bat.'[41] Well, I think that there is something much more mysterious in that there is something it is like to be us, and I suspect that, even if I had stayed in neurology, I would have remained as puzzled today as some people are not (and I think quite unjustifiably not) puzzled that there is such a thing as redness rather than responses to a particular wavelength of light striking the retina. The problem of redness is extremely odd and one which I think people are far too confident about solving. They believe that ultimately it's an emergent property in the way that liquidity is an emergent property of H_2O molecules put together in a certain way. John Searle at Berkeley believes that consciousness emerges in exactly the same way as liquidity or conductivity emerge from certain configurations of physical matter.[42]

Another example cited is bioluminescence. We didn't know how it was that a firefly or a glow-worm could switch lights on and off. Well, we solved that; we know that an enzyme called luciferase catalyzes an oxidation reaction, which releases a photon. No problem. But unfortunately there's a curious tendency to try to equate bioluminescence and consciousness as if, in fact, consciousness were simply a brain-glow: an observable thing, an emergent property which came out of putting together matter in a certain way. So we have this weird, paradoxical situation, in that we know that it's nothing other than matter put together in a peculiar way, but the idea that matter put together in a peculiar way can yield content and excitement and things like redness and coffee seem to me to be beyond our understanding at the moment, and I suspect beyond our understanding at any future moment that we can imagine.

Nevertheless, it seemed worthwhile to go on in neurology even if, in fact, the problem of experience, the problem that the philosophers call *qualia* would remain insoluble. There was lots of other work to be done, and it was not, as Patricia and Paul Churchland at University of California San Diego insist, a counsel of despair to say that this would never be solved.[43] There's plenty of work to be done – we will approach this problem asymptotically and never arrive at it, but en route to it all sorts of extremely interesting things will be solved with regard to our ability to calculate, to remember, to distinguish colours, and so on and so forth. And also to raise our arms without being able to contract our muscles knowingly.

Now, what on earth connection could all that have to the theatre? Well, one of the things which became clearly apparent to me was that the work I did as a diagnostician in neurology sensitized me to the demeanour of people. A good clinical neurologist could probably do 30 per cent of the diagnosis by the time patients have got from the door to the chair, and could do it without having to use any sort of technical instrument but by merely watching the demeanour, the behaviour, the gait, the facial expression, and the way in which they address him and give an account of their illness. In fact, the performance of a patient sensitizes you to behaviour in a way that is completely transferrable, wholesale transferrable, to the theatre.

What are we doing in the theatre? We are getting people to pretend to be people they are not, which is very hard to do. You watch actors down in the canteen after they have rehearsed – and usually rehearsed very badly – trying to be someone they're not, but down in the canteen they are totally at ease with themselves when they order coffee and talk to their fellows about what they're going to do next. One is immediately struck by the peculiar discrepancy between being yourself and pretending to be someone else. And what it is that actually happens, as you rehearse and get better at being someone you are not, starts to concentrate the mind wonderfully on the problem of what it is to be oneself in the first place. Once you start getting people to pretend to be someone they're not you have to start breaking down the modules of behaviour, and it focusses your attention on the spontaneous performance of self because you're actually asking people to pretend to be selves that they're not. And you can watch the incompetences, the failures of performance of an actor, in exactly the same way as you watch the failures of performance of a damaged patient. I'm not saying that actors are damaged, but actors are 'damaged' until such moments that they have actually gone onto the stage with what they believe to be – and what the audience agrees to be – a satisfactory performance. There is a long period of individualism between the moment when they are given the text and yield the final performance. And by observing that long invalid period when they are handed a text consisting of lines which have not occurred to them but for which they have to give the audience the impression of uttering and meaning them – in that long invalid period, by watching what it is that goes into that incompetence, you learn something about what competence itself consists of.

So there was an almost seamless transition for me. I found there was no awkwardness or difficulty or inconsistency about having watched damaged patients whose motor systems were off, damaged patients who were unable to recognize their relatives, and watching actors. All of these things which I saw in neurology seemed to have a bearing upon the things that people were doing when they were rehearsing. I also found a very interesting reciprocity between being a doctor and being a director: in addition to finding that the work of observation – which I had been trained to perform as a neurologist – lent efficiency to my directing, I also found that the observations I made in the rehearsal room could feed back into clinical work. I found myself going back to the wards and seeing things my clinical colleagues had missed. People often say, 'Well, of course, the reason why a doctor finds it so easy to be a director is that you're dealing with mad people, disordered people. We all know actors are potty in some way.' It's got nothing to do with that. Actors are not potty; actors are perfectly ordinary and often rather humdrum people who sometimes spring into a more colourful existence when they're pretending to be someone other than themselves. But that's not the appeal. The appeal is not that you could help people – actors – who are damaged, but rather that, in seeing people who can't quite get round being someone else, you are actually focusing on what goes into being a self in the first place. So I went into the theatre. I found it a very intellectually profitable way of simply extending the work that I was trained for in the years that I had actually been studying clinical neurology.

The rest of my work time in the theatre I spent working on what one could loosely call 'the classics.' I worked on texts, on scores, which are inherited from the relatively distant past, works which probably have had a longer posterity than their makers could have imagined. It's extremely unlikely that Monteverdi and Shakespeare ever in their wildest dreams imagined that their works would be bequeathed to others who were so fundamentally and recognizably different from them and from their audiences. It's very hard to put ourselves back into the imaginations of people in the sixteenth or seventeenth century and to conceive the notion of posterity as visualized by them. We know that most works were, in fact, composed for the occasion, so we have this rather peculiar and interesting philosophical problem of what to do with works intended for an occasion, and which have been retrieved and revived and undone by people who are utterly different from the people for whom the works were intended.

The phrase I constantly invoke in describing this is what I call the 'afterlife' of plays and operas. With very few exceptions, I think you can say that almost all forms of art have what you might call their natural life –

a life for which they were intended, an audience for whom they were intended. And then at some time which is very difficult to date accurately – and it may not even be reasonable to *want* to date it accurately – they enter something which you could loosely call their afterlife. They are now being seen and visualized and retrieved and valued and reconstituted for reasons completely different from the reason for which they were composed and enjoyed at the time they were done. So there is a deep procedural problem about what to do with these works from the distant past, which fall into our world like meteorites from another part of the cosmos. I became fascinated by the problem of how to perform something when you don't know what it was intended for originally and what the sensibility was of those to whom it was delivered.

I sometimes think that it's very similar to the distinction that was made in 1903 by the geneticist Wilhelm Johannsen, who distinguished between genotypes and phenotypes.[44] What you have in the form of a text or a score is something like a genetic instruction. It's a promissory note with a view to something which will be created by obeying the instructions. But what in fact is created as a result of following the instructions depends, as it does in biological organisms, on the environment for which those instructions are delivered. Subsequent performances of the dramatic phenotype will often be profoundly different on successive performances from the performance that was generated by the same genetic instructions at the origin.

This poses a deep and interesting problem about transformation and interpretation. Audiences – particularly in the United States where they're very conservative about opera – who believe that there is a standard phenotype which ought to be preserved at all costs, become terribly restless when it's not preserved. They believe that the genotype tells you what the phenotype should look like, and that the phenotype should be preserved as it was at the origin. But of course very few people have any idea what the original archetypal phenotype looked like. We don't know what the first night of *Twelfth Night* (1602) looked or sounded like at all. All that we have is this sort of rough DNA which has come down to us imprisoned in literary amber, which we can, as it were, prise out and put into modern actors and create a Jurassic Park of modern drama. There's no way we can ever backtrack to the original phenotype because we don't know what it looked like, and we certainly don't know what it sounded like.

There are only very incomplete reports of what the earliest performance of *The Marriage of Figaro* (1786), for example, was like. There's no way of knowing. And indeed if there were a way of knowing, there is a deep perceptual problem about how you obey the instructions of the phenotype as exemplified by a record.

Let me tell you what I mean by that. The problem is raised most acutely by forgery, which, in a way, is the prototype of the faithful performance of the original phenotype. Now, doing operas is a very expensive business, so you cannot afford to junk the performance of any given after the inaugural run. You've spent so much money costuming it and designing it and simply putting it on the stage the first time, that you have to go on reviving it at successive intervals. What you do is write down a series of parallel instructions, in addition to the score you inherit from Mozart or from Verdi. There's a prompt book, which says: 'A moves downstage left, sits down, and turns contemptuously towards B.' And after the first year, by reading those circumstantial prompt-book instructions, you can reconstitute an approximation of that inaugural phenotype of the performance of that particular production. After about four or five years, when the instructions in the prompt book are no longer being read by someone who was there at the time they were written down, it becomes extremely problematic as to what those instructions really mean. You can work out mechanically what they mean. A little arrow pencilled in shows A moving downstage left, and you can say, 'Well, darling, what you do is you move downstage left,' and then the actor or the singer will turn to you and say, 'Well, *why* do I move downstage left at this point?' And you look it up and say, 'Oh it doesn't say. It doesn't say why.'

What would have happened if we had had a perfect, faithful videotape of the first night of *Twelfth Night*? Well, there is an interesting perceptual problem in copying a performance which is visually in front of your eyes and ears at the time, and there is a deep procedural problem about what goes into copying something. To use Nelson Goodman's term, what do you think the example exemplifies?[45] Which aspect of it is important? More often than not, you may have at your disposal in the first three or four years an assistant or a stage manager who was present at the time of the original performance who could say, 'Oh, what you see on the videotape here does not exemplify what people wanted in that inaugural performance; it's a fault. It's something which is not a realization of what was intended. It's a genetic error, a misprint, a mistranslation of the instructions.'

Now, what happens when people consult the videotape 15 or 20 years later? How do they know which part of it is, in fact, the part which ought to be copied? They have to start looking at it with a view to what they think is interesting in the example, and this brings me back to the question of forgery. Forgeries are by definition the prototype and the epitome of the faithful phenotypic reproduction. All forgeries become apparent after about 30 or 40 years. Why? The most interesting illustration about that is the story of van Meegeren's forgeries of Vermeer during the Thirties. Van Meegeren was an envious, failed artist, who felt that the only way in which he could attract attention, or prove to a disbelieving art world that he was, in fact, a genius of some sort, was forgery. Since people didn't like his original work, he said, 'Well, I will show how good I am by reproducing a work of someone who is widely admired, which will thereby prove that I'm as good as he is. I will do Vermeers.'

Now, there's no point in doing Vermeers everyone knows already because they would obviously be copies of Vermeers, so what he had to do was produce original Vermeers. When he delivered his original Vermeers, the art establishment in The Hague was taken in by the paintings and said, 'These are indeed interesting examples of the early Vermeer of the period of *Christ in the House of Mary and Martha* [1655]' (which you can see in the Edinburgh Gallery). And then something rather fascinating happened: he stupidly sold a couple of his pictures to the Germans, so that in 1945 he was had up in front of a Dutch court for collaboration, for selling a national treasure to an occupying army. Van Meegeren now had to say, 'Well look, no, those are in fact by me. I was not selling Vermeers. I was only selling van Meegerens and who cares a damn?' The court then said, 'Well, prove it.' So he painted another van Meegeren. Now here something deeply intriguing happened, as Nelson Goodman points out in *The Languages of Art* (1968). In the knowledge that these two or three he had done were, in fact, van Meegerens, the genuine Vermeers which were previously seen as imperceptibly the same as his forged Vermeers now became quite clearly distinguishable.[46] Now, this isn't because people were just being wise after the event. Rather more interestingly, it shows what goes into being wise after the event, what being wise after the event consists of perceptually.

And as Goodman points out, once you have circumstantial, independent evidence to the effect that groups A, B and C are van Meegerens, whereas the groups from D to M are in fact true examples of Vermeer, you can see it. Once you have a perceptual incentive to see the difference, the difference is glaringly apparent.

Now, this is related to something the great Harvard taxonomist and systematist Ernst Mayr pointed out. During the 1930s fireflies in the Caribbean comprised no more than about four or five different species, based on morphological grounds. After the Second World War, new electronic methods of recording the flash frequencies of fireflies showed that on flash-frequency criteria there were at least 14 or 15 different species. When the flies were caught and sorted into enamelled trays according to their flash frequencies, morphological differences which had previously passed unnoticed suddenly showed that there were as many species on morphological criteria as there were on flash-frequency criteria. In other words, there was a perceptual incentive to *look* for differences that had previously passed unnoticed.[47]

Something very similar happened with Gilbert White, the author of *The Natural History and Antiquities of Selborne* (1789). Two types of hedge bird, what we now know as the meadow warbler and the pippit, had previously been regarded as members of one species. When White observed them more closely and noticed that there were two song patterns, it became apparent that what had been thought to be one species actually split morphologically into two.[48] And that's exactly what was happening, I think, in the case of the Vermeers and van Meegerens.

Now, this is a roundabout route to asking the deeper question: why is it that now, more than 50 years later, anyone – not just an art historical expert, but *anyone* – going down into the basement of the Rijksmuseum and looking at van Meegeren's Vermeer forgeries will wonder, 'How was anyone ever taken in by it?' Again, this is not simply being wise after the event. Something much more fundamental is happening than what Goodman pointed out on the first occasion when the distinction was made. Why is it that people now, 50 years later, say, 'These are quite clearly not Vermeers.' They may not know that they're by someone trivial like van Meegeren, but they know that they're not Vermeers. It is clearly apparent by 1990 that they're not Vermeers, and the reason is simply this:

that what people thought Vermeer exemplified and what in Vermeer a forger thought was worth copying in 1932 were completely different from what people thought worth copying, even to the point of being indistinguishable, in 1990. So that even though the name of the game in forgery is indistinguishability, the forgeries become distinguishable with the passage of time, because time brings in a different view of what you think you are copying and what you are doing *by* copying something. In the act of copying something you are introducing a perceptual bias, some sort of idea of what you think is exemplified by the prototype – what you think is valuable in it, what is worth reproducing in it.

If that's the case with something like an autographic work, think how much truer it is when it comes to something Goodman has described as an allographic work, one that doesn't depend on reproducing an artefact but on simply obeying a series of verbal instructions with a view to a performance.[49] After all, there is a sense in which *Hamlet* doesn't exist between its successive performances. It exists in the form of these genetic instructions, but they're fixed in amber in the library. They can be read by people, but *Hamlet* itself in some plenary form doesn't exist until it is brought into intermittent and successive realization in performance. But the problem is how do you obey the genetic instructions? What do you think the genetic instructions exemplify? This deep interpretive problem arises with the passage of time. But even if you take the instructions and reproduce every single word of *Hamlet*, why is it that successive versions of the play look so different? Because what we think the text exemplifies, what we think it is an instance of, will vary with the passage of time.

This happens with anything that we inherit from the distant past. All of these works are in their afterlives. We value them for reasons totally different from the reasons they were valued by their maker, and also for reasons very different from the reasons they were valued by their audiences at the time they were first seen. Think of the Belvedere torso in the Vatican Museums in Rome – this armless, legless object; this strange, luminous, twisted torso which has no limbs at all. We know perfectly well that the author of that work would be extremely distressed to find it in that form. He would have to say, 'Well, you should have seen it when it had its arms. I'm very disappointed to think that you're exhibiting this mutilated version. It scarcely counts as an instance of my work.' And yet, in some odd way, it is in that mutilated version that we cherish it, so much so that we would be deeply distressed, I suspect, if by some sort of radiocarbon dating method we could find the original arms and put them back on again. There would be a sense that in some way it had been violated just as much as was the Michelangelo *Pieta* in the Vatican with its nose knocked off. The restoration is often seen by us as almost as much a destruction as a mutilation, and that is because it has entered our lives in the form that it has. Rodin, inspired by such mutilation, made some of his statues limbless or headless or armless because he got excited by the very form in which the work actually entered its afterlife.

I think any responsible director in the theatre, sort of like a plant breeder, takes these strange genetic instructions from the distant past and makes them into something intriguing and interesting to an audience in the late twentieth century; makes them recognizable. I don't want to use the word 'relevant' because I think relevance actually means that it always has to address current problems. I don't think things from the past are made interesting by torturing them until they deliver some sort of confidence about our situation. This is an example of what T. S. Eliot called the overvaluing of our own times, as if the works from the past exist in a sort of probationary relationship to our own times, as if they are interesting only insofar as they can address our problems.[50] That's going to the other extreme. I think there must be some way in which we actually treat them as alien objects, as something coming from something else, from elsewhen, from elsewhere; but nevertheless, unavoidably, they have to be treated as if they're going to interest us in some way without necessarily addressing our current interests. Not every version of a Verdi opera has to be set – as so many German colleagues of mine do it – in a concentration camp in order to be interesting to us. But there *are* ways of reconstructing and, God forbid, deconstructing them – one of the hideous new trends in the theatre these days. It's as if the genetic instructions are bequeathed to the modern director, who then does a lot of genetic engineering on the instructions themselves and actually transplants things and makes them mean something totally different from what they might have meant at the time. But I think there is a generic range of meaning that things might have, and if you go beyond that, you make a shambles of the work.

As I near my retirement from the theatre, I find myself confronted by this very peculiar problem of dealing with works which come from a long time ago.[51] One of the paradoxes of modernity is that it is characterized by extraordinary archival obsession with its inheritance. In 1700 no one would have expected to see a performance of a play or an opera which came from a hundred years earlier. Monteverdi was not performed for 300 years. He went into some sort of peculiar aesthetic hibernation. The idea of performing Monteverdi 25 years after his death would have been completely inconceivable, just as it would have been inconceivable to have performed something from 100 years earlier. Why is it that we are so fascinated with retrieving these works from the past, and why is it possible to go to a concert hall or an opera house and see works from three successive centuries in the same evening sometimes? You can get a work by Monteverdi and a work by Schoenberg performed in the same evening.

But a culture so energetically retentive and so eager to bring stuff back from the distant past makes problems for directors, producers and audiences. I think the audience has made the problem even harder for itself by insisting on the idea that there is a standard phenotype which must be preserved at all costs. In very big opera houses, such as the Metropolitan Opera in New York, where I've worked several times, audiences are deeply disturbed if they see a 'classic,' as they call it, transposed in some way – if they don't see lavish scenery, if they don't see what they think was the original phenotype on the stage. They have every reason to think that it was the original phenotype because they don't know what the original nineteenth-century version of Verdi looked like. I suspect they would probably be horrified by what went on in the nineteenth century. What happens is that modern audiences have another sort of psychological process going on not unlike Konrad Lorenz's imprinting of geese. What the audience thinks is the orthodox performance turns out merely to be the performance by which they were 'imprinted' the first time they were exposed to it. In exactly the same way as you can get a greylag goose to court a wastepaper basket (if that's the first thing it's exposed to, it will go on courting a wastepaper basket in exactly the same way), modern audiences will go on courting the operatic equivalent of wastepaper baskets in the form of a prototype of the first time they saw *Il Trovatore* (1853). If it departs from that, they think it's departing from orthodoxy. It's not. It's departing from what they were imprinted by, and the difference between that imprinting experience and the inaugural performance is probably very profound. If you were to compare the version they were imprinted by and found satisfactory, it would probably bear a very marginal relationship to what they think was the inaugural one.

Trailing clouds of glory?
New Yorker, 31 August 1963[52]

First the Birds and now the Kids. The old standards of innocence are under fire. Perhaps it was Henry James who originally turned the screws on the clean Wordsworthian image of childhood. Anyway, that romantic notion had long ago been knocked out of literature, and then Hitchcock smeared the Franciscan reputation of birds, leaving us with no fixed moral point by which to navigate. The world has become a Satanic sea, and we are adrift in a hurricane of evil, with the pole star of innocence gone forever. A few years back, in his imaginative and, one supposes, unsettling novel *Lord of the Flies* (1954), William Golding ruined whatever illusions we had left, stomping them to death with Hobbes-nailed boots. Professor C. B. Macpherson, in his recent book *The Political Theory of Possessive Individualism*, makes an interesting point that has a vital bearing on the main thesis of *Lord of the Flies*. He says that Hobbes' theory of the natural man – a nasty brute with a short, ferocious life – is not, as some have held, derived from some actual original state; it is a deduction from current naughtiness, a retroactive fiction that draws its gloomy conclusions from evidence in the here and now.[53] In other words, its pessimism works backward. While seeming to lay our present ferocity to the persistence of an original brutishness, it actually postulates that ancient state on the basis of the hoggishness we have at hand. It appears to be Golding's view that the public-school cherubs in his novel *revert* to a primitive state. In reality – to look at it the way Professor Macpherson might – they merely ditch a few courtesies and reveal a full-blown version of the bullying nastiness that they already showed back in England's green and pleasant land. And this is the strength of Peter Brook's remarkable film version of Golding's novel.

With an uncanny ear for locker-room chat, Brook, who both adapted and directed *Lord of the Flies*, has reproduced all the callow customs of the English public school. Far from being, as Golding had it, a universal allegory or a parable about the human condition in general, this is a brilliant local satire. For all its war paint and bonfires, totems and pig-sticking, it never departs from the classroom idiom, and in this it has a great deal in common with Robert Musil's *Young Törless* (1906). The desert island is a convenient dramatic counterpart of the Austrian attic where the young toffs act out their sadistic ceremonies. It's an undress version of familiar public-school vice, removed from the restraining hand of 'Sir' – an alfresco production of *Tom Brown's School-days* (1857), with Jack, the fierce young chorister, filling in for Flashman, the bully of the Upper Fifth. The satire gains strength by this adherence to local colour, and it is greatly to Brook's credit that he has not been seduced away from it by the booming generality of the book. All that stuff about mythopoesis is nice enough, but it shouldn't distract one from the humdrum exchanges between the actual boys, since it is in these that the satire really finds its meat. The details of 'picking up sides,' the furtive giggles at a bare-bottom beating, the wrangling over leadership, and the inky chatter of the younger boys are beautifully captured in Brook's free improvisations. This adds up to a drama that is far more piercing and, in the end, makes a far more convincing point than any of the book's anthropological ideas, which, when they are not trivial, are certainly dubious. Brook's direction has been attacked elsewhere for having his boys talk like young public-school boys and for failing to show them as young savages. Yet this seems to be its triumph. The picture's final burst of anarchy, for all its fierceness, is not a return to some hypothetical state of savagery; it's just schoolboys run wild – murderous and bloodthirsty, perhaps, but still schoolboys. When authority goes and misrule prevails, we do *not* return to a primeval condition but rush instead toward a more turbulent and hectic form of our previous, civilized condition.

There is an astonishing performance by Hugh Edwards as the myopic Piggy. Stumbling along the strand in his long, baggy shorts, this extraordinary young man has mastered the style of Golding's fat, cowardly pragmatist. Crippled by asthma and held up to scorn for his ridiculous figure, Piggy has all the dreary realism of someone whose physical handicaps have driven him to resignation. Disqualified by his bulk from the sporty heroism of his colleagues, he has a plodding common sense that provides a perfect counterpoint to their cruel Jungian fantasies. He is just too fat and breathless to be swept away by their athletic volatility of spirit. He is accidentally wise – unmoved by all the talk of monsters, not through any superiority of intelligence but because his fat boy's world of tea and telly simply won't allow such aberrations. He serves as ballast to the slightly Wagnerian extremism of his more streamlined schoolmates. Hugh Edwards carries all this off with magnificent aplomb, and the flat, adenoidal monologue in which he tells his mates everything about his home town of Camberley is an inspired episode, placing his role with perfect accuracy. Tom Chapin, as the ruthless Jack – a lanky, pubescent sadist – displays all the moody vanity of this type. Tom Hollyman's photography makes beautiful use of grainy close-ups, and the whole thing has been cut with sabre-toothed abruptness by Peter Brook and Gerry Feil. The soundtrack is conspicuous for a fine, harsh sibilance – the crackle of branches and the hot whine of insects.

Shadows of doubt

Atheism: A Rough History of Disbelief, BBC4, 11 October 2004

For his last major documentary project, Jonathan Miller attempted the first television history of atheism. This opening programme traced the ancient origins of disbelief.

It is some years since I was on the Staten Island ferry, and when I last looked back at it from here, the skyline was dominated by the twin towers of the World Trade Centre. It seems quite odd to think of it in the light of religion but its absence now reminds me of the religious implications of what one saw on television on that hideous day, and although, when it happened, many people said it was a cowardly act – atrocious, it certainly was – it really is quite hard to see it as 'cowardly' exactly, since it was perpetrated by people who sacrificed themselves in the certain knowledge of their forthcoming death. It's inconceivable that it could have been done *without* religion, for it is only in the name of some absolute assurance of a permanent life after death that someone would be willing to undertake such an act. And we know that the men who did so did it in the name of

ONE THING AND ANOTHER

a religion which they upheld against a society whose lack of religion – as they saw it – they deplored, and whose support of Jewish claims in what is called the Holy Land they were implacably opposed to. Therefore, the conspicuous absence of the twin towers, involving as it does the inherent conflicts between Christianity, Islam and Judaism, is I think one of the most powerful expressions of religious fanaticism in the late twentieth and early twenty-first centuries.

Understandably for Americans, the events of September 11th aroused tremendous feelings of hostility towards the religion in whose name the terrorists' act had apparently been performed. It drew attention to the difference between them, the Americans, on the one hand, and the Muslim world. But it's important to remember that you only have to travel a few miles from New York City to find yourself in the middle of a country which, far from being the secular world which was deplored and attacked by the Islamic fundamentalists, is in fact intensely Christian and therefore, in its own way of course, just as religious as the Muslim world that attacked it.

But for someone like myself who has nothing which you could possibly call a religious belief, or even feeling, the spectacle of September 11th is a forceful reminder of the potentially destructive power of the three great monotheistic religions that have dominated the world in one way or another for nearly 2,000 years.

I wouldn't want to say, and I think it would be entirely inaccurate to say, that my interest in or my objections to these religions was actually provoked by the events of the last two years. All the same, these events do bring one face to face with the consequences, both social and political, of beliefs in the divine, the supernatural, the holy, the sacred and the transcendent. Ideas which I, like many others, find alien, uncongenial and, to be frank, almost unintelligible.

I want to investigate the antecedents of my own disbelief and to consider the history of what I'm reluctant to call atheism. In fact, I'm rather reluctant to call *myself* an atheist. And that's not because I'm embarrassed or ashamed of it or because I fear for my life, as I might have done in the olden days if I'd announced that I was. Nor have I any reason to think that I might be socially disabled in a way that I once might have been. No, the reason I'm so reluctant is that atheism itself has acquired almost sectarian connotations and it hardly, as far as I can see, seems worthwhile having a name for something which scarcely enters my thoughts at all. For myself, as for many people, it's only in the light of such current controversies with regard to belief that I've found myself willing to explicitly articulate my disbelief.

I think it's important to make a series like this because at a moment when intense commitments to different forms of monotheistic religion have now acquired, or rather *reacquired*, such an intense political connotation, it's important to indicate that the widespread *suspicion* of disbelief is becoming a real threat to free thought.

It isn't as if atheism were a small religious sect. In fact, it's not another form of religious belief at all. And it's important to understand that disbelievers constitute a much larger percentage of the population than religious people, and especially politically-motivated religious people, would like to think.

I was born in England but my grandparents came here from Lithuania as Jewish refugees, and for Jews, spread as they are across the world, their religion has always seemed an essential part of their cultural identity.

(Miller enters the New London Synagogue in St John's Wood.)

This is the first time in almost 60 years that I've visited a place of worship for anything other than sightseeing. When I first came here it was in the name of religion, though not with any religious motive on my part. The fact is I was sent here by a Jewish father – sent here because he thought that I owed it to what he called 'my people.' The reason is that, quite suddenly, because he had been so appalled about what had happened in the Holocaust, and guilty about having escaped it, he felt that he and I owed some sort of identification with the group. Throughout the war, from 1940 – at which time I was six – until 1945 or '46, I don't really think that I knew or really understood that I was Jewish. When my father said that I *was* I didn't really know what he meant.

I came here to several services when I was about 11 or 12, on what were called the high holidays. But I came here not knowing what I was participating in. It was conducted in a foreign language which I didn't understand, written in a text I couldn't even read. There was singing but the singing was completely different to the singing with which I had grown much more familiar with by virtue of the fact that I was a prep-school boy and attended Christian prayers. So I found myself sitting right at the very back, as far back as I could from the main action, amongst a group of people with whom I felt no particular identity, in spite of what my father told me about my identity. And I stuck it out here during the services as long as I could, wondering just how long I'd have to stay before I could return and satisfy my father that I had in fact attended.

Well, my atheism – if that's what one insists on calling it – was not at any point a rejection of anything. What I was being introduced to scarcely seemed to be something against which I had to rebel. This all happened at a time when I simply felt myself to be an English schoolboy and the only thing that I was rebelling against…well, it certainly wasn't the dogma or the doctrine, because that was completely inaccessible to me and I hadn't been introduced to it earlier. It was simply the coming here on those occasions took up time, when I might otherwise be enjoying myself playing cricket.

And to be honest, I didn't feel alone in this. I suppose there were lots of boys for whom religion – Christian or Jewish – must have meant *something*, but my closer friends and I spent no time at all thinking about gods of any kind. Perhaps I was too dumb or just too interested in cricket or in girls to ask myself any questions about religion. If I had not been, I might have inevitably asked myself questions that have troubled sceptics and unbelievers for as long as men and women have been sceptical or have lacked belief. Is there really no God, and if there really is no supernatural dimension to the universe, why have so many people throughout history and in *so* many different cultures thought there was?

The problem, as I've already said, is that there are so many different forms of scepticism, disbelief and free thought, that it's quite hard to do a straightforward history of it, as if it were something that simply grew to become the fully-formed thing we know today. In any case, what it is to *be* an atheist is itself very complex and very questionable. The word is like 'atypical' or 'asymmetrical.' The word *a-theist* simply means not really theist, and that of course begs the question what *is* a theist?

Oddly enough it's quite difficult to find a simple, straightforward history of atheism on the religious shelves of your local bookshop, and although the subject is dealt with at considerable length in some of the more scholarly works, it soon becomes apparent that, in contrast to each of the three monotheistic religions whose articles of faith are explicitly affirmed from the outset and continue to be expressed throughout their subsequent development, it's quite difficult to identify a correspondingly explicit current of denial.

(Miller enters the reading room of Dr Williams' Library in London.)

In the case of Christianity, for example, more than a thousand years after its establishment you'd be hard put to identify an openly sceptical rebuttal of its supernatural claims, and that's hardly surprising when you consider the cruel penalties which were often inflicted on anyone convicted of subversive belief.

Paradoxically, some of the sources of disbelief are to be found amongst the arguments of *believers*. It's important to understand that Christianity was constantly redesigning its own dogma and theologians often formulated the most dangerously sceptical arguments in their effort to test the impregnability of their own faith, and in doing so they unknowingly furnished atheists with readymade weapons.

Now, what we're talking about here is disbelief, and that's a notion which presupposes something which it contradicts – in other words, belief. Because, in the absence of belief, the whole idea of *dis*belief would be unintelligible, so if we're going to trace a history of the various things that we call atheism, we have to understand what we mean when we use the word 'belief.' So I'd like to jump into what you might regard as the shallow end and consider some of the ways in which we talk about belief.

To find out more about that I talked to the English philosopher Colin McGinn at his home in New York.

MILLER: Before I start asking you about your beliefs and disbeliefs, I'd like to get into a little bit of an analysis of what we are saying when we talk about believing at all. There seem to be some situations in which one says 'I believe this, that… I believe *in* this, in ordinary things.'

MCGINN: These are usually implicit or tacit beliefs. Belief is a technical term, as it's used in philosophy and psychology. It really just means what you are going to take for granted, what you'll act on, what you'll assent to, what you might gamble on. That means you're committed to it being the case. Belief is just an umbrella term to capture all the varieties of assent, of takings to be true. That's a huge variety of different things, actually – all the way from 'I believe there's a table in front of me' to 'I believe there's no God or a supreme moral principle,' or 'I believe in democracy.' They're all valid uses of the word belief but different phenomena from case to case.

MILLER: In the case of believing, when someone *has* a belief or believes, they don't have to be in that state of mind consciously all of the time in order to be the upholder of a belief.

MCGINN: Exactly. You can say of someone fast asleep, he believes that Paris is in France – and it's true, because beliefs are dispositional. 'Implicit' is another term for it. They're unlike thoughts – a thought is an occurrent phenomenon. At a given moment, you take something and occurrently believe it.

The fact is it sounds rather odd, doesn't it, to say that someone is believing at a particular moment. One can't be in a state of belief all the time. On the other hand, that doesn't mean that we stop believing if we happen to have something else on our mind. It's just that belief is not in any sense an 'episode.' It's impossible to say at any moment that one is entertaining a belief. Now, that doesn't mean that the notion of time is actually inapplicable to belief. After all, someone can *become* a believer having not been one sometime earlier – in the case of St Paul, for example, who was dramatically converted to belief in the divinity of Christ at a particular moment. But once acquired, dramatically or otherwise, belief is not a continuously experienced mental state. In fact, it's somewhat questionable whether belief is actually a state of mind at all. It's certainly not one for which there is a corresponding state of brain that one might be able to identify using a CAT scan, allowing one to say 'Oh yes, he's having a belief at this moment.' Someone who believes in God, for example, isn't necessarily entertaining that thought – whatever it is – all the time. If he's trying to remember where he's left his keys, for example, the thought of God's existence or whatever isn't in or on his mind at the time; and when he suddenly finds his keys, the state of mind of believing in God doesn't suddenly reassert itself after having being pushed off centre-stage.

It doesn't *resume* its rightful state after what was, a moment earlier, a lapse of belief. It's not like that at all.

What I've said about belief is also true of knowledge. I *know* the alphabet. I know my multiplication tables. In fact, I know a large number of things without being explicitly conscious of any of them at any particular moment. But, although belief resembles knowledge, there's a very importance difference between the two. In the case of belief, you can say that someone believes X and that he was wrong, but it sounds rather odd to say that someone *knows* X and is wrong. It is part of the definition of *knowing* something that it is the case, whereas *believing* something to be the case is a state of mind about which you could be proved to be wrong.

My beliefs, religious or otherwise, represent dispositions rather than a particular state of mind which I might or might not experience at a particular moment. In other words, instead of being an episode in my mental life, my belief is expressed by certain tendencies – a tendency to entertain certain thoughts or feelings. And in the case of religious beliefs it also involves the disposition to participate in certain social actions which we call rituals – prayers, services, and so on – all of which dramatize in some way or another certain attitudes which I assume with regard to the meaning of life and the possibility of its continued existence after my death. In one way or another these rituals imply the existence of things or entities which I cannot *know*, in whose existence I must simply believe.

MILLER: Largely we tend to invoke the notion of belief when there is some sort of disagreement in the world around you about whether one does assent to this, that or the other.

MCGINN: Yes, that's when we bring the notion up, when we're having a discussion about 'What do you believe?' 'What are your beliefs?' means 'which questionable, debatable issues do you take a particular stand on?' And that's when we use the word 'belief.'

MILLER: So that it's about debatable issues.

MCGINN: I think that's how we use it. That's why primarily it's used in connection with religion and politics, because those are issues where people hotly debate the fundamentals of it, so they tend to say 'This is my belief about the political situation,' 'I believe we should not go to war with Iraq,' 'I believe there's only one God.'

I'm sure that Colin McGinn would agree with me that it's important to recognize the different implications which the notion of 'belief' has, in the case of religion on the one hand and politics on the other. You see, when it comes to politics and for that matter ethics, belief refers to how things ought to be: 'I believe in equal rights,' 'I believe in democracy.' And when I say any of these, I'm referring to moral preferences. Whereas, in the case of religion, although there are of course beliefs which refer to how things ought to be, the main body of religious belief consists of assertions as to the existence of this, that or the other.

Well, even at this point you can begin to see that belief is rather a complicated idea, and what makes it even more complicated is the extent to which it can be brought about voluntarily, if at all. And yet the states of mind associated with belief can seem so enviable that you might conceivably *wish* to believe. And in fact Colin McGinn, for example, says, indeed, that he would quite like to believe.

MCGINN: I would like religion to be true. I would like it to be true, because I'd like there to be immortality, I'd like there to be rewards for those who have been virtuous and punishments for those who have not been virtuous – especially the punishments would be good; there's no justice in this world! It would be good if there was some cosmic force that distributed justice in the proper way that it should be. It still is to me a constant source of irritation and pain that wicked people prosper and virtuous people don't.

But he *doesn't* believe.

MCGINN: So you feel disappointed and you feel, you know, the fact that death is death and that's the end of you. Most people find that difficult to take. So it would be nice if those things were there, but I just don't believe they're there anymore.

So what's the problem? Or to put it another way, is there anything that Colin could do to convince himself that he was after all immortal and that he would in some way or other survive his own death? Well, the fact is that those who do believe in such things often encourage those who don't to make some sort of effort. It's a question, they say, of making a leap of faith. Well, the problem is that it's quite hard to imagine the sort of exercises that one would have to undertake in order to make such a leap, if indeed it was a leap. The best one can do is to visualize the sort of experiences – misfortunes say, or even revelations – which might bring about a change of mind. But that's hardly a leap, and some people might simply regard it as a lapse.

Admittedly there are things that I believe in without being directly acquainted with them. For example, I've never actually seen a coelacanth with my own eyes, but I believe in them. Also, I believe that the Earth goes round the sun, although it certainly doesn't look as though it does. I take these things on trust for the simple reason that I recognize the authority of the people who say that they do. But then, on the other hand, you get a whole range of dubious entities such as ghosts, witches, spirits and immortal souls, which I don't believe in at all, but the people who *do* believe in them don't necessarily do so on the basis of trust or authority. The psychological origins of such beliefs can be traced back to certain predispositions that we all share simply as human beings.

The anthropologist Pascal Boyer has written at considerable length about the origins of the religious impulse in human beings.

BOYER: I think there are major themes that you will find in most religions in the world, but those things are not the things we are familiar with, so a concern for who created the world, for example, is not one of them. A concern for mortality – what's happening to me after death – is not one of them, in a surprising way. But the presence of unseen agents in the environment is one thing that you will find everywhere. You'll find that there is some notion that there are spirits, ghosts, ancestors – agents of that kind that are sort of counter-intuitive because they're not like you and me or animals. They don't have a physical body, but they have all the characteristics of agents – like a mind, intentions, and so on.

According to Pascal Boyer, this notion of 'unseen agents' is not quite as counterintuitive as it might seem. It may actually be hardwired into our brains. In a primitive community, the accidents and misfortunes that inevitably happen make more sense if it's assumed that somebody or something actually *intended* them to happen, and strange coincidences which are often genuinely hard to explain make more sense if it's assumed that there is some hidden intention behind them. And those assumptions are often still made today.

It may seem strange to suggest that we are hardwired to suspect that we're threatened by potentially malign, as opposed to merely harmful forces, but there may be good selective advantage to this tendency in a world in which you are surrounded by predators. Although there's always the possibility of making embarrassing mistakes and over-attributing agency – seeing intention where there's none at all – it's worth making the occasionally embarrassing false-positive, when the alternative is the catastrophic false-negative; in other words, when you land up being lunch. And it's only one short step from avoiding genuine threats to believing that other misfortunes may also be the result of malign intentional forces – that they may be the result of hidden, even invisible intentions directed against you.

MILLER: Now what is it that makes that religious as opposed to what one might call, or some people might call pejoratively, superstitious?

BOYER: Well, it's your choice of term, and I think it's just a human phenomenon that corresponds to what we generally call religion. What we tend to call religion is more this sort of institutional framework that uses those beliefs, or fosters those beliefs, but really those beliefs are there – institutional or not – and they're there in very simple societies where you don't have a church, but that's just one of the features. Another one you'll find is a propensity to organize rituals, to get together and do a whole set of things that are directed at those unseen agents in an organized way, with a script that has to be rigidly followed.

So if rituals based upon beliefs in spirits and witches represent the origins of religion, can we find the origins of atheism in these primitive communities?

MILLER: In these preliterate communities, would there be anything which corresponded to what in literate communities would be the village atheist? Is there a village sceptic?

BOYER: No, I don't think there would be a village sceptic. There are characters of that kind who would have become the village sceptic or the atheist in modern contexts. But in that kind of context that's not really a role that you could choose.

MILLER: Why not?

BOYER: The kind of person who would say 'witches do not exist' or that anti-witchcraft rituals are a joke, would be suspected of being a witch: 'who but a witch would go around saying there's no such thing as witchcraft?'

MILLER: So that even in very simple, preliterate communities with relatively simple social structures, there is a close relationship between village authority and village belief.

BOYER: Very much so. Most of those places are places where you do answer to calls, and answers to calls are about dead old men organized by living old men who have authority over everyone else.

So, one of the problems we have in telling the story of disbelief is that even in the most elementary social arrangements religious belief became almost inevitably associated with authority and power, and, as those social arrangements became more complex, with patriotism. Thousands of years later, nowhere is this association more obvious in the Western world today than it is in the United States of America, and few commentators have observed the phenomenon with more scepticism than the American playwright Arthur Miller.

A. MILLER: Certainly, the religious overlay of patriotism has come into fashion. It's always there of course, in this country. We've more people go to church here than I think anywhere, but it's gotten heavier now.

J. MILLER: Is that since 9/11?

A. MILLER: It was always here but it's gotten thicker, it's gotten heavier, because it's such an easy way to cuddle up to what they think the majority is about. They've convinced a lot of people to forget that this country was founded by people who were really escaping the domination of a governmental religion, and who breathed freely here with great gratitude that they didn't have to obey a church.

J. MILLER: One always gets the impression that the enterprise in Iraq had a sort of faith-based patriotism. It wasn't just patriotic, it was *Christian* patriotic.

A. MILLER: Oh yeah. Of course in wartime I suppose we did that in the Second World War to a degree, but it was never laid on with a trowel in this way. It's now being used as a means of persuasion. It's patent. It's obvious. They call upon God to initiate a programme, whatever it may be. They lard it over with some religious verbiage to make it seem as though if you oppose this you oppose the Lord. There are a lot of Americans – I think they're a minority, but they're very vocal – who are really aching for an Ayatollah.

And what Americans are aching for, certain American Presidents are tempted to supply. Certainly in 1987, George H. W. Bush stated that people who did not believe in God might have, at best, questionable rights to American citizenship: 'I don't know that atheists should be regarded as citizens, nor should they be regarded as patriotic.'[54]

So, in the United States no public figure and certainly no one who wished to enjoy popularity as a politician could risk it being said that he or she was a disbeliever, and yet there's a substantial minority in the United States who hold no religious beliefs of any sort at all.

It's interesting, as Arthur Miller has just pointed out, that the Christian faith is such a significant theme in American public life today. Because when this country declared its independence in 1776, it also enshrined in law that the church and state should be completely separate. The very first President of the United States, George Washington, for example, was a very unenthusiastic churchgoer who always walked out of the service before the congregation took the sacraments. And when the Rector of the church admonished him for this, Washington accepted that his sudden departure might after all seem to be a bad example, so he subsequently never bothered to attend the church at all. And the Presidents who closely followed him in that office were often on record as being considerably less than devout Christians.

God is an essence we know nothing of. Until this awful blasphemy is got rid of there will never be any liberal science in the world.
JOHN ADAMS

The clergy believe that any power confided in me will be exerted in opposition to their schemes, and they believe rightly.
THOMAS JEFFERSON

I have seldom met an intelligent person whose views were not narrowed and distorted by religion.
JAMES BUCHANAN

My earlier views on the unsoundness of the Christian scheme of salvation have become clearer and stronger with advancing years.
ABRAHAM LINCOLN[55]

Judging by the standards set by George H. W. Bush, it seems doubtful if any of these great American presidents would have been considered for, let alone voted into office today. All the same, it would be wrong to suggest that the United States is now an uncomfortable place for atheists. I feel entirely at home here and I'm more often than not in the company of people who have no faith and no time for the officially sanctioned 'sacred patriotism.' For them, as for me, the tenets of and the conflicts between the great faiths, even at their most frightening, are still faintly ridiculous.

The whole religious complexion of the modern world is due to the absence from Jerusalem of a lunatic asylum.
HAVELOCK ELLIS[56]

The Anglican Church in England is astoundingly moderate and accommodating. All the same, there's still a faint feeling that atheism is best kept under wraps. There's a kind of fastidious distaste about admitting it, for reasons which are really quite hard to identify.

(Miller enters King's College Chapel.)

It was here in Cambridge that I became an undergraduate more than 50 years ago, and I was surrounded by the architectural symbols of the Christian heritage. By the time I came here I'd already decided to study medicine and, although it's difficult and I think rather misleading to make a simple equation between science and disbelief, the biological sciences with which I was already acquainted left very little room for religious considerations. All the same, when you walk around these ancient buildings, the images and architecture of Christianity are inescapable and undeniably beautiful. *(Admires the stained-glass windows.)* These of course are stories and events which are deeply buried inside the imagination of any literate European. I don't believe a word of it. I don't believe the divinity of any of this, but I would be very impoverished if I didn't have these in my imagination. It would be a very thin form of life which didn't have these images.

It would be a mistake to think that my scientific training as an undergraduate confirmed my pre-existing disbelief in the existence of God. Many of my medical colleagues after all were pious Christians. No, the fact is that it was my exposure to modern linguistic philosophy which helped me to distinguish between my belief in genes or atoms – things which you never see directly – and my disbelief in supernatural entities such as Gods and spirits. The point is that philosophy, right from the outset, has concerned itself with the nature of existence itself – with what might or might not exist.

With thoughtfulness, and above all with literacy, thoughts themselves become subjects of discussion in a way that they wouldn't have been before they were written down. It's not until they are written down that they become stable enough to bear examination in the same way that physical objects themselves can bear examination, and indeed philosophy as such doesn't really emerge until literacy occurs, and even then not conspicuously until the Greeks who start to question the nature of reality itself. And it's with the philosophy of the Ancient Greeks that we finally get to what you might call the deep end in our examination of the history of disbelief.

[Surely] you don't believe in the gods. [...] What's your argument? Where's your proof?
ARISTOPHANES[57]

Here we are in the midst of the Elgin Marbles at the British Museum. It's an hour or two before the public floods in, and I find myself wondering what they'll make of these artefacts, retrieved as they've been from a civilization with which we really have no contact at all. The objects you can see here are the ruined fragments of effigies which were defaced some years after the adoption of Christianity by the Roman emperor Constantine, because they were seen as idolatrous threats to the new religion. Now, although idolatry was seen as the principal threat to Christianity, the culture represented by these statues also contained unillustrated themes which would later be recognized as a much greater danger, for there were certain Greek philosophers who expressed what were seen as subversive doubts of the role of supernatural beings in the natural world.

What we discover in looking for the first atheists is that, more than 2,000 years ago, there were men – whose names may not be as familiar as Aristotle or Plato – who began to make extraordinary claims about the origin and nature of the universe. Men such as Democritus. As far as we can tell, Democritus was an amiable man who felt that the greatest good was happiness and contentment. In spite of the fact that living 400 years before Christ he had absolutely no scientific reason for thinking so, he believed that all matter was made of atoms or indivisible particles, and that included the soul, if indeed the soul existed. He was also convinced that everything that existed had existed forever, and that therefore the Earth had never been created. The question that arises is whether or not this really is the beginning of atheism.

The historian Sir Geoffrey Lloyd has studied these early Greek philosophers.

LLOYD: What I think to be a fundamental question is what atheism means in different societies with the background of different religious institutes, because atheism in a polytheistic society is going to be very different to atheism in a monotheistic society, and most of the talk of atheism seems to me to be related to the religious institutions that we associate with Christianity. A fundamental question is who felt *threatened* by atheism, and what sanctions were available to get the deviants back into line. And if there isn't a church – as there wasn't in pagan antiquity, after all – then the whole thing looks very different. To be an unbeliever in the ancient world was much easier. I'm not underestimating the originality of the philosophers, because they produced new ideas and new arguments, and the arguments are of course extremely impressive and they have quite a life.

The first Greek philosopher to address himself explicitly to the question of the existence of God or of the gods was a follower of Democritus, namely Epicurus. And his argument is as vivid and powerful today as it was when it was first expressed 2,300 years ago:

> Is God willing to prevent evil but not able? Then he is not omnipotent.
> Is he able but not willing? Then he is malevolent.
> Is God both able and willing? Then whence cometh evil?
> Is he neither able nor willing? Then why call him God?[58]

In addition to his doubts about the existence of the gods, Epicurus clearly did not believe in a life after death.

> Why should I fear death? If I am, then death is not. If death is, I am not. Why should I fear that which cannot exist when I do?[59]

The importance of this early Greek philosophy is revealed by the way in which it was preserved and still celebrated 400 years later by the Roman philosopher and poet Lucretius:

> Long time men lay oppressed with slavish fear;
> Religion's tyranny did domineer,
> [...]
> At length, a mighty man of Greece began
> to assert the natural liberty of man[60]

MILLER: And those are the people who seem to survive, and then encourage what later became explicitly-called atheism in Christian Europe.

LLOYD: I wouldn't like to pronounce on which were the most important influences, but go back to the original writings and it's certainly true that Lucretius devotes considerable arguments to say that death is nothing to us, and considerable arguments to show that of course the gods have no role in the world. Now, the question then is, did they leave any room for gods at all?

> Fear is the mother of all gods... Nature does all things spontaneously,
> by herself, without their meddling.
> LUCRETIUS[61]

So throughout the ancient world we come across thoughtful people beginning to express doubts about the existence of deities and also about those who, for whatever reasons, chose to believe in them, or at least said that they did.

A tyrant must put on the appearance of uncommon devotion to religion. Subjects are less apprehensive of illegal treatment from a ruler whom they consider God-fearing and pious. On the other hand, they do less easily move against him, believing that he has the gods on his side.
ARISTOTLE[62]

In this subject of the nature of the gods the first question is: do the gods exist or do they not? It is difficult, you will say, to deny that they exist. I would agree, if we were arguing the matter in a public assembly, but in a private discussion of this kind it is perfectly easy to do so.
CICERO[63]

Religion is regarded by the common people as true, by the wise as false, and by rulers as useful.
SENECA[64]

Once the Roman Emperor Constantine adopted Christianity as the official religion of the Empire, pagan philosophy as a whole became somewhat suspect. In fact, in the sixth century the Parthenon itself was partly demolished, and what remained became one of the earliest churches devoted to the Virgin Mary. And at the same time, on the orders of the Emperor Justinian, the Greek philosophical academies were abolished. The 1,000 years that followed the closing of the Greek philosophical schools has come to be known as the Dark Ages. Like all such labels, it's not much more than a cliché. It's *never* possible, completely, to eradicate free thought.

Views and reviews
Vogue, August 1967[65]

In midsummer, art drops from the air like syrup off the limes. There's too much of it. It seems like chaos, and it only makes sense when you ignore most of it and bend what remains to some theme or theory.

The exhibition of Picasso's sculpture at the Tate Gallery until 13 August seems to dominate the month.[66] Not just in magnitude, or intrinsic importance, but by the way in which it seems to upset our ideas of what a work of art really is. The entire exhibition is overwhelming, and yet with some conspicuous exceptions, no single piece stands up very well on its own.

This is not to say that the minor works are there just to set off the important pieces. The show is a monumental whole, and nothing can really be taken away from it without diminishing the complete effect. As an exhibition, it goes a long way towards destroying the very idea of a masterpiece. Instead, it's a show of prodigious fertility, which relies for its stunning effect on the volume and variety of it all. Seeing it spread out, one begins to realize that there is an acquisitive obscenity in the idea of taking any *one* of these pieces and setting them up as an owned object in a private home.

The show is like a Neolithic site, full of masks, arrowheads, pots and idols, left behind by some absconded occupant. The artefacts only make sense when seen together.

Picasso seems to create art as spontaneously as one of these Neolithic craftsmen. No other artist living today seems to be so utterly at one with his materials. He seems to have dissolved the surface between himself and the substance he employs. He almost seems to be part of the world of nature from which he draws his forms. In some ways, the secret of his dreadful power is very close to that of nature itself, creating species with the same careless, wayward energy.

Picasso is already a myth in his own lifetime. This is almost a cliché, but his mythical role is not just a function of his fame. He is actually like something *out* of myth; half-man, half-beast, like the uncouth minotaurs he likes to draw. He is like a primitive mediator between nature and man, imitating the fecund productivity of the one in order to assert the ambitious creative independence of the other. Shaggy-thighed, nimble-fingered and comic, he takes off the grand act of creation, even going so far in the great Boisgeloup heads to produce huge, voluptuously obscene visual puns on the organs of human reproduction.

But there also seems to be a mythical curse at the heart of Picasso's achievement, at least with respect to the sculpture. He is like a melancholy

77

Midas. Everything he touches turns, perhaps too readily, into art, or something like it. As he grows older, he seems to be almost a prisoner of his own productivity, and actually seems to be straining to lose himself completely in the world of nature which so mercilessly provokes him to create. There is something Promethean about his situation, stretched halfway between the total creative capabilities of God, and the ordinary blundering mimicry of human craftsmanship. As John Berger has pointed out, perhaps this explains the painful sadness of those drawings where the artist impotently confronts the effortlessly created body of his model.

For Picasso, in fact, the separation of human beings into men and women for the purposes of reproduction is a tragic metaphor of his own situation as an artist. The artist faces the spontaneous creativity of nature just as men face the mysterious pregnancy of women. In both cases, the male role seems trivial and abbreviated. It is hardly surprising, therefore, that in the Boisgeloup series Picasso should make a wishful blend of the reproductive organs of the two sexes – suggesting a sublime androgyne where the begetting power of the stallion male loses itself in the conceiving capabilities of the woman as nature.

It is a special irony that Picasso should have become so extravagantly rich by selling off his life in bits. Owned in pieces like this, his work shrinks and one needs to be reminded, in these late years, of his achievement, by seeing it all in a huge coherent mass.

The recent exhibition of Tim Scott's sculpture at the Whitechapel put the problem of art ownership even more acutely.[67] It is slightly ridiculous to think of any one of these large, brilliant coloured affairs being in someone's private possession. Scott's show was an environment rather than a collection. It was a space filled and occupied by his work, any part of which, if taken away and owned, would tend to lose its meaning and become an awkward gaudy obstacle.

In fact, it is in the act of imagining the proper destination of these works that one goes some way towards understanding their appeal and function. Scott himself suggests that these huge coloured bulks belong in an enclosed space devoted exclusively to them. They would become nonsensical if put among other domestic objects. He also rejects the official alfresco of a municipal park. They should be housed instead in a special aesthetic gymnasium where the spectator is free to wander round exercising his mind just as he would on a set of trapezes, swings and parallel bars. With works of this sort, art has made a break with its traditional function and points forward instead to a more didactic future where the artist, instead of asking the audience to purchase parts of his work, will charge admission to an enclosure in which his work will challenge the spectator to a debate about space and its understanding.

For sculptors of the New Generation their work consists of solid acts of intellectual demonstration. The relationship between the surface and the enclosed volume of the piece is no longer clear. The pieces are sliced open in order to show how the inner space relates to the skin which encloses it. The whole question of what a surface really is becomes an issue here. By treating the skins with different colours and textures which vary from the rough matt to high polish, Scott gets the eye to scan backwards and forwards throughout the depths of his objects so that space starts to argue with the spectator. At one moment the gaze is stopped at the outer pellicle by the dense dullness of its painted surface. Or confronted by a huge transparent sheet of dark Perspex, the eye can choose to look right through and see the tinted space beyond, or, pulling back a bit, it can see instead the reflection of the world immediately in front. And this reflection, of course, includes the image of the spectator himself in the very act of choosing to see or not to see himself. And as a third choice the Perspex flange can be viewed as a thing in itself...in other words neither as a mirror nor as a plate glass, but simply as an interface existing in its own right.

These are early days for Tim Scott and for the New Generation of which he is possibly the most impressive protagonist. It is hard to see how artists of this sort will be financed in the future since they have so decisively cut themselves off from the older forms of patronage. It would be as absurd for an individual to own one of these works as it would be to own a large model of the atom. They belong in some as yet non-existent 'thinktank'...perhaps something like a planetarium which puts on spectacular demonstrations in return for a decent admission fee.

There are other exhibitions, of course, but for the purposes of argument one play makes more of a point in the context I have chosen here. Peter Dews and the Birmingham Rep have pulled off a difficult trick with their new production of *As You Like It* at the Vaudeville.[68] The setting is brilliantly stylized and set in a vaguely nineteenth-century limbo. I have never approved very much of playing around with period when producing Shakespeare. It rarely does more than tickle the palate of an audience bored with the original text. But in this case, largely because the setting is so cunningly blurred, the trick has worked in favour of the text. More than anything else Dews has welded his production into a sort of traditional panto which brings out the essential artificiality of the play itself. Artificiality in the best sense, though. *As You Like It* is *not*, as some of the more idiotic daily critics assume, a badly constructed piece of unlikely naturalism. It is a coherent piece of mystical formality, which rather like the Boisgeloup heads of Picasso, plays games with the puzzle of human bisexuality. The elaborate deceptions, transvestitism and so on are not just bits of idle Elizabethan tomfoolery, but essential features of hermetic Renaissance paganism. The contrived symmetries of the plot are as solemn and formal as a medieval zodiac or a Book of Hours. In fact the play is constructed almost like a religious diptych in which the two halves of human creation face each other like mirror images. Man and woman, brother and sister, vanquished and privileged, old and young. Around the axis of the mystical duality Shakespeare weaves an action which comes very close to Mozart opera. Dews has managed to focus this fugal formality and through the medium of a nineteenth-century operetta has restored the pagan mystery of the Renaissance.

Here and there, however, the modern gaiety of the production slightly obscures the elegant gravity of the original play. The wrestling match, for example, staged with dazzling sense of parody, takes away the mythical horror of Charles the wrestler. For this odd episode at the start of the play is just like something out of a fairy story. Charles is a sort of foul fiend with whom Orlando, the miraculous foundling, must struggle before he can begin his journey through the dark wood. A slight touch would have done the trick. Since the scene was conceived in terms of telly wrestling, Charles could have come on like Dr Death and the traditional parallel would have been completed at the same time.

But this is a rare and at times quite sublime production. It's a scandal that the audiences were so small both times I was there. Shakespeare, it seems, will only survive in this country when performed either by great stars or famous national troupes. Quality alone, it seems, is not enough.

Aboard the Victory O

Olivier: In Celebration, 1987[69]

The following memoir was prepared for a celebratory volume of essays by friends and colleagues of stage and screen actor Sir Laurence Olivier.

I first met him informally at parties after *Beyond the Fringe*. He saw the show and was, I suspect, slightly irritated by our Shakespeare sketch. He had sat in a box and it got backstage that he was not conspicuously amused.

My first *professional* contact with him was when Ken Tynan edited a television programme called *Tempo*, which was commercial television's answer to *Monitor*. With his wonderful flair for what is fashionable, Tynan had asked us to do a regular satirical spot. In the opening programme this was a pastiche of C. P. Snow written by Alan Bennett, a high-table scene of people drinking, wearing gowns and so forth, and bandying conversation about. On the same programme Larry was being interviewed by George Harewood about the opening of Chichester.[70]

We were on first but we began 'corpsing.' There were two takes, three takes, and Larry was obviously amused by the fact that the young lads couldn't do it. By the fourth take we could see him getting more and more impatient at these dreadful amateurs. It took something like 20 takes before we got it right, by which time he was thoroughly nettled, if only because we'd kept him waiting so long.

Then I didn't see him for some while, by which time I'd blotted my copybook quite badly with him. When I saw his performance as Othello, I told a journalist that while I couldn't help but admire the extraordinary bravura, energy and detail of it, I wasn't all that impressed by the performance as a whole. He was understandably annoyed by this – or I heard he was – and looking back I can understand just how he felt and I'm rather surprised he ever asked me to direct anything. However, some years later I was doing my first and only feature film – an unspeakable catastrophe – and was sitting in the commissariat at Elstree when a message came through saying 'Laurence Olivier on the phone.'[71] I thought it was Alan Bennett or Peter Cook. Anyway, a hoax. I came to the phone and heard this voice saying, 'Dear boy... This is Laurence Olivier here...

Joanie wants to do *The Merchant of Venice* and would love you to direct it.'[72] No question of him acting in it, no mention of that at all.

I was blushing at the thought of what I had said about his Othello. 'I would love to,' I managed to say and I mentioned doing a nineteenth-century version. He said, 'Whichever way you want to.' Later I saw from his book that *he* came up with the idea. It may well be that we both thought of it. But, anyway, it then gradually became apparent that *he* was going to do Shylock. Now, whether he had thought this all along and had decided to delay committing himself until he found out whether I had an idea which coincided with his own, or one which he could approve of, the fact is that he came to the first reading knowing the part perfectly. Not like the other actors.

This was so characteristic of him. He's very Machiavellian and although this has its drawbacks, there was always something glamorous about his political calculation. It was like working for Diocletian.

Before rehearsals I had a lot of difficulty eliminating ideas of which he had been persuaded by Ken Tynan, who had in turn been persuaded by Orson Welles. The idea, for example, that Bassanio should play all three suitors, including the black one, in order to get the right casket. There was another idea that Portia would present herself in court in a wheelchair. In any case there were a lot of encrustations – Tynan's rather than Olivier's – which I had to careen before I could find the clean lines of the play. Eventually we came to an agreement, which also involved persuading him to drop an enormous amount of make-up – false nose, ringlets, a Disraeli beard, all adding up to a sort of George Arliss.[73] I said, 'Larry, please' – as a Jew I felt embarrassed – 'please, we're not quite like that, not all of us.' He then said a wonderful thing: 'In this play, dear boy, which we are about to perform, we must at all costs avoid offending the Hebrews. God, I love them so.' 'The best way to do that, Larry,' I said, 'is to drop these pantomime trappings which are offensive and unnecessary.' He agreed to drop the ringlets.

But he had invested in extremely expensive dentures which gave him his strong prognathous look – based, I think, on a member of the National Theatre Board – and he was so attached to them in both senses that I felt I would have been a terrible spoilsport to object to them. He used to go round the corridors of the National Theatre seeing whether anyone knew he had them in. He would give interviews to journalists wearing them. He loved them so much and he looked rather good in them – and I couldn't bring myself to object!

In the event we did a lot of horse-trading. I would give *him* ideas and he would exploit them. He never tried to push rank. He has what all really great actors have – an expedient recognition of good business. If you have a good idea he'll take it from you regardless. If not he will go on to 'automatic pilot,' or rather he'll take over the controls himself.

I suggested the little dance, at the moment when Tubal tells him Antonio's ships have gone down. I also suggested that he entered bearing Jessica in his arms when he discovers her flight. This reminded the audience subliminally of Lear and Cordelia – another father 'betrayed' by his daughter. I suggested his crying at the end, though not in any way which he didn't utterly make his own. He always looks for a memorable effect at some critical moment and I remember him saying, 'Oh God, I've done a fit, a fall, I cannot possibly fart!' I said, 'Why not try humiliated, terrible crying. *I* can't do it, but I know *you* can.' Off he went and gave it this curious unparaphrasable energy and vehemence which did actually freeze the blood. I remember him saying, 'Oh dear boy,' and there was a look of brimming gratitude in his eyes. He has an absolutely wonderful, really humble magnanimity. If something is good, it doesn't matter who or where it comes from.

When the *Merchant* opened I became aware of his stagefright, as he called it. I didn't know it was that, not until three or four days into the run. He certainly never spoke about it during rehearsals or run-throughs or on the first night.

I was standing in the wings one night and could see – in that rather unnatural light coming from elsewhere which you see from the darkness of the wings – a look of shocked terror on his face, beads of sweat on the make-up, and his eyes staring as if they were behind a mask. I couldn't detect anything more than a hesitation. I knew, though, from brief moments of stagefright in *Beyond the Fringe*, that what to an outside observer seems like a thirtieth of a second is half an hour for the victim. He then confessed to me that he had these moments of appalling, shattering lapses in which he forgot his words and the Earth stood still. There was a night when he actually forgot the things that a Jew has: 'Hath not a Jew eyes?...' One was almost tempted to say, 'Hath not a Jew elbows!'

After the event he was wonderfully humorous about it, but I should imagine from the drenched and exhausted way in which he came off stage it was far from funny. I think it happens to a lot of people as they get older. It was obviously more than mere forgetfulness. It was the terror of a moment of standing outside himself and seeing himself suspended in the night sky of a theatrical performance, illuminated by all those lights, watched by dimly visible faces – and frozen. It must have been a horrible experience.

But he seemed to recover from it because far from retiring as he threatened to do, he came back with redoubled vigour in *Long Day's Journey into Night*.[74] He has this curious and startling immortality, which became part of his charisma. He would be fatally ill one moment and the next moment he'd be back on stage doing a part of heroic length with some superbly accomplished piece of business, giving the performance of his life. Everything about him as a public performer is to do with being unexpected, unpredictable – Machiavellian in fact.

His ability to shift with the tide is also absolutely astonishing. There was a time when, despite the noble glamour of his roles in *Henry V* (1944) and *Hamlet* (1948), he belonged, for a lot of younger people, to another era. The slightly clipped tones, the romantic, matinée idol; nothing whatever to do with us, and we all thought he was yesteryear. Then quite suddenly he was doing Archie Rice with brilliant modern seediness.[75] He took on the very thing which denied everything he *had* been. In place of the glossy, beautiful, noble, grand creature of earlier days, he was suddenly scratching the inside leg of his awful check-trousers as a seedy comic, offending all the ladies who had adored him. He renewed himself in this act of metamorphosis – a sort of phoenix performance. It's part of his Machiavellian strategy: be unexpected, come back as something else. If they think you're dead, spring to life; if they think you're passé, change your course. Identify with the enemy, join them, and then beat them. No one else could manage to be as protean, as Machiavellian, as self-serving – and remain so lovable.

Those of us who knew him as a father, as a leader of the National Theatre, saw he had what he had always wanted, as a great patriotic Englishman:

control of the whole show. He was always the great commanding officer. He would have loved to have been the captain of the flagship which sank the *Bismarck*. He always wanted to serve his majesty and there he was, in command of this grounded boat, 15 brass rings on his sleeve and a bridge of his own.

The very set-up of the National, the offices in Aquinas Street, were like Pompey's galley, or like the shacks on those HMS training ships which are on land. It was absolutely made for him. Whatever competitiveness he might have had among his peers was now sublimated into running his ship, dispensing largesse, interest, and patronage to younger actors. His eminence had been recognized and a lot of otherwise competitive energies were turned to totally benevolent purposes. He loved the thunder of feet on the companionway. He was always speaking down the tube, lots of clang-clangs to the engine-room, backings and churnings of propellers, and people brought up unexpectedly to the bridge. He had genuine interest in the welfare of his staff, like a first class Captain on a battleship. 'Sign on. Everyone is expected to do their duty.' And because of this he created an enormous competitive admiration and filial affection amongst those who worked for him.

In cold print
Listener, 17 March 1966[76]

Truman Capote has finally published his famous book on the multiple murders in Kansas. Which all goes to show that time is out of joint. Even before it got into print this book had an almost mythical reputation. It was one of those strange cases, not uncommon in the United States, where advertisements speak louder than words and publicity is as important as publication. The clamour was so cunning that when the book finally *did* appear it seemed like an aside, a printed summary of what was already known and approved from foregoing hearsay. This was partly due to the economics of modern American publishing where profits are tied to advance paperback sales, but it also says something about the public style of some recent American writers themselves. Capote has fallen victim to the same sort of crazy process which is practised much more flagrantly, perhaps, by his colleague Norman Mailer.[77] They seem to be in an indecent hurry to set up copper-bottomed claims to greatness in advance of the due process of literary judgment. In Mailer's case this takes the form of elaborate stunts – spectacular debates, suicidal showdowns with heavyweight boxing champs, and monstrous self-advertisements in which he announces that he will settle for nothing less than a total revolution in the sensibility of our times. Now Capote, on the edge of an otherwise modestly distinguished middle age, feels pressed to make big claims in advance of his own publication. With *In Cold Blood* he announces a breakthrough to an entirely new form of literature: the fictional documentary; the non-fiction novel. It would be unfair of course to judge the book in the light of this claim, but, equally, it is hard to ignore it entirely. Precocious manifestos raise the critical dander and make it difficult to consider a work entirely on the basis of its unannounced merits.

Following the outrage of a particularly bloody and apparently motiveless massacre in the mid-western state of Kansas, Capote went to the scene and rummaged out the details of everyone involved in the case. The painful thoroughness has become part of the myth. He filled thousands of pages with minute verbatim notes taken from the friends of the murdered family, the shocked neighbours, the law-men, and finally from the two murderers themselves. Everything was scrupulously scribbled down and from this grotesque potpourri, where sweet incidental triviality jostles with savage psychopathic incident, Capote extracted, by artful recollection, 280-odd pages of engrossing factual narrative.

The form is not entirely without precedent. Nearly half a century ago, Dreiser took the court records of another famous murder and built it up into one of the great American novels. With regard to the use of actual material, *An American Tragedy* (1925) stands somewhere about half way between *Le Rouge et Le Noir* (1830), where Stendhal simply used a real case as the occasion for his novel, and Capote's *In Cold Blood* where the facts make up the whole book. If Capote's work is new it is only by standing at the far end of a spectrum within a well-established genre of social literature. In the three examples there is the same ambitious social scope, the same effort to capture through the events surrounding a violent public act the overall tone of a national temperament. And in all three the human vehicle is curiously alike. An obscure, rootless hero (two in Capote's case), head filled with shapeless and extravagant ambitions, is driven through the middle of an indifferent community and collides with it in a gory climax. It's rather like the device used by the nuclear physicists in which a charged particle rushes through a sealed vessel of dark vapour, brushing up into brief visibility everything with which it comes in contact. Capote's work is notable, therefore, more for the contribution it makes to an established form than for any startling novelty of its own. And oddly enough, one could argue at least that the out and out novelists, free from binding obligation to the smallest details of the original case, get nearer to reality than someone like Capote who contracted himself in advance to forswear invention. There is no such thing as verisimilitude anyway, but finally only a choice between more or less convincing fictions. Documentary fiction is a much wider category than the one that Capote claims to have invented for himself, and he must finally be rated in terms of his performance within this recognized form.

The work falls into two rather unequal parts. He is least successful in the early pages, before the murder, minutely embroidering a picture of the doomed family, the mid-western town and the characters of the humdrum neighbours all around. There is a trivial accuracy about all this; true, one supposes, in detail, but sweetly overdrawn in general, rather like Norman Rockwell's vignette covers for the *Saturday Evening Post*. And too often this lapses further still into a Crawfie coyness.[78] Even in the better parts of the book, where he deals with the crooks themselves, their families, the arrest, trial and Death Row, he falls with unsettling regularity into a touch purple journalese. All this sends up a maddening fog which conceals the book's virtues. For Capote has caught, like Hannah Arendt with her book on Eichmann, the essential 'banality of evil.'[79] Following the pair in their destructive lurch through the south-west of America – cheating, charming, slaughtering, and hitch-hiking – we get the feckless dullness of criminal psychopathy.

He shows too the vapid alternation of moods. The brilliant theatrical improvisation as they pass dud cheques in a Kansas clothes shop, the lotus-eating languor of their après-kill holiday in Mexico, the outbursts of pathological hunger, and perhaps best of all that characteristic swing from callous violence to maudlin sentimentality: the very thing which led the early psychologists to name psychopathy moral insanity. Time and again through the dark glass of this dismal pair we see the features of another killer – the footling, dangerous dafty, Lee Harvey Oswald. They are the hazardous orphans of the Other America. It is a crushing irony that in a country hell-bent on fame and fortune, Capote should have won through tepid print what they tried to get by spilling cold blood. I hope he's satisfied.

King Lear in rehearsal

Squiggle Foundation, London, 11 March 1989[80]

I find it quite hard to talk about a play which is actually in rehearsal, although that is the subject of this talk. When you are in the middle of it, it is very hard to see the wood for the trees. I will try and describe both the wood and the trees, but I will describe the wood first of all.

I think the great problem with *King Lear* is that it is a play which in production in the recent past – for I suppose the best part of a hundred years – has been bedevilled by certain ideas of the cosmic. It has been inclined traditionally toward a Druidical representation partly because of that damned storm that takes place in it. Because of the iconography of that storm, in which you see a figure with a long white beard ranting at the clouds and the thunder, there is a feeling that the play is about large cosmic archetypal issues. But it has always been my sense while doing the play, and this is the fourth time I've done it, that the cosmic is really the least important aspect of it.[81] That doesn't mean that its themes are not large and eternal, that they are not themes which repeat themselves constantly, or that they aren't in fact deeply preoccupying themes, but I don't think that the play has anything to do with storms at all. The storm is rather as it were a ground bass against which entirely human actions occur.

It's also a play which people have been misled into thinking takes place in a sort of timeless antiquity, particularly a pre-Christian antiquity. People have been misled by its references to the gods, as opposed to God, and by what seems to be its conspicuous abstention from references to Christianity. But I believe at least one of the themes that has got to be brought out and developed in production cannot be understood unless you set the play in a period which is recognizably Christian.

In fact, although it makes no explicit references to the Christian religion or to God, and indeed it expresses a sort of quasi-atheistic nihilism by the time that it reaches its conclusion, *King Lear* is a play which I think is largely unintelligible unless you take into account certain Christian themes that would have been current and salient at the time when Shakespeare was growing up. We must remember that Shakespeare as a child, like anyone else in Elizabethan England, was a compulsory churchgoer – not a *compulsive* one, but a compulsory churchgoer. He was compelled to go to church as everyone was on Sundays. The reading of texts – of the Gospels and other passages from the Bible – was so repetitive, so unremitting, that their images and tenets recur as a central motif in almost all of Shakespeare's plays. They come to the surface perhaps more conspicuously in *King Lear* than in any other play.

One central notion of *King Lear* which cannot be understood beyond the context of Christianity, and beyond the context of sixteenth-century Christianity, is the notion that it is impossible to enter the Kingdom of Heaven unless you have actually gone through the experience of poverty. I think that a central metaphor of the play is the metaphor of trying to get a camel through the eye of a needle, representing the idea that until you have lost everything there is complete impossibility of gain. One of the words central in the play, as William Empson emphasizes, is the word 'fool,' to which I will return presently.[82] But I think that the word 'nothing' is the most central word, from which everything in the play develops. Lear has to learn in the course of the play the falsity of 'nothing will come of nothing' (I.i.90), as he says when Cordelia refuses to give him a protestation of her love. He has to undergo a rough tuition to learn, as so many of the other characters do, that it is only in the process of losing everything and gaining *nothing* that you actually are in a state to achieve everything. Nothingness and nullity are the centre of the play.

All sorts of losses are presented in the play: a loss of kingdom; a voluntary divesting of authority, power and privilege; an involuntary divesting of subjects' love and the love of children; ultimately an involuntary divesting of sense, sensibility and sanity. The play shows that it is only in the process of divesting yourself of all these things – of shelter, of clothing, of warmth, of love, even of sense and intelligence – that you can actually build yourself anew. This process of complete reduction calls to mind the notion of liminality that Victor Turner develops at length in his various books.[83] It is only by the process of undertaking the role of the 'liminal' – the person who falls between the cracks by divesting himself of all category and of authority – that you actually can restore your humanity and can develop a genuine sense of *Gemeinschaft*, as opposed to the formal structures of *Gesellschaft*.

Lear undergoes his losses without knowing that this is going to happen. He attempts to divest himself of authority and power while wickedly retaining all the privileges that go with kingship. He then enters a curious path which starts from a voluntary act of abnegation but leads on to a slippery slope where he has no control over the further things that are stripped from him, by virtue of the fact that he abdicates.

The issue of Lear's abdication brings me to another reason why it is impossible to set the play outside the period in which it was written. *King Lear* is a play which resists transposition either backwards into the notional antiquity where it is so often set, or forwards into a more modern period because you have to take note in it of a constitutional and political theme which is central to the seventeenth century. That theme involves notions of kingship and sovereignty which give blasphemous connotations to abdication. In 1605 Europe was still shaking from the experience of the abdication of Emperor Charles V, 50 years earlier. This abdication was regarded by the literate population as something blasphemous as a usurpation: not only was it seen as blasphemous to usurp a crowned and anointed King, it was seen as blasphemous for a crowned and anointed King to pre-empt the decisions of God and voluntarily to give up the office which was assigned to him by virtue of being crowned and anointed. One still sees traces of this in the reluctance of the present Queen to give up the throne in favour of her ageing son. The reason for this is not that she is obstinately enjoying the privileges of power, which are extremely dubious, I would have thought, at this particular moment in history. I think she still retains some sort of belief that it is not within the gift of the officer to resign what in fact is given to the officer by virtue of the fact that she or he has been incorporated into the immortal corporation of monarchy by the act of being crowned and anointed.

I would like to remind you of a medieval theory of kingship which was still current in the seventeenth century, of an idea dealt with by Ernst Kantorowicz in *The King's Two Bodies* (1957). That great work on medieval constitutional theory suggests that the King hath in him two bodies: a body politic and a body mortal. The body mortal was that part which died with the death of the officer, but the body politic was the immortal corporation of sovereignty into which he was incorporated by virtue of being anointed. By being anointed he was incorporated into an immortal pedigree of monarchs which had descended from the first act of anointing, which was of course the anointing of David by the priest Samuel. For the Middle Ages and for the Renaissance there was a fundamental theory that once the officer was incorporated into this immortal office of sovereign, it lay with him or with her until in fact his or her mortal life had been brought to an end by a decision other than his or hers. It was not within the sovereign's gift to resign, it was not within his gift to abdicate, just as it was not within the gift of perhaps a morally better-qualified monarch – such as, for example, Bolingbroke in *Richard II* – to usurp a frivolous Richard. In other words there was some notion of the office being more important than the officer. Even though the officer could be either a villain or a ninny, as soon as he was incorporated into that immortal corporation of sovereignty he was there for life.

This thought is expressed clearly in two images. One is found in the royal tombs at St Denis outside Paris, where you see the double effigies of the King. You see the King in his regalia, kneeling with his eyes wide open, wearing his crown, carrying the sceptre: the figure which represents the immortal corporation of sovereignty, while in a balustraded canopy underneath lies the naked body of the mortal officer. This is often taken to be a *memento mori* to remind the proud and the mighty that they must return to the state of the worm-eaten and the mortal. But it is not really a *memento mori*; it is much more an emblematic representation of the constitutional theory that once an officer had been incorporated into this corporation of sovereignty he had a divine power and a divine sanction. A similar image is to be found also in the famous practice of the royal touch. The royal touch was thought to be a sacred power which was invested not in the person of the sovereign, but in his person as crowned monarch. He could exercise that power and touch for the 'King's evil' (a tuberculous gland in the neck), could touch and heal this illness not by virtue of any particular shining characteristic that he had as an individual but by virtue of the power that was invested in the office that he was now a representation of after the act of anointing and crowning. It is almost as if the regalia were endowed with the power to heal, rather than the officer himself. You could see this ritual of the royal touch enacted year after year in the long line of French kings from the Capetian monarchs right the way through the Valois monarchs and the Bourbon monarchs. It was connected with the office of the King and, whether the officer was a villain or a ninny, his touch healed. He did not heal by virtue of his personal charisma, because he might have none at all; he healed by virtue of the charisma which was attached to the office.[84] It was not within his gift to withdraw himself from that office until he had died. At that moment, then, when 'the King is dead, long live the King,' instantly the role was assigned to the successor who continued the unbroken line of this immortal corporation.

So that when Lear undertakes almost frivolously to lay down the burden and 'crawl toward death,' as he says in the first act (I.i.40), there should be in his court a sense that something exceptional has happened. This is not simply a casual incident in which a monarch has said, 'Right, I feel my time has come to hand it on'; it's not a resignation of a secular office as it would be if the president of a business said, 'I am getting too old to do this properly.' There is no way you can get too old to do it properly as a King. You only get too old to do it properly when you are dead. So, at the moment when Lear actually tells the Court his intention to 'Unburdened crawl toward death,' it should produce a *frisson* because all the Court know that in fact he should be, when crawling toward death, still with the regalia on his head at that moment. The power would still be invested in him, even though crawling toward death, because the power of majesty and the power of monarchy are undiminished and uninfluenced by the diminishing power of the officer.

Lear then compounds that particular sin or blasphemy by doing something amiss which has no place in constitutional theory, but has a place in psychological theory. That is that he offers to divide his kingdom in terms of the avowals of love which will be given to him by each of his three daughters in turn. It is this act that in rehearsal makes you realize that you have to present King Lear at the outset of the play as partly mad already, not as someone who goes mad. He must be presented as someone who is already on the edge of some sort of mental disorder, in a state of depression, or some condition which makes him do something which, once again, is not within the gift of human beings. Just as it is not within the gift of a monarch to renounce his office, so it is not within the gift of any mortal to ask other mortals how much they love him or her. Still less can avowals of love be purchased, and still less can they be obtained by offering gifts in return for which you will get a certificate from your own children of how much they love you. One becomes aware at a very early stage in the play that something very eccentric and anomalous is going on with the King. His decision at the outset can scarcely look like a decision, but must look like a sudden capricious outburst which should startle the court and indeed even startle the two elder daughters.

Too often, I think, in rehearsal and in production, the elder daughters give their 'glib and oily' speeches automatically (I.i.226), implying that they immediately have at their disposal the eloquence which will satisfy Lear. But his demand has to come as a surprise to them as much as it outrages and comes as a surprise to the younger daughter who fails to give the avowal which Lear demands. Too often Goneril and Regan leap into their speeches as if in fact they had already-prepared manifestos, which means that they have anticipated what he is going to ask of them. But the demand on them should come as a total surprise, so that when the daughters actually start their flattery they must be seen as beginning to formulate it, asking themselves, 'How can I express this in a way which will convince this mad, eccentric father of mine that I do indeed love him?' So I believe in rehearsal it is necessary to work towards some pregnant pause as the elder daughters seem to formulate their speeches. It is very interesting that in the first line of Goneril's speech, when 'our eldest-born' speaks first (I.i.54), she actually anticipates in some way the thought Cordelia later expresses in saying, 'I cannot heave/My heart into my mouth' (I.i.91–92). Goneril is often condemned for being a glib daughter, but this is contradicted by her first line: 'Sir, I love you more than word can wield the matter' (I.i.55). In other words, she starts by saying that it is in fact difficult to utter such an avowal, that the demand is in fact as awkward for her as it later turns out for Cordelia. Cordelia actually follows through by refusing to meet the demand, but nevertheless Goneril announces that such an avowal is difficult for her and is not actually readily formulable. So she should pause in saying 'I love you…more than…word can wield the matter.' There must be pauses within the speech so that we see she finds flattery hard, although not as hard as does Cordelia, who actually withholds it. It must seem difficult for Regan too, for otherwise, as I say, you will presuppose that they both anticipate exactly what is going to happen, which makes the outcome of the play decided before the start.

This brings me to another issue which I think again often bedevils the play in production. That is, because we are so familiar with the play, and actors and actresses are so familiar with it, and because the outcome is ultimately so atrocious, there is a temptation to make these two wicked daughters who do such ultimately wicked things start out as wicked. If they start out as monsters, as they are perhaps most spectacularly in the Riemann opera version, as satanic punk monsters who cannot wait to humiliate and destroy their father, you might as well merely summarize the rest of the play and then say, 'it turned out pretty badly as well.'[85]

The reason why evil in the play takes time to develop is that we must be able to witness something which in fact is more than ever apparent to us now in this part of the twentieth century, and that is the strange imperceptibility of the individual steps towards an atrocious outcome. Actually, for each of those daughters, and for each of those sons-in-law, it should become hard for them to say, looking backwards over the course of the action, at what point they started to do something which was so unacceptable and so outrageous that it actually culminates in the gouging of an old man's eyes and the locking of doors to a demented father. It shouldn't be apparent at the outset that this is what is going to happen merely because we, who have read the play, know that's how it turns out. Too often when the theatre takes up this play it actually writes the end into the beginning, so that it seems to be already wound up like a piece of clockwork with an absolutely inevitable conclusion built into the first scene. So it becomes interesting in rehearsal to minimize as far as you possibly can the atrociousness, the wickedness, the expedience of these daughters, and to make them reasonable. We have to make them seem so reasonable that when we come to that wonderful scene before Gloucester's castle (II.iv) – after the stocking of Kent, when Regan and Goneril arrive and both try to persuade Lear that he does not in fact need a retinue of the size that he has – their position should be so ordinary that much of the audience should feel: 'My God, I've done exactly that to my parents in the recent past; I hope that this half is not going to be too long, I must get on the phone and see if Dad and Mum are all right.'

In other words, I believe it is the responsibility of producer and actors alike in doing *King Lear* to actually induce deep senses of uneasiness and misgiving in the audience *vis-à-vis* their own parents. They should not be able to distance themselves and say, 'well, that's what monsters do. We are unlike that.' There should be a banality of evil in this particular case just as there was in the case of the Nazis. It should be very hard for us to identify any particular point during the plot when we could say, 'that is when it happened, that's when the thing became irreversibly atrocious.' These steps should be minuscule and imperceptible, both for the protagonists and I think for the audience, so that they begin to feel merely a cumulative sense of a tragic outcome, rather than knowing at any particular moment that the predetermined outcome is now on its way.

In this particular production that I am working on I have tried to stress this by casting the children, for the first time, as grown-ups. Perhaps this is due to the fact I've been rehearsing the play on and off over the last 25 years, and have grown that much older in the time myself. When I first directed the play at Nottingham many years ago, I cast young daughters and young sons, a young Edmund and a young Edgar. Now I find myself quite inevitably, without actually consciously thinking of it, casting daughters in their fifties and sons in their fifties as well. This is partly because I have been struck by the curious discrepancy in the age of both parents and their children, which didn't strike me earlier. Why is it that this man who is meant to be more than 80 so often has children of no more than 20? Why is there this 60-year difference between father and children? Might it not be more reasonable to assume that both sets of children, sons on the part of Gloucester and daughters on the part of Lear, are in fact the same age as I the producer, and have actually gone through experiences comparable to the ones that I have had with my parents and that people of my age have had with their parents, and perhaps also have had with children of their own?

As soon as you start to play the children at that age, suddenly the production starts to take on a different shape. I found certain lines which previously remained almost inaudible suddenly start to shine with a strange salience which had remained unnoticeable to me before. For instance, in the little letter that Edmund forges to persuade his father Gloucester that his brother is in fact a villain, there are things which until now simply remained inaudible to me. Edmund says in the letter:

> This policy, and reverence of age, makes the world bitter to the best of our times, keeps our fortunes from us till our oldness cannot relish them. I begin to find an idle and fond bondage in the oppression of aged tyranny
> (I.ii.46–50)

Now the fact is that this is a villain trying to present a letter which will convince his father that villainy is afoot. It's a very peculiar choice of motive that he actually writes into that letter; he writes of the sense of dissatisfaction which is felt by children who in fact are growing old themselves, old enough to feel that even if they come by their patrimony they are on the edge of being too old to enjoy it, so that they are experiencing a 'fond bondage in the oppression of aged tyranny.' If you start to develop groups of children who in fact are old enough to feel that they cannot enjoy their full independence, cannot enjoy full self-determination until these ageing parents are out of the way, the play suddenly becomes much more interesting than it would be if these are merely Satanic youngsters who are destroying venerable old creatures.

So the casting of older children in this production has made a difference not simply by virtue of the fact that people in the audience of a particular age will recognize something common to us all at that age, but also because it makes it possible to avoid what I think is an impossible obligation to represent metaphysical wickedness, wickedness which is transcendental. You remember when Hannah Arendt wrote about Eichmann, she was puzzled by the fact that in witnessing him it was very hard to understand how someone who looked as ordinary, as commonplace as that, could have done something as monstrous as he did.[86] The thing is that we want the monstrous to be visibly monstrous. We want those who perpetrate the outrages to look Satanic in some way so that we can, as it were, confidently identify them before they do it. But it is in the nature of human life that the atrocious creeps upon us imperceptibly, so that we cannot identify the moment when the process becomes irreversibly atrocious. Once you play these children as older – merely impatient, merely looking for what they believe is their due – you actually start to relieve yourself of the false necessity of presenting them as outrageously sadistic creatures.

This consideration of the children brings me to another issue which is related to the Christian theme. One recognizes around these grown children a range of relationships, motives and ideas which are very similar to the ones which ordinary people here and now still experience, and indeed hate themselves for, and would like to conceal and not to acknowledge. But there are also other aspects of the children which are I think emblematic of certain great Christian issues which I mentioned at the beginning. Without wishing to say explicitly that Edgar is Christ and Edmund is Lucifer, I think there are undoubtedly resonances to that effect. For instance, when Edgar gives an account of the whole course of his action to his brother at the end – when Edmund lies dying, and Edgar is describing the death of their father Gloucester – he says, 'I asked his blessing and from first to last/Told him our pilgrimage' (V.iii.194–195). I think that the choice of the word 'pilgrimage' is very significant. The view that Edgar presents of himself, and that we have of Edgar, is only intelligible if you see it contrasted with a certain view of Edmund. This contrast lives in the light of the relationship, I think, between Christ and Lucifer. Again, I am not saying that Edgar is to be seen as Christ or that Edmund is to be seen as Lucifer, but nevertheless there are metaphorical affinities between these two pairs. The course of action that Edgar undergoes in the play – his pilgrimage, or ministry – culminates in an emblematic fight at the last day with Edmund. A challenger must come forth, if you remember, 'by the third sound of the trumpet,' and indeed Edgar appears 'Upon this call o' the trumpet' (V.iii.112–113, 117). When Edgar answers the third trumpet, and throws down his brother Edmund, Shakespeare requires us to see some sort of metaphorical representation of the final struggle between Christ and Lucifer.

The way in which Edgar humiliates himself – becoming a Bedlam beggar, a wanderer in anonymity on the heath – and undergoes mockery, disdain and humiliation, only to return as this great soldier of Christ at the end, is I think unintelligible outside the mesh of Christian iconography. In contrast, Edmund is to be seen in some respects as a representation of a Miltonic Lucifer. Shakespeare represents in Edmund the pride of a rootless intelligence, an intelligence that is unrelated to life and to family affinity. Edmund is prompted entirely by expediency and commodity, like the bastard in Shakespeare's *King John*. He is prompted by nothing other than pure ratiocinative self-interest, whereas Edgar is prompted throughout his ministry by the process of love, by the urge to reconciliation with his father, and above all by forgiveness. When you think for example how easy it could be for him to exult in his father's misfortune, having gone through his terrible experience as a result of his father's failure to recognize that he is in fact the loving son, you begin to see the extraordinary act of generosity on the part of Edgar.

This act I think is a transcendental one, and a prescription for a Christian type of love and forgiveness. Also I think it has relationships to the healing of the blind man in the Gospels. Edgar heals Gloucester of his blindness by actually making him go through that absurd self-mocking ordeal of the fall over the imaginary cliff. It is only when Gloucester 'falls' over the cliff and goes through the experience of total despair that he actually recovers the sight of which he has been deprived at the hands of Cornwall. Now if he does indeed heal a blind man, but restores to him not physical sight but moral sight, we see in the action of Edgar once again the exercise of a Christian ministry which is concluded and brought dramatically to its end when Edgar and Edmund encounter one another in a great emblematic battle.

This is rather like the great apocalyptic battles which are mentioned again and again in Norman Cohn's book *The Pursuit of the Millennium* (1957). In these there will be a final struggle in the East when Lucifer and Christ will meet one another, and justice and the Last Judgement will in fact prevail. I think this is what we are being invited to consider in *King Lear*. Of course, in the context of a pre-Christian, Neolithic antiquity this falls apart; it simply has no meaning at all. It has to be rooted in something which inspires a Christian recognition on the part of the audience.

We also see in Gloucester and again in Lear the process of Christian renunciation. Lear starts by a spurious act of renunciation. He renounces nothing because he will keep everything: he will keep his hundred knights; he will keep all the respect due to a king; he is divesting himself only of the burdens of kingship, only of the duties. What he has to go through is the experience of being divested – as opposed to divesting himself actively –

of being divested of everything. And so also does Gloucester, who, by his gullibility and by his failure to recognize the virtue in his son Edgar, must himself be robbed of everything before he gains anything at all.

In fact all in *King Lear* have to go through the experience of being reduced to nothing before there can be any gain. I believe the central metaphor of that diminution and reduction to nothing is contained in that wonderful moment on the cliff when Edgar describes the appearance of things from the top. This is often merely regarded as a prelude to a farcical piece of drama in which someone simply falls over a non-existent cliff, or as an opportunity for Shakespeare to word-paint a wonderful picture of what it looks like from the top of a Dover cliff. But something much deeper is going on in that Shakespeare is giving us in one image two versions of nullity and diminution, while at the same time he is giving us perhaps the finest representation in literature of Renaissance perspective. We see the gradual reduction of the appearance of things as they recede from the gaze down to the tiny fishermen that walk like mice upon the beach: 'Half-way down/Hangs one that gathers samphire, dreadful trade' (IV.vi.14–15). As we see these objects diminishing in size we actually are beginning to see in that a representation of shrinkage, of annihilation, and of progress towards nothingness. But at the same time, by choosing a vantage point at the top of a cliff in order to achieve that, Shakespeare provides another metaphorical resonance. That is the idea that from various kinds of great height all things look small, and never more than from the great height of social authority, of majesty, from the height which you enjoy by virtue of occupying office. We and Gloucester are being encouraged to consider what it is like to look down not merely from a cliff, but also what it is like to look down from a social cliff, at the people below who in fact look like nothing more than mice from that height, and with whom it is therefore impossible to sympathize. You feel how difficult it is to sympathize with things that look like mice when in fact you feel the size that you are and they look the size that they appear. Therefore Gloucester, even if only imaginatively and notionally, has to tumble amongst them in order to identify with their genuine humanity. Edgar correspondingly has to play two roles. First he has to play the role of a commentator on the top of the cliff. Then, when Gloucester falls down over the notional cliff, he has to play the role of one of the imaginary fishermen who previously were mice-like. He has to comfort the fallen victim and present him with the sympathy which Gloucester was unable to extend to the fishermen when viewing them from the great height of social authority.

I think I may have said this in public once before, and if any of you have heard it forgive me for repeating myself, but I believe that is very like what happens in *The Third Man* (1949) when Harry Lime takes Holly Martins to the top of the enormous Ferris wheel in the Viennese Prater Park. You remember that in order to justify his actions in dealing in diluted penicillin, Harry Lime pulls open the sliding door of the carriage and says, 'Would it really matter to you, old man, if one of the dots down there stopped moving? A thousand dollars each one, tax free, old man – would it really matter?' And indeed from that height, as those dots move stochastically below on the pavement, it's quite hard even for you as a cinema spectator not to say, 'well, perhaps it doesn't really matter, if they are nothing more than dots after all.' Holly Martins himself tumbles amongst them, or is made to tumble amongst them, when Calloway the Security Officer takes him into the hospital where he sees full-sized children dying of meningitis. It is at that moment, if you remember, that Martins decides to turn in his friend because he would be doing the greater evil by allowing him to continue his actions.

I believe that what we are seeing in that imaginary fall over the cliff in *King Lear* is something closely analogous to that. This brings up the way in which you actually stage it. I believe it is terribly important that when you stage that moment of the description, Edgar himself must be seen to close his eyes, in order to abstain from what is visible so that he can concentrate upon what is in front of his mind's eye. So we should at that moment dramatically confront two blind people, one who is permanently blinded by Cornwall's sadism, and the other someone who, as it were, is voluntarily abstaining from sight in order to be able to concentrate on something which he is imagining. There should be a paradox when Edgar says 'how fearful/And dizzy 'tis to cast one's eyes so low' (IV.vi.11–12), because he cannot, and does not, actually do this. He must stand there and give an imaginary account so that we see two differently blinded people standing side by side: one giving a commentary on something which is not in front of his physical eyes but which is in front of his mind's eye, broadcasting it into the head of someone who will never have eyes at all, but nevertheless retains the capacity to conjure visions before his mind's eye which is still intact. The moment then when Edgar says 'I'll look no more' (IV.vi.22) actually, paradoxically, should be the moment when he opens his eyes.

'I'll look no more' signals the moment when Edgar starts to look because he is actually saying, I will look no more at what I'm imagining. That moment seems to me to be the still centre of the play with respect to the trajectory of Edgar's and of Gloucester's pilgrimage. We are seeing two people who are going through the experience of loss and reduction, because not only is Edgar acting as a spiritual physician for his father, but also because he himself is undergoing a spiritual discovery.

I feel that in the representation of Edgar, not only should we have in mind a Christian image, but also some sort of vision of figures similar to the holy fools in Dostoyevsky. Edgar should present a Prince Myshkin-like figure who almost seeks the role which is forced upon him by misfortune. Indeed he shows a curiously rhapsodic eagerness when he anticipates how he is going to play poor Tom. Immediately after Kent falls asleep in the stocks, suddenly Edgar appears and simply announces that he is in flight. It might seem he is merely putting on a 'base' disguise for protection. But the way in which he chooses the disguise that he will assume makes it look as if he has sought all his life this particular form of self-humiliation, for he shows a rhapsodic, ecstatic excitement when he anticipates the role that he is about to undertake. He says:

> No port is free, no place
> That guard and most unusual vigilance
> Does not attend my taking, Whiles I may scape
> I will preserve myself,
> (II.ii.174–177)

Up to that point it seems that this is merely expedient. But he goes on:

> and am bethought
> To take the basest and most poorest shape
> That ever penury in contempt of man
> Brought near to beast.
> (177–180)

And it then becomes a scherzo of excitement:

> My face I'll grime with filth,
> Blanket my loins, elf all my hairs in knots
> And with presented nakedness outface
> The winds and persecutions of the sky.
> The country gives me proof and precedent
> Of Bedlam beggars, who, with roaring voices,
> Strike in their numbed and mortified bare arms
> Pins, wooden pricks, nails, sprigs of rosemary;
> And with this horrible object, from low farms,
> Poor pelting villages, sheepcotes, and mills,
> Sometime with lunatic bans, sometime with prayers,
> Enforce their charity.
> (180–191)

The excitement now culminates:

> Poor Turlygod, poor Tom,
> That's something yet: Edgar I nothing am.
> (191–192)

In the process of discovering what it will be like to be the most humiliated and basest thing in nature, he discovers the intense and euphoric excitement of suddenly annihilating his previous identity as Edgar. He as it were launches himself out into this act of self-discovery which he then reiterates, if you remember, in the scene on the heath immediately after the storm, after the blinding of Gloucester, when we actually hear him exulting in his nothingness. He says here, immediately after the blinding:

> Yet better thus, and known to be contemned
> Than still contemned and flattered. To be worst,
> The lowest and most dejected thing of fortune,
> Stands still in esperance, lives not in fear.
> The lamentable change is from the best,
> The worst returns to laughter.
> (IV.i.1–6)

This is as if to say that only in the state of liminality, only in the state of nothingness where your own identity is completely obliterated, is there the chance of joy. Bertrand Russell once said in one of his essays, 'only if you recognize that the world is horrible, horrible, *horrible*, can you begin to enjoy yourself.'[87] I believe that in fact Edgar makes this wonderful act of self-discovery that in the process of paring yourself down to the minimum where you have nothing, not even what our basest beggars have, where you actually have reduced yourself below the level where you need anything, can you actually be safe from the ordeals of existence. But then of course he discovers that, when you think you are at the worst, you are likely to be surprised. In saying, 'The wretch that thou hast blown unto the worst/ Owes nothing to thy blasts' (IV.i.8–9), Edgar says in effect, 'here I am at the lowest level, and I can actually have euphoric enjoyment of being nothing.' Then suddenly his new-blinded father appears on the horizon and he says:

> But that thy strange mutations make us hate thee,
> Lie would not yield to age.
>
> O gods! Who is't can say 'I am at the worst'?
> I am worse than e'er I was.
>
> And worse I may be yet; the worst is not
> So long as we can say 'This is the worst.'
> (IV.i.12–13, 27–28, 29–30)

In other words he says that there is no possibility of escaping from the worst while you are still able to formulate that you are at the worst.

Nevertheless there is this movement towards some moral asymptote at which you gradually approximate to zero but never actually reach it. Always you can be defeated by the practical jokes the world can inflict upon you which can make it worse than your worst anticipation. Even so, Edgar undergoes a strange euphoric self-discovery in finding that, in the process of ridding yourself of everything, you actually have the possibility of being in some respects invulnerable. This ridding is of course what all the characters in the play, certainly Gloucester and Lear, actually undergo. Although they don't see it that way and are not regenerated by it, the daughters also discover that they are stripped of everything. All that Goneril can find in this is the fact that she has a 'hateful life'; she actually uses that

103

phrase (IV.ii.87). What we see in the play, and it is almost too self-evident to insist upon, is an elaborate symphonic development upon the notion of nothingness and stripping, of reduction to some sort of hypothetical zero which in fact is never reachable because there is always the possibility that the world will do something worse to you than what you have actually anticipated.

This happens to poor Lear himself at the moment when he has been reduced to nothing and is just about to be restored to his daughter. Then he loses his daughter and ultimately he must die, and one feels that Shakespeare actually punishes him for what he does at the beginning of the play. It is in fact a pessimistic ending because you do not get in Lear a recovery, a reconciliation, or a discovery. Or if there is one, it is never a discovery which enables him to say 'I did wrong.' He believes that he behaved wrongly to Cordelia but at no point does he ever seem to acknowledge how wrongly he behaved to all his daughters, and how wrongly he behaved to his society. He has glimpses of this and he occasionally glances at the fact that he has taken too little note of it, that pomp should 'take physic' and that he should encourage himself to feel 'what wretches feel' (III.iv.33, 34). But all his advances in this direction are tentative, and never complete themselves in the way they do with Gloucester, and with Edgar. So there is this marvellous death of Gloucester which is so unlike the death of Lear; we are told Gloucester's heart 'burst smilingly' (V.iii.198). There is no sense in which Lear's heart bursts smilingly. It bursts tragically and to no good purpose. He has learned nothing; he has picked up fragments of wisdom but has not achieved a comprehensive moral vision in the way that Gloucester has, or certainly in the way that Edgar has.

Let me say something briefly about interpreting the Fool because that is something that I have always remained fairly constant about in rehearsal. Once again there is an aberration which traditionally bedevils the play, and that is the capricious capering youngster who is so often cast as the Fool. People have been misled I believe by the word 'boy.' Because Shakespeare makes Lear refer to him as 'boy' (I.iv.105) he is often played as a young falsetto creature who crouches and clutches the calves of Lear and, rather nervously gnome-like, presents strange/wise formulae. But I believe that the things which the Fool says are so wry, so ripe in the sense of 'Ripeness is all' (V.ii.11), that they are inconceivable in the mouth of such a creature. I believe that we have been misled for years by the wrong connotation of 'boy,' and that in *Lear* it means no more than '*garçon*' does to a waiter, or no more than 'boy' does when a Southern Colonel addresses his black body-servant. The 'boy' Fool is simply someone who is politically junior to Lear, or socially junior, and nothing more than that.

Indeed, I believe that the moral of the play becomes much more clearly recognizable if in fact you make Lear and his Fool two creatures who are nearly indistinguishable; two old boys. One of them has grown fond and foolish in his old age, and one has grown wiser and more mature with age, but they both must otherwise be absolutely on a par with one another. I was prompted to do this in the first production I did of *Lear* by reference to King Louis XIV's body servant Bontemps, who was the only man in the court who was allowed to call Louis, 'Louis.' He had grown up with the monarch from the age of 12, had always stayed with him, had grown old with him, and knew him inside out. I believe that if the Fool is presented as an old man who is exactly the same age as Lear, who has grown up with him, every single one of his otherwise gnomic, runic formulae becomes understandable. He is like an ageing coachman who utters wisdom which would be incomprehensible in the mouth of an adolescent. If we put the Fool's country wisdom in the mouth of an old man who has known Lear as long as he has been monarch and probably longer, suddenly we find an intelligible relationship. What you see is simply two people who differ from one another merely by virtue of the office that they have been assigned; one has been assigned the role of monarch, one has been assigned the role of numbskull, of nothingness, of someone who in fact means nothing. But by meaning nothing the Fool can say everything. Therefore he is in a position to have a reciprocal relationship with his master which actually allows him to be his conscience, and so allows him to say the things which go some way toward restoring Lear's sanity.

It isn't until Lear undergoes the restorative process of becoming completely insane that the Fool can disappear. People often ask, 'why does the Fool vanish at the close as he does?' and the traditional tedious answer, which is a purely scholastic one, says that 'the Fool vanishes because he is actually played by the same person as Cordelia, and so when Cordelia comes back...' and so forth. That is a boring piece of Mermaid Theatre mythology which simply doesn't help one to rehearse the play at all. Merely knowing that the two roles might have once been played by the same person could lead you into the disastrous choice of following suit, which I think leads to nonsensical outcomes. It is much more interesting to ask psychologically, rather than as it were historically, 'why does *that* fool disappear at the point that he does?' He disappears at the point when Lear takes full leave of his senses, after the joint-stool scene in the farmhouse (III.vi). At the end of that scene Kent says to the Fool, 'Thou must not stay behind' (III. vi.98), and the next time we see Lear he has incorporated into himself all the wisdom that the Fool has had. Apart from those wonderful passages of completely demented discourse where he hallucinates brown bills and a mouse which he pursues with a piece of toasted cheese, everything Lear says afterwards is sane, and wise, and almost indistinguishable from the sorts of thing which the Fool had been saying in the previous act. So the Fool no longer has to be a ventriloquial presence who stalks King Lear through the action; he is now incorporated into a Lear who, through the process of fully taking leave of his senses, is beginning to take possession of them again.

The Fool has become incorporated into Lear in that moment of divine insanity on the cliff when he comes up with the wisest political insights which are in the play. All the wonderful things which he says then are folly:

KING LEAR: What, art mad? A man may see how this world goes
with no eyes. Look with thine ears. See how yon
justice rails upon yon simple thief. Hark in
thine ear: change places and handy-dandy, which
is the justice, which is the thief? Thou hast seen
a farmer's dog bark at a beggar?

GLOUCESTER: Ay, Sir.

KING LEAR: And the creature run from the cur – there thou
mightst behold the great image of authority: a
dog's obeyed in office.
Thou, rascal beadle, hold thy bloody hand;
Why dost thou lash that whore? Strip thine own back,
Thou hotly lusts to use her in that kind

For which thou whipp'st her. The usurer hangs the cozener.
Through tattered clothes great vices do appear;
(IV.vi.146–160)

These remarks are level-headed and sane, but they only acquire that sanity by virtue of the fact that Lear has acquired the wise folly which Erasmus praised in his "Praise of Folly" (1511). So we see that the Fool has vanished because he is actually present now in Lear, and is present there as a sane person. And so we see the restoration of reason through the loss of sense.

This is a much more interesting reason for the Fool's disappearance than expedience. It leads to the question of interpreting one of Lear's final lines: 'And my poor fool is hang'd!' (V.iii.304). All this week I have had a long and interminable argument with Eric Porter about what that line means. I believe it refers to Cordelia, and that Lear says 'And my poor fool is hang'd!' not because she once was played by the actor who played the Fool but because his term 'fool' is an endearment. Eric Porter doesn't think that. He actually wants Lear to say that line because he is tying up a loose end and letting the audience know that his Fool has been in fact hanged. I actually think that Lear's 'my poor fool' is a reference simply to the dead body of Cordelia which is in front of him, not that he sees her metaphorically as his Fool but that it is simply a phrase of great pathos when he confronts the body of his young daughter.

Which brings me to one final point about Cordelia. I have mentioned all the other daughters and haven't talked about Cordelia at all, about how we actually rehearse her and present her. I in fact have cast someone who is very young to play Cordelia, so in this production there is a wide separation between the two elder daughters and the younger one. It is as if she really is an afterthought, someone who was produced from even another wife, for whom Lear has a rather peculiar and distinct feeling, and who is virtually unknown to the other daughters. If you play the other daughters as 50, so they have gone away and lived elsewhere and hardly know this child, they will have a natural sense of resentment about the larger part of the kingdom being given to someone whom they don't know at all, who is in fact a step-sister.

There isn't much more I can simply say now because, as I say, it is extremely hard to describe rehearsal when you are actually in the middle of it. I can only do what I have tried to do, which is to sketch some of what I believe to be the salient themes of the play.

Foreword to *Ivan*
May 1986[88]

In 1984, BBC2's science strand Horizon *transmitted Miller's film profile of Ivan Vaughan, an acute sufferer of Parkinson's disease. The documentary provoked a powerful response from the viewing public. Here, by way of an introduction to Vaughan's own memoir, Miller reflected on their time together.*

In 1817 the English physician James Parkinson described a disease of the nervous system in which the patient was progressively afflicted by a stooped, shuffling rigidity accompanied by a coarse, disabling tremor of the limbs. Although Parkinson referred to this condition as a 'shaking palsy,' it is not really a paralysis in the obvious sense of the term, because although the patient's movements are slowed, sometimes to the point of statuesque immobility, it is possible to overcome the rigidity and under the right circumstances the patient may surprise onlookers by moving with unexpected speed and fluency.[89]

Viewers of the BBC documentary on Ivan Vaughan found it hard to reconcile the apparently normal running sequence at the start of the film with the strenuously awkward ritual of dressing in the morning. In order to make this transition, Ivan had to tumble off the front steps of the house and it was only by taking advantage of this self-inflicted emergency that he was then able to jog for several miles. And even then a trivial interruption, such as an unexpected encounter with a dog or a friend, could easily bring him to a standstill, at which point the trembling rigidity reclaimed him once again. The disorder displays many paradoxes of this sort. And as one clinician wrote in 1895, 'Parkinson's disease remains so utterly inexplicable...that we are constantly drawn to it by the lure of the mysterious.'[90]

The last 80 years have seen remarkable progress in neurological research, and Parkinson's disease is not quite as inexplicable as it once seemed. For instance, although there is still some dispute over whether the various examples represent one disease or several, the fact that so many of them are associated with degenerative changes in the same part of the brain – in the so-called *substantia nigra* – has convinced most neurologists that Parkinson's disease is, after all, a pathological entity.

Even so, the precise cause of the condition is still obscure and, although an important advance was made when it was discovered that the affected region of the brain is conspicuously deficient in the neurotransmitter dopamine and that startling remissions could often be brought about by administering L-dopa – a metabolic precursor of dopamine – the treatment remains to all intents and purposes symptomatic and the improvement is not necessarily maintained when the drug is administered over a long period of time. Besides, it is notoriously difficult to stabilize the dose and, unless the progress is frequently monitored, the patient can easily exchange one set of disabling symptoms for another. The limbs may now be affected by slow twisting movements and, although these can usually be corrected by reducing the dose, some patients claim that even when it is working favourably the drug tends to induce a disturbing sense of coercion. So while Ivan Vaughan would be the last to deny the blessing of L-dopa, he would be the first to insist that the blessing is a mixed one, and that there is an enigmatic sense in which he is more 'himself' when he is off the drug than when he is relieved of symptoms and on it.

For that reason, and also perhaps because he is an unusually curious patient who regards his condition as something to be explored as well as endured, Ivan juggles with his own treatment and, in the knowledge that he can always run to the drug for shelter, he sometimes takes pharmacological holidays so that he can experiment with the transitions from one state to the next.

As far as the medical profession is concerned this sort of therapeutic improvisation is short-sighted and irresponsible, and any adjustments are best left to those who are in the know. But for an intelligently introspective patient such as Ivan Vaughan, having the disease is just another way of *being* in the know – and since the paradoxical experiences of the disease are quite literally unknowable to anyone except the sufferer, Ivan feels that he has valuable contributions to make and that the experiments are not simply frivolous self-indulgences.

The problem is that, although doctors pay lip service to the principle that all patients should be listened to, the intelligent sufferer often comes away from the clinic with the distinct impression that he or she has been seen without actually being heard. And since many of the vicissitudes of the disease cannot be observed and have to be described, the patient's spoken testimony is one of the most valuable sources of information.

Unfortunately it is only too easy for the busy clinician to confuse a garrulous patient with one who is helpfully eloquent, and when it comes to someone like Ivan Vaughan – who sees himself as a partner in the research as opposed to being a submissive patient – professional hackles are raised and there is an understandable, but not altogether forgivable tendency to close ranks and disparage such contributions as the ramblings of an eccentric amateur.

In that respect Ivan is undoubtedly an awkward customer, and it is not difficult to sympathize with the suspicion that he arouses – not only amongst neurologists, but also amongst the members of the Parkinson's Disease Society, who prefer to maintain a cooperative relationship with the profession and feel that Ivan Vaughan's individualistic experiments rock the boat unhelpfully. All the same, as medicine becomes more scientific, its official literature leaves less and less room for the subjective accounts provided by the patient, and as the discourse becomes denser and more impenetrable, it becomes harder and harder to hear the voices of those for whom the benefits are designed. It is only by dint of his heretical awkwardness that Ivan Vaughan has succeeded in making at least one of those voices audible, and although both doctors and other Parkinsonian sufferers have argued and will continue to argue that Ivan's case is atypical and that his film appearance was both misleading and alarming, I feel now, as I felt when I reluctantly accepted his original invitation to visit him, that Ivan has a certain wisdom to impart and that anyone who is interested in this perplexing disorder has something to learn from him.

I can still remember my own irritation on hearing the thin, importunate voice at the other end of the telephone when Ivan rang me out of the blue with the request that I should come up to Cambridge and hear what he, a sufferer from Parkinson's disease, had to say about it. What, I thought, made *him* so special? Why did *he* rather than anyone else deserve a visit? To my shame, I tried to put him off, pleading business, not to mention a lack of requisite qualifications. But fortunately he refused to take no for an answer, insisting that I could surely spare an hour or two and that it was precisely because I was *not* a member of the neurological establishment that I might perhaps hear details that had gone unheeded by the better qualified.

It became apparent immediately on my arrival in Cambridge that my irritable misgivings were ill-founded. Ivan and I spoke for many hours and I soon became aware of the fact that, in some altogether mysterious way, he had succeeded in surmounting his disease by regarding it as a treasured possession and not just as an abominable affliction. As far as he was concerned, Parkinson's disease was simply another mode of existence filled with intriguing paradoxes, the introspective study of which might perhaps lead to a better understanding of the nature of normal will and action. After discussing the possibility of collaborating on a book, it was finally agreed that the subject might be broached more successfully in the medium of film – and from the awed fascination shown by the crew, I was convinced that my own interest was not peculiar and that what Ivan had to say and show would intrigue and enlighten the ordinary viewer.[91]

The book in which Ivan now develops these themes will probably arouse just as many objections as the film did. His description of what it is like to suffer Parkinson's disease is unarguably idiosyncratic and no doubt fellow sufferers will claim that their experience does not square with his. And neurologists will probably take exception to Ivan's unremittingly combative attitude to the treatment that is now on offer. All the same, this controversial narrative provides an indispensable supplement to the 'official' history of Parkinson's disease. As Carlo Ginzburg says in the introduction to *The Cheese and the Worms* (1976), historians who might once have been 'accused of wanting to know only about "the great deeds of kings" [are now] turning toward what their predecessors passed over in silence, discarded, or simply ignored' – namely, the personal experience of anonymous people whose lives are often omitted from official descriptions of a particular period.[92] Apart from the fact that Ivan's account has an undeniable value for its intelligence and for its inquisitive curiosity, and because extended subjective descriptions of this disease are so rare, its heretical tone of voice is just one of the things that future historians will find intriguing.

The amateur theologian rediscovered by Ginzburg represents the voice of an ordinary person who finds himself in conflict with the official dogmas of the Catholic Church and is prepared to risk and lose his life in the effort to reconcile his own beliefs with the teachings of the Vatican. By retrieving this story Ginzburg has amplified and enriched our picture of moral and intellectual life at the end of the sixteenth century. I'm convinced that the future will recognize Ivan's contribution in the same light and that his argumentative heresies, which could so easily have been passed over in silence, will eventually be seen as a valuable document in the history of medicine.

I won't pay for the trip:
no chemical routes to paradise
Vogue, 1 September 1967[93]

The first time I ever took a drug was when I had my tonsils out. I was 12 at the time, but I can still remember the mortal chill of the gas, and the way the voices of the staff became very loud, over-meaningful, and then vanished altogether. It's one of my strongest memories, but the wooziness and falling asleep seem now to be no more than corollaries of the main attraction. It's the *smell* of the ether which I recall more than anything else. Not that you could properly call it a smell – there's not enough body in it for that. That's why the name is so perfect: ether! The cold vapour has such an empty keenness that it rocks the mind long before it actually stuns the brain. It smells like nothing on earth, except a threat. It's a smell which glitters, like a blade perfectly sharpened to slit the throat of consciousness.

The actual process of going under has never appealed to me much. The singing in the ears, the loss of grip and so on are empty by comparison with the retrospective knowledge of the blackout which follows. It's only the oblivion, or rather the threat of it, which I find exciting. I am just the same with sleep. I am a sleep junkie, hopelessly addicted to long dreamless draughts of the stuff. It has nothing to do with dozing, or any of the hallucinating reveries that go before. The trip to unconsciousness can't be too short for me. I do not enjoy the deliquescent imagery you get halfway between full awareness and actual coma. I like oblivion, but I like to contemplate it with every faculty intact. The *thought* of unconsciousness, the view from the brink, is perhaps the most psychedelic experience there is. But it can only be got by paying minute attention to the details of what's involved. The kick comes from grasping the intellectual contradictions – from knowing that as you get snuffed, only a thin trickle of personal experience vanishes at that moment from the grand stream of the world's onward motion. It comes from knowing that for some time at least your body stays just as it was, preserved in every detail, just as the owner left it.

I just love the way one leaves the body there – like a bag left on a seat, reserving a place in the world, awaiting the owner's return. It's one of the oddest experiences to watch one of these slow-breathing proxies waiting for *its* owner to slip back into the place kept warm for him by that provisional presence, snoring away on the pillow. Just thinking about this can drive away sleep altogether, as one imagines one's forthcoming absence. After a while the mind reels with the metaphysical implications of it all.

I am not denying there are thrills to be had from alterations of consciousness a long way short of complete oblivion; it is nice to jar the appearance of things and feel for a moment the primeval oddness of simply being-in-the-world. In the normal way, everything around us becomes more or less invisible through habit; but that is just as it should be, of course. We could never get on with life if we were pulled up short by everything that touched our senses. We could never find our way about if we had to attend to the tickle of the clothes on our back or listen to every one of the million sounds which did not have immediate importance. We seal ourselves off from most of what the world has to offer, in order to make the best of the few things we *can* set our minds to.

But every now and then the mental insulation breaks down, and the world floods in to overwhelm us with its raw, complicated foreignness. In these rare flashes there is no focus and no perspective. Everything seems to bear down with equal importance, and the will is paralyzed with an *embarras de richesses*. Nothing seems quite as it should be; everything goes topsy-turvy. Familiar sights glow with unjustified novelty, and new experiences are greeted as *déjà vu*. Luckily for us these episodes only last for a minute or two, but in that moment the world seems to gleam with high romantic value, and our spirit is renovated as it is brought face to face with the vast unmanned enormity of the physical creation.

Paralyzing and impractical though these moments are, they are so disturbing and so beautiful that it is not surprising if people seem to spend so much time trying to improvise the condition at will. At one time or another there is always a recipe going the rounds for a sure-fire milk-of-paradise: alcohol, laughing gas, breath-holding, mushroom juice, morning-glory seeds, or hard drugs. But *I* have always been completely cut off from any of the chemical routes to paradise. Alcohol gives me scalding heartburn, and 'pot' gets me no further than vertigo followed by a fitful sleep. I daren't try any of the more powerful agents, as I know they would unhinge my mind forever, or hustle me into an eternity of hellish vomiting. It's no good saying that this is not what such drugs do – they would with me. I have never even got a glimpse of Xanadu through the thick poison clouds of nausea. There must be thousands of people like me, pharmacologically underprivileged, who will never know the delights of chemical psychedelia; but all of us want a share of the transcendental cake. What hope is there for us?

Let me say for a start what I don't need. I am not really interested in hallucinations. Nor do I really want to see colours brighter than I do already. In fact, I can do without any of the optical displays. To judge from the reports, these retinal shows are as brilliantly monotonous as the best Op art, and they wouldn't hold me for more than a minute or two. In fact, I don't really want any improvement in my powers of peripheral sensation.

What I really want, if it can be arranged, is simply a sharper sense of how odd it is to be here at all. Therefore, I insist on preserving the full power of my critical and intellectual faculties. So far as I am concerned, there is no point in having one of the varieties of religious experience unless I am in a position to describe and amplify what I have known in words. Half the pleasure in any new or extravagant experience lies in being able to fix the whole thing. Most of the reports brought back from drug trips have a gaudy mediocrity. They are affirmative without being descriptive, and I am just not interested in an experience which slithers out of the bottom end of the mind, leaving nothing more than a sense of conviction behind.

There are said to be good substitutes for drugs. These usually take the form of violent assaults on the senses: flashing lights or unbearable noise.

Well, that won't do either. I resent the idea that I can be raped into the higher sensitivity. Anyway, it doesn't work. Shows of this sort simply drum me into a state of mindless idiocy.

That leaves hard work as the only effective road to paradise. Not common-or-garden hard work but the sort of hard work which takes everyday experience and, by paying careful attention to it and rubbing its tarnished surfaces, brings the whole thing up with a supernatural glow. Chesterton says somewhere that it is only after seeing something for the thousandth time one can suddenly see it again for the first.[94] But it doesn't come easy. One has to use all sorts of mental tricks in order to achieve this sense of freshly-peeled newness. It's no good looking at the world straight on. You have to get at a peculiar angle to it before it will show its secret. It is rather like a gardener who improves his sense of colour by occasionally looking at the landscape upside down between his legs.

One method, which I find works like a charm, is to take a trip to a foreign city. Any old city will do, since the actual scenery has nothing to do with the strange psychological effect of arriving. The place can be as dull as dishwater and without a single tourist attraction. In fact, glamour of any sort would get in the way of what I am after. The dizzying, ecstatic mystery of the experience comes from simply dislocating one's self from the familiar stream of life and from arriving in a place which was there long before one arrived, unaware of one's existence. No drug on earth can produce such a cataclysmic heightening of consciousness. I got the feeling for the first time many years ago when I went to Paris. I arrived late one afternoon at the Gare du Nord. As I stepped out into the golden railway sunlight of that Parisian five o'clock, I was overwhelmed at once, not by the Gallic charm of it all, not by the boulevards, the smell of Gauloises, or any of the usual tourist clichés, but simply by the sense of civic otherness.

I had stepped out of the London timestream, where I had an unquestioned existence and some sort of quotidian pedigree, and had stepped into a Parisian sequence where I had no past whatsoever. All around, Parisians were scurrying backwards and forwards, trailing an invisible string of Parisian encounters and incidents, and on their way to more of the same. I, on the other hand, stood on the steps of the station without a single fragment of Parisian past. I felt that it would be almost indecent to walk off into the hurrying crowds and join them without a past like theirs – I must have been as conspicuous as if I had had no clothes on. Free from the weight of shared memory, I felt as if the Parisian gravity just didn't apply to *my* body, and that if I took a single step, I would float off into the evening air like a whiff of transparent gas.

It was only years later that I realized how unnecessary it was to go so far as to cross the channel in order to get this feeling. Any city would do, so long as it was the same sort of size as London. So long as it was big, black and busy. So long as it had rush-hour crowds hurrying to buses and subways, just as I would have been doing if I had been at home. The important thing was to arrive in a place similar in almost every respect to the city I had just left. In fact, the only feature it would *not* have to have was my previous presence in it. For against this plain backcloth of civic similarity, one's lack of past and future stands out in brilliant contrast. At one simple manoeuvre I am turned into a creature with instantaneous existence; a point in time whose feelings are therefore concentrated to infinity.

All this scores over drugs in achieving its effect by the unaided activity of the mind alone. There is no sharing the credit with chemicals, and since the intellect is intact, you get none of that blooming euphoric confidence which goes with drugs. The descriptions do not decay as normality returns, and unlike drugs, the dosage works in reverse. Simply with practice, you can get the same effects with smaller and smaller bits of travel. I don't even have to travel outside London now. I can get the effect by moving from one part of town to another, at an unusual time of day, or by taking a new bus route and by coming on familiar places from a strange new angle.

There is a weird railway line, for example, which runs around the back side of London, above ground and yet hidden from the streets by hoardings and factories.[95] As soon as you move out of the station, you are knocked out by a sense of *jamais vu*. Landmarks which seemed perfectly familiar now stand out as if seen for the first time, and with the train's eccentric course they change positions in all sorts of remarkable ways, and take up places that they couldn't possibly occupy according to the rules of common sense. And for some unaccountable reason, this backstage railway land is bathed in a sulphurous nineteenth-century light, so that nothing seems quite real; and, as the train rattles on towards Kew and Richmond, you seem at last to be on a celestial railroad bound for Avalon.

The point is that ordinary reality is always on the edge of hatching apocalypses like this. The world is a miraculous chrysalis which cracks open under the heat of attention, yielding angels which whir about your head like dragonflies. It doesn't need any drugs to bring on the transformation – attention is enough.

You can sometimes get the effect in the middle of the English countryside, on a hot, silent summer afternoon. Three o'clock seems about to go on forever, and the heat-stunned stillness seems like the edge of doomsday. All around, the trees stand ankle-deep in the lifeblood of their own shadow; birdsong stops for a moment, the insect machinery switches off. The whole of creation sweats with expectation. There is no knowing what the scene is about to deliver. In one sense it is irrelevant. The expectation is all; fulfilment can only be an anti-climax.

And yet, these sacred instants can pass by without ever being felt. Drugs would simply blur the experience or reproduce it best in a chaotic form, so that its sacred precision would be lost.

All I want is some device which keeps me constantly in touch with the bizarre 'there-ness' of the world in which I have been formed.

Fortunately, the world itself comes up with stimuli which jolt the mind in this direction. Once you are in practice, small changes of climate even will do the trick. There is nothing like a sudden wind, for example, to switch the mind into high gear. Or a sousing, catastrophic downpour of rain. Or a snowstorm when the whole city seems suddenly to have been seriously burned, then bandaged and consigned to a darkened invalid silence. The point is, once the muscles of the mind are in tune, very small changes of sensation, mood, climate or interest can produce quite startling alterations in consciousness.

The world is always tugging at one's sleeve in order to impart its secrets. It's just a question of being on the *qui vive*. Judging from the traveller's tales, psychedelia would be too vague a place for me, a vivid but somehow smudged version of the world at large. Most of it seems spectacularly vapid. Convincing, but thin. The fact is that it always seems to border on the exotic, when what I'm after is the apotheosis of the humdrum.

It's significant, I think, that psychedelic trips are spoken of in terms of inner space. I am sure that the pharmaconauts journey to the same sort of dizzy emptiness as travellers in outer space. In both places, physical substance thins out and finally vanishes, giving way to a mindless region filled with methane and stardust. It's not for me.

The strongest influence in my life
BBC Radio 4, 27 May 1975[96]

It is very hard to make an accurate or truthful estimation of personal influences in one's life, because, usually, the choice one makes is determined by hopes or regrets about the sort of person one is at the moment. I think that, in making choices about strong personal influences, one is really looking backwards and making judgements about oneself, so that, at this particular moment in my life, when I am reconsidering my life in the theatre, and whether I will continue in the theatre, my choice of a biology teacher and a philosophy teacher – at school and at Cambridge respectively – is strongly determined by new feelings; and although, undoubtedly, I was powerfully affected by my first exposure to my biology teacher, I do not think that his influence would have worked strongly if I had not had some sort of interest in the subject before I met him.

At the age of 12, I was started on the path towards biology by a gift from my father. He gave me a large Victorian brass microscope, perhaps hoping to lure me into medicine as he was a doctor himself. I do not think there was anything quite so calculating, but he gave me this present and it had a very powerful effect on me. At night, with a desk lamp, I used to stare down this long barrel, this well-shaft, into a brilliantly illuminated world. I used to look at hay infusions and blood films and the surfaces of leaves and collections of diatoms and foraminifera – slides which I had bought with my spare pocket money from rather dusty microscopical shops in Soho. And, without quite knowing what I was looking at, and without quite understanding why I was even looking, I became intrigued by this peculiar basement at the bottom of the world – as if someone had opened a staircase to a level of the world which I had not suspected existed at all.

In some ways, perhaps, I was moved, in that mood of adolescent vanity, by the figure that I struck at my desk, as much as by the sort of things that

I was looking at down the microscope. I had been weaned on the scientific romances of H. G. Wells and was already very powerfully influenced by the idea of a serious, heavy, studious world of South Kensington science, of heavily moustached savants moving gravely between teak benches with these brass taps and these great microscopes, indulging in serious controversy – the world of Conan Doyle and Professor Challenger, as well as the Wells scientists.

By the time I entered my public school, my microscopic experiences had already convinced me that science was what I wanted to do, but I entered the school on the classics side, because, as usual in English prep schools, science was looked down upon: it was regarded as a slightly artisan skill. I remember wandering, in the lunch-hours, around the biological laboratories, and looking in through plate-glass windows. There I could see boys dissecting, opening dog-fish, again rapt and studious in the South Kensington sort of way. And, at the teacher's end of the room, I saw this mysterious, rather agricultural figure of the biology teacher – rather tweedy, rather apple-cheeked, fair hair and tawny moustache – moving backwards and forwards behind his desk, sucking at his pipe, and occasionally writing things on the blackboard. And, for some reason, he stayed in during his lunch hour, when other masters were out either on the sports field or having their lunch.

This silent spectacle behind the aquarium windows of the biology laboratory began to intrigue me. I felt that in some way this was a sort of Eden or Paradise from which I was being excluded, and that I was being condemned to a prison of the classics. Finally, in desperation, I went to the headmaster and said that I wanted to change to the biology side. He tried, in a last desperate move, to retain me for classics, by saying that even if I wanted to become a doctor I should stay on the classics side because I would learn the Latin names of diseases, and would therefore be able to christen my discoveries with more panache; but that did not work, and I finally entered the biology side and came under the influence of this very remarkable man, Mr Pask.

I can remember very little about the actual quality of his mind, nor can I even remember any burning enthusiasm on his part. I can only infer his enthusiasm from the results upon us, and upon the extraordinary institution which he had managed to create. He was known very affectionately amongst the class as Sid, and I can remember a very touching occasion, 15 or 20 years after I left school, in which a whole series of generations of biologists and doctors got together to celebrate Sid's fortieth anniversary at the school, and it was strange to see this cavalcade of scientists all of whom had been influenced and shaped by the enthusiasms of this man. I can remember no distinct ideas which he imparted to us, and yet, at the end of four or five years, I had accumulated a systematic knowledge of biology which must have been imparted to us by him.

Perhaps he did it by putting things in our way rather than by actually instructing us, and this, in a way, is the most potent form of instruction. He assumed that we were adults on a small scale. He equipped his library on the scale of a university library – he did not have elementary textbooks, he had the textbooks which one would have used for Part II of the Tripos at Cambridge.[97] I can remember the heavy, august volumes of Ray Lankester, Sedgwick textbooks of zoology, Strasburger botany. I can remember the spinach-coloured covers of the botany volumes, and the brighter green of Parker and Haswell's textbooks of zoology.

Perhaps, in some ways, he created for us a science which it is no longer possible to practise, a science which is associated with people more like Darwin than with Francis Crick, a science which was descriptive, classificatory, rather than biophysical and mathematical. He himself had been trained in Cambridge under the great anatomists of the 1920s, and I think he brought to us the world of South Kensington. The effect of Mr Pask was so powerful on all the boys of my generation, and he had trained us up to such a high level that, by the time we entered our universities, and particularly by the time I went to Cambridge, we really were almost ready to take the final exams.

One discipline which I had never encountered at school was the philosophy of science. At the hands of Mr Pask, science was all content, rather than a method of thought. The idea that there might be some system of thought which would question these classifications, and, indeed, question the whole nature of inquiry itself, never really occurred to us. When I first went to Cambridge, I came under the influence of a philosopher of science who turned my world upside down. He made this world of opaque objects transparent to the influence of philosophical thought. He introduced me to the idea that one would have to consider the whole nature of science itself – to question the enterprise of scientific inquiry, rather than take on scientific inquiry as something which was given.

He was an American called Norwood Russell Hanson. He was tall, very muscular, robust, a Johnny Appleseed figure – great mane of hair, trousers that were always too short, thick rubber-soled shoes, and he would bounce behind his desk, demonstrating to us the principles of thought rather than the principles of science. I was supervised by him, which meant that I used to take my essays to him once a week and we would sit knee to knee in a tiny office at the top of a rickety staircase, in a place called the Whipple Museum of the History of Science, which housed a few rather ancient microscopes, one or two astrolabes, and some rusty collections of seventeenth-century instruments. There, over a faltering gas fire, in the early Fifties, we would discuss the philosophy of science.

Now, here was a man the content of whose thought I can actually remember. He created no décor; for him, there was no question of establishing a series of objects, or setting up a library, or introducing us to appearances – it was simply the stream of his thought which affected me. Perhaps the most important thing which he did was to introduce me to the philosophy of Wittgenstein, who had died a year before I went up to Cambridge. And, in some sense, this was a road to Damascus: the whole idea of inquiring into the nature of language, and discussing the relationship of language to the world which it supposedly described, fell upon me like a thunderclap. Language had seemed completely transparent to me before. I had not thought of it as a model, or a picture of the world; and quite suddenly, under the influence of this man, language became an opaque object of interest in its own right, and its descriptive powers and capacities suddenly became a subject of interest.

From that moment my interest was diverted, to some extent, from the object of science. I became interested in the logical connections between the ideas, rather than in the ideas themselves. With Norwood Russell Hanson, the very notion of an idea itself became completely intoxicating. One would spend hours, sometimes much longer than the supervision was meant to last, simply discussing the nature of perception, discussing the nature of the statement 'I see a bird,' discussing whether in fact this is a statement about oneself, or a statement about something going on in the world. And, in doing this, science suddenly reorganized itself in my imagination.

Now, I have been away from both science and philosophy for nearly 20 years. I became a practising physician, and then drifted into the theatre. But when I awake sometimes early in the morning, in those awful, dark hours when one has regrets and remorses for what one might have been, the images both of Mr Pask and of Norwood Hanson stand rather vaguely and accusingly at the bottom of the bed, pointing their fingers at me for having fallen away from the thoughtful creature I might have been, instead of the frivolous flibbertigibbet that I have become.

The heat-death of the universe

Beyond the Fringe, 1960[98]

Some years ago, when I was rather hard up, I wanted to buy myself a new pair of trousers – but, being rather hard up, I was quite unable to buy myself a *new* pair. Until some very kind friend whispered into my earhole that if I looked sharp about it I could get myself quite a nice second-hand pair from the Sales Department of the London Passenger Transport Board Lost Property. Now before I accepted this interesting offer I got involved in a great deal of fastidious struggling with my inner soul, because I wasn't very keen to assume the trousers which some lunatic had taken off on a train going eastbound towards Whitechapel.

However, after a great deal of moral contortion, I steeled myself to the alien crutch, and made my way towards the London Passenger Transport Board Lost Property Sales Department in Portman Square, praying as I did so, 'Oh God, let them be dry-cleaned when I get there.' And when I arrived there, you can imagine my pleasure and surprise when I found, instead of a tumbled heap of lunatics' trousers, a very neat heap of brand new, bright-blue corduroy trousers. There were *400* of them! How can anyone lose 400 pairs of trousers on a train? I mean, it's hard enough to lose a brown paper bag full of old orange peel when you really want to. And anyway, 400 men wearing no trousers would attract some sort of attention. No, it's clearly part of a complex economic scheme on the part of the London Passenger Transport Board – a complex economic scheme along Galbraithian or Keynesian lines, presumably. So over now to the Economics Planning Division of the London Passenger Transport Board Ops Room:

'All right, men. Operation Cerulean Trouser. Now, we are going to issue each one of you men with a brand new, bright blue pair of corduroy trousers. Your job will be to disperse to all parts of London, to empty railway carriages, and there to divest yourselves of these garments and leave them in horrid little heaps on the floors of the carriages concerned. Once the trousers have left your body, your job ends there, *and I mean that!* All right, now – are there any questions? Good – now, chins up and trousers down!'

And they disperse to places far out on the reaches of the Central Line. Places with unlikely names like Chipping Ongar; places presumably out on the Essex marshes, totally uninhabited except for a few rather rangy marsh birds mournfully pacing the primeval slime.

And there in the empty railway carriages they let themselves separately and individually into the empty compartments; and then, before they commit the final existential act of detrouserment, they do those little personal things which people sometimes do when they think they're alone in railway carriages. Things like…things like smelling their own armpits.

It's all part of the human condition, I suppose. Anyway, it's quite possible they didn't even take their trousers off in the compartments but made their way along the narrow corridor towards the lavatory at the end – that wonderful little room, where there's that marvellous unpunctuated motto over the lavatory saying, 'Gentlemen lift the seat.' What exactly does this mean? Is it a sociological description – a definition of a gentleman which I can either take or leave? Or perhaps it's a Loyal Toast? It could be a blunt military order…or an invitation to upper-class larceny…but anyway, willy-nilly, they strip stark naked; and then, nude – entirely nude, nude that is except for cellular underwear (for man is born free but everywhere is in cellular underwear) – they make their way back to headquarters through the chilly nocturnal streets of sleeping Whitechapel – 400 fleet-white figures in the night, their 800 horny feet pattering on the pavements and arousing small children from their slumbers in upstairs bedrooms. Children, who are soothed back into their sleep by their parents with the ancient words: 'Turn your face to the wall, my darling, while the gentlemen trot by.'

Foreword to *On the Side of the Angels*
2012

Miller's mother Betty was a prolific writer of both fiction and non-fiction. For a new edition of her sixth novel, originally published in 1945, he provided this foreword.[99]

I can't remember exactly when I first became aware of the fact that my mother was a writer, although I knew that she was a devoted scribbler. During the war, when paper was in short supply, I would see her soon after my father went out to his work as a military psychiatrist, sitting at the dining-room table carefully opening envelopes with a paper knife and writing preparatory sentences for what she would type out some time later in the afternoon. I had no idea what she was writing about and I was completely unaware of the fact that she had already published several well-received novels. I assumed, albeit vaguely, that she was a typist of some sort but I had no idea for whom she was performing this service. I do remember the peculiar way in which she performed on the keyboard, poking at the letters, one by one, with her elegant index fingers. The fact is that she was almost entirely uncommunicative about her work, and even if she had disclosed what she was engaged in I doubt if I would have shown much interest since I was more or less indifferent to the idea of literature and I suspect that she regarded her work as something which had to be done under cover, and that family life intruded rather inconveniently.

It wasn't until I was about 16, by which time I had begun to develop some sort of intellectual interests of my own, that the two of us engaged in discussion, and even then I suspect that her most intimate intellectual relationships were with women writers of her own age – Marghanita Laski for example, Inez Holden and Olivia Manning. So I only learnt what she felt about things by reading her books, and I have to admit that I didn't do that till long after her early death from Alzheimer's disease.[100]

All the same, from the occasional conversations that we did have, and the subsequent reading of her books and many literary articles in journals such as *Horizon*, I see now that she had a considerable influence on my work in the theatre and that her own preoccupation with the seemingly negligible details of human behaviour became one of my articles of artistic faith. In one of my own productions, for example, I owe an undeniable debt of gratitude to this book, in which she describes the regrettable misbehaviour of what must have been some of my father's medical colleagues once they got into military uniform during the Second World War. Professional men who had previously behaved with commendable propriety as long as they were dressed in civilian clothes occasionally took advantage of being in military disguise.

In my several productions of Mozart's *Così fan Tutte*, an opera which is traditionally regarded as an exposé of women's treacherous susceptibility to seduction, my mother's book persuaded me to visualize the opera in terms which are just as critical of men.[101] Under the influence of her book it became increasingly apparent to me that Mozart's work was about identity rather than fidelity and about the dangers of pretending to be someone other than your previous self. Ferrando and Guglielmo trustingly lend themselves to a scheme which Don Alfonso assures them will reveal the inconstancy of their lovers, but what actually happens is something comparable to some of the things that go on in *On the Side of the Angels*. In the disguises which will allow them to deceive the girls, the boys discover unsuspected versions of their own personalities.

I wish I had the opportunity to tell my mother how much these productions of mine owe to her post-mortem inspiration.

3½
New York Review of Books, 20 February 1964[102]

Three movies about competition, property and rank: *Knife in the Water* from Poland, *It's a Mad, Mad, Mad, Mad World* from the USA, and *Billy Liar* from England. All three are chases and each with a beast in view, but only the American film actually runs away with itself down a nightmare slope of greed and violence. The other two are painful enough but generally well in hand; especially Roman Polanski's *Knife in the Water*, a vigilant, metallic piece set on board a small sailing boat. In fact this movie is so artfully cool, so muted and slit-eyed that it sometimes seems downright camp. Two men compete for the favours of a bored girl who wishes the hell with both of them – a spare sexual isosceles which is nicely symbolized in clean, stripped images of sail, sky and water which group and re-group in triangles and trapeziums of grey and white as the boatload of trouble skims trimly across the lake. A stylish three-finger exercise on the theme of pride.

But there is something else which brings this film into line with the other two. For it's also a political story about privilege and envy. It was made after all in a country which has begun to emerge from social and economic austerity – from a section of the world which is seriously embarrassed these days by the liveliness of the acquisitive spirit. We have a journalist who has worked his way, apparently from a position of great poverty to one of comfortable privilege. He comes on at the start in a nifty little German car and unloads a bundle of expensive dacron sails for his racing dinghy, the cabin of which turns out to be an Aladdin's cave of ritzy sporting gear – shipboard cookers, inflatable water toys, frog-flippers, chronometers, and a whole trove of outdoor stuff from some Polish Abercrombie & Fitch. The student who hoists himself aboard this pleasure barge is understandably consumed with envy and resentment – not to mention a certain ideological dismay at all this middle-class hedonist equipment. Before long the two men are engaged in a silly tournament of wit and daring as the student's envy provokes him to score off the older man's vanity. But while they are both challenging each other's manliness in this way they are also locked in a concealed political dispute, about who does and who doesn't have a right to expensive personal property. Even the wife is reduced to a sullen chattel for whom the men are haggling, along with all the other tackle.

Polanski has played a cool trick by taking this ordinarily social squabble out of the city and putting it down in the middle of a watery nowhere. In this way the two men, one deprived and the other privileged, are isolated from the familiar evidence which they might otherwise call upon to explain the puzzling difference in their fortunes. Out in the wild like this, without legal credentials at hand, everything seems to be up for grabs and the only way of establishing rank and rights of ownership is to fall back on natural selection. And by these improvised criteria the tables are turned and the poor student gets the girl and takes over the ship. Moral: the rights of ownership do not cover the possible effects of wind, water or acts of God.

It's a Mad, Mad, Mad, Mad World by Stanley Kramer is a raucous, wraparound Cinerama farce which somehow goes seriously out of kilter and zooms off into a mirthless crescendo of injury and violent punishment. It was clearly modelled on the Sennett formula but the simple chase plot gathers unto itself a disproportionate momentum which carries the film to an inconceivably crushing climax. Part of this can be explained by Cinerama, which is so bloody enormous that almost any violence that takes place on its surface has the force of an overwhelming personal concussion. By contrast, the accidents that went on in the movies of Harold Lloyd and Mack Sennett were pleasantly distant. The idiotic staccato of the old cameras made everything seem reassuringly artificial. But in addition to that everything was choreographed with some tact. Collisions were delicately timed, syncopated even, so that each one had the entertaining *form* of impact but without the actual shock. On Cinerama every crash seems absolutely deadly, and painful as hell.

But all this only partly explains the exhausting brutality of *It's a Mad, Mad, Mad, Mad World*. The film is internally violent. It is intrinsically and deliberately vicious. All the characters are mean, cruel and greedy. They lie, steal, cheat, smash and wreck with single-minded depravity, for which they are punished in the end by a series of excruciating physical torments. The violence of the crimes and the severity of the punishment are completely out of scale for comedy and so the movie fails in this respect. Nevertheless, it is more than just a comedy gone wrong. It has a positive vileness which is almost a virtue. It is as if what started out as a comic extravaganza broke down under its own weight; and then, instead of falling to bits, got taken over, lock, stock and barrel, by something else which then drove the dilapidated mechanism at a ferocious pace in the opposite direction. In fact it's an interesting example of the evacuated shell of a bad comedy being seized by seriousness and turned over to the service of a deadly Puritan theme. All that remains of the comedy is subordinated to the prevailing sternness, and the comedians themselves dwindle to the scale of those tormented clownish figures in a Hell by Hieronymus Bosch.

There is an unshriven demon abroad in America these days; a free-floating collective remorse looking for a place to dramatize itself. *It's a*

Mad, Mad, Mad, Mad World has been taken over by this poltergeist. It's a haunted film.

Billy Liar is a sturdy little film made with austere flatness by John Schlesinger. It's about an ambitious but flimsy young clerk in a funeral parlour who improvises lies, fibs and footling fantasies of grandeur to make up for the actual defeat of real life. He secretes a haze of euphoric hallucination, in which he guns down employers and nagging parents, struts triumphantly at the head of a regiment of victorious Fidelistas (how punctual fantasy can be!) and generally drowns his ambitions in a sea of wish fulfilment. The background to this cut-rate Quixote is splendidly drab, rather 'down,' and very 'Sixties' English. It is more permanently English, however, in the way in which the admirable cast seem to get odder and more memorable as they are further from the action. In this respect the film is very close to Dickens. That is to say it uses a childish perspective – in the sightlines of which adults, who surround a young central character, loom up with impenetrable oddness. A great deal of English comedy depends on the psychological opacity which develops in the characters who are viewed from this primitive egocentric perspective. It distances the adult scene down what then becomes a comic vista, and characters, placed beyond the understanding of the viewer, automatically become inexplicable, grotesque and odd. This optical trick of Dickens is repeated almost angle for angle in *Billy Liar* and although Billy is cockier and naughtier than any of Dickens's sexless young prigs, at heart he is all of a piece with Pip, David and Oliver – an ambitious young innocent, a gentile *nebbish*, pressed in upon by a crowd of gibbering grown-up gargoyles.

Through Dickens this movie establishes connections with another well-known English situation. Billy is a descendent of a line of thwarted young intellectuals – or marginal intellectuals – stifling in the depths of the lower middle class. There is David Copperfield consumed with snobbish disdain for his colleagues at Murdstone and Grinby. Hardy's Jude panting after academic recognition in the obscurity of a stone-mason's yard? Poor Leonard Bast making an ass of himself in front of those snooty Schlegel girls with his idiotic cultural malapropisms. Wells's Kipps and George Gissing himself. On the brighter side there are those garrulous Fabian burglars of Bernard Shaw. Billy comes off rather badly by contrast with this lot who, sad as they are, at least show a flailing heroism. Even dismal old Leonard Bast has a lucky end and Jude's scholastic odyssey has an almost Homeric grandeur. With all the supposed advantages of the Opportunity State, however, Billy just rolls up in a cocoon of fantasy.[103] And yet the closer one looks, the worse his predicament seems. For, in a sense, he is the wretched victim of the very opportunity from which his predecessors were so cruelly protected. He is a casualty of meritocracy. His talents, unlike those of the obscure Jude, have actually been exposed to open competition and found wanting. To the eager Victorian autodidact, failure and frustration could always be put down to something outside the abilities of the competitor. Nowadays, as it becomes easier to enter the competition, the self-esteem of the aspirants is more acutely threatened by the same token, and fantasy becomes the only resort of frustrated ambition.

Worse than that, society has even transformed the honourable ambition itself. Unlike the lean and earnest Jude, Billy has no intention of scholarly or artistic fulfilment. He has a fantasy in view. He wants above everything to become the scriptwriter for a sleazy radio comic, so that even the original aim belongs to the same masturbatory day-dream as the palliative. Ay me! the woods decay and fall.[104]

Directing Shakespeare
Interviewed by Ann Pasternak Slater
Quarto, September 1980[105]

First conceived in 1975 as a 'television library' of all Shakespeare's plays, the BBC's Television Shakespeare was initially led by series producer Cedric Messina. After two seasons and twelve productions, Messina made way for Miller, who was assigned to produce a further dozen. Of these, Miller would direct five: The Taming of the Shrew *(1980),*[106] Timon of Athens *(1981),*[107] Antony and Cleopatra *(1981),*[108] Othello *(1981)*[109] *and* Troilus and Cressida *(1981),*[110] *with the remainder assigned to Jack Gold,*[111] *Jane Howell*[112] *and Elijah Moshinsky.*[113] King Lear *(1982)*[114] *was handed to Miller after Shaun Sutton took over as series producer.*

The extensive interview which follows took place before transmission of any of Miller's productions, and at a point in time when the directors of his remaining plays were yet to be chosen.

SLATER: When you were Assistant Director of the National Theatre in 1973, you planned to educate your actors by getting lecturers from the National Gallery to talk about the seventeenth-century face, and so on. Did you have grandiose ideas like that when you took over the BBC Shakespeare?

MILLER: No, I knew that wasn't possible, because the BBC doesn't have a permanent body of actors.

SLATER: What were your problems with taking over the series?

MILLER: Mainly the original contract with the American co-producers; it had to be so-called 'traditional,' in the costume of the period, whatever that meant. There was no chance of shifting period – above all, no modern dress. That wasn't a difficulty for me – most of the things I wanted to direct in traditional costume anyway. But some of the best directors that I might otherwise have got refused to work under those conditions.

Also there are inadequate rehearsal facilities: you only have about a month to rehearse, and six days to tape. Most people who really take Shakespeare seriously feel that at least six weeks are necessary to rehearse, with 12 days of taping.

SLATER: You have said that you wanted to get Bergman and Peter Brook to direct for you.

MILLER: I would have liked to. None of that came off. Bergman wasn't available; I think he would have done a rather interesting *Timon of Athens*.

SLATER: Why?

MILLER: He's very good with eccentric emotions, like sudden onsets of paranoid rage at generosity being exploited. As for Brook, it's just important – if you're doing a series of Shakespeare plays which are meant to stand as a document – to have at least one version of a great director's work on tape. But he wouldn't do it, unless we worked with his actors, in his theatre, in Paris, filming under his own direction.

SLATER: Was that impossible?

MILLER: It's terribly expensive to get a film unit abroad, and also many of his own troupe wouldn't have spoken well enough for transmission in America.

SLATER: Did you have in mind a play for him?

MILLER: There was a possibility of his doing *Antony*, which I did in the end – and was very pleased to do.

SLATER: Who else did you try to get?

MILLER: Trevor Nunn turned it down. Bill Gaskill turned it down.

SLATER: Not a popular series!

MILLER: Indeed not. Ronald Eyre turned it down.

SLATER: Did the costume requirements make your own productions any more conventional? You're commonly criticized for pushing Shakespeare into different periods.

MILLER: It's an odd objection, because I have only twice done productions out of the period – *Measure for Measure*[115] and *The Merchant of Venice*.[116]

SLATER: What about the colonial *Tempest*?[117]

MILLER: No, it was very strictly seventeenth century. Possibly *Julius Caesar*: that was a surrealist limbo based on de Chirico.[118] I didn't do *King Lear* in the pre-Christian antiquity to which the play nominally refers. People do still try to make it look very Saxon – lots of leather – whereas I set it in the early 1600s. But otherwise all the Shakespeare plays have always been absolutely in their own period.

SLATER: What were the problems of directing for the small screen with the huge audience?

MILLER: There are specific problems to do with the institution of television, and specific problems to do with the medium of television. There is a temptation to introduce casting or production devices to seduce a supposedly unwilling audience. I simply haven't given in. I could be said to be catering to that sort of weakness by casting John Cleese in *The Taming of the Shrew*, but I cast him because I felt he would be right, not because he would attract a larger audience. Neither is my staging more attractive or less puzzling because of the size of the audience.

There are certain inevitable institutional requirements, however, like limitations on time, which perhaps make one less scrupulous about the composition of shots. Television is really a motor-car factory in which you are required to turn out products in fixed slots of time. If you don't you will muck up the factory. You're doing work at a more rapid rate than is compatible with the quality you think it deserves.

SLATER: What about other things, like the problems of doing battle scenes, for instance? You have them stylized on the stage.

MILLER: You simply have to find a corresponding form of stylization which is suitable for a television screen. On the stage there's a particular sort of rough stage technique which you can use. It looks ludicrous if you're looking through a camera, which gives you the impression of something much more realistic. You have to find a convention which is compatible with that kind of realism.

SLATER: So far as battle scenes go, what do you do? Superimpose shots?

MILLER: You might be able to use some of the things that are exploited in various pop programmes, like strobes, stopped action, slow motion, superimposition, action replays. One would hesitate to use them in the really important plays, but fortunately the really important plays don't involve battles.

SLATER: On the whole Shakespeare simply learned not to use them.

MILLER: Yes. Since they seem to take place in the less good plays, the introduction of electronic gimmickry could be an aid to covering up a second-rate play – rather than something spurious.

SLATER: Is there any point in trying to reproduce Elizabethan stage conditions on television?

MILLER: I don't think there's any way in which you can do that. What is characteristic about the Elizabethan stage condition is that the audience is part of that condition. They occupy the same physical space in which the events on stage take place. They surround the stage, they are visible to the other spectators, and they are part of the scenery. In television you automatically eliminate the audience. It isn't present at the production. It's absolutely hopeless to try and reconstitute the wooden O inside the electronic square.

SLATER: And similarly you wouldn't have approved of Olivier's *Henry V* for trying to do that?

MILLER: No, it's a mistake to try and set up within one medium the conventions of another. You have to start from the ground-floor again and simply redefine what the special characteristics of that medium are.

SLATER: Talking about imitating the ancients reminds me of something you said on *Saturday Night at the Mill* – that Elizabethan actors overacted horribly; we'd be appalled to see them now.[119] Is that what you think?

MILLER: No. I meant that they would seem to be overacting to us, because they were employing rhetorical techniques which were part of the idiom of Elizabethan rhetoric. It would seem very peculiar and stilted to us, because we are familiar with naturalistic acting.

SLATER: But we have the rhetoric of Shakespeare still, and we prefer not to have overacting to go with it…

MILLER: Yes, we do. But Shakespeare's plays came into existence at the same time as an extremely vigorous tradition of oratory was in existence.

SLATER: But it seems from things like Hamlet's speech to the Player – 'o'erstep not the modesty of nature. For anything so o'erdone is from the purpose of playing […] to hold […] the mirror up to nature' (III. ii.19–22) – that Shakespeare had the ideal of naturalistic acting.

MILLER: He probably had an ideal of naturalistic acting, but I don't think what would have counted as naturalism in the sixteenth century would be the same as what we think of as naturalism. When he mentions sawing the air, or making unnatural movements, he was thinking about departures from the idiom familiar to him. But the basic idiom is something which we would find very uncongenial.

SLATER: I would probably disagree with you, because there is so much natural action in the dialogue. And indeed the dialogue itself is so natural a lot of the time. Obviously it's rhetorical too, but if he'd simply had mannered actors, they couldn't have done all the natural things, like Leontes wiping his son's nose, Marina putting her fingers in her ears in the brothel scene in *Pericles*, and things like that which the dialogue demands.

MILLER: Well, yes. I suspect that Shakespeare's stage performances were hybrids, in which he was quite modern in the introduction of unprecedented natural idioms, but they were superimposed. Long speeches and soliloquies would have been presented in a mode which we would find unfamiliar, stiff and stylized. I'm sure our own idioms will seem as stylized: all attempts to represent nature presuppose that our mirror is featureless and actually reflects what exists, but all mirrors are distortions, having their own characteristics. Each age holds up what it regards as an undistorted mirror to nature, but with the passage of time the characteristics of that mirror become apparent to our successors.

SLATER: Yes. I certainly find the Stratford manner of production very artificial.

MILLER: And yet it's thought to be naturalistic, and was probably thought by people when they first saw it as being a great move towards naturalism.

SLATER: But it has very obvious verbal mannerisms, very much like the mannerisms of BBC reporting – pauses in absurd places.

MILLER: Absolutely. I am certain many of these were apparent from the word go, but more and more of them become apparent with hindsight. I don't think you can ever jump over your historical shadow and suppose that whatever you are doing at any given moment is actually the way things look. After all, just think of the successive ways in which painters have supposedly held up a mirror to nature.

SLATER: That's the theme of Gombrich's *Art and Illusion* [1960], isn't it?

MILLER: Yes. The *New Yorker* cartoon of the art class, with them all holding up their thumbs to a person who's posed like a hieroglyph. It happens again and again. There's a wonderful book by Anne Hollander about costume, in which she has a series of photographs of productions of films and plays about Queen Elizabeth I, going from 1920 to 1960.[120] Each of those periods presumably thought that they were producing an authentic version of the costumes, but what comes off each of the photographs is the period in which they were done rather than the period to which they refer.

SLATER: When I was watching you rehearse, you mentioned what you called the Bishop Berkeley effect. What did you mean?

MILLER: There are moments when the unused camera is browsing around the edges of the shot, and is often taking a fragment of those unlit parts of the set that are not meant to be seen. Very often you look at this marginal stuff on the monitors that are not actually recording the scene, and see a casual spontaneity of composition, décor and lighting, rather than of acting – because very often it's not shooting a bit of acting at all – which you cannot reproduce when you turn the cameras on formally and light it. I'm always trying to get the lighting people to bring on to the screen what is often only seen on the spare monitor.

SLATER: When I was watching you rehearse the last banquet scene in the *Shrew* it was a couple of waiting ladies sitting with their arms folded, chatting to each other in white aprons, in an unlit alcove, and it was very pretty.

MILLER: We managed to pick it up and use it.

SLATER: The other thing I noticed when I watched you rehearse was that you seemed to spend ages over tiny details, and yet there'd be some great flaw, like that an actor wasn't very good, which you simply seemed to bypass. For instance, Kate has to take her cap off. She did it with a very stagey gesture…

MILLER: That's right. I knew that had to be dealt with. Very often those big things are so noticeable that you simply leave them on the side, while you're dealing with apparently small, technical things which have got to be done there and then. You can go down [to the studio floor] when it comes to the important preliminary rehearsal, before you do the takes, and say: 'Now look here, that really is not good enough.'

SLATER: What is your technique? You seemed to have one single shot that you carry on for a long time, and then you slot in a lot of what you call 'specials.' Is that right?

MILLER: I'll sometimes do that. My general tendency is to avoid what I believe to have become the cliché of television shooting, which is to go ding-dong, backwards and forwards, between close-ups of each participant – an electronic ping-pong which I think is dull, and anyway runs against what I believe to be the essence of drama…

SLATER: Which is?

MILLER: Which is that in any given scene where one person has a long speech it is always a duet or trio with one or two people who happen to be silent. Their expressions during the speech are very important. You can't just take random samples of the expression every 30 seconds – in what are known as reaction shots, which assume that people only react every 30 seconds – because it is the continuous shadowing of a speech by a listener that constitutes the effect of that speech upon the listener.

SLATER: Do your actors know that this is your theory?

MILLER: Yes, and they're pleased, because they are of course acting continuously, not only when they're speaking or at representative moments. Therefore I like to shoot people at the same time and not go backwards and forwards between several cameras. There are moments, with very complicated bits of business, when you shoot what's called a master shot, and then you have to build in, mosaic-style, special pieces of detail.

SLATER: Kate putting her foot on the cap, at the end of the *Shrew*, would be an example of that, would it?

MILLER: In fact, I didn't cut away to her foot on the cap. I just showed her drop it on the floor. There again, there are those awful cutaway shots where you show a bit of mechanical business... I avoid them unless it's absolutely unintelligible otherwise.

SLATER: So what would be an example of some complicated business?

MILLER: In the *Shrew* where Petruchio throws away the food at the servants, you could have a very wide shot, establishing the relationships between everybody in the scene. But you also want to see a rhythmic series of close-ups of people wincing as lots of food goes over them. I took the scene once, to get the wide shot; then I simply did the whole scene over again, closing in on the servants, so that you saw a hail of meat and buns coming over their heads without seeing Petruchio at all. It gives more amusing detail and a rhythm to the scene.

SLATER: 'Rhythm' raises another question, which is your opera experience. Obviously it has affected the way you direct. You use musical metaphors all the time.

MILLER: I've become influenced by musical metaphors. Perhaps I always obeyed musical rules to some extent, without thinking of them explicitly. But now I've become more self-conscious about rhythm and have acquired a vocabulary.

SLATER: So you see scenes in rhythmic terms?

MILLER: Yes, with *scherzos*, and *rallentandos*, and so forth.

SLATER: Can you give me an example of a scene that struck you as musically particularly well-shaped?

MILLER: No. I think that every scene has a musical structure of some sort. At least, you can analyse it in terms of musical structure.

SLATER: Well, take the opening scene of *Antony and Cleopatra*. You have a frame of the Roman commentators, and in the middle you have Antony and Cleopatra swearing love. A narrow viewpoint framing grandiose vows. Can you see that also in musical terms?

MILLER: No, not there. And I would hesitate to talk in detail about a scene without the text. I have to have the score to demonstrate what's going on. But it is something I constantly think about. For example, building up the banquet scene in the *Shrew*: there is a rhythm of laughter, there are *scherzos* of mounting hysteria in response to the exchange of witticisms and abuse. The tempo slackens when Bianca and the ladies go out. Then it speeds up again. There are ways in which you can dot the notes, underline and emphasize the changes in rhythm, so that it avoids monotony, a uniform pace. It isn't just a question of being faster here and slower there, you've got to be more specific about pace and rhythm.

SLATER: In an interview you once said: 'I try to create as much complexity and indeed, as it were, strategic ambiguity as I can. I think that if you choose clear-cut, explicit lines what you get is fairly boring, instructive theatre, whereas if you create clusters of meanings, so long as those clusters are centred round a salient point, you get theatrical art.' Could you give me any examples?

MILLER: No. I can only give you negative examples, because it's very hard, when you go back over a production, to say how you arrived at what you hope to have been a rich palimpsest of ideas. By the time it's been achieved, you can't remember the components out of which it's made. You hope that it will seem to be complex. Negatively, I mean that I would never, if I could possibly avoid it, take one thematic line as the ruling symbol of the piece.

SLATER: But on the other hand you do have an overall interpretation of a play. You have said that your lack of an overall interpretation for *A Midsummer Night's Dream*, when you were directing it in Vienna, was one cause of that production's failure.[121]

MILLER: Yes, but by an interpretation I may mean nothing more than a ruling metaphor, generating a large number of subsidiary metaphors, images and interpretations. I often can't put my finger on what the metaphor is.

SLATER: What about your stress on 'kind' in *The Merchant of Venice*, as spanning the ideas of kindliness, and being good to your own kindred, or race?

MILLER: That would probably have been a subsidiary one which helped me to deal with the text as and when it came up. Certainly it was one of the literary themes I harped on a lot.

SLATER: But it was my impression that in your Greenwich production of *Measure for Measure* you made it one-sided, rather than ambiguous.

MILLER: Well, I certainly took one particular line *vis-à-vis* the Duke.

SLATER: Overriding one of Shakespeare's creative ambiguities.

MILLER: I really did take a clear line on that. Not in order to be didactic... My personal reaction to the idea of someone meddlesome – who eavesdropped on his own reputation, and who actually tried to play a *deus ex machina* – was so hostile that I had to, as it were, give him his comeuppance at the end.

SLATER: So that your view of the Duke relates to your view of Prospero, and what you have called the reality principle – that there are some things we can change, and many things which we can't. That was the lesson you said Prospero must learn.

MILLER: Yes, but quite apart from the Duke's meddling in people's affairs and playing God, I feel that the play is a seamless whole; to assume the Duke is above the general mixture of failings and virtues, to put him outside the action as a manipulating deity, makes the play lopsided in some way.

SLATER: I once saw an amateur production in Oxford where they made him very vulnerable about his reputation. He was tremendously offended to hear Lucio's slandering of him, and it worked very well. Shakespeare never makes any *deus ex machina* an absolute – they always overlook some bit in their plans: Prospero forgets about Caliban's attack; the Duke in *Measure for Measure* doesn't foresee that Angelo will go back on his word and execute Claudio.

MILLER: This is certainly true. But there are much larger lacunae than those specific oversights – which are small, by comparison with the glaring oversight, the great human error, of thinking that you can play around with lots of other people and you'll not yourself be an interested participant.

SLATER: But that's exactly what Shakespeare says, isn't it? One of the themes in *Measure for Measure* is that the Duke tries to control peoples' attitudes to death – Claudio in particular, and Barnardine as well. In both cases he fails. I think that the Duke, Angelo and Isabella are all absolutists in moral viewpoints, and they all have to modify in the course of the play.

MILLER: Yes.

SLATER: So that Shakespeare provides all of that, and you've spoilt the play slightly by taking an even more simplifying view of the Duke.

MILLER: Yes. It's probably because I am repelled by any sort of ostentatious nobility on the part of any character in Shakespeare; I feel that they all have to be equally suspect.

SLATER: Why don't you produce *Coriolanus*, in that case?

MILLER: I certainly would like to. I'm not, though, because I have to leave enough in the next 12 to make it worthwhile for someone else. If I took all the goodies, and left a pile of shit, it wouldn't do.[122]

SLATER: Michael Billington's 1972 profile said your great failure was that you weren't sufficiently aware of visual effect,[123] but in an interview you have said that you frame the production with all sorts of visual accessories which emphasize your point. Sometimes they may be elaborate emblems which you hope the audience will interpret correctly; even if they don't interpret in detail you hope they will set up imaginative overtones. So you're obviously very interested in the visual aspect.

MILLER: I've always taken great exception to that particular analysis of Billington's. It springs from a melodramatic insensitivity on his part to what counts as a visual effect. English theatre critics are, by and large, visually illiterate. *a.* They don't know anything about the history of art, and *b.* they are simply insensitive to the beauties of certain arrangements of space which are themselves spectacular visual effects. For Billington, a bare stage is a stage which is nonvisual. There are all sorts of theatrical minimalisms which may be extremely beautiful. The English critic is unfamiliar with the developments of contemporary painting and sculpture, which often play with very spectacular effects by using practically nothing.

SLATER: Could I divide your answer for you into two parts? – the use you make of art in your productions, and your use of visual effects which Shakespeare himself controls in the plays. If I can take the first – it's quite obvious that you use pictures all the time for your productions. For instance, your production of *Figaro*[124] was based on early David paintings and the *petits-maîtres* of the 1780s; you used Hogarth for *The School for Scandal*,[125] Velázquez for *The Tempest*, van der Weyden for *Richard II*,[126] and so on.

MILLER: They influence the way in which I light or arrange people, or colour a scene. Take my *Julius Caesar*. That was a more revolutionary departure from tradition. There I was quite determined not to have it set in Rome, nor to have it in modern dress – which is the other extreme – nor to take the middle line and set it in Elizabethan costume, but to find something which would somehow reproduce the Renaissance; suggest the world of twentieth-century European fascism without that plonking parallelism which would have been intolerable, and at the same time make references to the Rome that is obviously mentioned and referred to in the text. I found in de Chirico a painter who embodied all of those. The pictures are set in Renaissance squares and piazzas, there are fragments of Roman statuary placed on plinths, and also he gives one a feeling of that world of early Italian fascism of 1916. Drabness. Scenes of the semi-industrial edges of Ferrara. In addition, there is the extra bonus that his pictures are about intimations and premonitions of some unspeakable doom about to fulfil itself. They are pictures of waiting, and the notion of interim in *Julius Caesar* is a very important theme. The play is filled with images of premonition and foreboding, and of the surrealism of dream. The imagery of the horrible sights in the streets are all surrealist images, which are very, very consistent with de Chirico's own iconography.

SLATER: Did any of your audiences or critics pick this up?

MILLER: No. It was fairly well received, but it was just thought to be a piece of bizarrerie. Which it was in some ways, but it was also rather an intriguing one.

SLATER: What about the two productions you've just done. Have you got any comparable pictorial backing for those?

MILLER: In *Antony and Cleopatra* I was determined not to reproduce a straightforward, archaeologically literal-minded Egypt or Rome, because Shakespeare didn't have that in mind. What he had in mind was seen through the refracting medium of the sixteenth-century idea of those places. I therefore tried to go back to a painter who was working within the same 50 years, visualizing those or comparable locations. I looked at Veronese and tried to reproduce the sort of Roman antiquity which a sixteenth-century imagination would have visualized.

SLATER: Did that contain as many ideas as the de Chirico did for *Julius Caesar*?

MILLER: No, there aren't so many overtones in Veronese, nor could I find a painter who embodied so many literary themes so well. But it seemed a very satisfactory way of representing the sumptuousness and exoticism, without that straightforward, Golders Green exoticism of gold lamé skirts and green eyeshadow and Nefertiti hairdos.

SLATER: What about the *Shrew*?

MILLER: Well, there you have a relatively straightforward piece of sixteenth-century domesticity. The difficulty is that the Italians did not do genre paintings – interiors – in that period. I wanted something with the settled calm of a domestic interior. I've always been intrigued by Vermeer, and liked him very much. So I tried to use him – modified, obviously, in the costumes and furnishings, so that it gave the sense of an Italian interior – but also reproduced that extraordinary calm and prosperity.

SLATER: The other side of these visual effects are the details Shakespeare himself asks for. Can you think of any that you used?

MILLER: I don't specifically try to reproduce them; it so happens that, from time to time, the sort of effects he asks for automatically fall into place if you obey what happens in the dialogue. I did stage Cleopatra's reminiscences of fishing with Antony, and the actual occurrence of hitching him up into the tomb in such a way that there is a similarity in the staging. They're both shot from below, so that you see this object being pulled up.

SLATER: So that when Cleopatra says 'I will *betray*/Tawny-finned fishes' (II.v.11–12), did you pick up the 'betray'?

MILLER: No. If you ever specifically start to visualize things item by item, what you get is a pedantic catalogue of images. You really have to take things in the long phrase or paragraph, or speech by speech, and get some overall image or metaphor.

SLATER: There's a moment in *The Taming of the Shrew* when Lucentio is giving Bianca a Latin lesson, and Hortensio is tuning his lute. The lute is out of tune, first in the bass and then in the treble, and Hortensio gets it in tune just as Luciento and Bianca begin to hit it off in their Latin lesson: she begins to encourage his overtures just when the background music becomes harmonious. Did you make anything of that?

MILLER: No. There are points which come out much more clearly in a literary analysis. Once you start to strain after those in the action, you get bogged down in a fantastic amount of exegesis which holds up the action.

SLATER: What a pity – it must have been there for a purpose.

MILLER: I suppose so. It's partly carelessness; it's partly that one's getting on with other things which are more important.

SLATER: Did you have an overall image of your heroines then? What of Cleopatra? In rehearsal you described her to me as a Sixties beatnik – very attractive, but with dirty knickers.

MILLER: I was determined not to have the siren of the Nile. I was perfectly prepared to see her as exotic and Mediterranean, but not in the clichéd Hollywood manner into which Cleopatra has settled in the last 30–40 years. She's become a sort of middle-page spread in *Playboy* – a superlatively accomplished sexual athlete, who keeps Antony on the southern side of the Mediterranean because of some unspeakable skill which seduces him away from the frosty matrons in Italy. I don't think that's what makes her interesting or attractive. She's exotic because she's a fascinating, versatile chatterbox. She's up all night; she talks a great deal, has sudden, intriguing whims, and so is careless and shoddy, and probably inattentive to her own laundry – like those girls who are fascinating, whimsical chatterboxes who really don't care too much about whether their petticoats are clean.

SLATER: What about the glorious side of her? Do you just let that come out in the fifth act?

MILLER: Yes, she becomes glorious because of a stoical calm which falls over her. You really don't have to look for it, it plays itself.

SLATER: What did you make of Antony and Caesar? Did you pick up Shakespeare's stress on the age difference between them?

MILLER: Yes. I haven't made it an ostentatious feature of the production but they are people separated by very nearly 20 years: Colin Blakely is that much older than Ian Charleson.

SLATER: Is there a desperate last fling about Antony's affair?

MILLER: You do get a feeling with Colin that he's exactly what Caesar calls him, that 'old ruffian' (IV.i.4). He's not simply an ageing, attractive, greying-at-the-temples roué...more like one of those attractive boxers or rugby players, who has a lot of girls around him. You realize he's just beginning to fail, and is not going to be included in the first XV next year.

SLATER: Was there anything that you found particularly challenging in directing *Antony and Cleopatra*?

MILLER: The most challenging thing was simply getting it in on time.

SLATER: That's a very dull answer!

MILLER: Well, it really was the most pressing requirement. We had to shoot 30 or so scenes in the six days that were available to us. It was really frightful. The other challenge was to honour the musical character and ornamental exoticism of the speeches, without having them as a series of incantations. It's a play which is often just sung, rather than played. Trying to reconcile these two demands was very challenging and I can't say for certain that we've been altogether successful. All those last speeches, and the famous barge speech, are very hard to do convincingly if you sing them. On the other hand, if you simply vernacularize them, it's very hard to do honour to the verse. You have to get something which allows them to be definite, credible people with whom you can sympathize – not just simply verse-speakers who happen to undergo some unfortunate accidents.

SLATER: What about *The Taming of the Shrew*? That obviously didn't have the same problem. What was the interest there?

MILLER: Its great challenge is to retrieve a humorous play from the wreckage of facetiousness, the accumulated tradition of horseplay. It's a play about many important themes in family life: fathers who distribute their love unfairly between their children and then are surprised to find that the deprived child is behaving cantankerously; the failure of men to recognize who the truly valuable woman is and who see in cantankerousness nothing but viciousness; the failure of unsophisticated lovers to see that the young and the bland is more likely to be the shrew than Kate herself.

SLATER: What about Petruchio's training of Kate? How can you make it palatable?

MILLER: By not having so much cheerful bullying; not making him into a complacent, twinkling, thigh-slapping, moustachio-twirling cavalier. He should be someone who handles her firmly, sympathetically; throws back at her imitations of her own worst traits.

SLATER: In rehearsal, you compared Petruchio's treatment of Kate with techniques for problem children you'd seen in the Tavistock Clinic.

MILLER: That's right. There are ways in which a skilful therapist will gently mock a child out of a tantrum by giving an amusing imitation of the tantrum immediately after it's happened. The child then has a mirror held up to it and is capable of seeing what it must look like to others. Also behind the play lie all sorts of assumptions which I'm sure are based on Calvinism, and ideas about the sanctity of marriage as a sacrament within which order is reinstated in a fallen world. Because man is a fallen creature who inherits the sin of Adam, the best thing that can be done in this naughty world is to keep order – by undertaking to obey certain magistrates, either fathers and husbands, or kings and sovereigns. Shakespeare's conviction, which runs through all his plays, is that a society – whether the small one of the family or the large one of the state – will fall to bits unless obedience is shown to the sovereign. Not because the sovereign deserves it but because, without it, everything will be in disarray.

SLATER: So, in fact, you relate the play very closely to the histories, and indeed the tragedies?

MILLER: Absolutely. I think it has overtones on a miniature scale of *King Lear*: the father's failure to recognize the truly valuable daughter; the importance of maintaining order; above all, the Calvinist issue of recognizing that the virtue of your mind is all that matters, not the appearance of your body or your dress. 'To me she's married, not unto my clothes' (III.ii.116) and ''tis the mind that makes the body rich' (IV.iii.171). The very fact that Petruchio comes up twice with those remarks indicates to me a Calvinist line.

SLATER: So it's not simply an early comic success of Shakespeare's…

MILLER: It's one of his good, serious plays, cast in a comic mode.

SLATER: What are the plays that you're planning to do in the next season?

MILLER: I plan to direct myself the next three after *Timon of Athens*. I'm going to do *Othello*, the *Dream* and *Troilus*.[127]

SLATER: What are you going to do with *Othello*?

MILLER: I don't know for certain, because it depends very much on who I can get. It's eight months ahead, and very few actors will commit themselves. I'm interested in Ian Holm, among others, and someone like Frank Finlay as well.[128]

SLATER: What sort of conception of Othello do you have?

MILLER: I'd like to get away from the rather distorting myth of blackness which hangs around the play. So much of the story of previous productions has been how someone succeeded in blacking up so convincingly.

SLATER: Olivier, for instance.

MILLER: Yes. How someone like Olivier succeeded in getting the manners of a Negro. The emphasis falls on the accomplishment of a racial portrait rather than on the central theme, which is the juxtaposition of envy and jealousy. His strangeness and blackness are almost beside the point. It's something that is used to give the play an extra, jarring edge.

SLATER: Where do you find the envy?

MILLER: The envy of Iago for other people's getting on.

SLATER: His line on Cassio: 'He hath a daily beauty in his life/That makes me ugly' (V.i.19–20)?

MILLER: That's right. Iago is almost identical in some respects with Cassius in *Julius Caesar*. Both are characters that run through Shakespeare – the people who cannot bear the success of others, and are determined to undo them in some way. In the case of Cassius, he undoes Caesar by working on the mind of the apparently virtuous but hypocritical Brutus; in the case of Iago, he undoes Cassio and Othello himself by working on Othello's imagination, and by realising that he is susceptible to jealousy. He uses the jealousy of another to satisfy his own envy.

SLATER: Yes. I've always thought of the play as an exercise in jealousy on many planes. Iago's is not jealousy of the woman you love, but of absolutely everything. He's jealousy personified.

MILLER: Yes, he's jealousy, and restlessness, and misanthropy personified. And as far as Othello is concerned – taking the hint of the title, 'Moor' rather than 'Black' – I thought one might make a lot out of converting him into something much more recognisably Arab, rather than Negro. I always liked the idea of those Sandhurst-trained Arabs like King Hussein of Jordan, flying their own jets and marrying their white secretaries, and speaking in rather clipped Sandhurst tones, but nevertheless preserving the peculiar susceptibilities of their own culture – which would be this sudden, devastating sense of betrayal when Othello thinks he finds infidelity in his wife. I don't want to make him look too like King Hussein of Jordan, but one can take something and exploit it. Almost all actors, when building parts, and directors who help actors build parts, do so out of the bits and pieces of what they know – and what they know most vividly and justifiably are characters from newspapers, television broadcasts and personal acquaintances. The actor is, in Lévi-Strauss's sense, a *bricoleur*; he's an odd-job man who puts together a new creation out of the fragments which his culture has provided.

SLATER: What about Desdemona and Bianca – are there any traditional interpretations you want to avoid?

MILLER: I haven't thought too closely at the moment. All I want to avoid is Desdemona as the limp victim. She's amusing, and witty, and delightful, and would entertain Othello as much as he had entertained her.

SLATER: She doesn't give that impression in the play, though.

MILLER: No. But there are ways of shifting it.

SLATER: In fact, you're sometimes stuck with people having done it right for so long that you have to do it wrong, as it were, in order to make it interesting?

MILLER: In order to make it new. You have to keep raising the nap on a play.

SLATER: Most of the plays you've directed in the past seem to have been 'classics.' Are you interested in modern drama?

MILLER: I'm not uninterested in it. If I could find a play which I thought was worth doing, I would do it. But to find modern plays, and do them properly, you have to be much more conscientiously on the lookout for good plays. The most successful productions of modern playwrights have not been one-offs; they've all been the result of very close and often very long cooperation between a given director and a given writer. Peter Hall's long cooperation with Pinter, for example. Peter Wood's work with Stoppard. You can point to this again and again. Robert Lowell was the only one with whom I managed to do that, and that was for some irrelevant reasons of social accident – I happened to know him well, and we talked a lot about plays, and therefore it was quite inevitable that I would do his plays when he came to write them. I did them all apart from *Phaedre* [1961]. I worked with him for years, on and off, and spent a lot of time with him. Oddly enough, I knew him less when he came to England and remarried.

SLATER: What was he like?

MILLER: Well, he was mad a lot of the time. When he was mad, he was clinically very mad indeed. I saw him through about three hypermanic episodes. They used to coincide with the onset of one of his plays, partly due to the possibility of great fame hanging over him. That took the governor off the machine.

SLATER: Was his behaviour in madness interesting?

MILLER: No; it never is. Certain unpleasant aspects of people are exaggerated in madness. He became bullying, and tyrannical, and intolerant. He set off on hare-brained schemes. He would often write an extra act to a play one had already fully rehearsed. I remember once when I was doing *The Old Glory* [1964] he came in with 'I've got this fifth act here I think you ought to do…' – and an entirely new character is suddenly introduced – 'Sir Walter Raleigh's wife comes in holding this severed head in her hands. I guess the blood can be done with ribbons hanging from the neck… It has to be ghastly and at the same time very sensitive and tender…'[129]

Had he lived and gone on to write more plays I suspect I would have gone on working with him. But in a sense they are classic plays which happen to have been written by a modern poet, in that they have all taken place in the past. I have worked with very few modern writers. In order to do it, you've got to wade through oceans of shit.

SLATER: Stoppard has already got his director, but would you be interested in working with him? Or is he not your kind of playwright?

MILLER: No, he's not my kind of playwright.

SLATER: Not enough character, and too many ideas?

MILLER: It's perhaps too little in the way of character, and ideas in which I'm not particularly interested.

SLATER: Would the same go for Beckett?

MILLER: No, Beckett I would like to do very much.

SLATER: But then he directs his own plays, doesn't he?

MILLER: Sometimes. They are obviously the most successful versions. There's no doubt that something directed by Beckett is worth breaking a leg to go and see. I can't think of any other modern playwrights that I regret not having worked with. I found Edward Bond interesting in the early days and considerably less interesting now. *Saved* was a very remarkable play, but after that they have become rather Germanically didactic.

SLATER: What about David Hare?

MILLER: I like some of his plays, but again he's a very accomplished director in his own right and he's also found a very good series of directors already and works very profitably with, for example, Michael Blakemore. No. I don't turn my face from modern plays, but, with the works of the past, history's done the selecting for you and things have settled into readily recognizable ranks. Some of the priorities perhaps need reappraising, but you can be fairly certain that you're working on something valuable, because the real nonsense has dropped away.

SLATER: When you say there are people in the past who need reappraisal, who are you thinking of?

MILLER: Well, for example, I've always wanted to do Chapman's *Bussy D'Ambois* [1603–04].[130] And when I did Marston's *The Malcontent* it was only the third time it had been done since its first performance in 1606.[131] There are many other Jacobean playwrights worth going at again, and certain continental plays ought to be looked at. I'm very interested in Lenz's *Der Hofmeister* [1774] and *Die Soldaten* [1776]. I saw *Der Hofmeister* in Vienna about two years ago and was very, very struck by it. There are things by Marivaux as well. Molière is much harder. I'm not sure there's any way in which one can translate that into English, in the same way that I know absolutely for certain that there's no way in which Racine can make the transition.[132]

SLATER: Even in Lowell's translation?

MILLER: I'm not satisfied with that at all.

SLATER: What about the Scandinavians? Ibsen's often done; what about Strindberg?

MILLER: Strindberg I would like to have a go at. I've only done Ibsen's *Ghosts* [1882].[133] I've often thought of Scandinavian Expressionism as a way of presenting those plays. I've never seen that use of harsh primary colours and highly stylized settings. I would like to play around with something like that. I haven't used bright colours on the stage. It would help one get at the obvious stylization of the works themselves. Other things I would like to do are not conventionally thought of as plays. I would like to see dramatizations of famous dialogues.

SLATER: Plato?

MILLER: Yes, I did the *Symposium* on television about 15 years ago, and the *Crito* and the *Phaedo* as well.[134] They were so successful that I began looking around for others. In France they've often had great successes with things like Diderot's *Rameau's Nephew* [1761–74], or *The Dream of D'Alembert* [1769]. Also it might be possible to dramatize *Jacques le Fataliste* [1765–80]. That would be better done as a television film, rather than a stage presentation.

SLATER: Are there any English dialogues?

MILLER: Well, of course there's Mallock's *The New Republic* [1877], and there's Lowes Dickinson's *A Modern Symposium* [1905]. I don't think they'd be any more than rather mandarin, Edwardian pieces! Some of Hume's dialogues on religion, or some of Berkeley's dialogues, might be interesting. You could present some of the Plato dialogues on stage very successfully.[135]

SLATER: What, with action?

MILLER: Yes – well, not action; but certainly Pierre Fresnay did the *Symposium* with very great success in Paris about 30 years ago, and I think that the *Symposium* which we did on television in 1965 was very successful.

SLATER: The only comparable thing that I can think of is Shaw's *Back to Methuselah* [1918–20], which has fantastically long, static, philosophical dialogues. It doesn't work well on the stage at all.

MILLER: But then Shaw's flatulent, whereas Plato is interesting. Not right, but interesting.

SLATER: You have talked in the past about wanting to film Kafka –

MILLER: I've always wanted to do Kafka's *Amerika* [1911–14], yes.

SLATER: And Italo Svevo?

MILLER: Yes, I would like to do the *Confessions of Zeno* [1923]. But I think that's been done now.

SLATER: And Dickens was the other.

MILLER: I've probably got less interested in that…though *Bleak House* has always been a niggling dream.

SLATER: When I was watching you rehearse, you mentioned the influence Jacques Tati and René Clair had on your comic directing. Could you tell me more?

MILLER: I've always been influenced by the way they stage comedy. They'll never cut away to a comic scene. They'll allow things to happen in and out of the frame, and will let the audience pick up whatever it finds amusing. In both cases, but particularly Tati's, they understand that often the most comic things are events seen at a great distance, almost down the wrong end of a telescope – something almost bewildering and inexplicable down at the back of a set.

SLATER: Can you give me an example?

MILLER: Well, there's a wonderful example in the *Jour de Fête* [1949], where a village band is suddenly attacked by a bumblebee. There's a scene close up to show it to you, and then Tati instantly gets as far away from it as he possibly can, and shows you the cavalcade at a great distance, coming down the village lane. From this high, aerial shot you can see a strange mechanical disturbance in the crowd, and you know that the bee is getting among them. A shimmer, a little fidgeting occurs. You have to infer the cause of the disturbance, which is much funnier.

SLATER: Where have you done the same kind of thing?

MILLER: Let me see now… In *The Taming of the Shrew*, for example, I don't draw attention to the fact that there's a dwarf in the crowd at the beginning of the market scene. As the camera pans across, a dwarf happens to move with the camera, and buys a melon in the front of the shot, and you don't see him again. At the very end of the scene, separated by about 20 minutes from his first, unmentioned exposure, you see Katharina go angrily back into the house, and as she passes the very back of the shot, you can see her indignantly push over a dwarf in the street. You only see it in silhouette – the little dwarf, with fists up, pursuing her, way at the back of the shot, the main action at the front.

SLATER: It's curious that when watching or listening to things, rather than reading them, one has a much longer memory. You can pick up verbal or visual echoes like that in a way that the reader doesn't seem to.

MILLER: I go on this absolutely fundamental principle of perception. The only way I can illustrate it is by talking about the way in which you find your way around. There are many occasions when you've been on a car journey, or a walk, and then about six months later, without knowing the route, you find your way back. You do this not by holding in your mind a memory of the route, because that's already been obliterated. Nor do you seem to have in your mind, when you embark on the journey, any specific memory of anything seen on the route. But once you start, you're startled to find that you did appear to have taken a mental photograph of that shop window on the corner, which must mean that you had to take a left there – yes, and then 400 yards on I remember there was a peeling piece of paintwork on a bridge…you clamber your way from one or another of these apparently forgotten *mementi*. You can plant an image for reactivation later.

SLATER: Isn't that something you can do much more easily on television or in the cinema, than on the stage?

MILLER: You can do it on the stage just as well.

SLATER: Even though you've not got a selecting camera?

MILLER: You simply have them at the front of the shot – at the front of the *stage* – and they come across and do something, perhaps with some slight idiosyncrasy: a limp, or a sniff. Because the main action's what's going on, you don't pay any attention to it. But nevertheless the eye has photographed it. In *School for Scandal*, I had a servant who had a sniff when he came to the door to announce someone. About four or five scenes later, it had quite clearly developed into a running cold, and at the very end of the play the man was awash with handkerchiefs.

SLATER: You're very good with those little details. I remember your *Measure for Measure* had Isabella clutching a handbag and in brown lace-up shoes, which epitomized the buttoned-up quality she has.

MILLER: I do like assembling works out of these tiny details. I think detail is what a lot of drama is made of.

SLATER: That makes me think of you as a great naturalistic director. In terms of Shakespearean criticism, your analogue seems to be A. C. Bradley, with his painful detailing of character. You're very interested in the fullness of character, too.

MILLER: Well, I have two strains which might be seen as conflicting, but I prefer to think of them as complementary. On the one hand, I am extremely interested in minute naturalistic detail. That's partly associated with having been brought up in clinical medicine, where you are taught to look for the tiny, all-revealing detail. In this respect, too, a major influence on me is the work of the psychologist Erving Goffman. He wrote a number of books. The one which has most dominated me is *Relations in Public* (1971). He has a basic theme, which is a mixture of social psychology and philosophy, partly influenced by his reading of the Oxford philosopher John Austin's great essay on excuses.[136] He is interested in the way in which human beings offer to one another a series of accounts, justifications or mitigations for what might be interpreted as misconduct on their part. These may be misconducts for which formal excuses have got to be offered – which takes us into the area of crime and immorality – or they may be minor misdemeanours which are so small that you'd never notice them, but nevertheless constitute a very large part of the traffic that passes between people in society. You have constantly to offer a series of mitigations or excuses in order to restore your image in the eyes of the either offended or contemptuous other. So Goffman will say that when someone trips up in the street, though it isn't necessary, he'll ostentatiously go back and inspect the pavement, as if to announce to the world at large: 'I have tripped up, not because I'm clumsy, but because there's an obstruction which anyone would have tripped over, wouldn't they?' He calls that an all-round body gloss – a display of explanation which restores any fall in esteem.[137]

Now, I believe that this is happening all the time, literally *all* the time. There is a constant broadcast of these messages in society – simply in the effort to get in and out of a room, or to pass out of a door, or to say goodbye. People take so long to say goodbye, as Goffman points out, because the manner in which you do so runs the risk of repudiating the quality of your encounter. If you say it too perfunctorily, you are implying that all that had passed between you is in fact worthless. And therefore people tend to go through an extremely elaborate series of farewells, most of which are ways of saying, 'We have had a good time, haven't we?' Very often people will be so reluctant to convey the

153

impression that it might have been a bad time, that they will depart from one another under a smokescreen of future engagements. They'll say: 'So look, um, we'll, um, I'll be contacting you then, on Thursday, or failing that…'

Everyone knows all these things, but they are so negligible taken one by one that people will very often leave them out of a performance. You have constantly got to restore that line in the score, otherwise it's like leaving out the whole of the timpani section.

SLATER: The example I can think of is the little trial scene from your production of *Measure for Measure*, where Escalus asks the questions and Froth answers Pompey, the policeman he knows, rather than Escalus, every time. Didn't you say that you had picked that up from watching a court?

MILLER: I picked it up watching a court, and also I remembered it from *Great Expectations*, where Joe and Pip go to Miss Havisham. Miss Havisham asks questions about Pip of Joe, but Joe is so overwhelmed with embarrassment at addressing Miss Havisham that he gives the answers to Pip.[138] Now, you see, one's constantly got to watch those details, because actually the sum of them is at least 50 per cent of what is going on, however negligible they may seem taken individually.

SLATER: You talk about yourself as having two complementary sides as a director. One side is the naturalistic accumulator of detail – what's the other?

MILLER: The other, I suppose, is that I have a classicizing streak in me, which sees things abstracted, reduced and formalized. So that, for example, in a production of *Measure for Measure* that will contain thousands of those details, I will have staged it in the most austere, stylized way, on a bare stage with very little furniture, and with departures and arrivals formalized to the rhythm of a Schoenberg sonata, so that in fact it was all set up to coincide with certain notes played on a 12-tone scale. The whole thing was based on Schoenberg. Every single time the doors opened or closed, it coincided with a particular one of those tone-rows.

SLATER: This is the other thing which people will say about you – that you have absurdly intellectual ideas behind your productions, which nobody in your audience is going to pick up.

MILLER: Well, what happens is that some people pick up one, and some pick up the other.

SLATER: What about that *New Statesman* profile of you, which said that you were going down the primrose path to Pseud's Corner? It can be thought pretentious.

MILLER: Anything can be thought pretentious. The question is, does it come off, or not? One doesn't just present them in order to have a *roman à clef* in which people can score by recognizing the references. The reason I did that was not because I wanted to introduce Schoenberg, but because I wanted something that had a highly formalized, abstract skeleton.

SLATER: And all those doors at the back of the stage –

MILLER: They were highly formalized exits and entrances.

SLATER: They were the notes on the scale?

MILLER: Yes. Well, now, I suppose you could say, 'Good God, how pretentious and pseud to make those sort of references.' I can't deny it. I can't in any way wriggle out of the accusation. I simply have to say, 'That's what I do, because that's what I enjoy doing.' I like playing these games, and a lot of what one's doing in making art, even at the low level of producing plays, is in fact playful. You're making arrangements of sights, sounds, patterns of themes and references, some of which may be readily available to an audience, some of which may not. I'm often startled how swiftly and accurately members of the audience find out exactly what I'm up to in things which I thought were highly idiosyncratic, and often done purely for my own entertainment, such as that 12-tone reference, which three or four critics picked up. I didn't expect them to, and it certainly wasn't essential to an appreciation of the play. But it helped to rehearse the play – it gave a formal restraint, and an icy deliberation which is underneath the play.

SLATER: It's certainly there, even in the title.

MILLER: Yes, and the notion of 'measure' is a musical term as well as a jurisprudential one. That's what I mean by complexity: I like there to be lots and lots of puns and overtones and references.

SLATER: You said in an old interview that you wanted theatre critics to come and watch you in rehearsal as a way of seeing what you're up to. It seems a bit much to ask...

MILLER: Yes, it is. I don't really want them. It might be quite instructive to see that I go about these things less frivolously and facetiously than I think some of them believe. They could see that it's less of a pseud's business than it might appear from what I say in interview.

SLATER: But then have you got anything like that in your *Antony and Cleopatra*?

MILLER: No, less in that, because the play itself is so flamboyantly rich, it's so hyperbolic in its own terms that there's no need for it. With something austere it's not necessary to do it, but one often finds oneself inclined that way.

SLATER: People often say that you aren't true to Shakespeare: you distort him. It seems to me that you are working on Shakespeare, as a director, in exactly the same way Shakespeare the playwright worked on his sources. You've got raw material, both of you...

MILLER: Yes, that's exactly what does go on with interesting productions. But what you've said runs the risk of seeming to say that I'm of the same stature as Shakespeare, and of course that's nonsense. It just happens that making art is a series of dependencies on what has happened before. I quite self-consciously *use* Shakespeare in order to amuse myself. I'm not doing the plays in order to honour Shakespeare. Shakespeare isn't honoured by constantly and conscientiously reproducing his intentions. That may be one way. But Shakespeare is honoured in the complicated and plural ways in which he is attended to.

SLATER: You talked of Tati and Clair as influences on your comic directing; what about the serious?

MILLER: Only what I hear about the productions from the remote past. Meyerhold, perhaps. There's something about the staging that I gather from photographs – I can't explain what it is.

SLATER: What about Stanislavsky?

MILLER: Absolutely not at all.

SLATER: But he was interested in realism?

MILLER: Yes, but I get an impression that it's very laborious. Chekhov's own suspicion of Stanislavsky confirms my own.

SLATER: What about Gordon Craig?

MILLER: No. There's something about that rather austere, tasteful lighting and *rostrums*, and so forth, which just seems to be arch. I've always found myself intrigued by the work books of the Berliner Ensemble – some of those rough stages and bare platforms, with sudden pieces of very accurate architectural detail on the middle of an otherwise bare stage. Bits of canvas, poles…

SLATER: How does that differ from rostrums?

MILLER: The rostrums of Gordon Craig are shrouded in misty sunlight. They are locations for some possible, as yet unfulfilled, production of *Tristan*. I like things which you see are made out of wood and splinters, a clearly improvised platform.

SLATER: What about Eisenstein?

MILLER: You mean the staging of faces in Eisenstein's films? That interests me a great deal. I've often thought I would like to look carefully at his montages.

SLATER: He's got work books as well –

MILLER: Which I've looked at. He's got stunning visual sense. The things are lit so beautifully, and there's such an interesting attention to costume and to detail. Compositions of faces with ruffs staring out of the left corner of a screen. Wonderful. I like some of the Russian Constructivism of the stage: there are marvellous bits of platform with fragments of lettering, tubular-steel scaffolding… So that most of the things that have influenced me have been the archaeological remains of productions I couldn't possibly have visited. Occasionally, I've seen things on the stage that I've been bowled over by and thought 'My God, how nice it would have been to have done that' – Brook's *Marat-Sade*; Arianne Mnouchkine's *1789*, that great staging of the French Revolution which she did in the Roundhouse, in separate booths all round the hall. It had that dazzling, frowsty style of French theatre, dressed in decaying pieces of furnishing velvet. People struck huge, rhetorical poses with white faces and black lipstick. It had a visual flair we simply can't begin to approach in the English theatre.

SLATER: One last question. Don't you regret that so much of what you do is ephemeral?

MILLER: There are two attitudes I have. I'm delighted that it is ephemeral, because there is something very extraordinary about the way in which performances will not outlive their own time. It's one of the mysteries of the reproductive arts. The score which gives rise to the production is in some strange way immortal, transcending its own period; but the reproduction of that score is so absolutely characteristic of its own time that, after a certain lapse, it is a dead thing. But my other attitude is, it's a shame. Some people can look back to a production, and say it was good; others, who didn't see it, can only know the reviews, and say 'I hear it was awful.' And you can't say 'I've got it here; I'll show it to you.'

Man: the double animal

Are Hierarchies Necessary?, BBC Radio 3, 3 July 1972[139]

I want to describe an experiment which has acquired a classical status in the history of neurology. In 1903, Sir Henry Head and his colleague W. H. R. Rivers, the psychiatrist and anthropologist, agreed to undertake an experiment on the sensory nerves to the skin, and Head, a practising consultant neurologist at the London Hospital, offered himself as the guinea pig. At the London Hospital, with the help of a surgeon, the nerve supplying the forearm was severed under surgical anaesthesia. The cut ends of this nerve were then joined together with silk sutures. In other words, the nerve was put back again in physical continuity. The fibres, however, had been interrupted. Living nerve fibres will grow together again after they have been severed, providing anatomical continuity is maintained. After the acute phase of the injury had passed off, Sir Henry Head then subjected himself to a series of psychological experiments on the area of anaesthesia which was produced.

He would travel up once a week to St John's College, Cambridge, and in the quiet of Rivers' rooms there he would submit himself to a series of minutely detailed investigations on the recovering sensation in his own arm. This involved a series of graduated assaults on his skin. Rivers would test the temperature sensation in Head's arm by using warmer or colder water in a test-tube. He would use a series of bristles of various thicknesses to detect the touch sensibility, or a wisp of cotton wool. Or he would use pins. A whole battery of these tests was done and recorded. Areas on Head's arm were inked and photographed week after week. These results are now contained in five or six leather-bound volumes in the Cambridge Psychological Laboratory.[140]

One might have thought that the recovery of sensation would have proceeded by a slow encroachment from the edge of the lake of anaesthesia towards the centre – rather in the way in which a puddle dries up in the sun: the puddle of anaesthesia would get smaller and smaller until it returned to normal. However, Head and Rivers claimed to have discovered a different course of recovery altogether: instead of this simple advance, the encroachment proceeded in two phases. Sensation began to appear as the nerve recovered in the form of a sensation which seemed abnormal and unusual and, in Head's words, extreme. There was a much higher threshold, for a start. In other words, it needed a much stronger stimulus applied to the skin before any sensation was reported, and when that sensation was reported, it was extreme, painful, very poorly localized, and had a capacity to radiate beyond the actual location of the stimulus itself. The first phase of recovery, which proceeded concentrically towards the centre, resulted in a state of sensation which was totally different from that of a normal skin.

Once this phase had been completed, a second phase started to occur, encroaching over the surface of this first phase like a varnish spread over a picture. It began to appear within the course of a few months, and as it took place the skin gradually returned to its full complement of normal sensation. It was now possible to evoke a sensation by using the light wisp of cotton wool or the bristles, and the subjective feeling evoked by these stimuli was now normal. It was well-localized, it was moderate, it was graduated; with each increment of stimulus there was an increment of response by comparison with the previous state of recovery, in which there was either an extreme response or none at all. Eventually there was a more or less complete return to normal sensation in the skin.

Head and Rivers described these two forms of sensation as protopathic – the crude early stage of recovery – and epicritic. Epicritic meant the final varnishing of the recovered area of skin with normal, precise, accurate, graduated sensation. From this observation they went on to elaborate a theory of the central nervous system which they used as an explanation. The theory which they relied on was in one sense an evolutionary theory. What they claimed they had done was – to use a metaphor which Head himself did not use – to open a sort of manhole cover into the central nervous system and thereby observe a previous stage in the evolutionary development of the nervous system before it arrived at the human condition. In the protopathic stage of recovery we were having a glance at the more primitive stage of the nervous system, and in the subsequent stage of recovery we were returning to the fully-evolved condition of the human that we know.

Subsequent investigators, notably Wilfred Trotter, a neurosurgeon working at University College who had also shown a great interest in sociology, repeated the experiment of Head and Rivers, severing a skin nerve, but did not find the results proceeding in this strictly biphasic form.[141] I'm not saying, nor was Trotter saying, that Head was dishonest. The comparison shows, however, the risk of using oneself as a subject of sensory investigations.

The general theory which had helped to shape both Head's and Rivers' preconception was, of course, the theory of evolution; not necessarily that which was inherited directly from Darwin, but the one which was inherited through those who had been influenced by Darwin – notably the English clinician John Hughlings Jackson, a practising consultant neurologist working at the National Hospital for Nervous Diseases in Queen's Square. Jackson is hailed by neurologists today as the father of modern clinical neurology, and he's justly celebrated for a particular evolutionary notion of the effects of disease upon the nervous system. Jackson was studying the clinical appearance of epilepsy following injury or tumour or thrombosis in the brain. And he observed that, broadly speaking, the symptoms could be divided into two groups. On the one hand, you had the negative symptoms: the symptoms of loss. But in addition there were what he called 'positive symptoms': symptoms of release, symptoms which were due, or so Jackson thought, to the release of a more ancient part of the nervous system which had been held and suppressed and subdued by subsequent stages of refined higher evolution.[142] In certain movements in the epileptic fit, in certain regressions which the patient exhibited – particularly when language was lost – he noticed that the patients tended to retain swear words and violent emotional expressions, which indicated to him that here was an older, more emotional, more incoherent level of the nervous system being revealed now by the loss of the restraining higher levels.

Jackson derived this theory not so much from Darwin as from Herbert Spencer, who prior to Darwin had developed a fairly elaborate evolutionary notion of the nervous system, in which he saw, as it were, a double animal in each living creature. There was the higher, well-integrated, organized animal at the summit of its own evolutionary branch, and within it an older, more incoherent animal which represented its ancient, incapable ancestry.[143] Jackson then put this general theory of Spencer's into combination with his specific clinical observations to say that through disease we obtain a brief and incomplete snapshot of our ancestry – not, of course, a complete one, because the entire nervous system is not damaged. The old animal was coming up because of the absence of the restraints of the newer animal. It has to be remembered that Jackson was working nearly 40 years before the work of Head and Rivers. The great papers in which Jackson expressed this fundamental idea of evolution and dissolution in the nervous system appeared between 1850 and 1870.[144] But clinical neurology as it is taught today in medical schools is still framed by Jackson's notions of evolution in the nervous system, with the results of damage to the nervous system seen as a gradual climbing down the evolutionary tree to the level just below the disease.

While he derived a large part of his theory from Spencer, Jackson also referred to the work of a physician who is generally not mentioned in the history of medicine – a practising physician working almost at the same time at the Westminster Hospital, a pharmacologist called Anstie who was interested in the effects of narcotics (morphine and alcohol) on the nervous system. Anstie explained some of the effects of drugs upon the nervous system in terms of this notion of a duplex animal, although he never expressed it as explicitly and as vividly as Jackson was later to do.[145] He thought that some of the extreme sensations which were produced when a finger was inflamed were due not so much to a positive irritant of the poison in the injured part as to the fact that the poison removed an inhibiting higher function and had consequently released a lower form of function.

It's possible to attribute all these ideas to specifically biological theories of nervous function, and of animal function in general. But I believe there are other sources of inspiration for this notion of the double animal. The notion that the human being is in some respects double forms a part of the fundamental theory of Romantic poetry. In a letter to Miss Millbank, Byron says that poetry 'is the lava of the imagination, whose eruption prevents an earth-quake.'[146] Behind that proposal is the notion that there is something split about the nature of the human being, that there is a crust of higher or more familiar function beneath which are fluid, incandescent levels of activity held in by this crust. There are two ways of interpreting this duplicity. You could simply propose that all individuals are fundamentally and inexplicably duplex. This makes no reference either to our ancestry or to our individual development in the womb: it simply asserts that human nature is ranked in some way, that there is a familiar surface of highly organized, public, rather decorous function, and that underneath there is some other level. It may be conceived as a rather dangerous, violent level, or it may be conceived rather more favourably – as the Romantics conceived it – as the source of some higher, inspirational level of organization. In neither case is any reference made to the source of this duplicity.

This notion of ranking, of organization based on levels, is very old indeed. It goes back to Aristotle and perhaps even before. The great historian of ideas, Arthur Lovejoy, wrote a whole book devoted to it – *The Great Chain of Being* (1933) – in which he refers to the history of the notion that life was arranged in a scale of organization from the least complex to the most elaborate, from the lowly to the most exalted. This notion has undergone successive transformations in the history of European thought. It does not, however, until we get to Darwin, make specific reference to the genetic origin of this ranking: it's simply an architectural statement about the way the universe is put together, the universe at large, the universe of man himself and also the great zoological and biological scale of being. It makes no assertions as to the origin of this scale and certainly no reference to there being an ancestral or genetic relationship between the successive rungs of the ladder. It is this which brings the theory into very effective line with Jackson's notions, because once we get to Darwin the assertion is made, not just that nature is ranked in a series of scales of being, but that life itself has passed through these scales of being and has proceeded from one to the other.[147] By making this proposal, you open up the possibility of asserting that one of two things might take place. On the one hand, the creature might go on making his ascent, pulling up the ladder after it, showing no trace of its previous condition. Looking at these creatures, therefore, we could detect nothing about their ancestry. But of course one only has to open and look at animals to see that they do show affinity with their previous condition. And this is the second theory: that in proceeding upwards on the scale of being – in passing from one stage to another in evolution – the animal successively conceals fragments or residues of its older self, these being successively covered up by the more recent stage of evolution. One can now suggest a whole series of methods whereby one can recover some image of or insight into that previous condition by looking at a contemporary animal. For example, one can, by opening it, detect vestigial organs; this is a morphological recovery of the previous state. We look at the appendix of man and see in it a dwindled residue of what was once a more elaborate, functioning piece of tissue.

When looking at function, you can also recover some residues of the previous condition, but you have to do so by subjecting the animal to certain assaults or experiences, of which the most obvious is disease or injury. If you were to injure an animal about whom you have proposed that it has moved from one stage to another, it might be possible that in injuring him you would knock off the top levels and allow an older level to come up and express itself. But in order to make this a viable proposal, it's necessary not just to suggest that, like a series of Chinese boxes, these older functions are there passively awaiting this act of retrieval. You also have to suggest that they exist in an active but concealed condition, bound down and restrained by all that has developed subsequently. And once you propose this, once you propose that there is a dynamic condition of existence of this previous version, then you have to suggest on top of that that the higher function exerts two activities of its own: first, there are its movements towards the outside world, all the behaviours through which it negotiates with the outside world; but then, in addition, by the back door or through its own basement, there's an inhibiting function which helps it to sit on and suppress this jack-in-the-box of previous evolutionary condition. And this raises the notion of inhibition in the nervous system as an essential feature of nervous function. The nervous system is now conceived in terms of two sorts of neurological function. On the one hand there is the excitatory action of the nervous system, through which it responds to stimuli from the outside world and negotiates with them more or less successfully, and behind it there's a level of concealed inhibition – active neurological inhibition – which is keeping down the dynamic, springy, antique version of the animal which is concealed under this evolutionary heap of subsequent development.

I can now return to the work of John Hughlings Jackson and to the influence that Jackson wielded later upon Head and Rivers. We can see that both Jackson's and Head's and Rivers' results flow from the basic idea of a restraining higher level holding down some older animal. They were in fact proposing that the epicritic level – that refined, delicate, well-located, graduated function of the intact nerve – was exerting two functions within the nervous system. One was its positive function of providing accurate information about the outside world, and the other was a domestic, internal affair of suppressing the older protopathic animal that was crouched like a monster – like a dog beneath the skin, like something older which had had to be suppressed – which the injury had released and which for the moment was running rampant.

Wilfred Trotter and, later, a clinical neurologist, Sir Francis Walshe, criticized the theoretical basis of Head's and Rivers' conclusion on the grounds that, by claiming that the protopathic stage of recovery was a picture of an earlier stage of evolution, they were claiming something about the biological style of that older stage of evolution.[148] And what were they claiming? They were claiming that the older animal was incoherent, ungraduated in its response, gross, unlocalized, rather savage and also vague. Now, in claiming this they were making errors on two levels. First, it was a piece of conjectural biology: they had no grounds for saying that this was the previous stage. Secondly, it was an unjustified and unsophisticated biological assumption, since it proposed a sort of animal which would seem to have very little chance of ordinary biological success. What sort of animal could survive with such gross, incoherent and vague responses to the outside world? If we look at the insects, or

164

if we look at the lower invertebrates, their behaviour is as graduated, as well-geared, as well-localized and as discriminating as their life requires. There is no such thing as a protopathic animal. A protopathic animal is a damaged and injured animal, so that, simply on the grounds of ordinary biological ecology, this seems to be a fruitless notion. Head and Rivers were sophisticated investigators – why should they have committed themselves to a theory which even a moderate amount of thought would have shown to be bankrupt?

It's profitable to look at some of the sources of inspiration which are not declared overtly in Head's and Rivers' work, or indeed in Jackson's. It's important to remember that at the time when Jackson was writing his theory of evolution in the nervous system, England had passed through a series of social upheavals in which riot and public disorder had alarmed a large number of middle-class intellectuals. It was, moreover, less than a hundred years since the French Revolution had produced a sense of enormous anxiety about the incoherent, violent, ungraduated energies of the mob. It's interesting to note in this respect that when Jackson came to use a metaphor for describing the double symptoms of the central nervous system, he actually made reference to a social model: 'If the governing body of this country were destroyed suddenly, we should have two causes for lamentation: *1.* the loss of services of eminent men; and *2.* the anarchy of the now uncontrolled people.'[149] And this paper was written within a few years of the Hyde Park Riots in 1866.

The sociologist Bagehot also uses an evolutionary theory to describe the structure of society. He was the first, incidentally, actually to use the word 'atavism.' In his *Physics and Politics* (1872) he wrote:

Lastly, we now understand why order and civilisation are so unstable even in progressive communities. We see frequently in states that physiologists call 'Atavism' – the return, in part, to the unstable nature of their barbarous ancestors. Such scenes of cruelty and horror as happened in the great French Revolution, and as happen, more or less, in every great riot, have always been said to bring out a secret and suppressed side of human nature, and we now see that they were the outbreak of inherited passions long repressed by fixed custom, but starting into life as soon as that repression was catastrophically removed.[150]

If you were simply to remove the social words from that particular paragraph, it would almost be a paraphrase of Jackson's description of evolution and dissolution in the nervous system. In injury we have the catastrophic removal of the services of eminent men, and if we think of eminent men as the summit of the nervous system, offering their positive services to the community at large but also repressing the incoherent energies of the mob whom they rule, we see a perfect mirror image of this model of the nervous system.

I don't want to suggest that Head and Rivers were using their theory as a Trojan horse for the expression of a series of anxieties about the state of society. Nevertheless, it's important to note that Rivers himself, in addition to being a clinical neurologist and a psychiatrist, was also a social anthropologist. He was one of the most important members of the epoch-making anthropological excursion made in 1898 to the Torres Straits and headed by A. C. Haddon the zoologist – Haddon the headhunter, with McDougall the social psychologist – to investigate the condition of primitive society, and with Rivers to examine the sensory endowments of primitive peoples. The social preoccupations of anthropologists with an allegiance to evolutionary theory, and a concealed allegiance to certain fears which they shared as middle-class intellectuals, can be seen to have a bearing on a purely physiological experiment.

Head passed on to other experiments and to other interests in the functioning of the nervous system, but Rivers continued his psychiatric work and his sociological work. He later wrote a book called *Instinct and the Unconscious* (1920) in which he continued the vocabulary which Head and Rivers had together formulated. He believed that we could look at certain phenomena in society as being exhibitions of the protopathic man. The behaviour of the rioting mob is an exhibition of the protopathic state of society in just the same way as the removal of the epicritic levels of sensation reveals the protopathic individual:

> I have now to suggest that hysteria is the result of the abrogation of
> the modifying principle based on intelligence, leaving in full power the
> other and more or less opposed principle of suggestibility.[151] [...] The
> mimetic nature of hysteria provides another characteristic indication of
> regression. The mimesis of hysteria may be regarded as a throw-back,

166

partly to the dramatic character of the activity of early life, partly to the mimetic aspect of the activity of the gregarious instinct.[152]

We have here a picture of the mob which embodies a theory about the condition of primitive society. This is conjectural anthropology, in which Rivers is making an assumption about some sort of primal herd which exhibits a protopathic form of mental life analogous to the protopathic form of sensation that he and Head had revealed when they cut the nerve in Head's arm.

This theory continues to be expressed. McDougall, who had been a colleague of Rivers on the Torres Straits expedition of 1898 but had not taken part in the experiments, wrote a book called *The Group Mind* (1920):

> We may sum up the psychological characters of the unorganised or simple crowd by saying that it is excessively emotional, impulsive, violent, fickle, inconsistent, irresolute and extreme in action, displaying only the coarser emotions and the less refined sentiments; extremely suggestible, careless in deliberation, hasty in judgment, incapable of any but the simpler and imperfect forms of reasoning. [...] Hence its behaviour is like that of an unruly child or an untutored passionate savage.[153]

In that single paragraph of McDougall's you have a whole series of conjectures about primitive society, about the state of the child, and, behind it all, the phantom image of the nervous system as it was reflected, first of all, in Jackson's notion of the double animal, and later in Head's and Rivers' distinction between protopathic and epicritic levels of sensation. What we can see here is not a simple chain of cause and effect in the history of ideas, but what Lovejoy describes as a series of elective affinities between ideas which have some common origin – some common, general model both of society and of the individual. This model was based on evolutionary theory as inherited from Darwin and Spencer, but also on certain ideas about society as a structure dominated from the top by a refined elite, holding in restraint an incoherent, raucous mob of savages.

It's now nearly 70 years since the formulation of Head's and Rivers' great notion of the protopathic and epicritic nervous system, and the idea has undergone a great deal of modification in that time. However, it still exerts a considerable influence. In the teaching of anaesthesia, the levels of anaesthesia – as the patient gradually goes under with the gas – are often explained in terms of the successive peeling-off of evolutionary layers, until, as the patient lies on the table, we are witnessing a parody or a caricature of what he was before he became a man. It's almost as if the surgeon is going to work on a hairless monkey.

Competing with this notion is a theory of nervous function which is beginning to replace it. No one wishes to repudiate the notion that we have in fact climbed up an evolutionary ladder and have arrived at our excellent current condition through previous states. But what I think we would quarrel with now is the idea that evolution consists of a concentric series of restraints upon these older conditions, and that you can reveal these older conditions by injury or assault or by special procedures of one sort or another. It's quite possible that this vertical model of nervous organization is no longer useful for examining the nervous system that we now know. It's certainly the case that when the nervous system is injured, very dramatic symptoms are produced. What we have to ask ourselves, however, is this: is it profitable to view these symptoms in a simple evolutionary light, as the mere release of an older stage? Is it profitable to look at these symptoms with a purely vertical model in mind, a purely hierarchical model, in which we view the nervous system as something which is dominated from the top?

Beyond dispute
Times Literary Supplement, 27 July 1967[154]

The last hundred years have seen an astonishing growth in the scope and power of the physical sciences. In fact the growth rule of science is probably the most famous thing about it and the result is a public superstition about its developing capabilities nearly as strong as those it once succeeded in dispersing. The most sophisticated form of this superstition consists in the belief that science – whatever that might be – has reached a commanding height from which it will shortly control not just nature and the physical environment but the rest of human knowledge too. It is widely held to be a model, if not *the* model, for all meaningful description and that any proposal which hopes to make serious or lasting sense, on *any* substance, must either be capable of being assimilated to it or else be dismissed as gibberish.

The most powerful effect of this assertion has been felt in those departments of thought which have always faced both ways across the border between the two cultures. Psychology and sociology have summed up their own predicament in this respect by sometimes referring to themselves as the 'soft sciences.' This title may be ironic but it has a normative ring as well, suggesting through the medium of irony that these subjects should hurry up and assume the armoured hardness of the 'real' sciences.

It is, of course, by no means clear how, or even *whether*, such a transition is really possible. The debate on the subject goes back to Mill and Comte, or even further perhaps, to Hobbes. And of course it is not something upon which facts *have* a bearing, since the question of what *is* and is *not* a fact in these matters is precisely the point at issue. But the fact that such a trend exists at all might lead one to expect a nervous reaction on the part of those disciplines which share a frontier with the disputed territory. That is to say in the arts, and those especially which, like the 'soft sciences,' have an interest in human behaviour. But in fact, at the most general level at least, literature and drama have been more or less indifferent to the procedural conflict going on within the disciplines of sociology and psychology. Artists have quickly recognized that, at this level, the discussion of things like factual validity is of no immediate interest. This is partly due to the fact that art has never been self-conscious with regard to its fate as a coherent body of wisdom. There has never, for example, been, as there has in science, a superordinate philosophy whose agreed function it has been to adjudicate the systematic long-range ambitions of the subject as a whole. Science on the other hand is, by its nature, very self-conscious, and very profitably self-conscious, about its status as a system. It is bound therefore, as are any of its subsidiary disciplines, to be methodologically sensitive in a way that literature has no need to be.

The result is that literature has possibly had more effect upon psychology and sociology than vice versa, not through any explicit manifesto but simply through the insights it has to offer. For, eager though the 'soft sciences' are to assume the credentials of hard physical science, they are also embarrassed by the way in which imaginative writers will often arrive at social and psychological conclusions without having to use any of the respectable apparatus of surveys or statistics. They may even concede the vivid finality of literature to the extent of using examples from fiction or the drama to illustrate their own cast-iron generalities. But there has never been a good open discussion on the question of *why* an illustration *should* be necessary; or what could be said to count as an illustration and what its logical connexion with more formal analysis really is.

For except in the philosophically trivial sense, an illustration is *not* just something to break up the text with pictures. In any sense that really matters, an illustration which could be said to make a difference has a complicated structural relationship with its explicandum. Any illustration which is to be more than a picturesque tautology must actually add something to the propositions made in the formal text. Social scientists are characteristically rather vague about what this extra dollop of enlightenment actually *is*. They are aware that it exists and Max Weber even coined the term *Verstehen* or 'understanding' to cover the case. It has not been made quite clear, however, what this *Verstehen* is and why it should ever be needed. One never hears the term referred to in the physical sciences, where the theory, the formula or the equation *is* the 'understanding.' No extra clinching illustration seems necessary. This is not the place to go into the question, but its existence as an unsettled issue accounts for the way in which literature sometimes influences social science rather than the other way round.

Imaginative writers on the other hand are quite naturally indignant at the suggestion that they are only illustrators of respectable social or psychological theory. They may be happy to contribute, but for them, in the final reduction, literature is neither a docile handmaiden of the 'soft sciences' nor a larval form of something which the 'soft sciences' alone have succeeded in making adult. For them the pursuit of literature needs no other justification apart from the domestic critical standards of the subject itself.

Writers and dramatists may have been impervious to the more general calls of psychology and sociology but there still remains the possibility that they may have been influenced by the concrete data provided by these hybrid sciences. But does this possibility really exist? What is literature such that a fact, discoverable only by science, *could* have a bearing upon its development? In any of the recognized senses which make a work of literature unique or valuable, it is about nothing more than what its characters did or felt. Any failings which a work may have in this respect have nothing to do with shortage of special knowledge. For if this were the case, literature would become out of date in the way that effete scientific theories must. Seneca's plays would have died of antiquity just like the astronomical theories of Ptolemy. But in some odd way Seneca has outlived Ptolemy. Not because Ptolemy was dumber than Seneca but because his work made statements about the world in a way that made it critically susceptible to new facts and above all to new theoretical ways of expressing those facts.

For this reason Ptolemy's work was superseded by that of Copernicus. Seneca on the other hand made statements about the world in such a way that, while Shakespeare may have been better, there is no meaningful way in which he could be said to have superseded his Roman forebear. Not only have Seneca's plays *not* been superseded by those of Shakespeare, it is hard to understand just what it would be for them to have done so. It is this freedom from the risk of supersession which also makes literature somehow proof against the facts of science. By contrast with this, any so-called scientific theory which is proof against facts is not really a theory at all. A scientific theory has to be capable of being wrong in order to stand up as being right in any significant way. We never say that a work of literature is wrong. A novel or a play can be wrong-headed but never simply wrong. This suggests quite properly that the forces which determine the qualities of a work of fiction are an expression of the aptitudes of its author and not of any special facts to which he may or may not have had access. Special knowledge is really nothing to do with literature. It *is* with science. In fact science *is* special knowledge set out in such a way that it positively invites contradiction. Literature on the other hand is *general* knowledge, set out in a way which may be disliked or disagreed with, but never truly contradicted.

Although its subject matter may be general, this does not mean that literature cannot be abstruse. But this is because its expression is private, which has something to do with the handling of language and nothing whatever to do with any special disclosures which may have been made by another discipline. Nevertheless, the 'soft sciences' and especially psychology have had some influence upon the course of modern literature, but not in any way which upsets the principles suggested above. The influence of psychology, for example, has come from that part of the subject whose methodological 'softness' seriously embarrasses its claims to be a science at all. That is to say from psychoanalysis, the very department of psychology whose scientific status is most in doubt. It has influenced literature precisely because it is, in the very best sense, so literary itself. As an influence, therefore, Freud is far more like Tolstoy than he is, say, like Newton. His work affects that of other writers because it is part and parcel of the same affair. No logical rules are broken by saying that such an influence exists, because in fact the basic proposals of psychoanalysis are on the same plane of descriptive insight as those of literature. The data which Freud chose to organize are those that *any* imaginative writer could have handled too. And the sense which he made of these facts could also have been made by a literary figure, given Freud's genius.

This does nothing to diminish that genius, but is simply an attempt to recognize precisely what it consists of. For the sake of argument one can describe it all in terms of one magnificent move of the literary imagination. Freud simply carried into childhood, and into the fantasy world of dreams, the same imaginative sensitivity which other writers had expended on the world of waking adults. It was not so much that he brought *science* to bear on *adults* as the fact that he enlarged the scope of *literature* to include the world of *dreams and children*. Until Freud suggested otherwise, children had been seen by writers – if they were seen at all – as innocent apprentices of adult skills. Their souls were seen as nothing more than smaller, simpler and duller versions of their grown-up relatives. They were not therefore worthy subjects for serious literature. Freud saw, on the other hand, that the moral life of human beings began not just with social seniority but at the moment of birth, and that man is complexly human from the moment he takes the breast from his mother. He did the same for dreams, which had hitherto been regarded either as incoherent anomalies on the edge of waking consciousness or else as receivers designed to pick up messages from the future. Freud showed that dreams, like childhood, were an integral part of the moral life. Freud in other words was a literary essayist in the spirit of Montaigne. He was a radical humanist for whom not only was nothing human alien but everything human was of total and meaningful interest – dreams, babies, lunacy, the lot.[155]

Not only is the text of Freud's work literary and perhaps essentially tragic; unlike any other putatively scientific study, its intellectual pedigree

172

is strikingly literary too. It brings to the twentieth century a preoccupation with the irrational life of the imagination which is straight out of early-nineteenth-century Romanticism. In his interest in dreams, for example, he has far more in common with the Coleridge of *Biographia Literaria* (1817) than he has with any of the neurobiologists he admired and tried so hard to emulate.

And this of course is the Freud who has influenced modern literature. He licensed the surrealists by giving impressive credentials to the irrational, though of course it is hard to say how many writers of this and other sorts might not have gone on like this without his provocative permissions. Writers like Jarry for example are simply *contemporaries* of Freud, not dependents. The plays of Ibsen too read exactly like some of Freud's great cases, especially *Ghosts* and *The Master Builder* (1892). They would have happened, and indeed *did*, without Freud; just as Freud, a literary genius, could quite possibly have happened without Darwin or Charcot.

In fact, modern literature could no more be said to have descended from Freud than in the strict sense men could be said to have descended from the apes. Both modern literature and psychoanalysis are cousins with a common ancestry in primitive myth, symbolism and nineteenth-century Romanticism. Any influence there has been arrives from this purely literary parallelism. Whenever the work of Freud has been brought to bear *explicitly* on literature, the work of fiction or drama has suffered actual damage. This is particularly evident in the work of American writers, and above all in the work of American theatrical directors whose intuitive sensibilities are often distorted by trying to press actors to work through the recognition of dogmatically Freudian motives. But such strictures are not specifically connected with the doctrine of psychoanalysis. The unique genius of imaginative literary insight suffers *whenever* it is fitted to an idea which is misunderstood to the point of becoming a dogma. Plays or novels which are tailored to Marx suffer the same sort of mortification. The best plays of Brecht, for example, spring to dramatic life only when the larger literary vision of the dramatist assimilates the insight of Marx rather than being subordinated to the dogma of his disciples.

For literature is not and never can be a *forme fruste* of an unachieved super-discipline. It is a *ding an sich* which reminds us all that we are, as

173

human beings, of lasting special interest. Without it we cease to be *that* and the universe reverts to its primal vacuousness – a cracked vessel full of stardust and cuckoo-spit.

West side stories
New Statesman, 8 February 1963[156]

We sailed up the Hudson on the heels of a dying hurricane. Warm veils of green-house rain douched the running swell and blotted out the Manhattan skyline. The Immigration came aboard: joke-proof figures in shirtsleeves and dark glasses who took over the First Class lounge and set up their desks at the end of hastily improvised sheep-runs. Without looking up, the official took my passport and flipped the pages grimly back and forth.

'Whadja in the United States for?' He glanced unbelievingly at my photo.

'I'm with *Beyond the Fringe*, an English show, y'know – sort of satirical revue…along the lines of the Berlin cabaret but with a certain English… how shall I say–'

He cut me short with a molten look, stamped my visa and slipped an effusive, printed 'Welcome to New York' between the pages of my passport.

The city was damp and tense. Throughout the summer there had been a succession of violent crimes. Central Park had become so ferocious that the police had just launched a fleet of decoy victims – burly cops dressed as women who tart around in the gloaming, operating what one may flinchingly call a dragnet. New Yorkers talk and joke a great deal about the violence of their city, but once he has recovered his equanimity the visitor is surprised at the relative decorum. I have never been given a first-hand account of an assault, although nearly all my friends know people who were themselves mugged, rolled or senselessly beaten on the street. I am not saying I disbelieve these stories. As a protective incantation, I *do* believe in muggers, I do! I do! I do! But the generalized ache of fear which such reports produce takes on a life of its own and becomes a free-floating anxiety which weighs on the city's morale.

Scanning the real-estate columns of the *New York Times*, I would light on places which the experts would then discourage me from taking. 'That,' they would say, 'is the most dangerous street in New York.' Apart from a few pricey pads on the fashionable East Side, there seemed, from all accounts, to be few places where I could live without the possibility of finding my wife raped by a delivery boy or myself 'jumped' by a hungry junkie. Strangely enough, when I viewed the apartments and talked to the people who lived around, the position seemed somehow less alarming. 'This street's fine,' they would say. 'But watch out on 86th – it's one of the most dangerous streets in New York.' Distance made the heart grow weaker.

Each night I take the Broadway bus, juddering downtown to perform in that English revue with overtones of Berlin cabaret. Our opening was timed, with a certain black nicety, to coincide with the Cuba crisis. All that week New York was gripped with a dull, paralyzing fear. People seemed to be living from hour to hour, each of us nursing private visions of that first detonation, of the hot nuclear gales scorching down the empty avenues. The audiences turned up, though – to a man. They sat there in complete silence, fatuously attentive to our efforts, but silent. After a week of these unsettling previews, the crisis thawed and we opened on a wave of euphoric relief. Since then, it has been much like playing a show in London. Laughter and silence come in the same places, varying unexpectedly, just as they do in England. Only on Wednesdays, perhaps, is there any noticeable difference. Then we get the blue-rinse, hot-flush and menopause brigade: mirthless middle-aged ladies from the suburbs who pop into town, 'take in' a show and wind up the day with a spiteful little tea in Schrafft's.

Uptown, Broadway is all giant cafeterias, dry cleaners, laundries, delicatessens and funeral parlours – these indistinguishable from cinemas: Gutterman's Midtown Memorial, the Ortiz Funeral Home. Under the neon-lit canopies dark groups of matinée mourners spill across the kerb to the double-parked ranks of limousines. There are more old people on the Upper West Side than anywhere else in New York. Jewish, mainly. Tiny widows in Persian lamb who crowd the benches of Sherman Square, waiting for the sun to go in. Many of the hotels on 72nd Street, once grand, are now richly disreputable – peeling Nymphenburgs which give houseroom to old opera singers, Russian ballet teachers, sly masseurs and sorrowful widowers. These great hotels, with apartments for long lease and rooms for 'transients,' give the Upper West Side its provisional feel – post-war, bombed out even, like the Vienna of *The Third Man*. On Broadway, one half expects the cruising jeeps of the four-power Commission. Then there are the side-street flophouses, from the fairy casements of which flit the West Side's more flamboyant deviants: fags, queers, dykes and painted lulus, who catch one's eye with lingering cosmetic gaze. They shop at midnight in the 24-hour supermarket, petulantly pushing their wire carts from stack to stack, emerging finally with hopelessly primitive pansy provisions. Coke and strawberry yoghurt. Frivolous pixie fare!

The Upper West Side is being resurrected, though – slowly. After its grand decline in the Thirties, having once been a modish uptown venue, the area began to recover. Actors and writers, psychiatrists and Columbia academics were attracted by the low rents and spacious European style of the flats which had been carved out of the old mogul palaces. Since the war there have been deliberate efforts to accelerate this rise in tone. 'Live on the Golden West Side,' says one advert, and in fact two enormous high-rent apartment blocks at the top of 11th Avenue filled up while the builders were still in, no doubt because of the glowing social aura of the nearby Lincoln Arts Centre, the placing of which, at the lower end of Upper Broadway, has set off a minor property boom on the West Side. The concert hall is already in full use and the theatre is under construction. There are West Siders who resent this access of prestige in a district which had, and even now preserves, a shabby European vitality. It would be sad to see it pass over into the boutique dinkiness of the East Side.

Where is thy sting?

Spectator, 3 March 1961[157]

I was 19 before I saw a dead body and if I had not become a doctor, it is unlikely that I ever would have done. A doctor's initiation into the facts of death goes through a series of ritual stages, the first being the dissecting room. Here, for a whole year, the young medical student ambles through a leisurely dissection of the human body, nibbling away at ancient cadavers with an anatomy textbook propped irreverently against a greasy abdomen. I can remember that first morning, yawning with fear at my forthcoming encounter with the dead as I waited along with the other students outside the frosted glass doors of the dissecting room. We joked uneasily as to who would be the first to faint. The doors were thrown open by the attendant and we flocked gingerly into the long tiled room which echoed like a swimming bath. Instead of the stench of decay we were startled by the clammy aroma of formalin and red lead. Before us, laid out on 40 glass-topped tables, lay the 'subjects,' as the dissecting manual courteously referred to them. Our fears were unfounded. The subjects, most of them paupers, seemed to have little to do with life or death. They had died many months before and in the embalming process had suffered a sea-change which put them quite outside any human category. They lay in restless postures, grey as pumice, like the figures at Pompeii, fossilized in a moment of disaster. 'On the first day the subject will be placed on his back and the dissectors will proceed to the display of the structures in the axilla.' The biblical simplicity of this opening command in the manual set us to work on a task that was to take a year, reducing our 'subjects,' in the end, to a few knucklebones and a heap of giblets which were solemnly bundled into a corner of a pine box for Christian burial at some later date.

Our next formal encounter carried more conviction. Arrived at our teaching hospitals for clinical training, we were expected to attend the autopsies which were demonstrated each day, shortly after lunch. Here we came face to face with the unvarnished and unembalmed details of recent death. The bodies were those of patients who had died only a few hours before and they lay on the tables calm and straight, their faces composed in a Gioconda smile. Whilst the dissecting-room bodies had been inanimately grey through and through, when the pathologist cut into these corpses they were red as beef and smelled of slaughterhouses.

One by one the various organs were removed and laid on a side table, wet and vivid like a windfall of exotic rotten fruit. For a moment one was unnerved by the contrast between the pale austerity of the intact body and this unwarranted fiesta of intestine. We soon became inured to these sights and smells, although time and time again some physical feature would cause a twinge of human recognition which one never experienced in the grey, greasy confusion of the dissecting room.

Finally, in the wards we came across the actual moment of death, though here again one felt cheated of the truth, life seeming to slip away in a whispering glissando which left one with a sense of anti-climax. I had expected something more clear-cut. Something perhaps on the level of Aubrey's spectre which vanished with a puff of perfume and a melodious twang. In the final reduction I go a long way with the man to whom I had once to say that his wife was dead. He gave me a puzzled look. 'Dead, eh?' he said; and then, with a wistful glance into the middle distance, he said, 'Dead, eh? Blimey, it's a funny old life.'

But few people have any resources these days to cope with death. A few months ago I leafed through a Borough Register, and I was struck by the number of deaths which took place in hospital. The great majority, in fact. The registrar told me of the great change which had occurred in this way. Few families actually seemed able to cope with death in the home and many of the admissions to hospital took place at the request of the relatives who had panicked at the prospect of having to deal with a corpse. Today, few people know how to lay out a body. A piece of domestic technology, familiar in most Victorian households, has vanished, and the registrar said with the few deaths that did occur at home a district nurse had sometimes to be called to help out the frightened family. During a year as a house physician I can recall only one family who actually asked that the patient, in hospital at the time, should be allowed to come home to die; compared to the hundreds who insisted that we should stage-manage the last act. Of those whose relatives did die in hospital, few actually saw the moment of death or went in to view the body afterwards. In fact, the whole business of death is gradually being bowdlerized out of common experience, giving place to the Gothic fantasies of horror films which now seem more acceptable to the public than the chilly details of the real thing. They have no familiarity to blunt the edge of their experience: only the doctors nowadays can provide it.

Mesmerism in nineteenth-century England
BBC Radio 3, 24 October 1973[158]

At the end of the eighteenth century and for more than half of the nineteenth, Europe was seized with an interest in the occult. For more than three-quarters of a century, books, pamphlets and articles poured from the press on the related subjects of trance, somnambulism, table-turning, animal magnetism and miracle cures. Human beings have always speculated about a life beyond the grave and about the sort of existence that lies beyond the veil of everyday appearances. Mankind has always set high value upon the significance of dreams, and the subjects of trances or fits have been invested with sacred dread since time immemorial. Witchcraft and sorcery are as old as society, and the magical power of thought has always held a strong fascination. In this sense, the occult interests of the eighteenth and nineteenth centuries are no more than a continuation of an ancient tradition.

Nevertheless, there is something peculiar about the way in which the Victorians continued and revived these traditional interests – especially as the avowed principles of the period seemed so much at odds with such beliefs, and the growth of large towns had done a great deal to destroy the social fabric within which occult practices had a natural place. To judge by the official documents of the period, encyclopaedias and so forth, the occult was dismissed as a regrettable survival of primitive superstition – something which would disperse as popular scientific education became more widespread. But, of course, it is easy to select as representative of the recent past only those publications which conform to modern ideas of what that past was like. In those periods which we regard as seedbeds of modern culture, we emphasize the work which appears to provide respectable antecedents for our own beliefs, and neglect and even suppress anything which looks like an embarrassing inconsistency. This process of retrospective editing sometimes applies to the work of a single man. The reputation of Isaac Newton has been artfully managed in order to shape him into the dignified ancestor of modern scientific rationalism. His interest in alchemy, astrology and the Hermetic mysteries proved so embarrassing to the historians who had chosen to appropriate him as the forerunner of tough-minded empiricism that they carefully omitted any reference to the million words he devoted to occult subjects. The truth is that these interests were part and parcel of the real Newton.

My point is that the historian of ideas cannot afford to be fastidious. As Professor Palmer has said, 'The tendencies of an age appear more distinctly in its writers of inferior rank than in those of commanding genius.'[159] For anyone interested in the overall complexion of a historical period it is necessary to plunge into the undergrowth of forgotten publications: the anonymous world of pamphlets and broadsheets. And in the case of the Victorians, constant reference must be made to the enormous periodical literature – a task now made easier by the heroic *Wellesley Index to Victorian Periodicals*, a Mount Palomar telescope through which the night sky of Victorian thought can appear as a majestic panorama of genius and error.[160]

Although it is hard to find any mention of hypnotism or mesmerism in what we now regard as the orthodox writers of the late eighteenth and early nineteenth century, the topic springs into sharp relief as soon as one turns to the unofficial sources. I propose to follow the fate of mesmerism after its arrival in England in 1785.

Franz Anton Mesmer, its originator, was born on the shore of Lake Constance in 1734. After studying philosophy he turned to medicine and in 1766 published his MD thesis on the influence of the planets on human disease. He was prompted to do so, it is said, by his reading of a similar essay written by Isaac Newton's physician, George Mead. According to Mesmer, the human frame came under the influence of planetary motions through the medium of an impalpable fluid which filled the otherwise empty spaces of the universe. By the time Mesmer put forward this idea, the notion of an imponderable universal fluid had already gained wide acceptance, largely as a result of Newton's own suggestion that the presence of such a medium might be necessary in order to account for the propagation of light, heat, electricity and magnetism. In his book *Mechanism and Materialism in the Age of Reason* (1969), Robert Schofield has traced the vicissitudes of this idea, proving that it received favourable emphasis in many of the later popularizations of Newton's work. From 1740 onwards we get pamphlet after pamphlet advertising the importance of an imponderable fluid. Newton himself had suggested that this might explain the propagation of nerve impulses, and, if you look at the Croonian Lectures published by the Royal Society throughout the eighteenth century, you repeatedly come up against the idea that the hollow nerves were filled with a so-called ether, and that this weightless, elastic medium served to transmit the urges of the will down towards the muscles. On the assumption that the fluid which fills the nerves is the same as that which fills the void of the universe, it only requires a small leap of the imagination to conclude that the medium which links the mind to its muscles could serve equally well to link one mind with another. Mesmer took this leap, and, after making preliminary experiments with the therapeutic effects of magnets, concluded that the human frame was a reservoir of animal magnetism, and that through the medium of the ether one person could bring influence to bear on any other, without resort to metal magnets.

This is not the place to record the ins and outs of Mesmer's career. The story has been accurately summarized in Ellenberger's great work, *The Discovery of the Unconscious* (1970). The important point is that Mesmer encountered the hostility of the Viennese medical establishment and moved to France, where he started a thriving practice in animal magnetism. Throughout the late 1770s and early 1780s, mesmerism became a huge cult in Paris and throughout the French provinces. The subjects, clients or patients – it's hard to settle on the right title – grouped themselves around a tub or bucket in which, according to the Mesmeric orthodoxy, the magnetic fluid would accumulate. Gripping iron bars plunged into the fluid, the subjects experienced every type of trance, fit and transport. Every effort was made to encourage a susceptible state of mind: soft entrancing music, drawn curtains, and the master himself stalking the salon in a magician's robe. According to the faithful, all sorts of illness vanished under the treatment; there is a marked stress on rheumatic illnesses and on all those other disorders which have subsequently proved particularly susceptible to hypnotic influences. Schismatic culls were soon established, each with its own apostolic succession of practitioners. And in some cases the cosmic theory which underpinned the practice was used to promote a programme of radical social reform.

By 1784 Mesmer had aroused the angry suspicions of the French medical profession, and a commission was formed to investigate the claims of mesmerism. The commissioners, among them scientists like Lavoisier and Franklin, concluded that the effects – some of them admittedly very dramatic – were due to the influence of the imagination; that is to say, the expectation of powerful effects was enough to bring them about. In other words, there was no need to invoke the existence of a mysterious fluid, at least not in this context. This form of criticism was reiterated from then on, and by the time animal magnetism had gained a foothold in England there was a well-established tradition of referring to the influence of the imagination, if only to counteract the claims of those who invoked the agency of the universal fluid.

Following the report of the commission, Mesmer suffered a personal eclipse, and although animal magnetism continued to flourish in one form or another, the figure of Mesmer himself now fades into obscurity. Meanwhile, the idea had crossed the Channel, and struck root in England in the year 1785. A French practitioner, one de Mainaduc, established a mesmeric salon, and by 1786 the topic was reported widely enough for the surgeon John Hunter to refer to it in his lectures on surgery. As one might expect, he felt that any effects would flow from the expectant imagination. Hunter said:

> I was asked to go to be magnetized, but at first refused, because the spasm on my vital parts was very likely to be brought on by a state of mind anxious about any event [and] I feared lest [it] should be imputed to animal magnetism. But considering that if any person was affected by it it must be by the imagination being worked up by attention to the part expected to be affected, and thinking I could counteract this, I went; and accordingly, when I went, I was convinced by the apparatus that everything was calculated to affect the imagination.[161]

Writing in the same year, Joseph Priestley expressed the same scepticism and offered, by way of explanation, the same hypothesis:

> With respect to what you saw of *animal magnetism*. All that I ever saw was a poor woman thrown into an hysteric fit. [...] I have conversed with several persons conversant in the business, and have read a small publication, said [...] to contain the true principle of the practice, and see [only] what is usually called *imagination*.[162]

In 1788, when the magnetic enthusiasm was already at its height in England, a Bath physician, William Falconer, was moved to publish a long essay on the influence of the imagination upon the diseases of the body, formulating principles which could easily be applied to what was going on in the mesmeric séances of London and Bristol.[163] Twelve years later, Falconer's friend John Haygarth had the opportunity of testing these ideas, not against mesmerism, but against a therapeutic novelty which was closely allied to it. In the 1790s an American called Elisha Perkins had introduced a pair of iron tongs – he called them 'tractors': according to him the magnetic influence set up by these tongs would, when drawn across the skin, alleviate any form of painful muscular or skeletal disorder. Haygarth insisted that this was a perfect example of what he and Falconer were talking about. The patients' expectation of cure supplied all that was needed. Haygarth set out to prove this in what must be the first example of a blank clinical trial – one involving the use of a type of placebo. He obtained a pair of wooden tongs – that is to say, tractors which could have no possible electromagnetic influence – painted them with black lead to give them the appearance of metal, and then drew them across the patient's affected part. The result was just as good as it had been with the real tractors.[164]

Ironically, Falconer's caution did not extend to the spa waters from which he must have gained a large part of his living. He published a separate pamphlet on the subject of spas without any reference to the effects of the imagination, and yet pious expectation accounts for most, if not all, effects attributed to mineral springs.[165] It would be unwise, therefore, to over-interpret these medical theories of the imagination. They are not really contributions towards psychosomatic knowledge, but rather blunt instruments with which enlightened sceptics tried to put down any medical novelty which smelt, for one reason or another, of mysticism or superstition. None of the physicians who used this explanation in order to criticize the claims of mesmerism tried to explain how the imagination might wield its dramatic effects.

The odd thing is, however, that as far as mysticism was concerned, the theoretical justification for mesmerism was no less vague or mystical than the fluid theories which were widely favoured as explanations of electricity. Great scientists like Thomas Young were quite happy to suggest that the ether might serve as a medium for universal mental activity. In his *Lectures on Natural Philosophy* in 1807, Young says:

> nothing can be more fit to constitute a connecting link between material and immaterial beings, than some modification of a fluid, which appears to differ [...] in its essential properties, from the common gross matter of the universe, and to possess a subtility and an activity, which entitle it to a superior rank in the order of created substances.[166]

For all its Newtonian ancestry, the theory of a universal fluid was a thoroughgoing example of occult spiritualism. In fact, there is evidence that Newton was drawn to it himself for that very reason. Far from representing a break with the mystical traditions of antiquity and the Renaissance, the introduction of an imponderable ether merely revived a well-established belief in the so-called 'world soul.' This tradition goes back to the Stoics, and perhaps further. The Florentine Neoplatonist Ficino describes this principle in words which practically paraphrase what Thomas Young said: '[The cosmic spirit] is a very subtle body; as it were not body and almost soul. Or again, as it were not soul and almost body. [...] It vivifies everything everywhere.'[167] As D. P. Walker has said, Newton's speculations about the ether might become clearer if seen against the background of the long history of ambiguities and muddles generated by the concept of the spiritus or world soul. For this reason, perhaps, the English sceptics of the late eighteenth century were unimpressed by the Newtonian credentials of mesmerism. Not that they necessarily knew the extent to which Newton had been influenced by his readings in the occult tradition: few people did until this century. But they were probably suspicious of the mystical smell associated with the doctrine of an imponderable fluid, and, in spite of Newton's great reputation, chose to overlook his seal of approval.

Henceforth the current of opinion about mesmerism divides on this very issue. Those who rejected the claims of the mesmeric fluidists did so out of hostility to the whole tradition of imponderable spirits, while those who embraced the fluid doctrine did so precisely because it seemed to continue a lost tradition of magic and mysticism. The sceptical tendency initiated by Falconer and Haygarth, by Hunter and Priestley, culminates in the 1840s in the work of James Braid, a Manchester surgeon who practised animal magnetism extensively, insisting nonetheless that the effects were mediated through the imagination, largely as a result of the unnatural fixation of the subject's gaze. It was Braid who retitled the phenomenon hypnotism or 'nervous sleep' and who is rightly celebrated for putting the subject on a firm intellectual footing.[168]

On the other hand, those who remained loyal to the doctrine of a magnetic fluid did so as part and parcel of their mystical enthusiasm for the great traditions of alchemy, astrology and the Hermetic mysteries. Throughout the 1830s and 1840s we find mesmeric theorists whose publications in favour of mesmerism are thinly-disguised Neoplatonist tracts. In the first full-length English work on mesmerism, published in the 1830s, J. C. Colquhoun embraces the idea of a universal fluid:

[We may assume] a very subtile and attenuated ethereal fluid, probably secreted in the brain [...] acting under the command of the will[169] [...] the existence of a nervous circulation [seems to] render probable the external expansion of this [...] fluid – an expansion [...] supposed to take place with such energy, as to form an atmosphere [...] of activity [like those] of electrical bodies.[170]

He goes on to suggest that through the medium of this fluid the subject may be put in touch with the universe at large, entering into a mystical clairvoyant oneness. This idea was elaborated ten years later by the Reverend Chauncy Townshend, a friend of Lord Lytton. (Lord Lytton was himself a Rosicrucian enthusiast.) In his influential book *Facts in Mesmerism* (1840), Townshend exploits the fluid doctrine in order to advertise a thoroughgoing Platonism. According to him, the mesmeric trance, mediated through the magnetic fluid of the universe, released the subject from the blindfold of the senses. Here he is talking about the five senses: 'it appears that the apparatuses of the senses are contrivances for blunting, not for heightening, the sensibility. They are masks, and careful coverings to instruments of too exquisite delicacy to be bared or exposed to the outer world.'[171] Also, 'There are evidently but two ways of perceiving objects; – the one by being present to them in their essential verity; the other by communication with them through the intervention of types or shadows.'[172] This is little more than a summary of Plato's image of the cave, where the prisoners are condemned to view reality in the form of shadows cast from behind. According to Townshend, mesmerism offers the chance of escape from Plato's cave: 'Separated from the usual action of the senses' – by the mesmeric trance – 'the mind appears to gain juster notions, to have quite a new sense of spiritual things.'[173] And as Plato suggested, the mind thus released from its prison of sense also gains a more accurate moral insight.

Townshend writes:

The great indication of this elevated state of feeling is a horror of falsehood, which I have found common to all sleepwalkers. Sincerity is their especial characteristics; they cannot feign or flatter: they seem to be taken out of common life, with all its heartless forms and plausible conventions.[174]

We will find this moral strain in mystical mesmerism taken up by other authors in order to exploit the radical social possibilities of animal magnetism.

A more extreme example of the same strain is found in the little-known work of Mary Anne South. Born in 1817, she spent most of her life sharing the mystical seclusion of her clergyman father. She devoted herself explicitly to the study of alchemy, astrology and the Hermetic mysteries. In 1846 she published a short pamphlet on what she called *Early Magnetism*, explicitly identifying the universal fluid with the fundamental essences of alchemy. She saw alchemy, as its sixteenth-century practitioners did, as an experiment with the primal stuff of existence. The transformation of gold was simply a metaphor for the purification experienced in ecstasy and in particular during the mesmeric trance. In *Early Magnetism* she speaks of the magnetic trance as follows:

> [It conjoins] the mind to its lost universality, and [allows] consciousness [to pass] regressively through its many phases [...] to that long-forgotten life in reality [...] passing behind the murky media of sense and fantasy [to behold reflections] in the brightened mirror of our own intelligence.[175]

What we have here is a sort of indoor pantheism. With its emphasis upon higher forms of perception achieved by laying the five senses to sleep, the transcendental mesmerism of Townshend and Mary Anne South sounds remarkably like Wordsworth:

> we are laid asleep
> In body, and become a living soul:
> While with an eye made quiet by the power
> Of harmony, and the deep power of joy,
> We see into the life of things.[176]

Wordsworth paid no attention to mesmerism as such, but like the fluidists, he identified, albeit in a metaphorical sense, a spirit that rolled through all things. The mesmerists had simply conjured this mystical metaphor into a substantial reality.

It would be a mistake to assume, however, that all those who believed in the existence of a universal fluid were mystical spiritualists, or that all the nineteenth-century magnetists regarded themselves as the heirs of Plato and Paracelsus. In the 1830s and 1840s, another group of mesmerists appeared who turned the fluid theory to somewhat different ends. In order to show how this group came into existence, we must retrace our steps and show what happened to animal magnetism after its first appearance in England at the end of the eighteenth century.

Following the first magnetic craze, the vehemence of which should be seen in the context of some of the other millennial cults of the period – Joanna Southcott, Richard Brothers and so on – the interest subsided, and it is hard to find any significant mention of the subject until 1829. Presumably the war made it hard to bring evangelical reinforcement from the continent; in any case, its undeniable association with French radical thought would have made it politically suspect after 1793. Even so, it is hard to account for the long silence between 1815 and 1829. One can only suggest that the transcendental tone of mesmeric theory was at odds with English common sense, and that without the encouragement provided by a steady stream of charismatic foreign evangelists the English reverted to their characteristic indifference.

Meanwhile, the first significant revival began in 1829, as a result of five articles published in the *London Medical and Physical Journal* by Richard Chenevix.[177] Chenevix was a chemist who had already earned a reputation on the basis of his work in inorganic chemistry. He was also a fellow of the Royal Society. It's important to realize, though, that fellowship of the Royal Society is a much more impressive credential now than it was then. In fact, within a year after Chenevix's articles, a group of English scientists, led by the mathematician Babbage, mounted a campaign in protest at the state of English science, pointing out, among other things, that the oddly mixed membership of the Royal Society reflected an alarming confusion of intellectual standards. In fact, the articles are undistinguished and simply repeat the well-known claims.

What makes them interesting is the way in which Chenevix identifies the discredited wonders of mesmerism with the equally incredible but nevertheless widely accepted phenomena of electricity and steam power:

In my remembrance, they have wondered at hydrogen and oxygen;
at a dead frog jumping between two slips of metal; at gas-lights, and
steam-boats; and now they wonder at all who wonder at those familiar
themes. They would pity the wretch who would not instantly believe
[...] that the taste which his tongue perceives when placed between a
piece of silver and a piece of zinc, has the same origin as the thunder
which strikes his soul with awe.[178]

In the early nineteenth century, the cascade of new discoveries must
have made it very hard to discriminate between facts and fantasies. In spite
of the existence of the Royal Society, the scientific community had not yet
incorporated itself to the point where it shared firm intellectual criteria for
judging such matters. The next 15 years would see the establishment of the
British Association for the Advancement of Science, and the publication
of works like Whewell's *Philosophy of the Inductive Sciences* (1840) and
Mill's *A System of Logic* (1843), which helped to establish an intellectual
foundation for science in general.

The flood of new discoveries in chemistry and electromagnetism made
it easy for a tender-minded figure like Chenevix to claim that the facts
of animal magnetism were on a par with those made known by Volta,
Faraday and others. Curiously enough, Faraday was one of the men invited
to witness Chenevix's mesmeric séances: he dismissed what he saw, just
as he later rejected the claims of the table-turning spiritualists. In fact,
it was partly due to his experiences in these areas that he insisted on the
importance of improving the quality of scientific education and of thereby
protecting the illiterate susceptibilities of the general public from the
ravages of mysticism.

Another witness was John Elliotson, a physician shortly to be appointed
as Professor of Medicine at the newly-founded Hospital of University
College London. This was the first intimation of Elliotson's interest in a
subject with which he was to be controversially associated for the next 30
years. Born in 1791 and educated at Edinburgh and later at Cambridge,
he had an illustrious career, and although his reputation was somewhat
eclipsed by his subsequent association with animal magnetism, he was so
highly respected as a physician that he was accorded the honour of the
Harveian Oration in 1846, eight years after his humiliating resignation
from the University College Hospital. His early interest in the subject of

sleep and trance is shown by the rapid enlargement of the chapter on the subject in his successive editions of Blumenbach's *Physiology*.[179]

Of course, Elliotson was not alone in this. During the early years of the nineteenth century many authorities had become interested in the nature of sleep and in the related subjects of trance, reverie and somnambulism. However, in 1829 Elliotson expressed no more than a guarded interest in animal magnetism as such, and it was not until 1837 that he became an enthusiast. Once again, the change coincides with the arrival of a French evangelist – the Baron Dupotet de Sennevoy, one of Mesmer's apostolic successors. For some reason, Dupotet's public demonstrations fired Elliotson's imagination, and with the Baron's help he undertook the magnetic treatment of patients within the wards of University College Hospital. Fortunately, Elliotson's casebooks have been preserved, so that it is possible to trace the growth of his mesmeric conversion. One by one, patients are switched from conventional therapy to that of magnetic sleep, induced by passes made by the hand in front of the subject's face. But in almost every case the patients appear to suffer from what would now be classified as hysterical or functional illness. The most dramatic example of this is the case of two sisters, Elizabeth and Jane O'Key, who were admitted to the wards for the treatment of fits. With Dupotet's assistance, the girls were put into a magnetic trance, and in the first instance at least, appeared to undergo remission of their symptoms. The improvement was short-lived – not because the treatment was ineffectual exactly, but because it was to the advantage of both practitioner and patient to maintain a self-repeating cycle of complaint and treatment. This doesn't mean that there was any conspiracy or collusion between Elliotson and the O'Keys. Unconsciously, however, patient and practitioner satisfied complementary needs by their association in the magnetic relationship, and, in order to sustain this mutual dependence, the notion of cure gradually gave way to one of interminable treatment.

As with Charcot's famous patients at the Salpâtrière, the hysterical sisters flourished under the special attention which their behaviour in trance excited. As the custodian of a dramatic medical phenomenon, it would not have been in Elliotson's interests to cure and then discharge his colourful patients. Inevitably, therefore, the O'Keys became conditioned to show the signs which provoked Elliotson's approving curiosity, until, by means of an unspoken pact, patient and physician were locked inseparably together. The next stage was equally predictable in terms of what we now know about patient-doctor relationships. Whilst in the trance, the sisters began to acquire some of the transcendental abilities associated with clairvoyant mesmerism. According to the reports, they were able to visualize their own innards, and, as the trance deepened, their clairvoyance extended to the interiors of other patients. Before long, Elliotson was steering them around the wards, where they claimed to be able to diagnose the state of other patients' organs.[180] In this respect, the course of events closely follows the career pattern of the shaman, in which, as Professor Ioan Lewis has shown, a phase of involuntary possession, during which the subject is treated as a sufferer, is followed by a phase of repeated voluntary possession, at which point the subject graduates in the eyes of those around to the status of a shaman capable of supernatural vision or insight.

It is interesting to note that the O'Key sisters were not altogether unfamiliar with visionary experiences. In his memoir of Professor Elliotson, the then assistant editor of the *Lancet* pointed out that the girls had previously been members of Edward Irving's Catholic Apostolic Church in Regent Square.[181] The services of this sect were characterized by ecstatic interventions from the congregation, interventions in which the witness spoke in strange tongues – the so-called glossolalia. It is evident that the sisters were susceptible to hysterical fits of one sort or another, and unconsciously acquired the ability to enact them within a social context which assigned special importance to such behaviour. Naturally, the behaviour was subtly modulated in order to conform to the ideological requirements of the two sets of situation: in Regent Square they were Pentecostal prophets, whereas in Gower Street they became mesmeric shamans. Thus, as Professor Lewis points out, 'The link between affliction and its cure as the royal road to the assumption of the shamanistic vocation is plain enough.'[182] And in the case of the O'Key girls the course of events bears out his further thesis that such occurrences are frequently associated with socially unfortunate females, for whom the gradual assumption of prophetic power represents a fire-escape from a situation of intolerable social alienation. One is reminded once again of the miserable Miss Southcott.

By the spring of 1838, Elliotson was completely intoxicated by the situation, and the wards were in an uproar. He had become his own evangelist and was soon holding huge publicly-attended séances in the lecture theatre of the hospital. Fashionable London came in droves and he now set out to prove that the O'Keys were endowed with the ability to pick out mesmerically-magnetized coins and to see through walls.[183]

By this time the hospital authorities had become so outraged that they appealed to the Council of the College, who insisted that Elliotson break off the practice of animal magnetism and discharge the O'Keys.[184] Elliotson refused to obey, and resigned. During the last few months of the controversy he was ruthlessly mocked and criticized in the editorial columns of the recently-founded *Lancet*. Oddly enough, the author responsible for these attacks was a close personal friend of Elliotson, Thomas Wakley, a pioneer in medical journalism and a hard-headed radical who was obviously nauseated by the confused mysticism which he had detected beneath Elliotson's apparent materialism.[185] The point is that Elliotson was claiming the discovery of a new physical principle. Unlike his Neoplatonist friend Townshend, for whom the mesmeric phenomena bore witness to the existence of a transcendental reality beyond that of the physical senses, Elliotson insisted that animal magnetism merely extended the frontiers of physical reality to include a principle which operated according to the Laws of Newton. Like his successor William Crookes, Elliotson was claiming the existence of a previously unacknowledged force in nature. Wakley, however, was not impressed, and after a humiliating experiment which Wakley insisted on conducting at his own house, he showed to his own – and I think one must admit to our – satisfaction that the O'Keys' powers could all be accounted for in terms of the traditional five senses.

After his resignation from UCH, Elliotson did not retire hurt. He continued a prosperous practice and remained respected throughout the profession. His honesty had never been called into question. It is apparent from Thackeray's portrait of him in *Pendennis* (1848) that he struck those who knew him as a man of considerable intellectual stature, and his intellectual stature was matched by his warmth and compassion.[186] Throughout the 1840s he edited and largely wrote a periodical called the *Zoist*, subtitled 'A Journal of Cerebral Physiology & Mesmerism and their Application to Human Welfare.' In Elliotson's opinion, the study of the brain had stood still for at least 15 years, largely as a result of the obstinate refusal of the medical establishment to acknowledge the new science of mesmerism.

Other scientists agreed that the study of the brain had come to a standstill. In 1831, Sir David Brewster insisted that

> While new sciences have been created, and every other branch of knowledge has made the most extensive acquisitions, the philosophy of mind has almost remained stationary. [...] It has made no advances, and the whole of this extensive field, where experiment and observation might be so fitly and profitably employed, lies at this moment an uncultivated waste.[187]

According to Elliotson, the situation could only be repaired by paying serious attention to the phenomena of mesmerism. He forecast that the fruits of such research 'may transcend in value and utility all that man has yet dared to hope for from science.'[188] The pages of the *Zoist* are filled with accounts of animal magnetism used to effect dramatic cures and as an effective anaesthetic.

Given that Elliotson's assumptions are false or even meaningless, it is important to see what he made of them. He was convinced that the universal fluid existed, and that through its agency the brain could be brought to a state of unprecedented activity. If this heightened activity could be somehow perpetuated beyond the period of the trance, it might be possible to use cerebral physiology as a means for improving the moral and intellectual capacities of the human race. The millennial vistas were unlimited. 'Who,' says Elliotson, 'does not catch a glance of a mighty engine for man's regeneration, vast in its power and unlimited in its application, rivalling in morals the effects of steam in mechanics.'[189] In spite of editorial avowals, he was not really interested in descriptive physiology as such. What fascinated him was the possibility of engineering the improvement of society on the largest possible scale. Not through political upheaval, or by any of the radical manoeuvres which so alarmed the anxious liberals of the 1840s, but by improving the intellectual and moral faculties of the whole population. Before he became associated with mesmerism, Elliotson had been associated with Brougham's Society for the Diffusion of Useful Knowledge, with the foundation of Mechanics' Institutes, and with all those movements whereby it was hoped that social misery would be alleviated through the peaceful cultivation of the mind. In the light of these interests, the possibilities of mesmerism would obviously have been very intriguing. In place of the slow spread of useful and improving knowledge, improvements could now be pumped into society at high speed.

According to him, cerebral physiology indicated that certain people were predestined to exhibit socially unacceptable behaviour. They were victims of their own brains. But Elliotson, confirmed phrenologist and President of the London Phrenological Society, thought that it was possible to predict such tendencies by inspecting a man's skull. By combining the diagnostic finesse of phrenology with the cerebral influence of mesmerism, Elliotson supposed that criminal behaviour might be nipped in the bud. Once the location of the constructive instincts had been defined, these could be encouraged to the point where their heightened activity would outweigh any tendencies towards theft or murder. Prisons would be replaced by preventive clinics run on phreno-mesmeric lines.

Elliotson's utopian materialism found an echo in the work of Harriet Martineau. For someone devoted as she was to Comtean positivism – she was responsible for the first English translation of Comte – the utopian programme of mesmerism would have held an obvious appeal.[190] Miss Martineau arrived at her interest through the personal joy of a mesmeric cure. In 1839, while travelling abroad, this odd Unitarian blue-stocking suffered what sounds like a profound nervous depression, combined with a prolapsed uterus, which, as she wrote, consigned her 'to a life passed between my bed and my sofa.'[191] Lord Lytton recommended the use of mesmerism, and after a consultation with Spencer Hall, a travelling magnetist, she experienced the following: 'Something [diffused] itself through the atmosphere, – not like smoke, nor steam, nor haze – but most like a clear twilight, closing in from the windows and down from the ceiling and in which one object after another melted away.'[192] She added: '[An] improved composure of nerves and spirit has followed upon every mesmeric exhilaration.'[193] She wrote five long letters to the *Athenaeum* and these were published as a single volume, entitled *Letters on Mesmerism* (1844).[194] She became interested in the wider implications of animal magnetism, and, like Elliotson, Townshend and the others, emphasized its moral virtues: 'As far as I have any means of judging, the highest faculties are seen in their utmost perfection during the mesmeric sleep.'[195]

Nearly all mesmeric propaganda lays the same emphasis on the high spiritual tone achieved during the trance, and while this idea was partly introduced in order to offset the frequent accusations of immoral misuse of the new power, it is certain that the English mesmerists of the nineteenth century invested the subject with their highest spiritual hopes as they searched for certainties in a changing world. Hope springs eternal, it seems, and people are still searching. There is little to choose between Mesmer's magnetic bucket and Wilhelm Reich's orgone box: both rely on the notion that the universe is animated by a form of spiritual energy, whose exploitation will cure all.

Valete

Royal College of Physicians, Edinburgh, 29 August 1983[196]

For the eighth Edinburgh International Television Festival, Jonathan Miller was invited to deliver the keynote MacTaggart Lecture. His talk reflected on the prospect of multi-channel television and the current boom in home video, as well as broader observations informed by two decades of working in television.

I would like to say first of all that it is a great privilege to be allowed to lecture in memory of James MacTaggart, my distinguished late colleague in the BBC. I want to say also what a pleasure it has been working in this industry, although some of the remarks which will follow may in fact seem to undercut that claim.

I would like to begin by saying that I think it is extremely hard to identify any professional group which is more prone to parochial and pontifical introspection than the one which is assembled here this afternoon. I am not saying that this means that other groups fail to meet in order to discuss their shared interests. At the same time there is something quite peculiar and distinctive about the conventions which are attended by people in this particular media, if only because of the large amount of conjectural rhetoric that one hears on such occasions.

Now the problem I think is that, as the technology improves and multiplies, it creates, as in no other enterprise, an anxious sense of opportunities which might have been missed or abused.

What we have is a peculiar and in some ways quite unaccountable situation in which the credibility and self-confidence of the broadcaster is somehow related to his or her ability to fill stretches of time, as opposed to providing items of service. Now this doesn't mean of course that the attractiveness or worth of the items themselves is unimportant, but in the end the mere fact that an allotted time has to be filled begins to have an all-pervading influence on the service which is actually provided, and I think that it is this rather than any intrinsic feature of the medium which confers upon it most of its recognisable characteristics.

Moreover, I believe it is because the technology of the manufacture of images grew up within an industry and within a technology which in fact had also developed instantaneous radio transmission and got locked onto a news broadcasting device, that we actually got ourselves into the irreversible situation in which time had to be filled rather than items of service provided. I think the most obvious result of this linkage between the transmission and the manufacture of images is that we are now in a situation where we tend to manufacture material whose viability would be very hard to imagine if it had to be marketed item for item.

For example, I think it is quite unlikely that any of the quiz shows which fill up television would have survived if anyone had to go out and hire them in the form of cassettes or actually had to visit a cinema on an item for item visit. And I think that the same thing also goes for the serials which characterize television. I am thinking of things like *Coronation Street*. The unspeakable triviality of these shows, which seem negligible when the programmes are effortlessly available in the household setting, would, I think, become glaringly apparent and intolerable if someone had to make an explicit decision to fork out cash for them item by item.

You have to bear in mind, however, that over and above the effortless availability there is an added attraction of the transmission in this form, and that is due to the peculiar reward of knowing that one's experience of these items, trivia or otherwise, happens to be synchronized with that of innumerable and anonymous others. The 'did you see…?' phenomenon after which of course a television programme has been named.[197] I suspect that this is the main factor which makes the medium curiously, and I suggest irreversibly resistant to most of the efforts which have been made and will be made to market programmes that can be viewed as and when the individual requires it, either in the form of dialable cable, or in the form of purchasable cassettes.

Some people would say this is one of the more regrettable aspects of television. But I would also like to say that I believe that this also in some ways acts as a benevolent social consolidant. While in fact these things are trivial, their chronic availability and above all their *synchronized* availability in some way provides a medium through which in fact we feel ourselves part of a common community in modern industrial society. Those who regard it as a technique which will guarantee the consolidated idiocy of the society, believing that it is somehow emptied into a passive and unresisting nervous system of the great British public, I think overlook and underestimate the extent to which, when television is watched and experienced, it is actively being talked about, insulted, having things thrown at it. It is then discussed the next day so that it actually is itself subject to the scrutiny and criticism of those who have experienced it. So that the occasions which are broadcasts provide one of the media through which in fact we entertain social relationship with one another.

Trivial though *Dallas* might be, trivial though *Coronation Street* might be – and I am not entirely certain how trivial *Coronation Street* is, incidentally – trivial as they might be, they actually provide some sort of moral tale about which discussion might be convened, and therefore I think they represent an important part of social life. And this would not in fact be there if people had to purchase these programmes one by one and go out and get them. It is the chronic domestic availability of them which actually confers upon them this strangely benevolent, cohesive effect upon modern society.

I also think one has to consider the so-called serious programmes. I think the synchronized and chronic availability of serious programmes works to their advantage in a way which would not happen if they were not available in the way that they were. It would be very nice to think that if arts, science and documentary programmes were made for cassettes alone then their intrinsic worth, their intrinsic interest – whatever that means – would guarantee them a market, item for item. Again, I suspect that they wouldn't survive on the scale which would make it worthwhile anyone making them in the first place, and that much of their appeal lies in the very fact that they can be almost accidentally encountered, or they can be engaged without anyone having to consult an inventory of his or her previous interests. I think that those who look forward to the utopian freedom of choice, which is supposed to be ushered in by the development of cables and cassettes, again underestimate how hard it is for any one individual to identify all of his or her interests in advance and forget the extent one's interests themselves arise often as the result of being exposed to unsolicited experience.

In some paradoxical way it is the very triviality of what is made on television – the fact that you really don't have to care too much, that you do not have to consult something as painful as choice – that actually renders it so attractive. When, for example, the channels multiply, that in itself imposes a terrible burden of choice upon the viewer, who then has to think about what sort of person they are such that they might like this or that. The wonderful thing is to find one's interests developed by the absolutely unsolicited experience which you engage in, actually bumping up against the set and finding that that seems to be one which attracts your attention.

I would like now to talk a little bit about the so-called serious programmes and about what in fact happens as a result of their being on television. I believe amongst these unsolicited experiences which might or might not engage the interests of an audience, there are certain ones which seem to work intrinsically better than others. There is something intrinsic about the medium which somehow makes them work inevitably, and they are the ones which in fact exploit television for what it really is, which is a periscope.

Television can reach to places that no person can normally expect to get to in their lifetime, either for reasons of distance, inaccessibility, risk, scale, privacy, propriety or whatever. What television does is it acts as a periscope, as an endoscope, as a microscope and a telescope. It enlarges, it goes to smaller places than the eye can see, it goes into more distant places than normal people with normal finances can expect to get to. It goes to places that are riskier and more dangerous than any normal person can expect to get to. In that sense it provides us with an enormous enlargement of our personal experience.

But there are places where I think television falters. Although in fact very, very worthy efforts are made in this area and often extremely substantial achievements, television still falters. This is in the area which involves the promulgation and explanation of complex and abstract ideas. There are impressive achievements in scientific broadcasting and arts broadcasting, even historical broadcasting on television. But I believe there is a curiously unhappy and as yet unresolved relationship between imagery and words in these, which actually overlooks some sort of cognitive machinery that we don't yet quite understand about the relationship between words and pictures.

I believe that one of the moments when words and pictures seem to be happiest together is when in fact they are directly related to conversation and synchronized speaking faces or talking heads. These are much disparaged figures on television, but it is when talk is related to facial movement that it is in fact readily intelligible; in fact, that's what talk and vision were invented for. That's how we evolved. We evolved an increasing sensitivity to facial movement, to intonation and to lexical streams, and for that reason I think there are moments in scientific and in artistic broadcasting in which there are often strange sorts of slippage of understanding, precisely because I believe it is often not understood the extent to which these two modalities are addressing separate parts of the human brain – in fact, so separate that they are on opposite sides of the head. The right side of the brain is almost exclusively associated with the understanding and the decoding of instantaneous imagery, whereas the left side of the brain is more or less consistently and exclusively preoccupied with the decoding of sequential and particularly linguistic signals, and these two halves of the brain are not necessarily synchronized to one another. They operate at different rates because they are dealing with different cognitive modes. And there are moments, I believe, when there is a slippage between these two, when in fact you are probably alternating between the left hand side of the brain and the right hand side and actually nothing is coming across except a vague understanding, and then as you switch to the right side of the brain – as the imagery starts to work – you are actually failing to be decoding what is going on on the left side of the brain.

I believe that until there is much more sophisticated research about the way in which imagery and words can be used together, television will continue to falter at this, and even at the very best, the documentary, science and arts features will approximate to the conditions of articles in 'high life' magazines, at a fairly high level. And as one who has participated in programmes of this sort, I know this to my own embarrassment.

This brings me back to another point before I wind up. There are, I think, two areas in which television not merely falters but fails and also perhaps misses its aim altogether. There is, as I say, a curious insatiability of an image-making industry which is related to a transmission industry. When you actually have to fill allotted spaces of time, all material is potentially put-able on to the box. And as time goes on it becomes omnivorous and it casts around for material which was made for another genre altogether and I believe often disfigures it. Now, I would like to make the extremely debatable claim that the most conspicuous example of this is the one which in fact the BBC in particular preens itself on as being one of its highest achievements – and that is the making of the classic serial; the transformation of the novel into the dramatized serial.

I think that we will have to admit most of these represent major achievements in broadcasting, major achievements of acting, of directing and of art-historical accuracy. As time goes on they improve in almost every one of these respects, but I would suggest that paradoxically, as they improve, the failure, the *inevitable* failure of them becomes more apparent, and that becomes apparent for one very fundamental reason, which is to do with the distinction of genre. Novels are an absolutely untranslatable art form, except that is in the case of the trivial and the second-rate, when it doesn't matter what happens to them, and in fact being digested into the belly of television is probably the best thing that could happen to them. But in the case of what we would regard as the 'classic,' actually to identify it as such is to state the dilemma.

Once you have identified something as a classic, you have paradoxically identified it as the one thing which actually does not belong on television at all. Nor does it belong on film. That is because I believe somewhere in the back of the television programme-makers' mind there is a belief that novels are in fact plays unfortunately buried in a magma of unnecessary prose, and if only they could be chipped away and extracted from this material they would actually rise to their finest hour in the form of a television serial. This often involves, for example, not merely eliminating the descriptive prose with which the speeches are surrounded, but

199

supplying supplementary prose or supplementary speeches which were never spoken by the characters in question. Now, the reason why I think this is an absolutely broken-backed enterprise – one which in fact has misidentified the nature of the genre – is that novels are in fact works of art which cannot progress beyond the perspectives in which the genre itself exists. And this is something to do with the visibility of characters in novels and also about the nature of speech in novels.

It is an extremely interesting fact that when Flaubert was asked by one of his friends whether an illustrator could be provided for *Madame Bovary* (1856), he wrote to them fairly plainly that on no account must *Madame Bovary* ever be visualized by any one particular person, because if you had her in the form of an illustration, there you would have her fixed and unremittingly visual form which would forever fasten your image in that mode. It is part of the nature of the fictional character that they have this sort of provisional visibility which is never sustained, and the same also goes for the visibility of the décor – what is actually described around the character. I think, for example, of Jane Austen, where there are extremely perfunctory descriptions of scenery amongst which the characters move, and yet one is never conscious as one reads the novel that in fact they are not moving in the countryside at all and nor is this deficit made up by a series of images supplied by the reader. There are of course readers who in fact provide a florid supplementary series of images on their own, but there are just as many who live in the left hand side of their own brains rather than the right hand side, who do not in fact supply such images and are perfectly capable of extracting from the novel what the novelist intended by it.

Now, you might want to say, 'Ah…apart from the fact these things represent enjoyable achievements in their own right, this introduces people to the classics and that they are in fact invented for the people to go back to the book.' To which I will say the following: I believe first of all that aerosol versions of great works – in which is extracted what is believed to be the essence of George Eliot – these may persuade people to go back to the book, but they persuade people to go back to the book in a frame of mind which is not necessarily friendly to the reading of the book, because the book is now actually fraught with imagery which in fact was not originally provided. And it is not that you are surprised to find that Mr Knightley looks that way but more importantly that you are surprised to find that Mr Knightley has an appearance at all, and the fact that he has an unremitting appearance and goes on looking that way and on until the last titles start to roll. What is so wonderful about Dickens, for instance, is that quite suddenly one curious epithetic instance will be used; a detail will be plucked out of the air. For example, the rancid, molten fat stained with soot runs down the windows in *Bleak House* when the internal combustion has gone on in the room above.[198] First of all, that can never be realized on television, and if it was it would be absurd. Also, it would only be realized on television if you had to have the dreary rest of the window and the window frame and doors which would then have to be unremittingly present throughout the rest of the ghastly production.

Now let me say also that I am not trying to legislate and say, 'Let us make no more classic serials.' Rather, let's be quite clear what we are doing. We're making other forms of art which have got some sort of relationship to the original but should not be seen as faithful versions of them. In some paradoxical way, the more faithful they are, the more pedantically accurate they are, actually the less faithful they are in restoring the novel to its original form. It can only be restored by reading it. I believe that no matter what happens with television, one thing which will survive through all times is the book, precisely because of the peculiar unvisualized privacy of the experience. And this goes back to something which I have also raised when it comes to the science and the arts programmes. I believe that the difficulties of synchronizing argument and imagery are overcome in the book. In fact, when the illustrated book was introduced at the introduction of engraving – which could be set in the same form as the movable type – it actually introduced perhaps the ideal and unimprovable version of the transmission of audio-visual knowledge.

I would like to just briefly end by saying that there is one problem. It is less clear what the answer ought to be than the one which I rather arrogantly claim with regard to the novel. That is the problem of another form of art which was not intended for the box, and it is one in which I have been currently engaged in the last two years: do you take classic plays which were intended for another mode and put them on the box? After two years of having done it, I confess to a sort of embarrassed impotence about the possibility of doing Shakespeare on television. All right, as with a novel there is a sort of care-package missionary function – bails of literature to snowbound, distant people who otherwise wouldn't gain access to it. Nevertheless, I believe that in doing it some curious injury is done to the work in question. Not an irreversible injury, because in fact it is always possible to see them in the original context or to see them on the stage; but I believe doing works, particularly works from the sixteenth and seventeenth centuries, on television, actually has got insoluble problems associated with it. Some of which may be offset by the immediacy of speaking quietly to a camera immediately in front of you, but nevertheless it raises problems and it is again to do with visualization, particularly visualization of setting. It is well known Shakespeare wrote for an unfurnished stage, and he then lapsed after his death into 200 years of deplorable, picturey productions. The Georgian and the Victorian theatre swamped his works in visualization until the discovery of the drawing of the Globe playhouse and the work on the early quartos by William Poel. Until then, Shakespeare was in fact lost as a literary work. Poel identified them as essentially literary works, where in fact the visual setting was irrelevant to the play and in fact it would actually be unfriendly to the play; not merely because of difficulty changing cumbersome scenes, but also because it rendered visible what was not intended to be visible in precisely the same way as the novelist. I felt myself, in the course of the two years, that television inched irresistibly further and further towards increased pictorialization of these works on the box.

The reasons for which I will briefly outline. People say why would it not have been possible to have done all of the Shakespeare plays on television in this mammoth series – which in itself is a sign of the insatiability of television – why would it not have been possible to have mounted these in an abstract space, comparable to the abstract space in which Shakespeare set it upon the stage? And there has I think been only one instance, and I am thinking of Trevor Nunn's *Macbeth*, which has peculiarly come off, and I think that is probably unique to both *Macbeth* and possibly *King Lear* that they take place nowhere and nowhen.[199] But characters do not have to enter, they only have to appear. Almost every other one of Shakespeare's plays' entrances cannot be supplied merely by entering from the edge of a television screen; you have got to provide a setting. Now, on the bare unfurnished stage, entrances are understood – even on an unfurnished setting, because in fact you the audience are in a room which is actually geometrically related to the setting in which the action takes place. Someone arriving on the stage is framed by the proscenium arch which separates the audience from the playing space, so that entrance is quite clearly understood to be a walking entrance from off-frame/on-frame. Whereas if you were to set up something of that sort on the screen it would be complicated by the situation. If you were to try and realize for example the stage setting of Shakespeare – a comparable, bare stage-setting, which Poel rediscovered at the end of the nineteenth century for the theatre – you would have a double-framing device: you would have the framing device of the screen, which would be including a framing device which actually was known by the audience to be not including space in which they sat. There is no way of realising on a screen an abstract theatrical setting without creating this totally puzzling double setting of the screen frame and a theatrical frame, so that you find yourself therefore falling more and more towards the condition of the ordinary run of television drama.

So that you find gradually, as you start to put these kinds of plays on television, that you start to produce a sixteenth- or seventeenth-century mode which actually starts to work against the play in precisely the same way that Poel identified the pictorial hostility of the work of the eighteenth- and nineteenth-century producers. So I believe that there is perhaps no viable solution with Shakespeare. The only final virtue to be identified in doing these things for television is that it introduces a larger number of people to these plays than would otherwise happen, but it also I believe does exactly the same as the dramatization of the novel does. It introduces people once again to the regrettable belief that the works fall below par if they are not seen in the visual mode, so that they return to the theatre now disappointed by the fact that the theatre does not live up to the pictorial glamour that television provided. In other words, it produces once again a disjunction, a failure of understanding of the genre of the work. Perhaps this is one of the reasons I am finally leaving television altogether, along with the theatre.[200] And that is the point at which I would like to end, except that I would like, as I say, to give thanks to the people who allowed me to work in this medium for 20 years, and in particular, though he is not here tonight, to Huw Wheldon, who unwisely and very generously offered me the opportunity of editing *Monitor*, when I really came to him to ask if I could be allowed to make documentary films.

Native medicine

The Body in Question, BBC2, 15 January 1979[201]

In the mid-Seventies, Miller was invited to research and present a 13-part documentary series for BBC2 with the same intended prestige as Kenneth Clark's Civilisation *(1969) and Jacob Bronowski's* The Ascent of Man *(1973). The result was Miller's history of medicine and ideas,* The Body in Question. *Here, in the ninth episode, the presenter took a departure from Western thought in order to investigate tribal medicine.*

The Sudan is the largest country in Africa. It extends nearly 2,000 miles from the Muslim north to the equatorial jungle in the south, and it includes a great variety of tribal groups. For many years, the Sudan was a British protectorate, and for that reason many Sudanese became the subjects of early anthropological study. One of the first groups to be studied were the Azande in the south.

In the early 1920s, a young English anthropologist called Edward Evans-Pritchard came to live with them, and shared their life to a remarkable extent. He shared their food, he went hunting with them, he participated in their recreations, and learnt their language. Before long, he noticed what was for him a rather peculiar attitude to misfortune and illness. He noticed that the Azande tended to blur the distinction between the two; it was not that they failed to see the difference between, say, a broken granary or a crop failure on the one hand, and, say, an injured foot on the other, but that, as far as they were concerned, both types of misfortune had the same cause: personal malice on the part of friends, neighbours or relatives.

According to the Azande, this malice was the result either of witchcraft or of sorcery. In the West, we tend to use these two terms quite interchangeably, but Evans-Pritchard noticed that for the Azande they were quite distinct. A witch was someone born with a 'witch-organ' – a large cyst, which they claimed could be found in a post-mortem attached to the underside of the liver. When the witch became angry with someone, the cyst enlarged, became hot and broadcast its malignant influence abroad. It was quite involuntary and it was that that distinguished it from sorcery, since a sorcerer was someone who could skilfully manipulate potions, incantations, spells and medicines for the express purpose of causing injury, illness or misfortune.

The identification of witches and sorcerers is usually made by consulting the Benge, or poison oracle. As with any other oracle, the Benge's way of solving mysteries is by asking questions in a yes/no fashion. He administers a strychnine-like poison to a chick to see if the poison works. Grasping the chick between his toes, he murmurs magical encouragements while he drip-feeds the trial dose – inviting it, as it were, to prove its effectiveness by killing the chick. The magical character of what goes on is emphasized by the murmured spells which somehow encourage the poison to do its work. If the chicken dies, the poison is effective and the oracle is ready for use.

Even before he starts this, he has to prepare himself by abstaining from fish, red meat and sexual intercourse. In all magical procedures, there seems to be a special value in performing them on the margins of ordinary life.

Evans-Pritchard reported this 50 years ago, and when I went to the Sudan, I half-expected the oracles to have died out.[202] But, within three days, several old men offered to show me exactly how they worked. Although the villagers were at first embarrassed to admit that anyone now made use of such techniques, as soon as it was known that skilled practitioners were in the area, the local population flocked to the village. The local chief had arranged for the skills of a witch-doctor to be demonstrated as well, so all sorts of hopeful sufferers converged on the jungle clearing. One man – John Casena – had walked 12 miles for diagnosis of his swollen face.

The witch-doctor is a diagnostic expert, a doctor who finds witches by consulting his own imagination, which is stirred into action with a frenzy of dancing and drumming. He also has to observe a fixed procedure, and can only practise after a long apprenticeship. He, too, must prepare and purify himself and, unless he wears a proper uniform, his diagnosis will be invalid; even the rhythm of the drums has to be at exactly the right tempo.

The witch-doctor could apparently find no cause for John Casena's illness in this village, so the village chief, Chief Andrea, called for John Casena to come and tell his own story through an interpreter. His condition was obviously very painful, and I found myself lapsing into the Western mode of medical inquiry by asking questions about the physical cause of the facial swelling.

When he first became ill, he consulted the Benge oracle; the poison oracle consulted the chicken; and the chicken oracle, when asked questions, proved that this was the second of Evans-Pritchard's two categories of misfortune – that is, caused by someone making bad medicine. He then consulted a witch-doctor, who made the same diagnosis and said that this was the result of sorcery, or bad magic, rather than witchcraft.

Now, I think that the young man had a septic inflammation of the salivary glands – the ones which get swollen up in mumps – which sounds as if it spread from bad teeth. We could treat this with a Western antibiotic, but not wanting to interfere, one would have to do it through their system and consult the Benge to see whether Western medicine would be as much help as the medicine locally.

The old man and his poison oracle were still in the forest clearing, and in spite of the fact that so much care had been taken to test the poison, the old man seemed to be completely unconcerned that this chicken was twice the size of his test sample. Once again, there was a ceaseless recitation, this time including a rhythmic repetition of Casena's name. For those who practise magic, words are physical instruments – they *cause* things to happen, and the skilful mastery of these spells and techniques is held in high esteem.

Well, the chicken lived after all, so that meant that my medicine would not work. If the chicken had died, then it would have worked. So that's one in the eye for English medicine.

The Benge is the most important of a number of oracles, though not all of them involve the use of an expert. The Dappa – or termite oracle – can be used by anyone, rather like a Western thermometer. Inside a heap of hardened mud live the local termites, whose life is periodically interrupted by having two sticks – one sweet and one sour – thrust into their nest. The Azande warn the termites that the sticks are coming, and the insects are invited to nibble one or other of the two sticks to choose between questions which are then put to them.

Here the essential feature is the lapse of time. The skill is in reading the result and in knowing which stick has been nibbled. This kind of oracle is used to decide things like the best place for planting next year's crops, or the most profitable day to mount a hunting expedition. Like tossing a coin, it is a heads or tails result, and while we make only occasional use of such hit-and-miss guidance, the Azande will not take important decisions without consulting one or other of these oracles.

The third and most familiar oracle, the Iwe, or rubbing-board, relies on the same principle, although it produces a much quicker read-out. After moistening the surface of a small, polished tripod, the operator begins to rub it with another piece of polished wood. While he rubs, he asks his question, instructing the Iwe to stick after the third rub, for example, if the answer is yes.

The everyday tasks of Azande life are fraught with possibility of accident and misfortune. If, for instance, a well-made granary inexplicably falls down, witchcraft or sorcery are immediately suspected, and the oracles would be called into play. While to most people it would seem irrational to attribute all illness or injury to witchcraft or sorcery, the point is that our criteria of success and failure simply do not apply to the Azande. For them, magic is something which accompanies every aspect of life – it is as natural as breathing. Just as we throw salt over our shoulder, or avoid walking under a ladder, so they have productive and protective rites which accompany every single one of their important daily activities. So, naturally, the onset of illness automatically raises suspicions of witchcraft or sorcery.

If the magic does not work, there is always a standby explanation: perhaps the rituals were not observed in the right order, or the operator did not abstain from red meat or from sexual intercourse. In any case, no single episode of failure can do anything to undermine the overall belief in magic as a whole. One of the things that Evans-Pritchard found was that the idea of magic and witchcraft and sorcery were so all-pervasive, so total, that there was no way in which he could prove to his Azande hosts that they were wrong:

> I have often been asked whether, when I was among the Azande, I got to accept their ideas about witchcraft. This is a difficult question to answer. I suppose you can say I accepted them; I had no choice. In my own culture, in the climate of thought I was born into and brought up in and have been conditioned by, I rejected, and reject, Azande notions of witchcraft. In their culture, in the set of ideas I then lived in, I accepted them; in a kind of way I believed them. Azande were

talking about witchcraft daily, both among themselves and to me; any communication was well-nigh impossible unless one took witchcraft for granted. You cannot have a remunerative, even intelligent conversation with people about something they take as self-evident if you give them the impression that you regard their belief as an illusion or a delusion. Mutual understanding, and with it sympathy, would soon be ended, if it ever got started. Anyhow, I had to act as though I trusted the Azande oracles and therefore to give assent to their dogma of witchcraft, whatever reservations I might have. If I wanted to go hunting or on a journey, for instance, no one would willingly accompany me unless I was able to produce a verdict of the poison oracle that all would be well, that witchcraft did not threaten our project; and if one goes on arranging one's affairs, organizing one's life in harmony with the lives of one's hosts, whose companionship one seeks and without which one would sink into disorientated craziness, one must eventually give way, or at any rate partially give way. If one must act as though one believed, one ends in believing, or half-believing as one acts.[203]

Six thousand miles away, in Britain, people fall ill in much the same way. Like the Azande, they regard physical illness as something which they would rather do without. Most patients, like their African counterparts, would have treated minor ailments on their own, using simple remedies obtained without the advice or authority of an expert. But when the illness is serious or prolonged, they also seek specialized help.

For the African, medicine is called into existence when the occasion demands. Here, sufferers present their complaints to a standing institution which presupposes the continuing existence of illness in society. The very existence of such an institution means, perhaps, that British patients are less stoical about their misfortunes and discomforts.

For us, it may be the expert who recognizes that something is wrong in a person who believes himself to be healthy. A medical survey, for example, may detect an unsuspected abnormality in a routine blood sample so that someone may become a patient automatically without having a symptom to complain about.

The Azande would find it very hard to understand the concept of having an illness without being aware of it, and the thought of consulting an oracle without apparently having a problem to put to it would seem quite unintelligible. For example, one of the Western doctor's oracles, the ECG, works on completely different principles from those used by the Azande.

For one thing, the ECG provides information about the patient's body rather than his social relationships. And although there seems to be no obvious connection between the skin of the ankles, say, and the state of the heart, there is an underlying theory which connects the two, which allows the doctor to read the tracing and visualize an organ which he cannot actually see.

For the Western physician, illness is a process in time – not just an episode; it has a biography within the life of the patient, so there is always something to be learnt by following its progress at regular intervals even when the patient is apparently healthy. This may involve the doctor pursuing the patient – an idea which the Azande would find incomprehensible and perhaps even frightening.

In a long lifetime a Western patient can accumulate a fat volume of medical history, and such records are an essential prerequisite of accurate diagnosis. One illness may affect the course of a later one, and several separate symptoms may represent the continuing development of one disease. One could say, in fact, that one of the things that alters the prospects of a modern patient is not so much new drugs or new treatment, but the new conscientiousness about his past.

As things stand, the medical profession cannot cure illnesses like chronic arthritis. However, regular observation gives the patient the comfort of knowing that the doctor has his interests at heart, and that he is not simply being thrown into a limbo of incurable solitude. In any case, most doctors recognize that physical examination is often a treatment in its own right.

For all the technical skills of doctors, much of their effectiveness as healers depends on the confidence which is extended to them by their patients. And although this confidence is partly a question of a good track-record, the personal aura of a particular doctor is just as important.

The reason why the prospects of a patient in Britain are so different from those of John Casena is that the physician sees beneath the surface of the personal situation and visualizes, not malice and not witchcraft, but an interconnected system of organs and processes whose errors result in a consistent pattern of unwellness. And this is the cutting edge of modern Western medicine: the patient entrusts his personal unwellness to the collective wisdom which is invested in his family physician.

Although it is now fashionable to assume that there is some neglected wisdom in primitive medicine, that magic herbs, oracles and spells acknowledge some mystical unity of nature which Western medicine has arrogantly overlooked, the fact remains that it is only in the last 40 years that human beings have gained any control over their own health and well-being; and that this control is not the result of interfering with, but of understanding nature so that we can work hand in hand. Science, then, is not a blasphemy on humanity, although the wanton rejection of it is.

Producing opera
Interviewed by Harold Rosenthal
Opera, October–November 1977[204]

ROSENTHAL: I think we ought to start by knowing what it was that attracted you to the world of opera.

MILLER: I think almost the invitation to do one. I don't think I ever thought in the first place of opera. I was involved in directing plays and I suppose I began to get an idea that it would be nice simply to extend myself into another area of drama, and when someone invited me to come and do an opera it seemed like a nice idea.

ROSENTHAL: What was the first opera you were asked to do then?

MILLER: Britten's *Noye's Fludde* which I did at the Roundhouse, with an enormous number of children.[205] Then I was asked by the New Opera Company to do Sandy Goehr's *Arden Must Die*[206] and I enjoyed it so much that I felt, wouldn't it be nice to go on and do some more of it. It was very much the same way in which I drifted into the theatre.

ROSENTHAL: The world of opera and the world of theatre are so different – both artificial in their way, but is not one more artificial than the other?

MILLER: Well, I don't think so. I think that people overstress the differences between the drama and the opera drama. They are both artificial forms of representation, and of course music is what the opera is about, but they are musical *dramas* – they are plays which use, and are expressed through, music. And that of course makes very special conditions which you ignore at your peril. But, finally, what you are doing is making human situations through the medium of either speech or song.

ROSENTHAL: Is it not more difficult to realize the situations through a singer who, as well as having to act, must have a second part of himself thinking about the vocal side?

MILLER: I think that in great works of musical theatre, the singing is a spontaneous expression of the drama and it's almost inseparable. You don't experience a separate feeling that you have to first of all take care of the singing and then to take care of the acting. The acting and the singing are one and the same thing, and if you pay attention to what is dramatic in the music you will automatically take care of what is musical in the drama.

ROSENTHAL: So you do not subscribe to the rather commonly held idea that singers, on the whole, are rather stupid people who have been blessed with a voice and have been put onto a stage to do things that actors could do rather better.

MILLER: No, I think that singers are actors with a very special talent. I think there are certain institutional conditions of the opera which have, perhaps, stupefied singers; long practice of a particular form of opera may have stupefied their dramatic abilities. But if you have young, talented singers, they are, in fact, singing-actors.

ROSENTHAL: Have you never had a situation where a singer has said 'Look, you are asking me to do something impossible at this moment, because I can't breathe or I can't produce a tone that the score demands'?

MILLER: That has never happened to me. It is physiological common sense really. I mean, one doesn't hang people upside down to sing things; you don't tell them to sing while bent double, but, apart from that, common sense dictates what they must be doing. There are very few situations where a good singer can't sing. He'll tell you soon enough if he can't – and it's a matter for negotiation.

ROSENTHAL: How different is it for you, as a director in the straight theatre, to plan an opera production? Are the mechanics the same if you are doing a play at the Royal Shakespeare or the Aldwych?

MILLER: I think the mechanics of opera production are indistinguishable from the mechanics of a theatrical production. There is no difference at all – absolutely none. There are occasional awkwardnesses, perhaps, arising from the fact that the orchestra pit has got to be lit, and there may be moments in fact when you need a blackout and the leak of light that you get upsets the lighting balance on the stage. I suppose there are occasional awkwardnesses about being able to see the conductor, but I've never really found that that has got in the way of the drama.

ROSENTHAL: What about the time element? Is there much difference in the length of time needed to put on a new play or a new opera?

MILLER: I think that the time element is the same in each. The only thing that sometimes makes an opera production perhaps a little more lengthy than a straight theatre production is that you often have large choruses, and the organization and man-management of a large chorus is time-consuming. But otherwise it's the same, and there is a sense in which there's a tremendous release as a result of the music, because the music dictates stage directions so often that you might otherwise spend weeks trying to find out for a play. You know how many bars you've got to get someone across a stage or out of the room and so forth, and that actually is a tremendous relief.

ROSENTHAL: When you are planning a production of an opera, if there is a recording do you plan it having played the records or listened with the score?

MILLER: Yes, I plan always from records. I have to do that – I don't read music, and I don't think I ever will. I can see roughly what's happening by looking at the score but I certainly can't read the music, so therefore I'm at a disadvantage when it comes to a new opera which hasn't been recorded and I have to have it played through and sung at me for a while before I know what's going on. I think people again vastly overstress the advantages of being able to read music. There are certain drawbacks from time to time when I can't identify for a singer, when I'm talking to them, where it is that I want them to do something; it means that I haven't got a notation for referring to that moment in the music, but I can usually sing the bit I'm referring to and show them then. People say if you don't read music then you're not understanding the expression. Well, if that was the case then all human expression before writing came in would have been incoherent and this is simply not true. Music is like any human utterance and is designed to be heard, and the very fact that there happens to be a notation on paper is, in a sense, incidental. You learn what the expression or the utterance is by listening to it, and being musical is not really a matter of being familiar with the grammar of tonality or whatever; nor do I think it's easy to specify what musical sensitivity is – you can't print out the recipe for it. I think that I'm sensitive to what's going on in a piece of music; what it expresses is really, again, a matter for negotiation, and since there is a great deal of disagreement about what music expresses amongst those who *can* read music, I don't think my claims to say what it expresses are any the less valid than someone who actually reads the notes on the stave.

ROSENTHAL: The arrival in the world of opera of the man of the theatre probably dates from Max Reinhardt's being invited by Strauss to come and salvage *Der Rosenkavalier* at Dresden for the premiere; and the idea of a theatre director coming into the opera house began in pre-World-War-One Germany in 1911 or 1912, and then became established in Germany more than in any other country.

MILLER: Yes. Of course, that is not in fact much later than the advent of the director into the theatre. In the 1870s the Duke of Saxe-Meiningen introduced the idea of the director as a controller of the *Gesamtkunstwerk*; this in fact was an innovation.[207] Things were done much more haphazardly by stage managers and the leading actor, who controlled what was going to happen, and I think probably the same thing happened very much in opera. It's just simply a little bit later in opera. It's been held up in this country for reasons that are very hard to elucidate.

ROSENTHAL: The first time it really happened consciously in this country was in 1934 at Glyndebourne when Ebert and Busch between them came and established the *Gesamtkunstwerk*, as far as Mozart was concerned, and this was something entirely new; that, plus the visit of the Dresden State Opera to Covent Garden in 1936, opened everybody's eyes to the fact that opera was rather more than just a concert in costume.

MILLER: It is *Gesamtkunstwerk* or it's nothing; and what one has to do is act as some kind of chairman bringing together all the imaginative currents that make great opera into a dramatic experience, and that means, in fact, very close and subtle and humble cooperation with a composer if he's alive – and if he is not, with a conductor – and an ability to feed the currents from the visual arts and from other branches of literature as well, until finally, in addition to being music, opera is literature.

ROSENTHAL: The reason why any great work of art survives is because it's valid at any time for many people. So when you produce an opera, or direct an opera, do you feel that you must look at it from the viewpoint of the 1970s, or do you try to put it in its chronological context?

MILLER: I think one has to do the two things at the same time. All great works of the past which have an afterlife survive through renewal. There's no such thing as survival in its original form. All performing arts, all works of reproductive art, have to be reproduced anew every time. There is absolutely no way in which you can simply forge the original version; and even when you do try to forge it, you unconsciously introduce ideas and interests of your own time. We see this in the visual arts in the history of forgery; each forgery of a given picture introduces another layer of interpretation, even when someone is trying to reproduce the original work. So therefore what you get in fact is a very subtle and complicated compound of the context in which the work was produced, which you have to honour and investigate, plus the ideas which interest you at this particular moment in that work. It has got to grab the imagination of an audience living today. Now, that does not mean that you have to frogmarch the work out of its context into the twentieth century and make it relevant. 'Relevance' is one of the most ghastly words which ever comes up in the arts. All great works are bound to be relevant because they deal with fundamental and inextinguishable human situations which are the same in any period, but nevertheless you have got to refer to and honour the tone of the historical period in which it was created. But at the same time you have to animate the work in such a way that it is accessible and interesting, dramatic and engaging for a modern audience.

ROSENTHAL: Criticism is often levelled at opera directors today that they are apt to ignore the instructions written by the composer or librettist in the score. I myself do not feel very strongly about this. I think it is perfectly valid to ignore certain instructions and to introduce things yourself, if you feel that they are going to work into your concept and are valid for the piece in hand. What is your feeling about that?

MILLER: I think it's a most complicated problem. Again, there is no rule of thumb that you can apply. I think if you say that you must obey all the instructions, you do that at your peril; to say ignore all the instructions is equally perilous. What I think you have to do is to rely on your own discretion, and tact, and trust that your imagination will be nourished by the interesting things that the composer or librettist has said; one must also be confident in your belief that there may be things that could make the work more interesting now than it might have been if we simply obeyed what was written then. But you cannot write out a formal prescription for what you must do about the instructions written in a libretto. Very often the instructions are not actually written down – very often the instructions are implied in the score. If you listen to what Mozart is actually saying – not in what he (or his librettist) writes in the score as stage directions, but what he actually writes in the notes – you can generally tell when someone must turn, when someone must enter, when someone must embrace. There are phrases which melt, phrases which restrain, phrases which are themselves stage instructions; it may well be that the composer is wiser in his musical instructions than he is in his stage instructions, and who's to say which, in fact, one is to attend to? I think in the end you simply have to say, 'I'm going to attend to all the instructions that are written and I will make my choice about which ones are going to be most profitable.'

ROSENTHAL: As someone who says they are not a musician – you say you do not read music – I think that is one of the most musically satisfying answers I've heard from an opera producer.

MILLER: Great music is, in some strange and obscure way, expressive. I say obscure because it is very hard to say what it expresses and exactly

215

what it specifies. But it quite clearly does indicate something, and there are moments, in fact, when there is a compulsion in the music and you ignore that, really, at your peril. It isn't just simply a question of the music going faster or that it's in a minor key at a certain point. There are moments when cadences resolve in certain ways and they tell you how to resolve a phrase of movement as much as the phrase of sound – and all human movement is phrased as much as music is. I often tell singers this when I'm working with them, and when they sometimes resist what they think of as dance movements, I say, 'Well, look, regard your body and your vocal cords as part of one muscle: this is the system which you use for expressing yourself.' If you can sing expressively you're bound to be able to move expressively, and when you're moving and not singing, that movement is as much a musical expression as the moment when you're singing, and it's a way of extending the musicality, in a sense, rather than restricting it. Everything one does with one's body is capable of musical expression, and if there's musical expression eloquently put down in the score, there must be things which the body must do in response to it.

*****

ROSENTHAL: I suppose you've been lucky in the half-dozen or so operas that you've directed so far, because they span the operatic spectrum from Monteverdi (*Orfeo*),[208] through Mozart (*Così fan Tutte*)[209] via Verdi (*Rigoletto*)[210] to the moderns – to Janáček,[211] and to a gifted young contemporary composer in Alexander Goehr[212]…taking in Sullivan, by the way!

MILLER: I've been very fortunate in that way – it was partly by calculation. I do think that there are certain salient great works which it's worth working on. You feel yourself transfigured by having the privilege of working with such pieces. I don't know how I'd react to an opera which didn't produce this sense of transfiguration in me, and so far I have been very fortunate.

ROSENTHAL: In your approaches to all these pieces we have mentioned and to other pieces that you might well do in the future, the literary and artistic background of the period obviously plays a very important part in the way you plan your productions.

MILLER: This, in a sense, is what I feel as a neurologist, if you like. The human brain organizes and integrates the channels of the senses. What comes from the eye and the ear and the understanding are brought together in one common sense, and if you allow one to dominate, you're lost. What we are as human creatures are organisms that express and receive the world *in toto*. It's a seamless whole and I think to emphasize one at the expense of the other is actually almost a blasphemy. I think all works of any size or complexity reproduce the tones, the interest, the preoccupations of a period. Certain emphases are stronger at one time than they are at another, but I think that when the moral teaching becomes explicit then what you have is dull; but there is a sense, of course, in which all great art recommends certain conduct. *Orfeo*, after all, recommends restraint and submission as opposed to the unleashing of the passions, but it does it in such a subtle and complex way that you can't say that it is, as it were, a moral rearmament treatise on chastity; and who would wish to say that *La Traviata* was advice to a girl to behave well? Obviously there *are* complex recommendations written into the work – one doesn't come away from it feeling that one has been given a pamphlet in the street.

ROSENTHAL: Do you think that Dumas and Verdi would have produced *La Dame aux Camélias* and *Traviata* if the social conditions and conventions of that period hadn't existed?

MILLER: No, I think that each work tells you what people thought was commendable at any given time and what *we* think is commendable or despicable, obviously, is different from what they did. Their recommendations may be slightly different to ours, but nevertheless in the great works of art the part played by explicit recommendation is very small and it is subtly incorporated into the expression itself. One doesn't ever come away from a great work of art thinking that one has been given a series of precepts about how to behave.

ROSENTHAL: Returning for a moment to *Traviata* – obviously a production of that opera, especially in Victorian England, would have stressed the morality of Germont *père*'s case, whereas today our sympathies are all for Violetta; and so in producing a piece like *Traviata*, or other works of that genre, one is obviously conditioned by the morals and climate of 'today.'

MILLER: Yes, one's emphasis falls upon the motives of Germont *père*. One begins to say, 'Well, what did this man actually want? Does he want what he appears to want? Is it simply a relationship based on wishing that the girl would refrain from pestering his son, or is he, in fact, falling in love with the girl himself?' It's just that we have become slightly subtler about our view of human motives. We perhaps take human behaviour slightly less at its face value than they would have done in the nineteenth century, where they had slightly oversimplified and often very sentimental views of human motive. Now, you could well say that by introducing this idea of Germont possibly having designs upon her, or falling in love with her, you would be violating Verdi's original intention. Well, it might well be that Verdi had got these intentions without explicitly knowing them; and in a great work of art there are dark undertones, there are shadows, there are ambiguities, there are complexities which are perhaps not often on the surface. I use the musical metaphor of overtones, in that in addition to the tonic there are all sorts of other notes being played, and when you produce the work you may in fact – as a conductor does – bring up the instrument which is playing those other harmonics. They have to be there for you to bring them out, but if you impose them from without you do so at your peril. Anyone who is sensitive to the complexities of moral situations invariably finds in a great work of art that there are ambiguities and other things at work over and above what appears on the surface.

ROSENTHAL: I'm longing for your *Traviata* production, whenever that may be.[213] The operas that you've so far chosen to produce might almost be described as domestic pieces; but what is your attitude to the larger-than-life operas – the big, so-called 'grand' operas: *Aida*; the historical dramas like *Don Carlos*; or, on the next scale, Wagner and the Gods?

MILLER: I think that, as in the dramas, operas divide themselves fairly distinctly into two groups. I perhaps wouldn't use the word 'domestic' to describe operas which work on a comparatively small scale; I would say that they are directly and recognisably moral and that they deal with recognizable and realistic individuals and, although they are sometimes painted on a large historical canvas as in *Don Carlos*, nevertheless – as in Shakespare – you can recognize definite man-sized individuals who are in conflict with one another. For example, in *King Lear* the thing is apparently painted on an enormous scale, but really what impresses you is – to use your own word – the domesticity of the relationship. These are about fathers and daughters, and husbands and wives, and lovers, and that is the human scale. Then there are the works which produce mythical stereotypes, where the people on the stage are not necessarily to be seen as individuals but represent forces, parts of people; they represent certain aspects of a personality rather than *a* personality. When you are dealing with that, a different idiom of production and direction has to take over. *The Magic Flute*, for example, is not like *The Marriage of Figaro*. *The Magic Flute* has a series of extremely elaborate symbolic relationships about parts of the human personality in relationship to a tradition drawn from alchemy, and from the Hermetic mysteries, and from the Rosicrucian movement of the seventeenth and eighteenth centuries. You cannot hope to present *The Magic Flute* as a story of real people, whereas that is the only way in which one can represent the story of *The Marriage of Figaro*. *The Marriage of Figaro* is domestic in the true sense – not in the sense that it is 'kitchen sink,' but it takes place in a household and is the conflict of people who are the same size as all of us. Mozart makes them larger than us because he magnifies them through his art, but nevertheless they are still on the human scale. The figures that take part in *The Magic Flute* and, of course, in Wagner, are in fact mythical stereotypes. They represent either gigantic forces in nature or the personification of aspects of human behaviour – lust, power, avarice, self-sacrifice and so forth.

ROSENTHAL: From what we have talked about, it would seem that opera – because of its very complexity, embracing as it does theatre, music, the visual arts – is, in its way, more demanding on an audience than the straight theatre. I often feel that and I wonder whether opera audiences are more reactionary, if you know what I mean, because very often they are so unsophisticated.

MILLER: I think they are no less sophisticated than the average visitor to the National Gallery or the Louvre. If you stand in the National Gallery of an afternoon and watch the tourists hastening past the great works, they are looking at them often for illustration, pretty colours, or familiar images. They go to see the famous painting, or they go to see nice colours, or a pretty scene; and this, in a sense, is to diminish what the work is. So I don't think that opera, in particular, is abused in this way. The arts in general are very often abused in that people think that they are things that can be casually visited. I think that one can no more casually visit a great work of art than one can drop in on the communion service. You actually have to take the blood and body of the artist and experience, if you like, the transubstantiation that takes place in great art. It is an act of the Eucharist, really.

ROSENTHAL: In that case, do you not feel that the most important function a critic can perform is to help educate the public (i.e. the audience) to know what a work of art is about, rather than criticize minutely what a performer is doing on stage?

MILLER: Absolutely. I think that the critic stands in relationship to the work in almost the same way that the director does. The director's work is an act of creative criticism – it's an act of interpretation. The critic by presenting his piece is really doing a production without a performance – or he should be; and therefore he should bring as much imagination from as many sources to bear on his act of criticism as the director brings to bear on the actual production. The act of criticism is as much a *Gesamtkunstwerk* as the act of production, and therefore it is his job to interpret, demonstrate the sources – show, in fact, what is at work in what he has seen and heard.

ROSENTHAL: In other words, the opera critic ought to be something much more than just a music critic; a music critic doesn't always make a good opera critic. An opera critic ought to be informed about and keep pace with the developments in the theatre; know something about the visual arts.

MILLER: It isn't simply *knowing* about it. He has also to be as responsive and conscious of what a picture means, so that he can respond to what he sees on a stage as much as to what a piece of music means. It's no good just simply saying, 'Oh, I recognized a picture by Fragonard.' You have to say why the picture by Fragonard is actually relevant in this particular case – and why Fragonard rather than Boucher, for example, and whether or not it might have been better to have used Claude rather than Poussin. I don't think critics bring as much subtlety and discrimination to their visual statements as they do to their musical statements.

ROSENTHAL: Do you think it might be a good idea for a drama critic, who at least is not tone deaf and enjoys music, as well as a music critic to be invited to review an opera?

MILLER: In fact, I find on the few occasions when musically sensitive drama critics have talked about productions of mine, that I've got much more value from what they've said – even when they have disagreed. For example I had a piece written by John Morgan in the *New Statesman* on the *Così fan Tutte* that I did. He expressed certain disagreements, but they were interesting and informed and rather muscular disagreements based on his response to the literature of *Così fan Tutte*, the music of *Così fan Tutte*, and also the appearance of the production. I think there is a sort of stunning parochiality about musical criticism and opera criticism; some critics still write about opera performances as if the singers on stage were accidentally dressed up in costumes, and they were really listening to a lot of canaries.

ROSENTHAL: And not only critics, but lots of the audience! I think there are two kinds of opera audiences: the audience that goes to Covent Garden on smart nights, dressed up to the nines, and wants to hear A, B and C sing their top notes; the other audience, that will go to Covent Garden for *Jenůfa*, or *The Ice Break*, or to the English National Opera on most nights – they go to see a *work*, not just to hear A, B or C sing.

MILLER: This is exactly the same as you get in the great cathedrals; there are the dutiful gentry who appear in the great boxes at the front in order to be seen at an act of prayer, and there are the genuinely and enthusiastically pious who in fact recognize the Eucharist for what it is. Now it may be very pompous to say that art, and the participation in art, is in the nature of a sacrament, but I feel that in the end one has either to acknowledge that it is a sacrament or it's simply Olympic Games.

ROSENTHAL: Despite all these questioning statements and your feelings, you'll still go on, working if you can, in this amazing world of opera?

MILLER: Oh yes, I would like to go on as long as I've got breath in my

221

body. It's a totally fulfilling occupation and, of course, finally, a thing which I don't think people understand enough. It's in a way a very trivial thing, and being allowed to produce an opera is really like being licensed to go on playing with one's toys until one's an old man.

Self-recognition
On Reflection, 1998[214]

In 1998, Miller curated Mirror Image, *an exhibition at the National Gallery which focused on the pictorial representation of reflection. In this extract from the accompanying book, he considers the ability to recognize oneself.*

In 1886 the Austrian physicist Ernst Mach sat down in a *chaise longue* and drew a simplified sketch of everything he could see with one eye closed and the other fixed on a point at the far end of his room. In many respects the drawing is a misleading representation of what someone would see under such conditions. As we have already seen, the visual field does not have such sharply-defined edges and since the retina does not record visual details uniformly, Mach's sketch shows more resolution than it should. Nevertheless it truthfully includes something which we normally overlook: the extent to which our own physique intrudes on the visual field. Under normal circumstances we are completely unaware of the edge of our own nose and unless we undertake a manual task which requires visual control, we pay little or no attention to the way in which our arms intrude upon the circumference of the visual field. So in this sense Mach's sketch draws attention to a neglected aspect of visual experience. Even so, his picture is somewhat misleading since it reveals both more and less of ourselves than we normally see. If we are standing upright, looking straight ahead with our hands down at our sides, it is almost impossible to catch sight of ourselves at all. But conversely, by turning our head this way and that – up, down, right and left – we can take in much more of our own physique than Mach did at his artificially single glance.

But if we make an allowance for the way in which the drawing forgivably misrepresents the visual appearance of our own body, it draws attention to the fact that no matter how much we can see of our own physique – try as

we may, twist and turn – the part by which we would expect to be identified and recognisably portrayed is inescapably invisible, and that without the help of a mirror we would never be acquainted with the appearance of our own face. If we lived in a world without reflections, self-portraits would be inconceivable – or else they would have the strangely beheaded appearance represented by Mach.

How then do we succeed in recognizing our own reflection when we *do* catch sight of it? If we don't know what we look like until we see ourselves in the mirror, how can we tell, when we do see it for the first time, that the reflected face is ours?

One answer might be that in recognizing everything else that appears in the mirror as a duplicate of what we can see around us, we might deduce the identity of our own reflection by a process of elimination, since it would be the one item appearing in the mirror for which there was no counterpart in the immediate environment.

A much more significant clue about the identity of our own mirror image is the fact that its behaviour is perfectly synchronized with our own. Remember the famous scene in *Duck Soup*. But wait… If our facial behaviour is invisible, how can we tell that it *is* synchronized with the expressions we can see in the mirror? For the simple reason that we are directly acquainted with our own actions, facial or otherwise, without having to see them. I know that I am smiling, waving or frowning, not because I can see myself, but because I can feel it. Each of us has a so-called kinaesthetic sense of our own muscular activity. This sixth sense is based on two sources of information, only one of which is strictly sensory. When we move intentionally, the nerve impulses which are despatched to the appropriate muscles leave a copy of themselves in our central nervous system, so that we have a more or less conscious representation of the forthcoming movement. Since the ensuing action is then monitored by sense organs embedded in the muscles and joints which execute the gesture, we have detailed information about what we are going to do and about what we have just done. So, confronted by what happens to be our own reflection, we can recognize a correspondence between the actions of which we *know* or *feel* ourselves to be the author, and the visible movements in the mirror with which these muscular feelings are so accurately synchronized.

However, the fact that something changes its appearance in time with our own actions does not necessarily mean that we would recognize it as our own image. It is easy to imagine an experimental set-up in which an artificial configuration of squares, discs and rectangles was wired up to a television camera in such a way that it changed its appearance in step with changes in the facial expressions of the subject, who would inevitably recognize that there was a causal relationship between his own facial expressions and the mechanical movements of the Calder-like mobile in front of him.[215] But that would not lead him to think that he was seeing his own reflection. In order to *identify* with an image, as opposed to recognizing a causal relationship with it, the subject would have to recognize that there was a fundamental *resemblance* between him and it. In other words, he would have to see it as the same *type* of thing as himself and that there was an anatomical equivalence between some of its moving parts and some of his own. All this takes care of itself when and if the individual can see his own moving parts – in other words, the parts Mach could see when he looked at himself without the help of a mirror. For example, if I move my arm and can see myself doing so without the aid of a mirror, I have something visible with which to compare the visible movements of the reflected arm. If they look alike and move at the same time as one another, chances are that they are one and the same thing, and that I am in fact looking at myself. But when it comes to parts of myself which I cannot see without the aid of reflection – my face – then there *is* a problem. Admittedly I can feel the difference between opening my mouth and poking out my tongue, but how can I tell that what I can *feel* but not *see* myself poking out corresponds to what I can *see* but not *feel* poking out in the mirror? The fact that I *can* tell, indicates that I have an anatomical representation of my face, albeit a non-visual one, and that I can accurately map its 'felt' parts on to the corresponding features of a visually represented face. It could be argued that this correspondence has to be learned, but there is experimental evidence to show that it is innate.

In at least one study it has been shown that in the first ten minutes of life a newborn infant will follow or 'track' a face-like pattern in preference to a 'scrambled' one. Further research has shown that the infant reacts to such patterns as if it recognized the anatomical correspondence between the as yet invisible features of its own face and the visible features of someone else's. In 1977, Andrew Meltzoff and Keith Moore demonstrated that within the first few weeks of neonatal life, an infant will discriminatingly mimic the facial expressions of an adult.[216] That is to say, in addition to following a face with her eyes, the newborn infant will respond to the sight of someone protruding his tongue by poking out her own. If the adult gapes, the infant will accurately copy the expression with her own mouth. In order to rule out the possibility that this might be a crude reflex response, Meltzoff momentarily frustrated the reaction by putting a dummy or pacifier in the infant's mouth immediately before it was shown the test expression. In spite of the fact that the adult carefully assumed a neutral expression just before removing the dummy, the infant mimicked what she had just seen but had been prevented from responding to a moment earlier. It was as if she had retained a visual record of the mouth opening and then imitated it from memory.

All in all, then, the newborn infant *a.* can distinguish a human face as something peculiarly interesting *b.* can tell that someone else's face is sufficiently like her own to merit playful interaction *c.* in spite of the fact that she is unacquainted with the appearance of her own face, she can recognize the correspondence between the parts of herself that she can *feel* and the equivalent parts of someone else that she can *see*. In reacting imitatively to something which she recognizes as *similar* to herself, the infant is halfway towards recognizing something which happens to be identical to herself: her own reflection. All the same, it takes at least 16 months, and sometimes as many as 24, before the infant *does* recognize her own reflection. The method by which she does so is largely experimental. She plays games with her own reflection; challenges it almost. On finding that its behaviour is accurately synchronized with her own, she comes to the inescapable conclusion that she is looking at herself.

But what exactly does that mean? The statement 'Rosie recognizes that she is looking at herself' presupposes that Rosie is aware of something other than the reflection: namely, the 'self' with which she identifies it. The difficulty is that in contrast to all the other entities about which it is possible to make intelligible statements as to what they do or do not resemble, it is devilishly difficult to say what a self is, let alone what awareness of it consists of. Suffice it to say that the ability to identify ourselves in a mirror presupposes a distinctive form of consciousness – namely self-consciousness – and that human beings display it or have it to a remarkable degree.

However, the fact that human beings are endowed with a high level of self-consciousness does not necessarily mean that the privilege is confined to *Homo sapiens*. If it *is* a privilege – that is to say if having it confers a selective advantage and, as I shall argue later, there are reasons for thinking that it *does* – then we would expect to find traces of it in some of our closer relatives, perhaps even developed to the point where they too could identify themselves in the mirror.

As it happens, there is only one other primate species in which self-recognition is unanimously agreed to exist. Although comparable claims have been made for orangutans, for 'one' domesticated gorilla and even (predictably) for dolphins, the chimpanzee is the only other animal for which the evidence seems to be uncontroversial. The first experimental tests were carried out by Gordon Gallup in 1970.[217] He took a group of young chimpanzees reared in captivity and placed them in cages equipped with a large mirror. To begin with they reacted to their own reflections as if they were other members of their own species, displaying

226

social and sometimes aggressive behaviour. On other occasions they investigated the mirror itself, poking it and looking behind. After a few hours they began to behave as if they understood that their own actions were the cause of the reflected ones. Before long they began to use the mirror to inspect parts of their own body which would not otherwise have been visible: the inside of the mouth, the soles of the feet, etc. As Gallup goes on to say:

> In an attempt to validate my impressions of what had transpired, I devised a more rigorous, unobtrusive test of self-recognition. After the tenth day of mirror exposure the chimpanzees were placed under anaesthesia and removed from their cage. While the animals were unconscious I applied a bright red, odorless, alcohol-soluble dye to the uppermost portion of an eyebrow ridge and the top half of the opposite ear. The subjects were then returned to their cages [...] and allowed to recover. [...] Upon seeing themselves in the mirror the chimpanzees all reached up and attempted to touch the marks directly while intently watching the reflection. [...] In addition to these mark-directed responses there was also an abrupt, threefold increase in the amount of time spent viewing their reflection in the mirror.[218]

Gallup noted that when the same procedures were applied to various species of monkeys – macaques, etc. – none of them went beyond the first stage; they continued to react to their reflections as if they had seen another animal of the same species.

Apart from the fact that the natural opportunities for doing so are few and far between, it is difficult to imagine the biological advantage of a chimpanzee's being able to recognize its own reflection. This must mean that the skill which is so readily demonstrable in captive chimps can only be the unforeseen and functionless by-product of a capability which was selected for its usefulness. What could that have been? The most likely candidate is the one mentioned above: self-consciousness. In a sociable species whose individual members are bound to one another in a complex web of cooperation and competition, it might be a matter of some importance for the individual to recognize himself as the target for the same sort of Machiavellian designs that he entertains towards his fellows. In order to strike the most profitable balance between trust and suspicion, probity and deceit, it seems reasonable to suppose that the chimpanzee might develop or inherit a wordless hypothesis whose unstated premise is that members of his own species are fundamentally irrational – scheming, believing, desiring and expecting, just as he is himself. Since Premack and Woodruff's classic paper of 1978, this notion has been generally referred to as the 'theory of mind,' by which is meant a theory about the possession of mental states by individuals other than oneself.[219] The selective advantage of entertaining such a theory is almost self-evident, since it puts the individual in a position to predict and make allowances for the self-promoting schemes of others. It presupposes, and to some extent is constituted by, an awareness of oneself as an agent and as a believer. One of the consequences of such profitable levels of self-consciousness seems to be the predictable though biologically functionless interest in one's own reflected image.

But it would be rash to assume that the degree of self-consciousness *sufficient* to account for self-recognition necessarily implies the possession of a 'theory of mind.' The controversy still rages as to the extent or even existence of such a theory in the higher apes. But when it comes to two-year-old *human* infants, the evidence seems to support the belief that the moment of self-recognition coincides with the appearance of behaviour that can only be explained on the assumption that the child has a mental representation of the beliefs, wishes and interests of others. As far as some psychologists are concerned, failure to pass the mirror test by 24 months is taken to be a diagnostic sign of incipient autism, a condition which, as its name implies, is characterized by the inability to represent the mental life of others.

In contrast to chimpanzees who would not normally encounter their own reflections, whose self-recognition has to be experimentally induced, most human beings are born into a culture in which the mirror is already a significant artefact and where the act of self-inspection is so spontaneous and so recurrent that it figures as a prominent and varied motif both in literature and the visual arts.

With rare exceptions, the inaugural encounter between a child and its own reflection is never represented, and it is difficult to think of a painting in which mirror-gazing is represented as something prompted by objective curiosity, as if to say 'How odd, here I am and there I am again.' Broadly speaking, when human beings are represented in explicit relationship to their own mirror images the pictures fall into two recognisably distinct categories.

a. Ethically neutral, non-judgemental representations in which the mirror figures as one of many household appliances with which the individual might be engaged in daily life.

b. Moralising tableaux in which the subjects' preoccupation with their reflection is represented as the personification of either a vice or a virtue.

In genre paintings, the figure – almost invariably a woman – is using a mirror to check or change her appearance. The tone of such paintings is relaxed and easy-going and in most examples the subject is quite literally at home with her own reflection. Without any implied moral comment the act of self-adornment is represented as one of many domestic tasks dedicated to the blameless upkeep of appearances.

As Anne Hollander points out, in sixteenth- and seventeenth-century paintings the mirror is characteristically small and reflects little more than the subject's face.[220] To a large extent this must have been because of the unavailability of larger mirrors, but, by the nineteenth century, paintings and photographs show women examining themselves at full length. Although the larger mirrors revealed parts of the body which would have been visible without the aid of reflection, they did so from a viewpoint quite different from the one from which the subject would have seen herself without the aid of a mirror. As Mach's drawing shows only too well, the unaided view of our own extremities is steeply foreshortened, whereas the reflected view, being at a right-angle to the long axis of the body, corresponds to the appearance we have for others. By posing in front of a full-length mirror, the subject stages her social appearance and can rehearse the improvements as she would like them to be seen by her fellows. It is interesting to note that the sort of activities for which the mirror is necessary are characteristically the ones for which visual control is absolutely essential; that is to say, ones in which the effects of the actions cannot be judged without seeing them. Of course, there are many interactions between the face and the hand for which the visibility of neither is required. We can effectively blow our nose in the dark and accurately cup our hands to our ears without having to watch ourselves doing so. Dining tables do not have to be equipped with mirrors in order to guarantee the successful outcome of a meal. But when it comes to adjustments of personal appearance, reflection is the only way in which success can be judged. In tribal societies whose members employ elaborate forms of self-decoration, the absence of a mirror meant that each individual had to submit himself to the cosmetic skills of someone else. It was only with the arrival of European traders that self-adornment was increasingly performed with the aid of reflection.

Although many of the paintings that include mirrors are ethically neutral, they grade imperceptibly into representations in which there is an unmistakably moral attitude to the act of self-regard. Without any explicit statement to that effect, the disapproval is conveyed by the expression of self-satisfaction on the subject's face, or, as in many of Balthus's paintings, by a look of rapt entrancement. And in some cases the self-indulgence is collusively encouraged by smiling attendants. In such pictures the reflective surface is implicitly represented as a seductive trap in which self-regard can lead to culpable self-satisfaction.

A conversation with Susan Sontag
Monitor, BBC1, 17 November 1964

Jonathan Miller's tenure as series editor of the BBC's flagship arts strand Monitor *brought him to television and assisted in cultivating a career away from satire, but the resulting programmes received hostile notices. The opening edition featured a studio interview with the American critic Susan Sontag, which many critics found indigestible, due in part to its adoption of a loose and – for the time – unusual shooting style. The recording is now lost, but a transcript survives.*[221]

MILLER: I remember your saying to me – and you said it several times – that you're reading far less fiction and just simply going to the movies; you're spending more time in the movies now than reading books.

SONTAG: Well, you know, I think that has to do with the fact that the movies bring in so much more. That literature, that people who write books are mostly in a very phoney and inauthentic relationship to their own culture, their own personality, their own time; that it's all made up in a way that I don't feel movies are made up, that there's much less fantasy in literature, that it's just drier and narrower. Sometimes I just think it's because there are more good movies than there are good books – *many more* good movies, I think. The movies have a freedom to deal with all kinds of things, even with ideas, which I think is the most surprising development of all. Of course it's very rare, but in Godard's movie *Vivre Sa Vie* [1962] – I think that's an extraordinary movie because it's very intellectual in a really effective way. It's about the difference between the outside of a person and the inside of a person. It sounds very pretentious but it really comes off. You saw it, didn't you?

MILLER: No, I haven't seen that one. That's the one about prostitutes, isn't it?

SONTAG: Yes, yes. And when I saw that movie I was really stunned because I [had] thought that the one thing that fiction can do that movies will never be able to do is discuss questions, you know. I don't mean political questions or anything like that – people can have conversations about that and it doesn't matter one way or another – but the movie can really represent an idea; that I wasn't so sure about, but I think that it can.

MILLER: But you also like Thirties Hollywood movies as well. I mean, you spend a great deal of your time in and out of that New Yorker movie house...[222]

SONTAG: Oh, well… Yes, I find that for me in the last…this began about seven years ago. I was very depressed that year and I started going to the movies almost every night, and suddenly I went to a movie that starred Eddie Cantor, and I heard Johnnie Ray for the first time. And I'd never listened to popular music at all. I'd grown up reading, and listening to Beethoven quartets and things like that, and following a sort of almost classically culturally greedy adolescence. And then suddenly I discovered things like Johnnie Ray or certain kinds of Hollywood movies, all kinds… Popular music, I think, as much as the movies interests me now, although there isn't much one can do with it. I mean, it's a much more static thing in a way – you just listen to it and go…quiver, quiver to it. This is where life is. This is where real imaginativeness is. Energy. I think that's the thing that literature lacks – energy – compared to films and popular music; so does the theatre, I think…the American theatre…

MILLER: I think the English theatre as well. But do you think there is anything intrinsic to the theatre…I mean, in the structure of the theatre…or do you think it's just simply that they're not writing things for the theatre which allow energy to be shown? I think that a lot of this talk of the Theatre of Cruelty, which people are talking about a great deal here, is an attempt to infuse some sort of primitive energy: the dark god, ferocity, and things of this sort.

SONTAG: Well, I'll believe it if I see it. I have never seen anything in the theatre that impresses me or moves me as much as most movies do. Even the very best experiences that I have in the theatre don't come up to almost the average experiences that I have in the movies. The camera can go anywhere, it can be anything, it can bring you into a… Just the close-up for instance, something like that – you actually see faces. I think we all have an entirely different relationship to faces now, because of the movies; to eyes, to mouths, to hands moving. Theatre in a way is…well, it's a choreography scene from a fixed position of spectatorship, and it's more literary. It's very much closer to literature I think.

MILLER: Do you think it stands any chance at all in the future or do you think that the mere expansion of narrative possibility which you've got with the cinema has made the theatre, has pushed the theatre down to a level of spectacles, conjuring, lectures…?

SONTAG: I don't know, but I can't imagine myself being so taken in the theatre as I am in the movies. There's something about that infinitely wide screen, or so it seems if you sit up close. And those huge features of the face and the parts of the body, and the rapid movement, and the tremendous violence that can be communicated on the screen…and fantastic transitions. And also something we were talking about the other night: the sophistication by which a story can be told. I just don't see the theatre as having the resources…but somebody will come along and do it.

MILLER: But when they do do it, as there have been innovations, it's always been in terms of bringing the cinema into the theatre. That thing of having back projection and using Brecht techniques of screens that are lowered and you project things on. In fact, it's attempting to cinematograph the theatre. The theatre itself hasn't in fact advanced at all, very much.

SONTAG: Well it does seem that in the theatre you are more dependent on good plays in a way that in the movies you're not dependent necessarily on a good script. There are more sources of energy, I think, in the film. It can come through photography. It can come through an acting performance which completely transcends the script. Maybe in the theatre too, I don't know, but I think in the theatre you'd be more aware of it because I think in the theatre the thing could actually break off in a certain way, that you would say 'there's someone acting, and that's a marvellous performance, but the play is lousy and the supporting cast is very inadequate,' that it's just *that* performance. I can't imagine that happening in the movie – everything seems more organic in some way. You know Bresson says that he likes to use non-professional actors because he doesn't like acting – he says acting, that's for the theatre, and the theatre is a bastard art. He means that only in a very special sense, but I think that there is something more organic, more total in a film than there is in a theatre, where somehow you can't divide up the elements.

MILLER: Do you think that the quality of films… It was once possible to enjoy a large number of Hollywood films, and it's still possible to enjoy an enormous number of the old Hollywood films up to, I suppose, about 1943 –

SONTAG: '45, '46 even.

MILLER: – but from then on a lot of the qualities which you admire in these films really have vanished, haven't they? I mean, I remember it being a great shock of surprise and delight in New York seeing that movie which Mervyn LeRoy did – what was it called, *I Am a Fugitive from a Chain Gang* [1932]?

SONTAG: Yes, yes – with Paul Muni.

MILLER: Now, this was a film without any literary pretensions at all – it had absolutely flat narrative style. The story was simple. It was just about this guy going into prison and running away and being captured again and then his life being broken by it.

233

SONTAG: Yes. There's a tremendous cultural pathos that seems to be built into the art form of the film – the very fact that it's something that goes into a can and then you see it 30 years after it's made and you have an entirely different reaction to it from what you would have if you saw that film when it came out. You know, you might have felt very different towards it – in fact I'm sure you would have – and in fact a book is words and even if the words are the words of another generation or another period, it's still words, but all kinds of strange, surrealistic associations come into play when you see a movie of the Thirties or the Forties. You notice the shoulder pads in the women of the movies of the Forties, or you notice the double-breasted pin-striped suits of the Warner Brothers gangster movies of the Thirties, and a certain kind of music that's playing in the background, or someone saying 'Gee, that's grand,' and you know – nobody ever says 'Gee, that's grand' anymore, and it's touching, it's moving. I don't know what it is. I don't know what the name for that kind of feeling is, but movies are a kind of museum of one's childhood. They're a sort of permanent stimulus to some kind of pathos and nostalgia.

MILLER: You mean movies, then, are almost created for hindsight really? That the best way to make movies would be to allow all these Doris Day and Rock Hudson movies to be buried under Cleopatra's Needle for 30 years and then –

SONTAG: I don't know. I sometimes think that maybe it's true in that Troy Donahue will be just as touching as Paul Muni, but I really doubt it. No, I do think that they were better – partly because they were less self-conscious – but I think that this element of art is also an experience of one's own culture, and one's own human situation, and who one is, and who one has been. It's very important. I don't think people ought to talk about works of art in an abstract way as if they were some separate class of objects or things. The difference between, let's say, a movie of the Thirties and a bird or a chair of the Thirties is not so great, and – I mean, it's an object, it's part of one's experience, and then it's part of one's past, and it can be re-experienced, and that's very important; what they are the second, third, fourth time around. Maybe some of these movies now will have this kind of pathos, but then I think also movies are tremendously fortunate in that for a long time, at least in America, they were not being very self-conscious, and now they are, I think, perhaps.

MILLER: Then all that you create – as soon as you create a self-conscious movie – is you simply create an attitude above which another consciousness could then place itself, and judge that self-consciousness, so that the self-consciousness itself becomes a datum to be examined as a symptom of a period.

SONTAG: Yeah. I think that there are an infinite number of layers of consciousness that come into play in a work of art, and that one never talks about the work of art – whether it's a novel or a poem or a film or whatever – in itself. One is always talking about it according to certain angles, and the time thing – in relation to one's own time, especially if it's part of one's immediate path. If it's drenched with this sense of contemporaneity, or recently surpassed contemporaneity, is very important. In literature we just don't have that – literature is an old art, and we've learned to look at books for the most part as works of art in themselves and to forget you could read Scott Fitzgerald, and the way maybe you can see a Humphrey Bogart movie, and be all filled with a feeling about America in the Twenties or Thirties or whatever. But I don't think you can, really. There just isn't enough of America there – it's too private, it's too individual, it's too artful in a way.

MILLER: There isn't enough of the landscape there. I know for example that one of the most effective things that you get – from a Chaplin movie for example – quite apart from Chaplin's own brilliance and performance, quite apart from his brilliance in selecting minor parts to play with him, are those curious things that are blurred off at the side of the screen. For example, in *City Lights* there's that scene which repeats itself again and again and again with Chaplin coming round the edge of a corner where the flower seller usually sits, and you see people hurrying to the curb.

SONTAG: And the car.

MILLER: And the car.

SONTAG: Somebody said recently, I don't know where, that the most wonderful thing about the Mathew Brady civil war photographs is really not the dead – the dead young men, and all that – but it's the sight of this vanished rural America that existed in the 1860s. This extraordinary background: the abandoned farm implements, the little houses, the stone walls and so on. I'm not really sure of what all this means – I'm not sure what the role of nostalgia in one's experience is or should be, if there is any in this matter, but I think it's very important, and I think it's very unrecognized, and it's all the time influencing our reactions to things. And then, of course, in the end, some things just survive and others don't.

MILLER: But don't you think that movie-going itself, as a devotional activity, is a tuition course in nostalgia, which can become more and more refined and perhaps we're just innocents and apprentices in the field at the moment and that the Forties are the nearest back that we can get to the sense of the past, and that the more we do it the more refined our sense of nostalgia will become, and we really can get a great lift out of 1962 movies?

SONTAG: Well, I do. I think things are much more interesting now. I do get a big lift out of movies in the past four or five years, so I know it isn't…it certainly isn't just nostalgia that interests me in the movies. I just think there's an element that's not very much taken into consideration that's worth mentioning. Think of the raw, popular thing. The energy that goes into art when it is not totally self-conscious. And it might be furniture at one point or it might be architecture or it might be movies, and it can be literature sometimes, but I don't think it is now. I think literature is dreadfully self-conscious. It has perhaps a lot to do with the fact that it is a university subject. It's the thing that cultivated people do if they do anything – well, they probably read novels, or maybe even poetry at one time. Just because of its official nature, I think literature has lost a lot of its energy, its verve, its ability to encompass all the different things that are going on that people just don't talk about. But one thing, Jonathan. I think it would be very bad if one's experiences [of movies] were principally the nostalgic ones. I know that you've written recently in the *TLS* that you think that the avant-garde is finished, that there can't be any more really new important breakthroughs in the techniques and subject matters of the art.[223] I don't think this is true, and I would hate to think that we would all become such slaves to our nostalgia – that we would not

236

be aware of what is actually new and what is possible now. I just… What I think, rather, is that it's wonderful now that more people are aware of all the things that go on in so-called popular arts, or the mass arts, and that some of the old snobbery about high-culture versus low-culture has been dispelled, at least for some people. I know for me that these kind of words are absolutely meaningless. I don't give a damn about high culture or low culture, I don't think in those terms. Commercialization as such, the mass-produced thing, doesn't bother me at all. I think this whole thing that's been discussed for years and years and years – a sort of Marxist or Leftist, especially European kind of concern with defending culture against barbarism – for me this is really obsolete, really surpassed. And that I'm very grateful for, and I don't think it closes off the future.

MILLER: But don't you think that it does in the way that you said, for example, that literature has perhaps been destroyed by becoming an official subject, because it's been entered now in the courses and therefore everyone reads it as a sign of cultivation. Isn't it possible that by breaking down these barriers and now enlarging the notion of culture, the study of kitsch will itself become an official subject? For example, about two weeks ago in the *Observer* there was a review of a film, of a *Carry On* film, one of these *Carry On* comedies.[224] For the first time in this paper, serious attention was paid to this as a serious form of popular culture. And in the same piece the critic talked about a radio show which, in the past, has never been mentioned at all, it's been absolutely outside the pale…

SONTAG: You're one of the villains…you're one of the people who talked most eloquently in very phoney intellectual circles about *The Goon Show* and Lenny Bruce and things like that that had never been discussed.

MILLER: But perhaps…isn't this what is happening? By the extension of the disciplines of anthropology into discussions of culture, we're threatening the spontaneity of every single manifestation, not just simply the high culture, but indeed of everything. You see, for example, interviewers now go out and talk seriously to the writers of radio comedy shows. People who would never have been spoken to at all, who would have had to come round the servants' entrance before, are now regarded as culturally mainline. Isn't this going to do to them exactly what university courses have done to serious literature in the past?

SONTAG: I think, yes, it looks that way, except that I think in the end it won't, because I think that people who do this kind of thing anyway are too tough, or too insensitive, or too…and even being interested in money is a kind of salvation at this point. I think really deep down they would just ignore these people who are climbing all over them and trying to make sociology or anthropology or cultural prognostication about them. How do you feel when you write criticism, Jonathan – for instance, when you wrote for the *TLS* or the *New Statesman* or *Partisan Review* in New York? I mean, do you feel that you're adding to this immense burden of cultural self-consciousness? You do it and I do it too sometimes. Do you feel we're doing something wrong? How do you justify it to yourself?

MILLER: Well I tend to forget about it while I'm writing it, but if I look back at some of the things I've written, I do feel very anxious about it. Because I do feel in fact that all that's been created is this great Ziggurat of stories piled upon tiers, piled upon stories which are simply examining things, examining things, examining things. You get this great mirror-maze of reflections like this which just go on and on reflecting each other and never breaking out into a spontaneous enjoyment of life in itself.

SONTAG: Of course you know, it's funny, I was just thinking – I keep insisting very lamely without much argument that I'm hopeful that all these wonderful things will survive their critics, and yet it just occurred to me that I'm probably less committed now to writing criticism than you are, though we've both done it a lot in the past year or two. And that I think that I *am* getting off the train more or less for this reason – that I'd rather, you know, write a second novel and work on stories, than go on talking about what things are like, or how people ought to enjoy things that they're too inhibited, or too uninspired to seek out and enjoy for themselves. Because, I mean, I know for myself, when I have written criticism it's really been mainly with the idea of talking about things that I liked that might be ignored or passed over because of some kind of mental prejudice. I'm not interested in talking about things that aren't any good, because I haven't thought of criticism as a major occupation. And I think you have too been talking much more…like that marvellous piece that you did about Lenny Bruce for the *Partisan Review*[225] – showing people how to like something that they might not know how to get into the right sort of posture in relation to, that they might not be able otherwise to like; or writing about *The Goon Show* in the context of avant-garde art in that article in *TLS*. But I know, anyway, I have great misgivings about doing it… It's a pleasure to be able to communicate enthusiasm in the short run. That I think is what makes me do it, what makes you do it – but then one does feel one is just piling on. Let the people find out for themselves, you know. Maybe one should make these things instead of making words about them.

MILLER: So perhaps we should just cut the tape and dance.

Jokes and joking: a serious laughing matter
Queens University, Belfast, August 1987[226]

At the Manchester meeting of the British Association in 1842, a surgeon called James Bray tried to enter the topical but disreputable subjects of animal magnetism and mesmerism into one of the sections. He failed to gain admission and was forced to repair to the Free Trade Hall, where he was able to demonstrate the facts of mesmerism, which he then retitled hypnotism. (This was the occasion when the term 'hypnotism' was coined for the first time.) If a section labelled 'X' had existed in 1842, I have no doubt that the disreputable subject of animal magnetism would have succeeded in gaining admission. X is the lower end of the alphabet. X is a letter which is very rarely used, and then only for things that are out of the ordinary, out of the usual – for that which is in some way unclassifiable, or unmanageable. In his account of the concentration camps, Primo Levi recorded a hierarchy which existed among the inmates with regard to the numbers tattooed on their arms. Those with the lowest numbers, being the earliest arrivals, were the aristocrats; while those with the highest numbers, being the most recent arrivals, were the proletariat of the camp.[227] In our case, 'X, General' represents the disreputable end of the British Association. It is the unclassifiable; that which is opposed to the pristine respectability of 'A, Physics', and 'B, Chemistry'.

I think there is something quite significant about the fact that I am President of Section X, and that my subject is humour. For humour is an unclassifiable and unmanageable subject, something which has consistently defeated the attempts of scientists to explain it. It also has other drawbacks as a subject for discussion. While it fails to gain admission for serious consideration by scientists, it is also regarded by those laymen who take great pleasure in the experience of laughter as being too frivolous and too enjoyable to be treated by science at all. In fact, the journalists who usually come to these meetings take great pleasure whenever someone does deal with humour in demonstrating how unfunny the treatment of the subject is, rather as if it should be a qualification of a surgeon dealing with cancer that he or she should have the disease before operating upon it.

Humour is an extremely difficult subject to talk about and it is an even more difficult subject to be scientific about. We have to deal with the peculiar phenomenon of laughter, a respiratory convulsion which seems to be excited – whether we like it or not – by certain events which we experience. We normally regard laughter as an action, as something which we do – as a performance of some sort. But in fact it is hardly something in which we can be said to have competence. Laughter is not at all like a physical action. It is not like raising a hand, or making a fist. It is not like writing or speaking. Laughter is not something which we can undertake voluntarily: we cannot laugh at will. Of course, we can put ourselves in situations where laughter is the result, but there is no way in which we can make ourselves laugh. Someone who does make him- or herself laugh – an actor or an actress, for example – is indulging in what we call mirthless laughter. True laughter is not something to which we have direct voluntary access.

In this sense, laughter seems to be a cognate concept with things like sneezing and coughing. We cannot sneeze at will; and once we have started to sneeze, we cannot always stop ourselves at will either. Similarly we cannot laugh at will; and once we have started laughing, we cannot always stop ourselves. In some ways, then, laughter has features in common with sneezing and coughing, in the sense that all of these things belong to the area of the involuntary. Yet in other ways they all belong to the province of the will. For example, we can voluntarily suppress sneezing, coughing and laughter. Thus we may blame someone at a concert who sneezes or coughs, and we may blame someone at a funeral who giggles at the graveside. Thus each of these phenomena is distinguished from other forms of involuntary action – such as peristalsis – that cannot be either started or stopped at will. Someone, for example, who at the graveside produces audible borborygmi may be laughable, but they are not blameable. We cannot be blamed for stopping peristalsis and we cannot be praised for starting it.

So we are dealing with actions that are involuntary, in the sense that they cannot be started at will, but that are voluntary in the sense that they can be suppressed. Next, we must distinguish between involuntary actions like sneezing and coughing on the one hand, and laughing and blushing on the other. We think of sneezing as being an involuntary action which can be induced by putting oneself in a situation which produces it. For example, we may take snuff in order to sneeze. Similarly with laughing and blushing. We have to put ourselves in situations where joking matter is around in order to make ourselves laugh, and we have to be in situations which are embarrassing in order to blush. However, there is a distinction between snuff and laughing matter, just as I believe there is a distinction between snuff and embarrassing matter. Snuff is a physical stimulus which attacks the nervous system from the 'bottom up,' whereas laughing matter approaches the nervous system from the 'top down.' Snuff is purely physical – we do not have to understand anything in order to sneeze; but laughing matter is cognitive – we have to understand the situation before we can be tickled into laughter, or embarrassed into blushing.

It is interesting that we use the word 'tickling' because laughter does overlap into the sneezing area. We know that we can produce laughter by something as crude as a physical stimulus, and this does not require cognitive appreciation in order to work.

So far, I have simply been exploring some concepts that are cognate with laughter. It may be worth recapitulating my main conclusions. Laughter is involuntary in the sense that we cannot start it, even though we can stop it. Laughter has to be started by putting oneself in a situation where the stimulus is provided, but the stimulus to laughter is not like the stimulus to sneeze. We do not have to be in a frame of mind in order to sneeze, we simply have to have our noses tickled. But a frame of mind is required for laughter. This is because laughter is a 'top down' concept. In other words, it comes from higher, cognitive levels of the nervous system, as opposed to the other involuntary actions which attack the nervous system from the 'bottom up.'

The idea of laughter as a 'top down' phenomenon can be demonstrated by an interesting clinical finding, which is taught to medical students when they go on the neurological wards and see patients with strokes. This finding is one of the ways in which we distinguish between an upper motor-neurone and a lower motor-neurone defect. The illness called Bell's palsy attacks the seventh or facial nerve and causes paralysis of one half of the face. In this palsy, half of the face becomes slack; patients may dribble from one side of their mouth, and often the lower eyelid is everted. Bell's palsy is an extremely painful and embarrassing affliction. However, it is what we call a lower motor-neurone defect. It affects the lower part of the nervous system, the final common path through which motor impulses gain access to the muscles. In contrast, there are other, upper motor-neurone defects which involve the same muscles. For example, a stroke which affects the motor neurones in the cerebral cortex may also cause paralysis on one side of the face. However, there are sharp distinctions in the repertoires of patients suffering from these two different sorts of defect.

We pick a patient with a stroke and ask them to show us their teeth. We say 'Grin, please,' and they grin on just one side. We say for the second time, 'Grin, please, on both sides of your face.' Again, they respond by grinning on just one side. In other words, the patient does not have access to the other side of their face; not, that is, until we amuse them. Once amused, then there is bilateral symmetry in their performance. In other words, they do not have a total lack of access to their own face; they have access to their face with respect to a particular cognitive situation. If you amuse them, if they see a joke, they smile; but they cannot smile at will. In a patient with Bell's palsy – a lower motor-neurone defect – on the other hand, neither the order to grin nor amusement produces a symmetrical smile, because there is a block in the final path through which nerve impulses gain access to the relevant muscles.

The thing which is interesting here is the extraordinary situation of the stroke patient. He or she cannot grin to order, but they can smile when amused. This goes back to the question of how we gain access to

242

involuntary performances like blushing and laughter, which seem to be things over which we have partial and incomplete control.

If a Martian visited the Earth, he, she or it would be extremely puzzled by the strange respiratory convulsion of laughter, which sometimes sweeps through assemblies, and which people pay large amounts of money in order to experience. This strange phenomenon, which has been called a sudden glory, cannot surely be a respiratory convulsion alone. After all, there are other ways of being convulsed respiratorily from which we actually flee. Indeed, we flee from the sort of laughter which we can be tickled into. This sort of thing can be torture, whereas no one ever flees from a cabaret or a performance of a great comedian. People flee from the laughter which is induced by physical stimulation, but no one flees from the laughter which is produced by a cognitive situation.

Now, all of this leads us to ask an intriguing question: might there be some evolutionary significance in this curious performance of laughter, in this curious involuntary competence? Why is it that we pay so much money in order to put ourselves in situations where laughter results? Why is it that we pay so highly for people to do this to us, whereas we would not dream of paying someone to tickle our feet with a feather for three minutes? Could it be that there is an evolutionary pay-off in the pleasure which is associated with the cognitive situations which seem to induce this activity?

Presumably there is a selective pay-off in the pleasure associated with sexual intercourse. If there were no pleasure to be associated with sexual intercourse, we might forget to do it; in absent-mindedness, as it were, we might pass it up altogether. The same thing goes for eating. Both sexual intercourse and eating involve the use of scarce resources, i.e. the resources of physical energy in the pursuit and the consummation of these activities. Both are selectively advantageous and personally pleasurable. Without lapsing into the heresy of adaptationism – the assumption that everything we do has some specific evolutionary pay-off – I would like to suggest that what is true of sexual intercourse and eating may also be true of laughter. In other words, I propose that there may be positive selective advantage associated with the cognitive rehearsals which we tend to go through in undergoing the experience of laughter.

To discover this evolutionary pay-off we must consider what laughter is for. There are many theories of the origins of laughter. Michael Neve deals with one of the most famous of these theories, which is Freud's idea that laughter is simply the release of repressed material which has been prevented from expressing itself.[228] According to Freud, it is only through the medium of the joke, and suddenly, that repressed material is allowed us; and this provokes laughter. This is an idea which has gained wide acceptance in the psychoanalytic community, and I think there is something to be said for it.

Another, more biological theory of laughter was proposed by the French philosopher Henri Bergson.[229] Bergson claimed that we laugh at people in situations where they revert to a more automatic type of behaviour. When the herd observes a reduction in the versatility and flexibility of one of its members, it goes through loud respiratory convulsions which, as it were, ask the offending individual to 'pull its socks up.' A less flexible, less versatile individual endangers the biological integrity of the herd, and so the herd acts to protect itself. We laugh at the man who falls on the banana skin. (The man on the banana skin has become an emblematic figure in theories of humour, for reasons which have always escaped me.) Why? Because instead of retaining his versatility, his spontaneity and his flexibility, the man who tumbles is yielding to the force of gravity and is becoming something like a robot. He is becoming an inflexible object, and at that moment he is being reminded to pull himself together, to restore himself to a state of vigilant flexibility which will then make him into a valuable and productive member of the herd. Once again, it would be wrong to laugh this theory out of court; but as it stands, it deals with so little of the topic. This is a common feature of theories about humour: practically none of them cover the whole topic. There is almost always a series of exceptions which can be made to what purports to be a comprehensive theory of humour.

The last theory with which I shall deal very briefly is the idea that we laugh at situations where we see ourselves as superior to some victim. On this view, the victim of laughter is being reminded of his or her weakness by stronger members of the herd. In a performance that is an inheritance from our primate ancestors, dominant individuals put subordinates 'in their place.' This crude ethological view has been widely popularized, but I reject it out of hand because it overlooks complex cognitive and moral issues. This is why I prefer Erving Goffman to someone like Desmond Morris. Goffman perceived all of these things in their moral and social context, and not in terms of a crude inheritance from primate ancestors. Of course it may be possible to look at the motor performance of laughter and trace it back to certain primate roots; but at the cultural level I believe it has become latched on to something so elaborate, and so elaborately moral, that it is no longer useful to consider it in crude ethological terms. This, I believe, is why Darwin's book on *The Expression of the Emotions in Man and Animals* (1872) is such an intolerably tedious volume. It has encouraged even more tedious types of ethological thought in the last 25 years.

In contrast to all of these theories, I would like to raise what I believe to be a largely unconsidered theory of what humour is for, and what its biological value might be. In my view, the value of humour may lie in the fact that it involves the rehearsal of alternative categories and classifications of the world in which we find ourselves. Perhaps we should distinguish between serious discourse, on the one hand, and humorous discourse on the other. (This is really a way to avoid using the word 'joke'.) When we are in the domain of humorous discourse – i.e. those cognitive situations which actually bring about laughter – we almost always encounter rehearsals, playings with and redesignings of the concepts by which we conduct ourselves during periods of seriousness. When we conduct our ordinary business in the world – our practical affairs – we deal with things for the most part by rule of thumb; we mediate our relationships with one another through a series of categories and concepts which are sufficiently stable to enable us to go about our business fairly successfully. But if we were rigidly locked on to these categories and concepts, if we were inflexibly attached to them, we would not continue to be a successful, productive and above all socially cooperative species. What we require, then, is some sort of sabbatical let-out in one part of the brain and one part of our competence to enable us to put things up for grabs; to reconsider categories and concepts so that we can redesign our relationships to the physical world, to one another, and even to our own notion of what it is to have relationships.

Perhaps I can illustrate this idea of what humour is for with a cartoon from the *New Yorker*. The cartoon portrays two African explorers in a swamp. They are wearing pith helmets, and are surrounded by lianas, creepers, serpents and so forth. They are obviously in trouble because they are up to their necks in the swamp as they proceed from left to right of the cartoon. The figure at the back is saying to the figure at the front: 'Quicksand or no, Carruthers, say what you like. I have half a mind to struggle.'

Simply describing the cartoon causes something strange to happen. Even without seeing the cartoon, we tend to laugh. Now, why is this? A crude, ethological view would be, 'Oh, we are taking pleasure by laughing at the fact that we are not in the swamp, and they are.' Or again, 'We are taking pleasure by laughing at what is clearly a ludicrous view of their true situation.' I think, however, that if we parse the joke we can see that what is really going on is that certain categories with regard to the notion of volition are being played with. The cartoon actually throws up into the air the categories of will and action which we considered in relation to the notion of laughter as a voluntary or involuntary performance.

Consider the cartoon caption again: 'Quicksand or no, Carruthers, say what you like. I have half a mind to struggle.' Surely the core of this joke is not the situation of the swamp, nor the fact of our being outside the swamp and them being in it, but rather the fact that what we think of as struggling is not the sort of thing about which one could be in 'half a mind.' We cannot as it were consider struggling as the next thing on the agenda. We cannot say: 'We've tried firing warning shots into the air; we've tried hanging on to the creepers; now let's have a spirited go at struggling.' Again, we laugh at the very thought of applying the notion of decision to something which is at it were a paradigm of those things to which we do not have voluntary access. Sneezing, laughter and struggling are not things which you can be in half a mind to do. Struggling is not even something which you can be in full mind to do. It is not something to which the notion of mind seems to be relevant at all. It is something which happens flat out, whether you like it or not. It is something about which, in retrospect – if the struggling worked – you might say, 'I'm afraid I found myself struggling, although I know I ought not to have done.' In exactly the same way, you might say at the graveside, 'I'm afraid I couldn't help myself laughing.' You cannot be in half a mind to laugh, but you can be in full mind to try and stop yourself laughing, and in much the same way you cannot be in half a mind to struggle but you can be in full mind to try and stop yourself struggling.

What I am suggesting is that this joke rehearses what we customarily think of as hard and fast divisions between the voluntary and the involuntary. In this way, it introduces us to a concept that is fundamental to our relationships with one another and to the organized structures of our society. One of the things which makes our society coherent is that we have notions of what it is meet to praise and what it is meet to blame; what we send people to prison for, and what we award them knighthoods for; what we hit them for, and what we kiss them for. In other words, we divide things into a series of praiseworthy areas and blameworthy areas. The *New Yorker* cartoon is one of a battery of jokes which plays with our notions of praise and blame. By applying these notions to something which is clearly in the area of the involuntary, this joke rubs our noses in some of the basic ideas by which we live. At the same time, it allows us to reconsider these notions, and – if appropriate – to revise them.

I would like to make use of another example before I close. Twenty-seven years ago, when I started out in the humour business, I performed for three years in *Beyond the Fringe*. Each night I used to stand open-mouthed with wonder at my colleagues performing on the stage and making other people laugh. I was always amazed at their talent, but also I was amazed at the relationship between their performance and the strange noise of laughter that came from the audience beyond the footlights. After three years, I was able to analyse the performance in some detail, and it was here that this notion of humour as a disorder of categories came home to me. I would like to give you one example from a sketch which we used to perform every night. It was a sketch about civil defence in which there were three of us behind a table, and Dudley Moore was planted in the audience to ask questions. The question of civil defence was raised and discussed, and halfway through we issued an invitation for questions from the audience – hoping, of course, that Dudley would get in first. Dudley would say, 'Yes, I have a question. Following the nuclear holocaust, how soon will normal public services be resumed?' The answer to that was: 'That's a very fair question. Following Armageddon, we do hope to have public services working fairly smoothly pretty soon after the event. In all fairness, though, I ought to point out that it must needs be something in the nature of a skeleton service.'[230]

Now there are several pieces of 'joke-work,' as Freud would put it, here. All of them involve opportunities for us to throw previously rigid categories into the air, and thus to reconsider the concepts by which we think and live. The traditional explanation of this joke is black humour. We laugh at something which is so intolerable, so horrible in our predicament that we simply have to laugh in order not to cry. This is one of the traditional sort of push-me-pull-you views of humour, which does not help at all. Much more plausible, I think, is the idea that the joke involves a subversion of our concept of Armageddon. Armageddon is not one of those things, like Christmas, or Thursday, which has events following it. It is not something which you might, as it were, put in your diary; so that in response to the question, 'What are you doing November 11th?' you could say, 'Well, I've got Armageddon coming up; but once that settles down…' Armageddon just is not something which settles down, or which has a sequel to it.

Just as struggling is not the next thing on the agenda, so Armageddon is not an event after which there can be other events, least of all normal public services. Once again, I think, we are amused by a discrepancy – that is, the discrepancy between the magnitude of Armageddon in the form of a nuclear holocaust, and the extraordinary triviality of public services.

I would like to conclude with a well-known sequence in a Charlie Chaplin movie. All of us remember *The Gold Rush* (1925). In that movie, there is a scene in which Charlie is starving in a hut and is forced to eat his boots. The audience becomes hysterical at certain points only, and these are points where the categories are in danger. The audience laughs at the moment when Charlie twists his bootlaces around his fork and treats them as spaghetti, and again at the point when he tentatively cuts the sole, tries a small piece of it, and savours it. Once again, a discrepancy is the source of the joke. It is in the nature of boots that they are in the domain of the inedible. Here, however, someone is applying to the radically inedible the demeanour, the decorum and the finesse which normally applies to something that is the epitome of the edible – in this case, spaghetti and a very finely broiled steak. In this scene we are being brought face to face with categories by which we live.

This example takes us back to the issues raised by Mary Douglas in her book *Purity and Danger* (1966). There, Mary Douglas talks about the distinction between the dirty and the clean, the pure and the dangerous.

Boots are things which belong on the floor, and they become dirty when they arrive on the table. In exactly the same way, what makes us laugh in the scene from *The Gold Rush* is the jarring discrepancy in which an object is suddenly and forcefully reclassified by being taken out of the category of the radically inedible and placed into the category of the finely, the wonderfully edible. Once again, this scene rejuvenates our sense of what these everyday categories are.

The rehearsal of categories in humour need not necessarily entail their revision. The point about such rehearsals is not that they have short-term consequences or benefits, but rather that they allow us to play with concepts and categories and thus to put joints into life. We may not be faced with the possibility of having to eat boots. Nevertheless, by having gone through the delightful experience of humour, we have prevented ourselves from becoming the slaves of the categories by which we live. This is why humour is so often regarded as a dangerous and even a subversive thing: the joker and the satirist are regarded as dangerous fellows, and the card in the pack which upsets the hand is called the wild card, or the joker. I think what we are seeing here is the notion of the jocular as a kind of sabbatical section of the mind, in which 'off-duty' is celebrated. Being off-duty is bound up with refreshment and recreation. I would remind you that recreation is in fact *re-creation*. It is the rehearsal, the re-establishment of concepts.

In all procedures of life there are rules of thumb which enable us to go on to 'automatic pilot.' I am not suggesting that these rules of thumb are bad. Far from it, they are necessary labour-saving devices which give our activities some sort of momentum. We depend on the existence of these categories in order to go about our everyday business. Jokes allow us to stand back from these rules and inspect them. Anthropologists make a distinction between serious and humorous discourse, and Edmund Leach distinguishes between sacred and profane time.[231] There is a time in which we conduct our normal business – profane time – but there are always interludes in which the normal categories, social and otherwise, are suspended for the express purpose of undergoing sabbatical subversion. At Christmas time, for example, everything is up for grabs, and things are turned upside-down. (The historian Christopher Hill uses the phrase 'a world turned upside down,' in connection with the English Revolution.)[232] At Christmas time the pantomime dame is played by a man, the principal boy is played by a girl, masters serve and servants sit at table, a lord is crowned Lord of Misrule, a bishop is made of a boy, and so on and so forth. In short, the world is briefly and safely subverted in carnival time, in festival time, in order to allow us briefly to rehearse and revise the categories by which we live for the rest of the year. When the New Year comes, and we undertake the incumbencies and offices of ordinary life, we do so hopefully, in the knowledge that the categories and concepts by which we have lived in the previous year have undergone some sort of revision. Through humour we are not so much the slaves of the rules of life as the voluntary survivors of them. So perhaps there is something in Bergson's idea that humour restores us to the more versatile versions of ourselves, so that in joking we may be undertaking the most serious thing we do in our lives!

On Chekhov
Subsequent Performances, 1986[233]

At last, to the pleasure of all, Anton Pavlovich sent the first act of the new play, still unnamed. Then there arrived the second act and the third. Only the last act was missing. Finally Chekhov came himself with the fourth act, and a reading of the play was arranged, with the author present. As was our custom, a large table was placed in the foyer of the theatre and covered with cloth, and we all sat down around it, the author and the stage directors in the centre. The atmosphere was triumphant and uplifted. All the members of the company, the ushers, some of the stage hands and even a tailor or two were present. The author was apparently excited and felt out of place in the chairman's seat. Now and then he would leap from his chair and walk about, especially at those moments when the conversation, in his opinion, took a false or unpleasant direction. After the reading of the play, some of us, in talking of our impressions of the play, called it a drama, and others even a tragedy, without noticing that these definitions amazed Chekhov.[234]

The unnamed play Stanislavsky refers to is *Three Sisters* (1901). Chekhov was not only 'amazed' but 'left the meeting.' When Stanislavsky sought out the unhappy playwright, he discovered that the reason for his anger 'was that he had written a happy comedy and all of us had considered the play a tragedy and even wept over it. Evidently Chekhov thought that the play had been misunderstood and that it was already a failure.'[235]

Although Chekhov is a very different playwright from Shakespeare, his work similarly enjoys an afterlife and shares some of the problems common to works of art when they outlive their authors. This story, however, indicates that his intention was problematic even when he was alive and superintending a play reading. What has happened since Chekhov's demise? Initially his work was cared for by his widow who took on the dramatist's mantle and acted as the custodian to his intention. His plays have now become intricately connected with the slice-of-life realism and method of Stanislavsky. In England the misunderstanding of genre evident in Chekhov's time has been compounded by what I call the Keats Grove genteel, well-mannered school of acting that flourished in the late 1930s and post-Second-World-War period. His plays have often been performed by the English theatrical Royal Family – with leading actresses like Peggy Ashcroft – and a certain style of acting has been so consistently associated with them that people begin to think of the melancholy, pausing version as the only permissible one. When another style is introduced, and Chekhov's work is played much more rapidly, casually, even shabbily, they think that a beautiful work has been violated. This seems to me to misunderstand what is remarkable about Chekhov – that his work takes such pleasure in what is unbeautiful and mundane about life. I have directed *The Seagull*,[236] *Three Sisters*[237] and *The Cherry Orchard*[238] and in each case I reacted against the genteel approach, trying to make the work much coarser and more comic.

Three Sisters is a comedy in which someone is killed in a rather farcical and idiotic accident. Soliony has never struck me as a wonderful, sinister, duelling villain who with unerring aim kills Toozenbach. I've directed him as a rather drunken, resentful, solitary and harassed figure who was dangerous precisely because he was unexpected. Similarly, the sisters' failure to get to Moscow is *not* tragic; they simply have to continue having a dull suburban life – with an affair now and again – as time passes by. Chekhov says somewhere that in most of his plays people just have conversations and drink tea, and most of our lives are filled up doing that. In a sense, the feeling in the plays is rather like Beckett – it passed the time, and it would have passed anyway. This element, together with the comedy, needs to be brought out. The plays float on a rather indolent tide of undirected chit-chat, and unless time in rehearsal is given to that, we find people trumpeting and elocuting the lines as if singing arias.

In the process of rehearsing *Three Sisters* we discovered the recurrent themes of time and memory. There are references to the passage of time and the impermanence of strong feelings on almost every page. Starting with the first speech, when Olga says 'It's exactly a year ago that Father died, isn't it? This very day, the fifth of May –' we learn that Irena was prostrated with grief but that she is now radiant with happiness. The characters then attempt to date the significant moments in their lives – 'your Saint's day, Irena'[239] – and later Andrey asks Natasha when it was he first began to love her. 'Eleven years have gone by,' says Olga, remembering when they left Moscow, 'yet I remember everything about it, as if we'd only left yesterday.'[240] For some of the characters the past seems vividly present but to others it seems lost altogether. When Vershinin is reintroduced to the sisters, he has to admit, 'I don't really remember you, you know, I only remember that there were three sisters.' But he remembers their father: 'I remember your father, though, I remember him very well. All I need to do is to close my eyes and I can see him standing there as if he were alive.'[241] And the memory of Vershinin himself is incompletely distributed between the three girls. 'I don't remember you at all,'[242] says Masha, and then a few speeches later she says, 'Do you remember, Olga, there was someone they used to call "the lovesick major"?' With the return of this memory she adds, 'Oh, dear, how much older you look! How much older!' This raises the second issue with regard to time, and that is how things, especially people, are altered. 'Yes, I was still a young man in the days when they called me "the lovesick major,"' says Vershinin. 'I was in love then. It's different now.'[243] Again in the opening lines, 'It's exactly a year ago that Father died [...] I felt then as if I should never survive his death [...] And now – a year's gone by, and we talk about it so easily.'[244] Even grief, it seems, will be forgotten, both those for whom we grieve and even the bereaved themselves: 'You know, I'm even beginning to forget what she looked like. I suppose people will lose all memory of us in just the same way. We'll be forgotten.'[245] And then there is the effort to try and visualize what the oblivious future will be like: 'let's try to imagine what life will be like after we're dead, say in two or three hundred years time.'[246] And although, of course, they will be forgotten and no one will remember who they were or what they were like, they all, as Vershinin points out, have a stake in the forgetful future, for each one of them will have contributed to everything that follows. They cannot experience the posterity they imagine, but it will not come into existence without their actions. The happiness that Vershinin confidently anticipates is brought into existence by the suffering that we have to endure. In other words, it does no good to suppose that one could enjoy future happiness by hibernating until it comes into existence of its own accord, since it is brought into existence only by the misery that has to be endured.

As in Proust, the metaphor of photography is used to emphasize the experience of time. A group photograph is taken at the end of the first act and at the beginning of the last – two moments enjoyed and perhaps remembered by the participants, but whose visual record will be impenetrable and enigmatic to anyone looking at it hereafter. When they pose for the photograph, it provides a moment at which strange and unexpected smiles will be recorded – but they do not look like anyone's smile, because they are halfway between, their lips caught either on the way up or on the way down. When I directed this scene, the characters applauded themselves when the photograph was taken as though they had just performed and would see themselves on camera later.

Another metaphor of time is provided by the spinning top that briefly silences the company at the end of Act I while each of them contemplates his or her mortality as it spins, slows, falls silent, wobbles, and finally topples to a standstill. Suddenly the company see their lives winding down in miniature. The fact that things that seem so important at the time are soon forgotten pervades Chekhov's work. In *The Seagull* (1895), there is a similar effect to that of the opening of *Three Sisters* when Dorn says, 'By the way – where is Zaryechnaia now?' and the response, equally casual and throwaway, is 'I suppose she's all right.'[247] Things are soon forgotten; our lives pass with someone growing ill, having a stroke or dying. One of Trigorin's lines captures Chekhov's preoccupation with time: 'So we are going? More railway carriages, stations, refreshment bars, veal cutlets, conversations...'[248] That is the world of the plays – idle chatter, and the comic surface of social interaction.

253

While it is widely accepted now that genteel, pausing melancholy is not the way to perform Chekhov, I have always been very stringent about the amount of comedy that can be included in his work. Again, as with Shakespeare, the director has to be careful not to follow or fall into stereotypes. Those in Chekhov are much less famous than they are with a play like *Hamlet*, precisely because Chekhov's work has been with us for a much shorter time and it is not written on the heroic scale that attracts simple, prototypic outlines in performance. Even so, for years Trigorin has been played as a rather silvery, distinguished figure, reminiscent of a slightly disreputable English gynaecologist. Arkadina also invites stereotypes. She is usually played in a very English-actressy way, whereas it would be rather interesting to show her as a rather pudgy little spitfire played by an actress like Prunella Scales. This would bring out a particular sort of raucous, Russian vulgarity which is usually neglected. There should be a lot more of the eruptive gaiety that is characteristic of Russians – floods of tears followed immediately by hysterical laughter. Masha in *Three Sisters* is also a part that has fallen into a cliché by being seen as a star performance that should be played by a 'great actress.' In fact, Masha is a rather unlikeable provincial girl with ideas that would have suited the Bloomsbury set. She thinks she is much more sensitive and intelligent than she is – after all, she falls in love with the most boring, dull cavalry officer.

Another example is little Irena in *Three Sisters*, a part that is often played as a sweet innocent child, as indeed she is described by Chebutykin who, as it happens, is a sentimental old fool. I have always imagined her as a very hard woman and discovered this was realizable on stage by redesigning the delivery of one short line at the end of the play. This came about in rehearsal with Angela Down playing Irena. Usually when the Doctor enters with the news that Toozenbach has been shot, there is a melancholy and sad surrendering: 'I *knew* it, I knew it…'[249] Instead, I had her suddenly bite and slam her fist down on the ground, spitting out the words as though shouting an expletive. This totally transformed the character and retrospectively we had to reconstruct her.

Chekhov is quite clearly more realistic than Shakespeare. The characters speak lines that are very like those that ordinary people speak when conversing with one another. There are ways of enhancing that sense of being in the presence of reality, and it is most important to attend to what are called 'the rules of conversation.' These have been identified only in the last 20 years or so by psycholinguists who are very interested in what is called 'turn-taking' in conversation. Conversation has a certain internal structure which is determined by rules that we all somehow know without understanding how we acquire this knowledge. There are rules of listening, of not speaking until the other person has finished, learning how to take your turn, and all sorts of mutually understood rules for establishing how to become the next speaker, and how floor space is allocated. If the actors pay great attention to this, the plays can possess a glittering sense of social reality. Otherwise the speeches simply follow one another and become stale because they do not reproduce the rhythm of ordinary speech. I found it essential to be more slipshod, and allow more hesitation and pauses of the kind you find in any ordinary conversation. It is also useful to allow for things that Chekhov has not written – by which I mean interruption, reduplication and overlap, with people starting to talk when the previous speaker has not finished and then having to apologize. All these little characteristics of speech take a long time to recreate on stage but when the actors manage it the audience feels as if it is in the presence of a real conversation.

On the other hand, we have to recognize that there is a certain artificiality about the organization of the scenes in Chekhov's plays. Despite the fact that they are much nearer approximations to spoken conversation than Shakespeare, for example, they are still what we might call 'fourth-order approximations' and not real speech. In Chekhov's writing there is a hidden sonata structure. This draws your attention, as a director, to thematic recurrences and the shape of the plays. Certain themes are stated, developed, reduplicated, inverted and then returned again to the main theme. The sonata structure can still be preserved while encouraging the actors to speak in ways that are not written into the text. This is a rather complicated idea that needs some explanation.

When an author writes down a speech that he thinks of as being a genuine record of how people might speak, he inadvertently does something similar to what psychologists have recognized in perception and called 'regression to the real object.' This means that when we look at a scene, we are not aware of the fact that the objects arranged in space create images on the retina that are very much smaller as they get more distant. All that we are aware of is that the objects appear as we know them to be. Similarly, in recording speech a naive draughtsman writes down the speech as it is understood – its clear meaning, rather than its actual sound. On the page, we see the meaning of what is heard and not what is *actually* heard. So, the speech appears to be much more grammatical than it would if it had been spoken, and lacks the hesitations, the incompletenesses and the overlaps you might find on a tape-recording of the conversation. In a strange way, if you want to make the speeches seem real you have to overlook the way in which they are written down and try to remember how people actually sound, recognizing that what you have on the page is something that has regressed to the real object.

In order to return Chekhov's over-clarified speeches to the state of real conversation, it is necessary to break them up and pay very close attention to the processes involved in conversation. This means having to listen to all the verbal and non-verbal accompaniments of conversation that regulate the process of turn-taking. This can be captured only from memory and most actors do *not* remember. They remember what the speeches mean, and everything else – which is so vital to the production and belongs to social exchange – is disregarded. Most people will reproduce what is on the page without realizing that the text provides only a clarified picture of what the characters mean. They forget that the lines do not convey how they might actively be spoken. In Shakespeare's play we are not presented with this problem because, writing in the particular verse form and rhetorical idioms that he did, there was no need to pay attention to the dynamics of conversation. The verses follow one another with their metrical structure and we cannot insert hesitations and interruptions, nor can we have people mumbling and interjecting with agreements. Yet Chekhov invites these little details which have been rinsed out of the script because they are actually inaudible.

With great care and attention these details must be consciously restored to the speeches, and when this happens successfully, Chekhov's lines take off and become animated. It also means you can shorten the playing time by allowing for overlap.[250] One of the reasons that Chekhov traditionally takes so much time is that pauses, instead of merely indicating lack of response, are self-indulgently wallowed in and given melancholy significance.

Chekhov's dramas are often family affairs and when silence falls in the home, it is not felt to be an enigmatic pause but simply a moment when no

256

one speaks. In contrast, there is an unease about silence in a social situation such as the scene where Vershinin enters; everybody tries desperately to make conversation, and feels tremendously relieved every time Vershinin says something, as it fills in the gap. In order to show that they are not being inhospitable, the family goes on reacting long beyond the need to respond to his remarks. Erving Goffman describes the very complicated requirements placed on each of us in a social scene.[251] These not only require us to show ourselves in the best possible light, but to support other people involved in the exchange. What often happens in conversation is that, if somebody rather rudely or abruptly interrupts, they then have to overcompensate and apologize to the speaker they have stopped by over-agreeing and denigrating what it is they actually want to say. The dynamic of conversation is not scripted in Chekhov, so the director simply has to remind the actors that this is what happens. It can be very exciting when actors suddenly understand what you are asking them to do, and again it is an element that is very variable in performance.

By simply remembering what the idioms would be in a normal conversation, the actors have access to a generative grammar. It is not something you can learn rigidly line by line; what happens is that the cast understands the rules of conversation and generates the sequences accordingly. These rules, very loosely, are what Grice describes in his "Rules of Conversational Relevance".[252] This means that whatever contribution somebody makes should be relevant and not redundant and should not overload the listener with information. These very simple understandings are built into any conversation. Similarly, there are rules of courtesy that require us not endlessly to interrupt other people unless we have extremely good reason to do so. Actors have to internalize these habits in a performance, and then they can generate these differently every night. It was an intuitive awareness that prompted me to rehearse Chekhov in this way. I have since read a great deal about the structure of conversation, and listened to yards of carefully analysed tapes made by specialists so that my hunch as a director was later informed by other more authoritative sources.

Far from imposing his or her will on the actors, the director should be simply reminding, and releasing performances that only the actors' competence can bring to life. Most of the points I am making about Chekhov are familiar to us all; we do these things unthinkingly when we behave according to rules of conversational decorum. Offstage we never go through conversations without, in fact, offering a constant barrage of remedies – apologies, excuses, glosses – for potential or actual offences.

I have already mentioned many points with regard to intonation and inflexion that are not written into the script, but there are also interstitial features that are not part of what is being said, but rather linguistic and paralinguistic performances that affect how something is being said. Again, this is usually done without thought but it affects the audience's perception and understanding of the various relationships – familial and social – in Chekhov's plays, which are so full of the comic surface of social interaction. Often, actors become more sure of a character when they discover for themselves the sort of performances that their fictional part might give of these remedial actions. For example, they might find that one particular character violates turn-taking procedures more than another, and never apologizes for the violation, or does so in a way that heightens the offensiveness of his or her social behaviour. This aspect of performance is much more revealing than any produced by the archivist director who researches historical setting in minute detail. Obviously, certain details need to be checked to avoid anachronism, but Chekhov's short stories are probably the best prefaces to his plays. Descriptions of people's conduct and their mannerisms are conspicuous by their absence from the plays, and in reconstructing them it is very helpful to read the stories, which are full of accounts of gesture, and tiny physical detail. It is as if, confronted by a play-script by Dickens, you found inspiration for details in its performance by looking at the novels, which are full of wonderful vignettes, like the one of Mr Pocket, Herbert Pocket's father, who is seen picking himself up by the hair.[253] It is possible by looking at the stories to effect a kind of internal transfusion of personal mannerisms – those little touches that are rarely written down in plays. A playwright like Shaw does include such details, but he is such a bad observer that his descriptions of personal mannerism are just as much regressions to the real objects as the conversations he writes down. Dickens and Chekhov both excel in providing unexpected oddnesses of behaviour, which, incorporated into a play, can be quite breathtaking. One detail that Chekhov does provide in *Three Sisters* is an odd description of Soliony, who is described as constantly dabbing his hands with cologne. It is an interesting and rare little foible in the script and a very odd gesture that he makes because he hates the smell of his own hands – rather a Dickensian oddity. What makes any Chekhov production lift-off is this morbid sparkle of tiny, subliminal details – idiosyncrasies that are curious but never extraordinary.

Another example of this occurs again in *Three Sisters* where, idling away an evening, they are sitting over the samovar and drinking tea, gossiping while Irena sits playing patience. Chebutykin says something as he turns over a book: 'Balsac's marriage took place at Berdichev.'[254] A moment later, Irena repeats this phrase to herself but she is not responding; she has not been listening attentively. There is no connection between the two speakers; they are merely talking alongside one another, but people often struggle to find some profound significance in this repetition. It is, in fact, what is called echolalia, and unless it is treated as such, the effect is lost. It is a masterly inclusion of something that gives the genuine rhythm of undirected speech. Irena is preoccupied with turning over a card and the phrase has simply gone in one ear, and she faintly repeats the sound. Chekhov's plays are simply concerned with showing the chronic coming and going of fairly undirected discourse. Often, the so-called philosophical conversation suggested by characters is treated with too much reverence. When Vershinin says 'Let's do a bit of philosophizing,' the response reads 'Yes, let's. What about?' […] 'Well…let's try to imagine what life will be like after we're dead, say in two or three hundred years.' This is usually played with pace, firm intention and ferocious academic enthusiasm, but people rarely talk like this. It is a game and they are merely trying to fend off boredom and pass the time. The line might go: '*(yawn)* What about? *(Pause.)* Well *(pause)* let's – try to – imagine – what – life – will – be – like *(yawn)* after we're dead, – say – in two – or three hundred years.' Then there might be a long gap.

Chekhov has been performed too often by people trying to sing the lines. There are no arias in Chekhov – only a diminishing sonata that is written in very atonal music. Subsequently, the characters need to be fairly radically redesigned so that they are neither too romantic, nor too attractive, nor too melodramatic. The ordinariness must be emphasized with the humour, although I have allowed some eccentricity in casting when in one production of *The Seagull* we had Fenella Fielding playing Arkadina. In another production it was Irene Worth, who was very funny

259

but perhaps too grand.[255] Arkadina is, after all, rather vulgar. Chekhov's characters are very provincial, small-town people, not really gentry, who while away the time playing lotto and going on uneventful journeys. Conversations and veal cutlets – that's all there is to life.

The horror story
Interviewed by Dr Christopher Evans
BBC Radio 3, 23 December 1971

Three years on from his television film of the short story "Oh, Whistle, and I'll Come To You, My Lad", *Miller was invited to reflect on M. R. James's skills as a writer of horror.*[256]

> Now there began to be seen, far up the shore, a little flicker of something light-coloured moving to and fro with great swiftness and irregularity. Rapidly growing larger, it, too, declared itself as a figure in pale, fluttering draperies, ill-defined. There was something about its motion which made Parkins very unwilling to see it at close quarters. It would stop, raise arms, bow itself towards the sand, then run stooping across the beach to the water-edge and back again; and then, rising upright, once more continue its course forward at a speed that was startling and terrifying.[257]

EVANS: This is an enormously effective piece of writing because it conjures up in one's mind, immediately, something…the 'something' that James has caught there, which isn't merely the lack of description. He introduces something about the motion of the thing which is alien and unpleasant. This seems to me to be the essence of James.

MILLER: Well, it's very significant in fact that what is described is really a paraphrase of what psychologists would give of the appearance of objects as they present themselves on the edge of the field of vision, in that part of the retina which is not equipped to provide detailed information but can only provide very vague outlines: differences between light and shade, and differences of movement. We know for example that the human eye is divided into two sectors – the central field of vision, which is equipped to deal with detailed pattern, and the peripheral field of vision, which is designed just to tell the difference between light and shade and states of movement. Objects which are on the periphery of the field of vision can never be seen in detail. They produce a state of alarm because they are alerting you to the existence of something which might or might not be threatening. And as long as it's on the field of vision, it's always potentially threatening. Brought into the central field of vision, where its details can now be seen, it can be diagnosed, accurately classified and appropriate action undertaken. But so long as it remains out there on that edge of the field of vision, where you can't quite tell what its shape is, or what its colour is, or what its form is, it is still in that unclassifiable area and therefore is potentially a risky object. I think what James has intuited here is a very, very refined description of his subject's capacity to analyse the fact that what he was seeing was something which did not have the characteristic form of an ordinary, organic object, but was unclassifiable and peculiar in its motion.

EVANS: This business about not being too detailed in your description of the ghost – do you think that this…if it's going to be successful, do you think this partly accounts for the relative lack of success of ghost figures in the theatre and in movies?

MILLER: I think it's one of the reasons. I think it's extremely hard to create a visual counterpart to a ghost because it's hard to put on a screen something which is going to occupy the periphery of the vision of the audience. To put it on the screen is instantly to place it on the centre of the retina of the audience, and therefore it's there in all its detail and can instantly be classified and seen for what it is. I think the way to do it is simply to produce events and incidents which are themselves quite natural, but they're in a context where they shouldn't actually happen. In other words you don't need to present anything which visually is in itself abnormal, but you simply need to present two normal incidents which shouldn't be there at all.

EVANS: Now does the interpretation that the audience puts upon these juxtaposed events have to be a supernatural one?

MILLER: Well it depends how you arrange it. For example, in the James "Oh, Whistle, and I'll Come to You, My Lad" [1904], one of the most

261

successful moments in the written story is the finding of the upper bed by the maid, the discovery that the bedclothes have been mysteriously ruffled in the night – that it's been slept in.[258] Now, you don't need to see the creature that's done it; you merely need to know that only one person has been in that room and that therefore the bed should have remained unruffled. So what is upsetting here is no particular 'appearance' which is supernatural, but the juxtaposition of two incidents which together add up to a supernatural occurrence. A ruffled bed after all is a ruffled bed, but a ruffled bed in a room in which only one person has been sleeping is an extremely unsettling idea.

EVANS: So the problem with the ghost in the theatre and in the movies is that both are so visually…both are visual arts in the sense that they present things, they demand that you look at the thing in the full frontal vision, and it simply doesn't work because no one is prepared to accept anything in the peripheral.

MILLER: Well there are two visual tricks which you can use, I think, to present the thing visually. One of them is to present an extremely fleeting vision; in other words, the very rapid cut so that the mind hardly has time to fasten on the object, and that's the equivalent of placing it in the periphery of vision. You can place it in the centre of vision but it's there so fast that the mind hasn't got time to scan it, and that I think is always the trick which is used. Or else you pan very rapidly over the object of horror, *or* you present the object in a very anomalous form so that you can't quite tell what it is. For example, I had a number of technical difficulties, when doing *Whistle and I'll Come to You*, with the object on the beach in the extract that you've just read. We spent two whole days handling elaborate, concrete, physical machinery to try and create this fluttering drapery moving across the beach. We had meteorological balloons with long strings suspending a strange polythene object, and I'm afraid that on the screen it simply looked like a large polythene object suspended from meteorological balloons. It wasn't until we actually used something far simpler, and none of the technical devices of the BBC Visual Effects Department, that we really succeeded. What we did in the end was to hang a piece of dirty dishcloth from a string about 20 feet from the camera, from two beanpoles which were placed just on the edge of the frame, so that you couldn't see the beanpoles and nor could you see the strings. All that you could see was this dirty dishcloth. We then started to move the beanpoles very slowly towards the camera so that the wind caught in the cloth and began to wave it. It had no particular shape, no particular outline. It just fluttered in a rather unsettling way. We then stretched the film, and that's to say we printed every frame twice, thereby slowing down the movement of the thing, and also giving it a curious, anomalous, jerky progress. The actual effect of this was to reproduce a movement which was quite unlike any movement which could possibly occur with an animal or with a mechanical object. It had a strange, jerky, syncopated, glutinous movement which was extremely disgusting when it was on the screen. You couldn't quite tell what it was at all. It was too far away to tell it was a dishcloth. All that you saw was a sort of filthy turmoil in the middle distance.

EVANS: And no doubt M. R. James would have been proud of it.

MILLER: I think he would have been quite pleased!

EVANS: Of course James can also do detail beautifully if he wants to. The case that I think of is in "Lost Hearts", there are one or two images in that: the creature seen in an old bathroom, lying in the bath, through some frosted glass. A tremendously powerful image. And also two children seen in the moonlight outside a window, and here his very sharp writing and quite a bit of detail is equally effective.[259]

MILLER: It's also significantly detailed in "The Mezzotint" [1904], where the minutely detailed account of the movement of the figure on the lawn is reproduced almost with the same grain as the engraving itself.[260] But here of course he's producing a sense of the uncanny by a different technique altogether. It's to do not so much with the appearance as with a disorder of classification once again. After all, pictures are known to us as things which do not move, which are embalmings of states of affairs. The whole essence of a photograph or of a snapshot or of a picture is that time is *stilled* and fixed at that moment. And what James does is to reverse the classification and present us with, in fact, what now is very familiar to us: a moving picture on a framed screen.

EVANS: It's interesting, isn't it, that James really scorns the invisible creature, which was quite a fashionable type of ghost, although a limited one. I'm thinking of "The Horla" [1887] for example by de Maupassant, where a man is plagued by a totally invisible being. Now, that is a horrific notion. None of us would like this to happen to ourselves, and yet it's got limited potential because you can only have so many stories about totally invisible creatures. What do you think are the reasons for James's enormous success? Because he does zig-zag back and to between a piece of intuitive writing, such as in "Oh, Whistle, and I'll Come To You, My Lad" where something is seen in the periphery of vision, to something with a lot of sharp detail.

MILLER: I think there are two or three things which contribute to James's success. One I think is that he is a first-class naturalistic writer. There is an authorative sense of realism, a tremendous sense of physical authenticity about the time and place which he conjures up. He reproduces a world of late-nineteenth-century English academics and clerics –

EVANS: Which he was one.

MILLER: Which he was one himself – who live in a clearly recognizable world of studies and manuscripts and palimpsests, and it's by reproducing the dreary physical detail of this life and then slightly altering by four or five degrees the events which occur within it, which bring these into some startling relief. It's very important when writing a ghost story not to magnify the incident and not to make the incident too extravagant, because once you do that you stretch belief beyond the point where the subject becomes interested in the story.

EVANS: For example, a long chase, featuring a ghost chasing you endlessly through…no matter how horrible the house, the chase gets less and less exciting the longer it goes on.

MILLER: In a sense it's very like pornography, in this way. Pornography is really more successful when it sets itself in a very clear, dull, recognizable circumstance. In rather extravagant circumstances, one's interest begins to flag because it reproduces a world with which one can't identify. Therefore it only needs an extremely small shift of reality to produce a very large shock, either of erotic or supernatural sensation.

EVANS: One thing that James does is to set up, to make his background authentic, *doubly* authentic. He not only gives a lot of attention to local detail but he also introduces the apparently solid themes of archaeology, antiquarianism, and also the church very strongly featured in his stories:

the vicar who has the church service and yet, nevertheless, he still finds himself briefly face-to-face with something that is beyond him. In "The Treasure of Abbot Thomas" [1904][261] there's a whole lot of initial story which merely deals with the antiquarian's attempt to find this particular box. He lowers himself down the well and even now it's nothing more than almost an archaeological adventure story until he finds the box, opens it, and something reaches out and puts its hands around his neck…that is the total story in effect. He then runs away from the well and there's practically nothing much more to it.

MILLER: Well it's a very good lure, you see, and the reader is drawn in by his fascination with a very esoteric expertise. One of the reasons for the success, for example, of that architectural programme *Animal, Mineral, Vegetable?*, was to hear experts talking in detail about the physical arrangements and matter of the various exhibits, and this is exactly what James does. He plays a game of Animal, Mineral, Vegetable with us and then, quite suddenly, presents a fourth category which is neither animal, mineral, nor vegetable.

Can English satire draw blood?
Observer, 1 October 1961[262]

It is significant that the opening of The Establishment should capture the front page of the *Observer Weekend Review*. It is also slightly disturbing, since it shows an interest the very benevolence of which could well disarm the toxic intentions of the project.

The original idea of the club was born 18 months ago in Cambridge, conjured out of the amber haze of an all-night drinking session. Nicholas Luard, an undergraduate, was entertaining Peter Cook, another undergraduate, who had already startled Cambridge with his bizarre contributions to the Footlights Revue. Cook had been fascinated, on his visits to the continent, by the famous political nightclubs there. Luard, who had spent a year painting in Paris before coming up, shared Cook's interest. Between them they realized the exciting possibilities of starting the same sort of thing in London.

They reckoned that the time was ripe. The English theatre had begun to stir in its sleep. The fall-out from the Osborne explosion was already yielding its genetic changes as were the satirical *non sequiturs* of N. F. Simpson (Cook had played in an ADC production of *A Resounding Tinkle*, and his own sketches bore the scratches of this new surrealist attack).[263] Beckett's ragamuffin metaphysics, Pinter's psychotic menace and the success of Joan Littlewood's saucy productions had all sharpened the climate of the London theatre. There was, as yet, however, no place where an audience could sit and for the price of a drink enjoy the harsh impromptu satire which had for years been an accepted feature of the continental scene.

Revue, with its rapid montage of sketches and songs, seemed to offer the best form for the satire that Cook and Luard were aiming at. Unfortunately, at that time revue was stifled by the values of Shaftesbury Avenue. Cook had already written many of the numbers for the highly successful *Pieces of Eight* (1959), but the bony outlines of his contributions were softened and blurred by their gay commercial setting. Tinselly dance routines, a-fidget with glow-paint and fishnet, would follow one of his dour, screwy little numbers and promptly erase it from the mind of the audience.

In our revue, *Beyond the Fringe* (1960), we tried to rinse away some of this gaudy sediment. We abandoned décor, dancing and all the other irrelevant dum-de-da of conventional revue, hoping to give the material a chance to speak for itself. Even then, however, the full effect was dulled by the demands of the Lord Chamberlain. Until one could escape his bloodshot gaze there was no real hope of putting the last edge on the satirical scalpel. The privacy of a club offered a unique opportunity. There is a satisfying irony in the fact that the final choice of premises should have fallen on a disused strip-joint.

In France and Germany social and political satire has always been readily available. It is an ancient idiom and part of the popular culture of the continent. The cabaret, the chansonnier and the night-club were a natural focus for comic satire. In Germany and Austria there was a strong tradition which stemmed from the stylish buffoonery of the eighteenth century *commedia dell'arte*. The popular ballad was commonly exploited. By juggling with the lines of well-known songs, twisting the verses and shuffling the stanzas, the singer would produce a sort of musical collage which often had a strong satirical effect. Then there would be sketches, recitations and lampoons.

The targets of these attacks were often very local. While some of them were extremely witty, many of the sketches relied for their effect on simple name-dropping. The audience gained considerable pleasure from hearing the names of local luminaries merely mentioned in the comic context of the cabaret. In this respect the artists were enacting a primitive social ritual which springs from the magical belief that the pronunciation of the opponent's name somehow reduces his power – an extension of the Rumpelstilstkin story.

Even today, this naming ritual plays an important part in political cabaret. It is to be seen in the Paris chansonnier where many of the acts consist of an elaborate *double entente* upon the names of politicians. Even Mort Sahl sometimes uses the technique. He started one of his acts by simply reeling off the names of Eisenhower's Cabinet. The audience squealed in delight. He helped to puncture the McCarthy myth as much by naming him as by any witty construction.

In the austere intimacy of a café or a nightclub this name-dropping is an effective and legitimate device. In the extravagant and impersonal setting of a full-scale theatre revue it can become vapid and irritating. One can see this rather nicely in some of the recent English revues. Alerted to the prestige that was attached to political comment, some contemporary revue writers have tried to gain favour with the critics by conscientiously peppering their otherwise perfectly conventional sketches with roguish references to well-known politicians.

Naive attempts such as these are clearly hopeless, but it is also doubtful whether genuine satire could *ever* succeed in the context of conventional revue. Comment is muffled by glamour and in a large theatre the mere distance between performers and audience dissipates the effective energy of a satirical statement. In the café and the intimate cabaret, on the other hand, artists and audience are bound together in sceptical conspiracy. They hatch the satire between them. At The Premise, in New York, for example, the audience suggest the topics they would like to see dealt with. After a short interval, in which the players go away and discuss the suggestions, a new act is produced which is neatly tailored to the issues of the moment.

The café set-up in Germany and Austria ensured the same fertile intimacy. The cafés and bars were, and still are, important social centres. The cabarets performed in these places simply crystallized and put in a more epigrammatic form the conversational topics of the clients – a sort of comic feedback. The café proprietors were always on the lookout for new stunts for filling their large premises. A good, sharp cabaret fitted the bill nicely.

The performers were often students and young artists; the productions, done on a shoestring, consisted of sketches and ballads built around a compère who provided a caustic commentary. There were geniuses of the idiom such as Aristide Bruant in Paris and Karl Valentin in Munich. The drama of Brecht shows the signs of his early association with such performances, with their ballads and commentaries.

These cabarets drew many creative currents, especially from the area of the graphic arts. In the quick, improvised décor of these shows the young artist George Grosz, for example, found an exciting platform for his work. It was at the Cabaret Voltaire, in Zürich, in 1916, that a group of young *émigrés* which included Kokoschka, Tristan Tzara and Hans Arp started the Dada movement. Brecht showed a lively use of back-projections in his productions of *Mahagonny*.

Cabaret of this sort is a natural product of the restless European scene. The political flux of the continent generates a creative scepticism which had a readymade vehicle in the traditional forms of popular entertainment. The ceaseless *va-et-vient* of princelings, parties and politicians, the wars, the revolutions, the barricades and all the other furnishings of turbulence prevented the formation of that stifling sense of Establishment which marked the English scene from the accession of the Georges. European satire thrived best under the old-fashioned, indolently repressive regimes in which offensive comment was punished by short terms of imprisonment rather than by execution. The sort of regime, for example, which would fine Phillipon 6,000 francs for his famous pear-face cartoon of Louise-Philippe, or imprison the Austrian comedian Nestroy for his attacks on the malpractices of the local tradesmen.

Such satire is soon stamped out by the more streamlined repression of the modern totalitarian state. In France today, for example, the rather outdated paternalistic absolutism of de Gaulle is a good atmosphere for the chansonnier and for journals such as *Le Canard Enchaîné*. These, however, would soon wither if the more extremist elements succeeded in unseating de Gaulle. East Berlin does, in fact, boast a few cabarets but they deal with the abuses of a bureaucracy; a form of satirical criticism which is tolerated and even encouraged by the communists. All-out political satire, on the other hand, would not stand a chance.

American cabaret presents a different aspect altogether. Isolated from the baroque traditions of European satirical theatre, the idiom of American satire draws its inspiration from slick-tongued confidence tricksters or the old frontier: the tall-story-teller, the peddler of patent medicines and the hot-gospeller. The modern American cabaret performer is a distillation of this wiseguy tradition, by Mark Twain out of *Elmer Gantry*.[264] It is the apotheosis of pure talk.

Today there are many clubs devoted to such acts, where fast-talking hipsters keep up a breathless commentary on the social and political scene in a language which combines urban jargon with the rural, cracker-barrel accents of the West. In San Francisco there is the hungry i where Mort Sahl first made his Custer stand. Chicago has the Second City. New York has The Premise. There are many others.

Mort Sahl is the natural spokesman of this group and it is unfortunate that his true talent should have been so shabbily distorted in his recent visit to England. America spawns these new humourists as fast as satellites. In the first wave came Sahl, Lenny Bruce and Bob Newhart. Up and coming are Dick Gregory, Mel Brooks and a host of others. Sahl's favourite victims were the golfing Magoos of the Eisenhower Administration, although he is now upsetting his Democrat following by sniping along the New Frontier. Mel Brooks takes a swipe at the sentimental heroism of the New Astronauts ('What do you plan on doing up in space?' 'I guess I'll puke my guts out.'). Bob Newhart has a routine which involves Khrushchev being rehearsed for a television appearance ('There's too much glare off his head; we'll have to use a head-spray on the night.'). Lenny Bruce produces an imaginary conversation between Eisenhower and Nixon in which Eisenhower tries to explain why the Vice-President's Latin American tour was such a disaster ('It's your wife, Dick. She overdresses!'). The American air is a-buzz with these hornets.

While America is stung into a new political insight, the English satirical scene displays an oily calm. English satire, unequalled in the eighteenth century both for ferocity and point, has dwindled to a whimsical form of self-congratulation. The small plays of Fielding, the pamphlets of Swift and the cruel cartoons of Gillray and Hogarth were the last flowering of a formidable national talent for political criticism. The growth of good manners and the rise of the philistine values of an industrial elite soon suffocated this native genius. There is a record of a guest at a house party in the early part of the nineteenth century causing monumental offence by passing round a sheaf of political prints – prints of the kind which only 30 or 40 years before were the accepted currency of a satirical entertainment.

It is the same spirit that makes it a breach of good taste today to discuss politics or religion in the intimacy of a club. Such a spirit coincides, I imagine, with the development of the nineteenth-century English public school, with its emphasis on loyal and unquestioning service: with the rise of a new class, anxious to establish itself with unshakeable values and a reputation for reliability and sound judgement.

'Theirs not to reason why' is here an expression of praise and approval rather than a signal for a rain of scorching contempt which such blinkered loyalty richly deserves. 'Bloody fools' is the only healthy reply on hearing the news of the Light Brigade fiasco. It is to be hoped that when The Establishment opens its doors, the cry of 'Bloody fools' will ring loud and clear through Soho and down the courtly reaches of Whitehall.

Good manners have suffocated English satire more effectively than any secret police. The smug courtesy of the public school sixth-former, neatly adjusted to the demands of loyal service in a growing Empire, takes all the lifeblood out of satire. John Osborne, Nigel Dennis, Pinter and Simpson have gone a long way towards blowing the top of this *Fifth Form at St Dominic's*.[265] The sturdy, sterling figure of the school prefect is at last becoming an object of ridicule.

Forster had already effectively knocked against this tradition in the novel, but the philistine values persisted in the theatre. The Establishment represents a research station in which we might see developed the weapons necessary for the final overthrow of the Neo-Gothic stronghold of Victorian good taste.

As I mentioned earlier, however, the success of this project is seriously threatened by a subtle defence with which the members of The Establishment protect themselves against these new attacks. It is the threat of castration by adoption; of destruction by patronage. Cook is already somewhat disturbed by the number of applications for membership which bear the postmark SW1. We have begun to experience the same threat in our revue. Each night, before curtain up, sleek Bentleys evacuate a glittering load into the foyer. Some of the harsh comment in the programme is greeted with shrill cries of well-bred delight which reflect a self-indulgent narcissism which takes enormous pleasure in gazing at the satiric reflection.

It is the same spirit that moves the *Queen* magazine to make smart talking points out of misery and squalor. One might get something like this: 'Everyone is talking about trachoma, the beastly eye complaint which blemishes the eyes of millions every year. Holiday in Bizerta and see it for yourself. The beaches in this disaster-struck Tunisian town are unparalleled in Europe.' Cook and his associates will have their time cut out slipping the dart through the complex defences of this group.

The ranks are drawn up and the air resounds with the armourer's hammer. When battle is joined one can only hope that blood will be drawn; that The Establishment will be attacking from without rather than firing off popguns from within, for the entertainment of one big happy family.

A conversation with Richard Dawkins
The Atheism Tapes, BBC4, 8 November 2004

In the process of making his three-part documentary Atheism: A Rough History of Disbelief, *Miller conducted a number of interviews. The main series could not accommodate the full extent of these conversations, so it was decided that six additional half-hour programmes would be transmitted, each focusing on a single speaker. In the case of biologist Richard Dawkins, Miller knew that 'the theory of evolution provides support for his growing disbelief, but I wanted to know why atheism was such a pressing issue for him.'*

MILLER: Why is this argument so important at this point in the twenty-first century, when you and I can see that it's a settled issue – yet we find ourselves in an embattled position?

DAWKINS: As a scientist, to me it is important because I *do* regard the hypothesis of a supernatural designer… As a scientific hypothesis, I think it's a wrong one, but it actually *is* science. I don't have much patience with theologians who say, 'Well, we're really not disagreeing. It's just that religion concerns itself with morality and science concerns itself with how the universe is, and there's no problem between them.' To me there is a problem because the moment you talk about a supernatural creator, designer, *anything*…you are advancing a scientific hypothesis which is either right or wrong. A universe that has a supernatural intelligence – a supernatural over-mind in it – is a very, very different kind of universe, from a purely scientific point of view, than a universe that hasn't. And it's a very interesting difference. It's a *massive* difference. And I think it's scientifically interesting to hold a view of the universe, which I do, that there's no super-mind. Well, there may be minds far superior to ours but they will also have come into existence through a slow, gradual, incremental process. They were not there from the start. People who hold the opposite view, that there was a supernatural intelligence right from the start [that] was responsible for it all, are advancing a very, very diametrically different scientific hypothesis which has got to be either right or wrong. Even if we cannot finally decide whether it is right or wrong, we must at least admit that it is a different hypothesis, a very different hypothesis, and therefore it *matters*.

MILLER: I often encounter religious people who argue in the following way – they'll say, 'Well, it's not really, and we don't think of it as a scientific hypothesis. We think of it as something which involves a leap of faith.' In other words, it's not something which they say can be proved right or wrong. There's no way in which it can be proved right or wrong, because it belongs to a domain of existence and entities about which that sort of proof, disproof and research are irrelevant. There is something which they call the leap of faith which identifies you with this Creator.

DAWKINS: Well that sort of thing just leaves me cold, and I can't really even begin to empathize with it. I understand that it may be in principle impossible to demonstrate one way or another, so there may be no scientific test you could *ever* do to decide the question and that I could believe, but to me that still leaves the point that either it is true or it isn't. A leap of faith – which just means that a person has an inside, internal feeling of revelation which is not shareable with anybody else and which can't be demonstrated to anyone else – to me that just sounds like a mental delusion.

MILLER: Why is it, then, that people actually invoke the notion of a leap of faith, not as a weakness on their part but as some sort of virtue which is lacking in people like you and me; that there is some sort of peculiar willingness, and a willingness which indicates some sort of spiritual generosity, which we somehow don't have.

DAWKINS: Well, firstly it's important to stress that the kind of person you are now talking about is a very much more sophisticated animal than the sort who argues about creationism and that kind of thing, because those people really *would* think that there was some intervention by the deity in the world. But your people, with their internal revelation, presumably accept that their God doesn't actually intervene in the world. Otherwise they would have to concede that it is a scientific hypothesis. So, the domain in which He or it works seems to be a rather strangely detached-from-the-world domain purely concerned with internal feelings that people privately have.

MILLER: But the implication is that it's a domain from which we are unfortunate enough to be excluded.

DAWKINS: That's right.

MILLER: It's a lack of some sort of talent, generosity or blindness on our part which cuts us off from the beauty and majesty of this domain.

DAWKINS: Like not knowing what it's like to fall in love; being deprived, being deficient in some important way. Yes, I can understand that, and I could actually imagine that we're not so deprived, because you and I probably do have feelings which may very well be akin to a mystical wonder – when we contemplate the stars, when we contemplate the galaxies, when we contemplate life, the sheer expanse of geological time. I experience it and I expect you experience internal feelings which sound pretty much like what mystics feel, and they call it God. And I've been called a very religious person for that reason. If I *am* called a religious

273

person, then my retort to that is you're playing with words, because what the vast majority of people mean by religious is something utterly different from this sort of transcendent, mystical experience. What *they* mean is an entity which interferes in the world, which actually has some kind of impact upon the world and therefore is a scientific hypothesis. The transcendent, *mystic* sense – that people who are both religious and non-religious, in my usage of the term, [use] – is something very, very different. In that sense I probably am a religious person. *You* probably are a religious person. But it doesn't mean that we think that there is a supernatural being that interferes with the world…that does anything, that manipulates anything or, either way, that it's worth praying to or asking forgiveness of sins from, etc.

MILLER: But once we concede that… I know this is what I call 'the clergyman in the laurel bushes,' that as soon as one makes any concession in the direction of wonder or a sense of majesty, of mystery – and it's not confined to the large things… Just simply contemplating mitochondria produces the same sort of Blakeian feeling that he had from grains of sand – they…the clergyman in the laurel bush, leaps out and says 'Ah! You *are* one of us after all.'

DAWKINS: Yes. It's happened to me over and over again. I think it's deeply dishonest and I think it's fooling around with words and not understanding, or not honestly dealing with the way ordinary people use words. And so I prefer to use the words like religion, like God, in the way the vast majority of people in the world would understand them, and reserve a different kind of language for the feeling that we share with, possibly, your clergyman in the laurel.

MILLER: As soon as one does admit that and admits the unknowability of things, there is always the implication from the religious – not necessarily from the orthodox religions, but the people who are susceptible to energies and vibrations and aromas and so forth – that they often say, 'There must be something…'

DAWKINS: Well okay, but it just doesn't follow. It's just…

MILLER: Well, my answer when they say 'There must be something' is, 'Well yes. There is. It's everything. It's *there* without any super-added nonsense.'

DAWKINS: I think I would hit back harder than that, actually, and say that the sense of wonder that one gets as a scientist – contemplating the cosmos, or contemplating mitochondria – is much grander than anything that you will get by contemplating the traditional objects of religious mysticism.

Satire's brightest star: Peter Cook
Guardian, 10 January 1995[266]

Following the death of Peter Cook, Miller was invited to share memories of his Beyond the Fringe *co-star.*

In 1959 a meeting was convened in a Euston Road restaurant by John Bassett, who was putting the revue *Beyond the Fringe* together for the Edinburgh Festival. Dudley Moore, Alan Bennett and I were immediately overwhelmed by the astonishing improvisational productivity of Peter Cook's imagination, which seemed to come from some source completely alien to the person in front of us.

Peter was much more elegant, handsome, assured and good-looking than us, which was quite at odds with his disruptive surrealism. When we saw our costume – uniform grey-flannel suits – he was the only one who looked good in it. He was very puzzling to confront. I had seen him in the Footlights – an astonishing, strange, glazed, handsome creature producing weird stuff, the like of which I'd never heard before. I remember his first line when I was shot upright in my seat by him. He was playing some person in a suburban kitchen concealed behind a newspaper. He didn't say a word, but all eyes were drawn to him. Then he rustled the newspaper and simply said, 'Hello, hello, I see the *Titanic's* sunk again.' One knew one was in the presence of comedy at right angles to all the comedy we'd heard.

I have no idea where it came from. Peter himself, I think, was mystified by it. He ought to have been an extremely successful young diplomat. You felt you were with somebody from the Foreign Office who had suddenly gone completely bananas. He was like one of those discreet people shadowing Douglas Hurd. His father was a colonial diplomat, so that was the world Peter came from. He was a master of linguistic paradox, phrases which you can't invent. I don't think he ever set himself the task of being disruptive. He saw strange obsessional people, and in a strange, almost ventriloquial way, they took possession of him. He had a grasp of a character's idioms, so that people like E. L. Wisty or these mad upper-class judges are memorable in exactly the same way as some of the great Dickens characters.

Peter was always rather distant from us. Later there were reunions, when we would sit at a table and laugh and joke. He was always interested in this strange world of showbiz, celebrity golf, football. Yet he had this phoenix-like capacity to re-emerge. There was that revival when he did those four wonderful and inspired pieces with Clive Anderson a year ago.[267] He hadn't had his time. If anyone could come up with what he did for Anderson, at a time when he was said to have not fulfilled his promise, they would be very grateful.

The fulfilment that he did give was so much greater than what has been given by most people, and at such a level that it would be rancorous discontent to complain of a lack of other things that he might have done. He gave a great gift to British theatre, and the British comic idiom. There was no one quite like him.

The call of the wild
New York Review of Books, 16 September 1976[268]

In the fifth year of the new Republic, a group of peasants in a small rural district of south-western France reported that they had seen a naked youth scampering through the woods, apparently searching for acorns and roots. After a series of captures and escapes the child was finally secured and referred to a local orphanage, on the written understanding that his peculiar case deserved the attention of an expert. By this time the mute, ferocious child had attracted great interest among the local intelligentsia and, for the next month, there was a heated dispute over who should take charge of him. On 29 January 1800, the director of the orphanage, who had already completed a long preliminary account of the child's appearance and behaviour, received the following official letter from Paris.

If it is true that you have currently in your orphanage a young wild boy, twelve years old, who was found in the woods, it would indeed be important for the progress of human knowledge that a zealous and sincere observer take him in charge and, postponing his socialization for a little while, examine the totality of his acquired ideas, study his manner of expressing them, and determine if the state of man in isolation is incompatible with the development of intelligence.[269]

The writer went on to suggest that these studies should be conducted in Paris under the supervision of a committee chosen from the newly founded Society for Observers of Man. The request was backed by a high-level ministerial directive and, in spite of their understandable reluctance to surrender such an interesting specimen, the local authorities arranged for the boy's transfer to Paris.

On his arrival he was admitted to the Institute for Deaf Mutes, which was at that time supervised by the Abbé Sicard, a founding member of the Society for Observers of Man and a notable authority on the retraining of the deaf.

As far as the members of this society were concerned, the 'savage' child represented an ideal case with which to investigate the foundations of human nature. In fact, when a similar case had been discovered earlier in the previous century, the Scottish philosopher Monboddo had announced that it would prove to be more illuminating than the discovery of 30,000 new stars. By studying a creature of this sort, just as they had previously studied savages and primates, Red Indians and orangutans, the intellectuals of the late eighteenth century hoped to decide what was characteristic of Man. Perhaps it would now be possible to weigh the native endowment of the human species and to settle once and for all the part that was played by society in the development of language, intelligence, and morality.

It was obviously important to know how much the child could be taught. Was he incurably mute, or could this strange, grunting person be persuaded to acquire language? In a lengthy report, painstakingly translated for the first time by Professor Lane in *The Wild Boy of Aveyron*, the psychiatrist Pinel came to the conclusion that Victor, as he was now christened, was in all probability a congenital idiot and that he therefore had not the necessary ability to profit from remedial instruction. Still, the Institute had contracted an obligation to try and, in December 1800, Sicard appointed a young surgeon, Jean Marc Gaspard Itard, to take charge of the boy's education.

Unlike his colleagues, Itard was comparatively optimistic about the child's potential. According to him Victor's problem was not so much that he lacked intelligence but that any intelligence he had had been starved and distorted by isolation. Itard was a devotee of Condillac's theory of human intelligence – as indeed were the more sceptical members of the Society – and as such he believed that the rehabilitation of the child was largely a matter of restocking his undernourished senses and of directing his natural curiosity into paths of profitably stimulating experience.

In the first half of his admirably researched book – much of which consists of reports, letters, and descriptive memoranda, many retrieved and published for the first time – Professor Lane traces the course of this pioneering experiment, taking great care to show how the procedures were systematically underpinned by the epistemology of Condillac. As the narrative slowly unfolds so does one's admiration for Itard's courage and ingenuity. This, it seems, was no ordinary physician but an educational pioneer of the first magnitude.

When confronted by a child like this, the modern therapist brings to him an elaborate apparatus of well-tested theoretical assumptions. Most of these are inherited from the experience of Itard, who had to work them out as he went along. In an atmosphere of gentle reassurance and systematic encouragement, the child was reintroduced to the varieties of his own sensory experience. Consistent regularities were acknowledged and reinforced, and from day to day Itard tried to build up familiar and convincing associations between concrete experiences, personal appetites and certain conventional signs. By teaching Victor to classify his experiences, Itard hoped to reconstruct the ruined mind from its primitive sensory elements. The experiment had only a modest success and, after a few years, Itard abandoned the project entirely. The boy, still unable to learn to speak, died in 1828.

Perhaps the child had deteriorated too far already. Perhaps Pinel's diagnosis contained more than a grain of truth. In any case there were no theoretical precedents to support and maintain Itard as he conducted the experiment. It is true to say, however, that the principles which he succeeded in extracting from this encounter form the basis of modern pedagogical theory. Itard went on to elaborate them in his work with deaf mutes and mentally retarded children. His protocols, modified by Maria Montessori and other nineteenth-century educators, are now part of the conventional wisdom. In play groups, nurseries and remedial establishments throughout the world, children and teachers are still profiting from the enormous discoveries made during the course of this heroic failure.

Of course, the myth of the 'savage child' has an ancient pedigree. It is easy to understand why. Apart from the fact that it dramatizes a widely-shared fantasy about the negligence and cruelty of our natural parents, the idea that an abandoned infant might be able to survive and even flourish in the wilderness counteracts our normal fears of the indifference or hostility of nature itself. In fact, the will to believe a story of this sort is so strong that if there had not been any 'savage children' we would certainly have invented them. When genuine cases do occur, fact and fiction tend to become hopelessly confused. Even now. For instance, we still read the claim that these children have been raised by wild animals, although the evidence on this score is very shaky to say the least. In one of the most fully documented accounts of this century – the case of Amala and Kamala, the Indian wolf children – an otherwise reliable witness insisted that the two children were found in the company of wolves. This part of the story did not hold up to closer examination, however, but when the case was included in a subsequent survey of so-called 'feral' children, the author himself reverted to the traditional account, as if it were the only way to explain the children's 'bestial' behaviour.

And yet these children don't really behave like animals at all. Admittedly they are dumb and uncouth, they make peculiar sounds, rock on their hunkers, and a careless observer could, I suppose, confuse their eating habits with those of a dog, say. But in fact their conduct is much more characteristic of *abnormal* human beings than of any *normal* animal. So how does the belief in animal upbringing arise in the first place and why does it persist? According to Bruno Bettelheim it is not simply a matter of careless observation.[270] The theory helps to explain facts which might otherwise imply something unacceptably bestial in human nature, and once you opt for a theory which insists that these children must have been *taught* their peculiar habits, it is almost inevitable that the observations will be edited and shaped until they too confirm the theory of acquired bestiality.

Curiously enough, when it came to the creation of an *imaginary* character of this sort, the theory of animal upbringing was not invariably invoked. The 'wild man' of the Middle Ages is a case in point. As far as the medieval storytellers were concerned, enforced solitude was quite enough to deprave the human personality, and although their purely fictional biographies of the 'wild man' sometimes include an 'animal' childhood, many of the stories account for his dumb ferocity in terms of loneliness and hardship. In his remarkable book *Wild Men in the Middle Ages* (1952), Richard Bernheimer suggests that the repressed desire for unhampered self-assertion may finally be projected outward as a colourful fiction representing someone 'who is as free as the beasts, able and ready to try his strength without regard for the consequences to others.'[271]

To judge by the widespread appearance of this entirely mythical character, the desire in question must have been very strong indeed. In addition to his frequent appearance in literary romances, the 'wild man' peeps out of monumental sculpture and illuminated manuscripts and his place in daily life was commemorated in almost every conceivable form of folk art. In fact, the invented image of feral man is so colourful that when genuine cases occurred they were bound to be described in terms that were borrowed from the antecedent fantasies.

This is one of the reasons why the case of Victor is an important example in the history of ideas, quite apart from any influence which his career might have had on educational theory. From Professor Lane's account one can see that for the first time a conscious attempt was being made to reduce the confusing influence of fantasy and folklore. For instance, in one of the first reports on the child, the author takes special pains to note that there were no roughened calluses on the hands or on the knees, as there would have been, presumably, if the traditional picture of four-footedness were true. When the Swedish taxonomist Linné tried to paint a generalized portrait of 'feral' man earlier in the eighteenth century, he confidently and without any good reason included four-footedness as a leading feature.[272]

By the end of the eighteenth century, we are, in Charles Coulston Gillispie's happy phrase, on the edge of objectivity,[273] and as Professor Lane's interesting new material allows us to see, the authorities who took charge of the 'savage child' did their best to describe what was in front of their eyes. Even so, there are touching reminders of traditional superstition. For example, the accounts repeatedly claim that the child would laugh when the weather became stormy, and although this may have been true, it can't be altogether irrelevant that one of the most consistent features of the folkloric 'wild man' was the way in which he was said to sulk in the sunlight and roar with savage laughter whenever it thundered. Evidently the myths of antiquity die hard and, although these students of human nature would have been shocked to acknowledge it, their accounts are recognizably contaminated by elements drawn from traditional fantasies.

But even if they had been able to rid themselves of traditional bias, the attention which the members of the Society gave to this case was bound to be influenced by the vested interests of their own time. Just because these interests happen to be more sophisticated, more recognizably 'scientific' than anything hitherto, it does not mean that their reports are necessarily reliable. In fact, the relative credibility of late-eighteenth-century thought makes it even harder to distinguish the truth. The difficulty is that the intellectual assumptions of the eighteenth century are just close enough to our own to make one believe that the facts gathered under their aegis *might* be true, but not quite close enough to make one absolutely certain that they are. In other words, although the investigations of the 'savage' child were prompted by interests that are not altogether foreign to our own, it would be optimistic to imagine that the reports could be filed along with modern researches on the subject of child development and the origin of language.

It is not that the published facts are wrong or even misleading. They simply don't have the right character to count as science; and although Professor Lane has performed an important historical service by retrieving so much previously unsuspected material, anyone who hopes to gain scientific enlightenment is bound to be frustrated and even bored by these amiably talkative reports. They certainly give the impression that the authors belong to the modern world, but it is largely to the extent that the writing, unlike the previous literature on the subject, is refreshingly free from scholasticism and superstition. In this sense it is like reading Stendhal as opposed to, say, Chrétien de Troyes. Or like looking at the head of a madman by Géricault rather than at a gargoyle on a choir-stall. But compared with the forceful inquiries of a contemporary chemist and physicist like Lavoisier, for instance, these careful observations do not really begin to rate as scientific literature.

Perhaps it is unreasonable to make comparisons between the analyses of Pinel and Itard and the others in Lane's book, and those of a quantitative science like chemistry, but the fact remains that chemistry only became quantitative when Lavoisier's thought had developed the necessary logical structure. And this is precisely what is missing in the case of the wild boy of Aveyron. General curiosity about the existence of innate ideas was not enough to promote a fruitful line of investigation, and although Itard's inquiries were inspired by the epistemology of Condillac, it is hard to deduce any intelligible program of research from Condillac's metaphor of man as a sensitive statue.

To my mind this is why the attempt to diagnose Victor's condition is now doomed to failure. Through no fault of his own, Professor Lane's material cannot really be expected to throw any further light on this issue. A clinician reports his cases in the light of his own diagnostic interests and the questions which a modern investigator would want to ask would not have occurred to a physician in the late eighteenth century. For instance, it is almost impossible to know what the boy's hearing was like. He certainly was not deaf, but a modern paediatrician would want to know whether there had been any selective impairment. The psychiatrist Pinel believed that the child was an imbecile, but without a number of subtle cognitive tests it is almost impossible to weigh this conclusion retrospectively. In any case the diagnosis of idiocy would seem hopelessly elementary to a modern clinician who would want to discriminate between many more conditions than Pinel could possibly have suspected.

As far as diagnosis goes, Itard's conclusion seems much more plausible. According to him, the child's uncommunicative simplicity was probably due to the absence of human tuition at what might have been a critical phase in his linguistic development. In the light of modern work on the acquisition of language – which suggests that children are peculiarly susceptible to learning language only for limited periods after the age of two – this is at least a plausible suggestion. At the same time, it is impossible to know whether Victor had been in the wilderness as long as this theory would have needed him to be. Although there is no reliable evidence to support his assumption, I tend to favour Bruno Bettelheim's suggestion that we often overestimate the length of time children of this sort have been on the run. According to Bettelheim, children like the wild boy may be abandoned because they are defective and not the other way around. He adds, however, that they may have become defective through being psychologically abandoned while still nominally in their parents' care.[274] The garrulous accounts reprinted here provide tantalizing glimpses of what may have been an autistic child. But it is almost certainly a waste of time trying to clinch the issue with the available evidence.

It is interesting to note, however, that Itard seems to overlook what might have been the influence of *emotional* deprivation. According to him, Victor's simplicity was caused by a gap in his cognitive training, through not having been exposed to normal language at a critically impressionable phase in his mental development. And we now recognize, of course, that cognitive ability can just as easily be impaired by early failures of emotional attachment, and that intelligence can wither in the absence of sustained parental love. By insisting on a cognitive cause for a cognitive defect, Itard was affiliating himself with the mechanical empiricism of Locke, La Mettrie and Condillac – a tradition which made little or no allowance for the intellectual effect of so-called moral experience.

This is ironical since Itard's associate, Pinel, was a pioneer in the 'moral' treatment of insanity, and although the pedagogical regime of Itard was justified as based on scientific epistemology, it would be a great mistake to overlook the facilitating effects of permission and respect. In fact, when, at the end of the nineteenth century, Maria Montessori commandeered Itard's method and successfully applied it to the education of normal children, she explicitly emphasized the need to encourage what the child himself brought to the educational experience – that is to say, an energetic and spontaneous urge to explore.[275]

This was not a new idea of course. Something like it had been vividly expressed by the statistician Sir William Petty in the seventeenth century. Writing to Samuel Hartlib in 1647, Petty suggested that children should be introduced to things rather than to a 'rabble of words.'

For we see children do delight in drums, pipes, fiddles, guns made of elder-sticks and bellow's noses, piped keys, etc., for painting flags and ensigns with elderberries and corn-poppy, making ships with paper, and setting even nutshells a-swimming, handling the tools of workmen as soon as they turn their backs.[276]

In other words Petty insisted on the serious significance of play. Although this was later to be dignified as a scientific principle, the recognition of play expressed a new *moral* attitude to the child, acknowledging his personal interests as an essential part of the learning process.

To judge by the career of another memorable child, creative playfulness is not the only road to educational fulfilment. Less than ten years after Itard had given up his experiment with Victor, James Mill successfully steered his infant son through the very 'rabble of words' despised by Petty. No tinkering with painted flags for John Stuart Mill: 'I have no remembrance of the time when I began to learn Greek,' he wrote. 'My earliest recollection on the subject, is that of committing to memory what my father termed vocables, being lists of common Greek words, with their signification in English'![277] No doubt it would be foolish to extrapolate from the career of such an exceptional child; in any case, it is comforting to assume that Mill's famous depression in early adulthood was a delayed after-effect of this Gradgrindian infancy. All the same, at a time when middle-class parents in England and America are becoming increasingly alarmed by the results of an education founded on 'creative play,' it is understandable that there should now be a widespread nostalgia for vocables – even English ones.

It is probably unreasonable to panic about the affable incoherence of the modern primary-school graduate, and anyway there is a substantial body of opinion which argues plausibly, although not altogether convincingly, in favour of such an outcome. Nevertheless, the current suspicion of verbal mastery shows signs of becoming a dangerous cult, and although it would be irresponsible to trace the origins of this cult back to Itard, the fashionable interest in Truffaut's film *L'Enfant Sauvage* (1970), not to to mention Peter Handke's play about Kaspar Hauser, indicate that the image of the speechless child has infiltrated the popular imagination to become, perhaps against their authors' wishes, one of the charter myths of a new primitivism.[278] In fact, as far as a large part of the general public is concerned, the hero of these remedial encounters tends to be appreciated for the way in which he *resists* rehabilitation. (The boy in *Equus* (1973) is a more mischievous case in point.)

There is a growing tendency, in other words, to identify the therapist with all that is corrupt and depraved in modern society and to see his efforts at rehabilitation as an elaborate and persuasive form of cultural kidnapping. Nearly 20 years ago Jacques Barzun recognized the danger in the following words:

> Whatever is formed and constituted, whatever is adult, whatever exerts power, whatever is characteristically Western, whatever [...] embodies complexity of thought, is of less interest and worth than what is native, common and sensual; what is weak and confused; what is unhappy, anonymous and elemental.[279]

It would be a shame if these regrettable tendencies were allowed to overtake and obscure the significance of an important and valuable book. *The Wild Boy of Aveyron* is not a sentimental account of noble savagery but an indispensable contribution to the history of ideas.

Alice in wonderland
Vogue, December 1966[280]

I believe it was Lillian Hellman who first put me up to doing *Alice*. Sitting on the edge of a New York cocktail din we somehow got around to children's books and agreed that *Alice* was a rich, sombre book full of special promise as a film. It had been done before, but they had always missed the point. They had been too jokey, or else too literal. And certainly they had always come unstuck by trying to recreate the style of Tenniel's original illustrations.

Alice is an inward sort of work, more of a mood than a story, so that before it could be turned into a film we had to discover some new key with which to unlock its hidden feeling. Tenniel's drawings are fastened to the printed page. They belong to the world of ink and type and just refuse to translate into photography. All those animal heads and playing cards look fine on the printed page. On celluloid they look like awkward pantomime drag. So we had to go deeper into the text, under the scratchy texture of the print, to find some commanding image which would provide a picture, as inevitable for celluloid as Tenniel's illustrations were for paper.

What was Charles Dodgson (alias Lewis Carroll) about? What is the strange, secret command of *Alice's Adventures in Wonderland* (1865)? Nostalgia and remorse, of course. Like so many Victorians, Dodgson was hung up on the romantic agony of childhood. The Victorians looked on infancy as a period of perilous wonder, when the world was experienced with such keen intensity that growing up seemed like a fall and a betrayal. And yet they seemed to do everything they could to smother this primal intensity of childhood. Instead of listening to these witnesses of innocence, they silenced them, taught them elaborate manners, and reminded them of their bounden duty to be seen and not heard.

Perhaps the adults were frightened and, long before Freud, knew the anarchic vigour of the child. Whatever the reason, they were two-faced about youth, secretly longing for the very condition which they took so many efforts to stifle and restrain. They were caught in a cleft stick between the incompatible claims of duty and sensibility. They knew very well that in growing up they must sacrifice the glory and the freshness of the dream. And yet they realized, too, that only by doing this, by ignoring the splendour in the grass, could they apply themselves to work, to duty, and to substantial public accomplishment.

For above all, the Victorians were prodigious workers with an almost obsessional sense of the dignity of labour. The world pressed down on them with a burden of serious obligation, and anything which interfered with the discharge of this obligation seemed like a frivolous intrusion. Life was short enough without having to waste time on the petty sensitivities of childhood.

Yet the Victorians knew, or suspected at least, the damage they were doing by hurrying on to maturity like this. Deep down, in moments of sentiment and remorse, they realized that infant sensibility was more than a frivolous luxury – a core of precious spiritual vitality without which life was a meaningless drudge. It is significant that when John Stuart Mill fell into a depression in early manhood, he was comforted not by work, but by the poems of Wordsworth.

Alice is another Victorian's quest for consolation in childhood. Both books are about the pains of growing up. In *Wonderland* and *Looking-Glass*, a sombre punctilious child reaches hesitantly toward her own seniority, realizing as she does so the terrible penalties of the adult state. Right at the start of *Wonderland* she feels herself growing bigger, only to feel with an awful shock that by doing so she can no longer get down the passageway and out to the garden with its cool fountains and bright flowers.

The journey which Alice then makes takes her deeper and deeper into the mesh of adult obligation – into a world where punctuality is the cardinal virtue and where disobedience is punished by having your head off. And the story converges on an occasion which is surely the epitome of adult responsibility: a trial. At the end it is not the Knave who suffers but Alice herself, who is finally accused of having grown too big.

Everyone Alice meets on the way to this climax represents one of the different penalties of growing up. One after the other, the characters seem to be punished or pained by their maturity. The Queen is infuriated, the King is browbeaten. The Caterpillar is a fossilized pedant and the Duchess a bibulous old frump, prompted by morals and mottos.

Even the congenial characters are bowed down with pathos and remorse. The Gryphon and Mock Turtle sink into senility with a few tattered reminiscences of their school days to comfort them in their shallow grief. The Hatter lives on riddles; the Dormouse snoozes into his dotage. The whole book is a panorama of corruption and decay.

The animal heads and playing cards are just camouflage. All the characters in the book are real, and the papier-mâché disguises with which Carroll covers them all up do nothing to hide the indolent despair.

Once this was clear, the way to make the film fell neatly and inevitably into place. No snouts, no whiskers, no carnival masks. Everyone could be just as he was. And Alice herself? Not the pretty sweetling of popular fancy. I advertised for a solemn, sallow child, priggish and curiously plain. I knew exactly what she would be like when I found her. Still, haughty and indifferent, with a high smooth brow, long neck and a great head of Sphinx hair.

Seven hundred kids answered the advertisement and for three months I riffled through an album of bouncing, bonny Mods. It seems that every girl in England sees herself as Alice, or at least some jolly sweet version of her. Half of them came in as holiday snaps, knee-deep in estuary water, with a bronzed brute of a father about to throw some coiled rope out of the background. But the real Alice, my little white whale, was elsewhere.

Then my Alice turned up. Just as I'd imagined her. She was the only child I interviewed out of the 700 who applied. She had no wish to become an actress, but her mother thought that a summer stint like this would do her good – bring her out a bit. She was too much with her books and a bout of jolly acting might bring some roses to her cheeks.[281]

She was the reincarnation of Alice. In scene after scene she met the distinguished cast with the same indifferent courtesy with which in the story Alice meets everyone. Oddly enough this child required the least direction of all. Her nature supplied everything that needed to be done. She cruises through the film with prissy hauteur.

Not once did this girl do what I feared any child actress might have done. She never emoted, and best of all she never showed any surprise. She just spoke her lines and carried herself straight. As a dreamer, after all, Alice is the landlord of her estate and the characters are her tenants. She must come on like a stuffed Infanta, cold and gorgeous.

The film is very elaborate in its setting. This is not strictly true to the nature of dreams, most of which are rather slipshod about the details of décor. Dreams are only intermittently elaborate in visual detail. But I wanted to recreate, in addition to a dream, that bursting, fatal ripeness of Pre-Raphaelite surrealism.

I wanted the child to move through a world where every detail threatened to blossom with some dreadful vision. Grass blades, dewdrops, bricks, silk brocade, violets and lace. The awful pristine imminence of physical things. So in one set, for the trial, my designer, a magpie genius called Julia Trevelyan Oman, loaded the scene with 4,000 movable props.

It seems that the film contains the entire visual contents of the child's mind. Every object and surface she has ever seen and forgotten looms up with fatal clarity. We ransacked the Tate Gallery for all this. Pictures by Millais, Holman Hunt, Calderon, and Arthur Hughes were digested and assimilated into the décor. Everything to help recreate the nauseating intensity of the Pre-Raphaelite vision.

And then we prayed for heat. We petitioned for that special, syrupy English summer heat when insects play cellos in the grass and oak trees stand stock still on their own doilies of midsummer shadow. Because that's the sort of afternoon when Alice fell to drowsing. We wanted pollen and midges, long drugged silences and the flash of sunlight off a laurel leaf.

Tall order for an English summer, but we got it all. Except for the drugged silences. We didn't get too many of those. American bombers saw to that. Short of going to Ireland there seemed to be no hope of escaping the Strategic Air Command. Even at 38,000 feet a Boeing cuts across the Pre-Raphaelite scene with shattering irrelevance. But we steered a course between the flights, and only once does an aero-engine intrude. We pass it off as a hornet.

We toured three months looking for the right locations. As the summer opened we took off each day into the secret hinterland of rural England. It was ten years since I had been in the depths like this and I had forgotten how mysteriously rural much of England still was.

We took a wide sweep in each of the four quadrants of the compass. And I realized how different each one was – like a different temperament or humour, almost. There was the dry sedgy East: Tennyson country, with huge upholstered skies, cold marshes, and flights of honking swans. And the West, mythical and sleepy, drowsing under swathes of poppy-milk mist. And the Western rivers, too: sleek green and oily, like small Limpopos.

This odyssey through England put me right in the mood for filming. *Alice* is saturated in an intense feeling for the English countryside. It's quite clear that Carroll understood the awful apocalyptic mystery of English nature – its terrible, damp, mossy fecundity, with hobbits and angels ripening like dragonfly larvae in the ooze.

If you stand for a moment quite silent, in an English orchard, say in Gloucestershire, on a hot afternoon in July, you can hear the *Alice* fauna creeping among the grass stems. That's why I filled the movie with dwarfs and midgets. I wanted the best human counterparts for all those jewelled regiments of vermin that crawl down at ankle level in the English grass. And we dressed the dwarfs and midgets all à la Velázquez so as to get Empire of Habsburg insects.

We filmed in the midst of all this for about nine weeks. We forgot where we had come from, and when the end came someone suggested that we just carry on – no film in the camera, sham takes and all – sinking deeper and deeper into the somnolent magic of Alice's last summer as a child.

Breaking out of the box
Interviewed by William F. Condee
Theatre Design and Technology, Winter 1991[282]

Condee writes: 'Miller was in Athens, OH in October 1989 to give a lecture at Ohio University for the Kennedy Lecture Series. During a dinner with many faculty of the university I requested a breakfast interview and suggested a time. Miller quickly accepted, but asked, "Are you sure that will give us enough time? Can't we meet a little earlier?"'

CONDEE: I was reading articles that were written about your staging techniques and in a number of them you were quoted as saying that you were influenced by painting, that you've studied painting a great deal and that whenever you're in a city, you run off to the museum. Would you say that because of this importance of painting you're more inclined to work on the proscenium stage?

MILLER: No. My study of painting is not with a view to making my productions look as much like paintings as possible. I think that would be awful – just *tableaux vivants*, and so forth. It's simply that paintings, drawings and so forth are the only evidence we have of what things looked like in the past. And if you want to get some sort of indication about clothing, posture, the fall of light and even, indeed, in some cases, the organization of space, paintings are the only way in which we can derive some information.

Of course, you also get a lot of information from looking at the disposition of buildings around public spaces as well. They are themselves theatrical organizations. A place like the Campidoglio in Rome is a theatre space; so is the Piazza della Signoria in Florence; so is the great public space outside the public palace in Siena. They are all theatre spaces. They are designed for spectacles and presentations of seigneurial power and so forth. But apart from architecture, the only valuable information you can get about the look of the past is a painting.

But no, I don't particularly favour proscenium arches. In fact, I'm often rather impatient of them.

CONDEE: Why would you say that?

MILLER: Well, I find that the frame is a little bit too insistent. It comes down too much on the sides. I'm always wanting to break it out, violate it in some way, push stuff out through it, blur it and so forth. I find recently at the Old Vic, for example, which has got a very rigid picture-frame-like proscenium, that I've always been getting my designers to disguise it, to mask it, to break the stage floor out, to disguise the edges of the picture frame.

It's not that I'm necessarily in favour of the theatre-in-the-round or even three-quarter theatre, but I would prefer to see a theatre which wasn't so rigidly defined to a gilt frame. It may be that my objection is entirely confined to the character of the frame, to the fact that it's a gilded frame. But just recently I've found that that frame makes me impatient.

CONDEE: It's interesting at the Old Vic, because you've got on the one hand the advantage that it's a beautifully restored theatre. But that gorgeousness could make it too insistent for some productions.

MILLER: Well, it is. I suppose that my favourite theatre space, if I was really going to choose a theatre space, would be [Peter] Brook's Bouffes du Nord in Paris. There you have a conventional theatre, so it isn't one of these high-tech modern boxes which is featureless and soulless. It contains remnants and residues of something rather romantic, then burnt and scorched and destroyed and a lot of its structure ruptured. So that you get the best of both worlds in some ways...

I suppose more and more and more I find myself seeking warehouses – spaces intended primarily for something else – which you improvise in rather than theatres. I'm not really interested in theatrical spectacles in the conventional form any more.

CONDEE: Have there been productions there where you've found that gorgeousness of it particularly appropriate or inappropriate for the particular production?

MILLER: No, it's always inappropriate really. It's never been what I've wanted. I've never done those sort of Drottningholm-type productions, which would be favourable to that basically Georgian theatre architecture. It just doesn't interest me.

I did *Lear* recently and I broke the thing right open. We built great big, huge, black-brick towers around the proscenium arch and took the first row of boxes out; we dismantled them and made entrances off into them and put a great platform out towards them, which in fact corresponded to the platform thrust that Olivier had had when he had the National Theatre in the Old Vic. Then I simply took the whole stage right back to the back wall, painted the whole back wall black. It had a little bit of masking at the sides, but made it absolutely visible out to the wings. It was an attempt to try and make it back into a warehouse.

And I think that if I had my choice I would move more and more toward very small spaces, which I like very much. The happiest time I had was doing a play which I made out of Ryszard Kapuściński's book on *The Emperor* (1978), which we did in the Theatre Upstairs at the Royal Court, which I think holds 60 people. That was wonderful.[283]

CONDEE: In those kinds of warehouse spaces have there been instances in which you've incorporated the existing architecture?

MILLER: Yes, very often, if the architecture is not, as I say, high-tech. And that's why custom-built theatres, buildings and spaces – like a Cottesloe, for example – are not very attractive to me. They're featureless.

And I think more and more directors are looking to theatre spaces which do not start out their life as theatre spaces. I suspect that the era of building theatres is over.

CONDEE: Back to what we were talking about yesterday – Erving Goffman's frames. Some people who I have spoken with, who are very much against incorporating theatre architecture or allowing the theatre architecture to be part of the production, would say that they don't want the audience to be reminded of that frame of existing reality; they don't want the audience to be out of the production, or reminded about that which is not part of the world that they are creating on stage.

MILLER: Well, I think that's a misunderstanding of what in fact the audiences take for theatrical reality. What happens, I think, is that very often if the architecture of the place is incorporated, the audience is simply reading it as part of the action or they are merely neglecting it. Otherwise you have an extremely sharp and rigid distinction between the world which is meant to be a representing world and the world which is meant to be the overlookable space of you the spectator, in which nothing is meant to be visible at all, although necessarily might be visible even if you darken the auditorium.

I think that people who get fussed about that totally underestimate the extent to which audiences can voluntarily and discriminatingly disregard certain aspects of what is visible. So that they say, 'I will count that as part of the scene and I will discount that as part of the scene.'

We're through with the days of having custom-built places designed to focus your eye on a spectacle. Films do that: put a hole in a wall and a completely pitch-black featureless auditorium, because the only thing to be watched is the window in which the thing happens.

CONDEE: You mentioned in the *New Yorker* article that you were very interested in the use of the 'Sprecher' in painting – a figure that gazes out from the picture plane at the viewer, while the others are preoccupied with the scene depicted.[284] Do you find that there is a counterpart to that in the theatre and that you consciously use that counterpart, in that sense of including the auditorium space?

MILLER: Yes, occasionally. Of course, it's there, written into certain plays, because we have asides. And indeed, to some extent, soliloquies. A soliloquy is in fact performed by a Sprecher, who speaks to the audience, literally.

It's actually quite interesting to know what the character of certain soliloquies really is; you have to be quite sure what the mode of address in any given soliloquy might be. In some cases, a soliloquy is not in fact the act of a Sprecher – you the audience are eavesdropping upon an out-loud meditation, which is not addressed to you at all. And in some cases it is quite clearly the character taking the audience into his confidence, in which case it is a Sprecher. And one and the same speech can be treated in either of those ways, according to what the director or the actor wants. I have done *Hamlet* in which 'O, what a rogue and peasant slave am I!' [II.ii.485] has been either meditated inwardly – taking the front of the stage as a glass through which you're not meant to hear – and on other occasions I have deliberately made those meditations confidences directed to the audience, in which the character for that moment takes the audience's presence into consideration and confides.

CONDEE: And that's a very different meaning.

MILLER: Yes, that's right, a very different meaning. One is not a Sprecher. The Sprecher actually looks at you. And it is a paradox that he should look at you, because he looks at you from not just simply a different physical, geographical space, he's looking at you from a place which is 'elsewhen,' and the shock of the Sprecher, the shock of him upon one, is not simply that someone standing in Holland is looking at you in – as it happens in the Prado – Madrid, but that a young man in the seventeenth century addresses his descendants in the twentieth century, so that it has a double sense of bewildering and delightful paradox.

In many productions that I do, I put one in: someone in the middle of a violent action suddenly turns quite silently and unnoticed and engages the audience, as if to say, 'Look, something very big's going on elsewhere and elsewhen.'

CONDEE: For your production of *Così fan Tutte* several years ago in St Louis, which was on somewhat of a thrust stage, you mentioned in an article that you were trying to use it in a certain sense like the Teatro Olimpico.[285] Could you explain what you were doing with that?

MILLER: Strictly speaking, it's not true, because of course the Teatro Olimpico actually is a flat-on format, but I think that I was using the stage as if in fact the façade, as if the proscenium of the Teatro Olimpico were not there and you merely had the radiating vistas.

I think there are two ways of looking at the Teatro Olimpico. One is to take advantage of that flat, architectural façade and the platform as being the essential thing, and more or less disregard – or not regard as important – the vistas which are visible through the archways, delightful though they are. Or, in a rather more radical deconstructive mood, as one might have in, let's say, the Bouffes du Nord, say, 'Look, let's see what would happen if that whole ornamental façade could be removed.' And what you had instead were these three Scamozzi perspectives.

CONDEE: Like those Scamozzi vistas, there is an architectural piazza in Rome where you can view three streets with the buildings receding in perspective. It's a wonderful example, too, of scenery that is imitating architecture and then architecture that is imitating scenery imitating scenery.

MILLER: Yes, that's why I say that public spaces are just as theatrical. It's very hard to say which comes first. Because of course with early theatre, one knows that before there were buildings designed for theatre, the theatre spectacles were using the city as a site of the spectacle. I think there's a complicated reciprocal relationship between them.

CONDEE: In another example of painting influencing your staging, you mentioned for one production you had been reading the historian [Robert] Rosenblum about foreshortening.

MILLER: That was the end of the eighteenth century, about Neoclassicism. This was about the notion of fore-and-aft squashing which you get in late-eighteenth-century Neoclassical art, conspicuously in David and Greuze and so forth. What happens of course is that you get fore-and-aft flattening so that the action is more and more confined to a shallow platform which runs parallel to the picture plane and – wherever possible – either curtains are draped, or rows of columns or indeed just simply a wall is placed, to arrest the gaze and keep it from going too far back. Instead of having the deep space of the Baroque, you have an extremely shallow, frieze-like space, in which characters are confined to this ledge or platform. It's something I've always been interested in.

For example, if I were going to do some Gluck, say *Iphigénie* or *Orfeo*, I would be tempted to try and do a ledge stage, a shelf stage, and have it absolutely like a frieze – even to the extent perhaps of having a jasper-blue backdrop, featureless, and paint the characters white so that they looked actually as if they were on a Wedgwood vase. But in any case, I would make every effort to squash them flat, because I think it is compatible with that art of the late eighteenth century. It's a format I find rather pleasing.

CONDEE: Some people have said that any play can be done in any space, whereas other people maintain that for certain kinds of plays you've got to have the right kind of space in which to do them.

MILLER: I don't feel that there are complicated, really insistent generic requirements. You will often surprise yourself by finding that while you thought that the period or the genre demanded one space, you can discover that another space liberates and releases certain qualities which are inherent in it which you had previously not seen.

In many cases, what you're doing is constantly trying to arrest the audience's attention by making sharp contrast with what they expect. They've got used to seeing it in a deep space and you say, 'Have a look and see what happens when it's all squashed flat.' You're constantly pulling the lens, zooming it and, as with a long lens, you get tremendous squashing. That's why when you look at a horse race through a long lens, the horses never advance. They're endlessly moving, because they're squashed into a very narrow plane.

There are great interests in changing the optics. If you have it on a very long lens, it's all squashed very flat and there's not very much fore-and-aft movement, or you can have it on a very, very wide-angle lens, in which case there's a huge sort of vertiginous perspective. Each of those releases things which are unforeseen and often you're just making a sharp break with an accepted spatial tradition. And I don't think there are any unbreakable generic rules about that.

CONDEE: Do you feel that there is a fundamentally different approach required for staging in thrust theatres as opposed to proscenium theatres?

MILLER: Yes. You can't organize consistently pictorial scenery on a thrust. Once it breaks out of the frame – it depends on how far it breaks out – once an audience is broaching to such a position where they can view each other across the stage, then there's no way in which you can really convincingly represent a *verismo* reality.

I do miss sometimes the possibility of truly pictorial spaces in a deeply-thrust stage. I quite like pictorial spaces. A funny thing is that a lot of the avant-garde directors in Europe are quite given to pictorial spaces. Chéreau uses quite pictorial spaces in Bayreuth. You're definitely looking into a space rather than all being around something which is breaking out into your space. The same, actually, is true, I think, to a very large extent, of the Schaubühne.

I'm not very patient with spectacle at the moment. I just think, 'Well, this is a very tiresome thing to do. I'd rather be encountered with the people.' Shakespeare, certainly. I think Shakespeare shouldn't be visual at all, really. I think it should happen sitting in the same room: be right up next to Othello and Desdemona. Which I believe is one of the reasons for Nunn's success with *Othello* just recently. They're doing it at the Young Vic.[286]

CONDEE: When you're coming into a theatre space that you will be directing in for the first time, what do you look for, or what do you do?

MILLER: Take it on its merits and demerits. You just simply say, 'Well, I think I can do something with this.' There are certain theatre spaces which are very insistent and it depends what sort of license you have to alter it. The first thing I asked the Mirvishes when I went into the Old Vic was, 'How much can I muss this up?' Because it is extremely insistent, not just merely *vis-à-vis* the frame, but it's very insistent in the sort of presentation of itself as a theatre, in that it already implies something about gentility, decorum and a middle-class theatre-going public, which is rather unpleasant, I think.

CONDEE: It's a very self-consciously impressive theatre, right from the lobby when you come in.

MILLER: Yes, it is. It's too damned genteel. I don't like that. And I took it on because it was the only chance I had to run a theatre. But given the opportunity to have the Roundhouse or the Old Vic, I wouldn't hesitate at taking the Roundhouse, except that the Roundhouse has got no money.

CONDEE: Do you find that there is a fundamental difference that affects your productions, in the sense that in a proscenium theatre most of the audience is looking up at the performance, while in most thrust theatres most of the audience is looking down at the actors?

MILLER: I am really interested in quite profound alterations of relationships. You say quite rightly that there is a deep concavity about thrust stages, that there is a steep downward look. I wonder what it would be like if in fact you built a thrust stage which was the particular reverse, where in fact there was a steep upward look. Of course, there would be a limit in that. Unfortunately people couldn't go to the centre of the stage because they would become invisible.

The reason I ask that is that there are a number of painting styles which are called *sotto in su*, in which the whole point is that you look up at steeply foreshortened people, looking arrogantly down at you from high ledges in those great anamorphic ceilings, where characters are ascending into heaven: steeply foreshortened, looking down from great heights, standing on ledges. You look up their nostrils. It obviously is not altogether an impossibility as a theatrical format, because these are theatrical formats, because these are theatrical spectacles designed by people like Pozzo and there are lots of Renaissance artists of the seventeenth century who do that. It is the *sotto in su* format.

But it isn't strictly necessary that the arena stage is concave. It could also be a mountain rather than a pit, except of course the sightlines of a mountain are much, much harder, unless there are simply one or two things on the pinnacle, whereas you can always look down across on a concave format.

But I wonder what it would be like if in fact one did have to crane. One could have, for example, a spectacle which was a proscenium arch, or at least a frontal, end-on format which was shallow, where in fact everyone craned at this great, huge, arrogantly-placed spectacle high up.

CONDEE: The kind of maxim that many people have said to me about this is that putting the actors up high puts the actors in the 'power position,' as it were, whereas putting the audience up puts the audience in the 'power position.'

MILLER: Well, it does or it doesn't. It might or it might not. It depends on how the actor behaves. It depends on how the gaze penetrates the space. If they act as a Sprecher and gaze arrogantly down from their height to the audience – in other words, acknowledge the audience's lowliness – then it becomes dominant. Otherwise it is merely no more dominant than the gawping look of an audience down in the street looking at construction workers at a great height. Only if the construction workers look down and jeer at the spectators in the street is there a relationship of dominance to them.

People are very, very naive about space as being automatically, self-sufficiently an expression of dominance. I think it depends what the people are doing on that height and what they are doing on that depth.

There is a kind of arrogant contemptuousness which could be thrown upwards from below. For example, the medical students that look down from the arena, down to watch the surgeon operate; the surgeon every now and then glances up to them. That glance upward can be just as contemptuous as a glance thrown downward. The authority is invested in the role of the person and the relationship that he has by virtue of the authority invested in his glance, not by his spatial relationship to the audience.

I remember having been in one of those pit-like auditoriums – which is for an operating theatre – and someone happening to cough and the surgeon merely looked up, like that. Just the look. It wasn't the look of a prisoner down in a pit.

Think of the timid, fearful downward glance of the suicide on the ledge, looking downward on the myriad of people down in the street.

I think people get naively fussed about spatial relationships of that sort and don't take into consideration much deeper psychological factors which really ultimately determine the relationship.

CONDEE: Going back to what we were talking about before – certain kinds of plays in certain kinds of spaces – many people maintain that farce can only be done on the proscenium stage.

MILLER: I think that's probably right. I suspect that farce is a mechanical device which depends on a sort of ledge-like format. It is as mechanical as those processions of mechanical devices which pass on a shallow stage in those clockwork devices in the sixteenth-century south German towns. And therefore there has to be an extremely sharp edge I think, probably, to make that device work. It's totally mechanical anyway, farce, and therefore you need something which as it were sharply delineates the margin of what's mechanical and then what is not. I suspect it would be quite hard to have farce in a deep setting. They're much too real, the characters, when they come out at you on a thrust stage. Farce demands that they shouldn't be much like us – in some ways that they be very, very oversimplified.

And I think that oversimplification requires a sort of brilliantly lit, shallow separation.

CONDEE: Have there been instances in your directing experience in which the approach to a given play has emerged from the place where it is to be presented?

MILLER: Oh yes, I think that has happened. Certainly when I did *The Emperor*, this Kapuściński play, I think it was one of the best things I've ever done. That was very powerfully determined by that little narrow corridor of a room [upstairs at the Royal Court]. I made it even more like a corridor. We built artificial doors into it so that people were looking down a sort of palace corridor through which people emerged. It was a sort of an enclosed, rather hermetically-sealed world in which there was a sense that there were larger council rooms elsewhere and that the people were leaving a larger elsewhere to come into the space and hold confidential, hurried confabs.

CONDEE: What about instances in which productions have been moved from one theatre to another?

MILLER: Oh, well they've always been disasters. The *Hamlet* that I did at the Donmar Warehouse was unwisely moved for reasons of finance; the Albery organization wanted to pay off the expense of doing it in a small place by getting a larger audience and they played it for another eight weeks at the Piccadilly Theatre. It simply underwent an explosive and damaging decompression. The format was really profoundly unfriendly to it, because we designed it to be a little tiny room, really.[287]

CONDEE: Is it a good idea when a production moves to reconceive it for the new space?

MILLER: Usually the idea of reconceiving it is probably misplaced. There's no such thing as reconceiving a design which itself is constitutive of the production and you undertake the production for that particular form. To reconceive it is really another way of saying that you've settled for something less than perfect. I usually almost disown it.

It hasn't happened to me very much. I haven't had to do it more than twice, I think. In one case it didn't matter: the *Candide* that I did, which was done originally at the Theatre Royal, Glasgow and then came to the Old Vic, was designed for both.[288] The box in which it was set was suitable for both the physical spaces, because they were both proscenium arch and so therefore there was no loss. In fact there was a slight gain because the Old Vic was a little bit smaller.

The Emperor was taken from the upstairs theatre to the downstairs theatre at the Royal Court and it was very damaged; it just got blown apart. That hermetically-sealed privacy of being in on something very secret just simply vanished. And that was what it was about. It was about secrecy and namedropping and surveillance. Here you were simply watching a spectacle. In there [the Theatre Upstairs], it was as if you were part of the conspiracy.

CONDEE: At the Old Vic has your choice of play been influenced by the theatre space?

MILLER: No, I've been able to be fairly free with the format. As I say, with *King Lear*, for example, we just smashed it all open. And I suspect that if I do what I want to do next year, which is to do an adaptation of Kafka's *The Trial*, I'll break it open.[289]

I'd like to be much more experimental with the seating and perhaps bring things right out – build a catwalk out. Sometimes I do quite deliberately lose the first two, even three rows, in the stalls. When I did *The Tempest* with Max von Sydow, I broke the thing right out into the auditorium as well.[290] But there is a limit obviously as to what you can do with that theatre.

I've often thought how nice it would be to be a little bit more fundamental and perhaps put a row of bleachers up on the stage and really have a double view of the thing. But it's early days yet and if I do stay on there I think I'll try all sorts of things. And also, ultimately, I hope that if I do stay on there for another two years that they'll give me the annex next door, where I can do small stuff. That's the old paint frame and everything, which belonged to the National Theatre originally and there's a quite large rehearsal space there, which is appropriate for a, say, 200-seat or 150-seat theatre. The Mirvishes rented it out to the National Theatre, where Peter Gill has his experimental studio, but it reverts to us next year.[291]

CONDEE: And you can't wait to get your hands on it?

MILLER: Yes, can't wait to get my hands on it.

Cambridge diary

Varsity, 6 November 1954[292]

Sleep doesn't play much of a part in Cambridge life; at least, not in social life. Every now and then, however, you come across people sleeping out of context, and that is off-putting and alarming.

Being awake in a bedroom when someone else is fast asleep is bad enough, but coming across sleeping forms in libraries and reading rooms, lavatories, barber's shops and lifts, is a 'strong' experience and gives you – well maybe not you, but certainly me – a powerful sense of something disturbing, 'plant' and oak-like in even the best of us.

Sleeping men do not resemble the dead. They are alive, and powerful like moss-covered roots in an old forest; they snort and shift and their faces look heavy. This awful druidical plant *thing* is there, *with* us and claims us in sleep. ('Or snorted we in the Seven Sleepers' den?')[293]

That's why it's so off-putting being in a reading room when someone goes to sleep; no wonder everyone is frightened, and tries to cover up their terror by nudging their neighbour and giggling at the slumbering man.

I don't like it, one little bit.

Alternative worlds
Royal Institution, London, 6 April 1971[294]

I'd like to start this rather mystifying talk by introducing perhaps an even more mystifying quotation with respect to 'alternative worlds.' I want to quote from Michel Foucault's *The Order of Things* (1966) in which he refers to one of the possibilities of reconstructing an alternative world. He talks of the fact that

> This book first arose out of a passage in [Jorge Luis] Borges, out of the laughter that shattered, as I read the passage, all the familiar landmarks of my thought – *our* thought, the thought that bears the stamp of our age and our geography – breaking up all the ordered surfaces and all the planes with which we are accustomed to tame the wild profusion of existing things, and continuing long afterwards to disturb and threaten with collapse our age-old distinction between the Same and the Other. This passage quotes a "certain Chinese encyclopaedia" in which it is written that "animals are divided into *a.* belonging to the Emperor *b.* embalmed *c.* tame *d.* sucking pigs *e.* sirens *f.* fabulous *g.* stray dogs *h.* included in the present classification *i.* frenzied *j.* innumerable *k.* drawn with a very fine camelhair brush *l.* et cetera *m.* having just broken the water pitcher *n.* that from a long way off look like flies."[295]

Perhaps this is the model or the paradigm of a conception of an alternative world, a world in which we conceive of a classification which is utterly new to us, which conceives of the entities of reality in a way in which we have never previously seen.

Now, it's perhaps an irony – and it is also rather fit – that we should approach this problem right here in the Royal Institution, because it was here at the start of the nineteenth century that the very first possibility of an alternative world was thrust upon the general public. For it was here, from the Royal Institution, that the facts of science, as they were then, were first introduced to the public at large. It was here that the scientific lectures of Faraday were made and where Faraday himself presided over the advertisement of the new world of physical sciences at the start of the nineteenth century. He presided here for over 50 years; and he presented a world, and an alternative world, and perhaps a world which contained new classifications, which seemed to certain writers to represent a threat to the old world.

It is not surprising, therefore, that the author of the *Ancient Mariner* should have felt anxiety in the face of these developments. And although Coleridge himself was indeed familiar with the sciences, was familiar with Newton – a person, unlike many writers today, who read [Colin] MacLaurin's work on Newton and was familiar with the *Opticks* (1704) – nevertheless he felt that Newton had proposed a world which was a threat to the sanctity of the human imagination. And he wrote to [Robert] Southey in the early years of the nineteenth century, and he said:

> Newton was a mere materialist. *Mind*, in his system, is always *passive*, – a lazy *Looker-on* on an external world [...] there is ground for suspicion that *any* system built on the passiveness of the mind must be false, as a system.[296]

And he continues to say 'how flat' and 'how wretched' is David Hartley's solution of the phenomenon of memory.

> Believe me [...] a metaphysical solution, that does not instantly *tell* you something in the heart is grievously to be suspected as apocryphal. I almost think that ideas *never* recall ideas, as far as they are ideas, any more than leaves in a forest create each other's motion. The breeze it is that runs through them – it is the soul of state of feeling.[297]

What was it that Coleridge felt was lacking in the world that Newton had constructed? What was the 'risk' of this world that Newton had built for us? Presumably what Coleridge saw was this grand, august, architectural world of Newton, in which objects and men were moved around like billiard balls, and in which there was no room – apparently – for the benevolent initiatives of the spirit.

It is undoubtedly a mistake on the part of the writers of that period to have conceived of such a world as a risk to the imagination. The imagination was still self-evident; it was still self-sufficient. It can be relied on in its own terms. Nevertheless, the world constructed, apparently, by Newton, seemed to them to be a place of emptiness – and it was meaningless. It's not surprising therefore that misunderstanding the impulses of science, and perhaps failing in their allegiance to the imagination, large numbers of intellectuals at the start of the nineteenth century felt it was necessary to reconstruct some sort of compromise – a compromise which restored the energy of the soul, which restored the energy of the imagination, and all sorts of parascientific superstitions grew up. In particular, at the start of the nineteenth century, coming from France spread the idea of animal magnetism, of mesmerism – the belief that some sort of influence could pass from one person to another in such a way that people could be impelled, their imagination suppressed or enlarged, at the will of the hypnotist, or the mesmerist as he was called then. This, perhaps, represents a reaction to the idea of the passiveness of the mind, the mind which David Hartley said was simply the vibrations of particles which made up the nerves. This was a reaction which suddenly put the emphasis upon the activity, upon the emission of the mind, rather than upon the mind simply as a passive receptor of the impulses of the outside world.

Of course, the impulse which this suggests goes back into antiquity. Perhaps it has roots in witchcraft. It had roots in primitive animism, but it acquired special reinforcing credentials at the start of the nineteenth century, and it must have pleased intellectuals like Coleridge in being able to use Newton to defeat him at his own game. For in the *Opticks* Newton had proposed that to transmit the mysterious power of gravity, the universe was filled with an ultra-fine, a subtle, ethereal medium which could transmit gravity, electricity and heat. This idea was leapt upon by the intellectuals at the start of the nineteenth century because it seemed to them to give them the medium through which scientific credentials could be supplied to the original, primitive, sacred notion of the activity of the soul as such; and in animal magnetism, it was believed by many writers and intellectuals that they had found a compromise which managed to have all the credentials which were accorded to Newton, but at the same time all the original excitement and power and sanctity of the soul as it was originally conceived in primitive antiquity.

Many forms of this superstition developed throughout the course of the nineteenth century – in particular, spiritualism, which was simply a transformation of the notion of mesmerism or animal magnetism. It's very interesting to see how little confidence was expressed by the intellectuals in the middle of the nineteenth century in the mind's activity as a thing in itself. In its own *terms*, it was enough to simply introspect and see that the mind was active, that the imagination had, as Coleridge said, this esemplastic power. Nevertheless, they were so suborned by the impressive achievements of Faraday, so impressed by the mysterious equations which were now growing up between electricity and magnetism, that they felt it was necessary somehow to kidnap scientific ideas in order to reinforce the credibility of the activity and meaningfulness of the soul. So what you get are very peculiar chimeras or hybrids of the following sort.

In the 1860s, T. H. Huxley – Aldous Huxley's grandfather – gave a lecture to a working man's college in East Anglia, in which he first introduced into England the notion of protoplasm: the substance which bore life, the substance in which life was grounded. And this was a very respectable notion indeed, and it had all the credentials of German biological science behind it. It wasn't surprising, therefore, that the spiritualists who had already been having their table-rappings and table-turnings for the previous ten or 15 years, leapt onto the notion of protoplasm and invented their own 'plasm' in which the mind could be couched, and we get this peculiar substance called ectoplasm; and indeed it was photographed, and emitted from mouths, and in this substance it was believed, finally, the sanctity and reality of the soul – which Newton seemed to have called into doubt – was once and for all established.

It seems that throughout the nineteenth century, apart from these rather marginal or fringe encounters with science, throwing up these rather meaningless hybrids, the work of literature and the work of science pursued parallel courses and didn't really interfere with each other. There were of course classical encounters which produced literary work like *In Memoriam* (1849), but by and large the growth of fiction, for example, more or less proceeded on its own with self-confidence and did not feel it necessary to incorporate the ideas or the notions of science in order to give itself credibility. There was, however, inevitably, a fatal convergence towards the end of the nineteenth century, in which – it was bound to come, because of the achievements of science, because of the *impressiveness* of the scientific establishment and its various achievements – it became somehow necessary to incorporate the furniture of science into the work of fiction.

In Jules Verne you get the first spectacular example of the incorporation of very elaborate scientific images into a creative work of fiction. And yet,

I maintain that in the work of Jules Verne you actually see a completely unsuccessful incorporation of scientific images. What you get in fact is a familiar, Victorian clubman's world, furnished with all the elaborate furniture of the nineteenth century projected into an arbitrary outer-space. It's simply a Victorian drawing room extended to the moon. The men make their rather ponderous, Rotarian excursions into this outer-space, furnished in smoking jackets. There are flaring gas-jets on the walls of the capsule, and they return to redeem their wager, but at no point do we feel that the scientific imagination has entered into the work of fiction and created a successful new species of literary enterprise.

When we come to Wells, one feels that once again there has been no successful incorporation of the scientific notions into the work of literature. You feel that two entities have been jammed together and no successful new order of creation has arisen. For example, in *The War of the Worlds* (1898) when the capsule lands on Horsell Common – how very significant that it lands on *Horsell Common*. It's the quiddity of that Horsell Common which seems so important.[298] There it lands, and the genius of Wells is not here expressed in the scientific imagery but in the atmosphere of foreboding which he expresses and in the atmosphere which he generates, which is, after all, in the end very similar to the feeling which we had here in England in August 1940 just before the Blitz started; and one feels that it is quite possible, and it would in no way destroy the story, if a Wehrmacht officer were to step out of that capsule instead of that suede soufflé which in fact does.

The essential character of Wells, then, it seems to me, in his most successful scientific romances, is simply to use certain abnormal or unusual circumstance to bring us into a more clear consciousness of simply what it is like to live at that time.

Here I come to the question of science fiction, a subject which I don't know much about, and the reason I don't know much about it is because I find myself unusually repelled by it. In preparing this talk I asked my producer to send me a pile of famous science-fiction stories, and I waded my way through several volumes of this material. And I was struck throughout, while reading this, by some strange familiarity. I couldn't quite tell what it was. I'd read this before, I felt, in some way, and then I remembered that the thing which it was most similar to was pornography. Not in the sense that I was meant to be excited in some unusual or illicit way by it, but that there was a curious, meaningless monotony about the atmosphere; that there was a vacuous, hypothetical quality about it all, and that it didn't really matter. There was a sense of inviting the audience to agree that 'Wouldn't it be interesting, wouldn't it be funny, wouldn't it be disturbing, *if...*' rather than, as it seems to me is the essential work of literature, to invite the reader to agree, 'Isn't it funny, isn't it disturbing, isn't it interesting *that...*' In other words, to bring you to an awareness of things as they are, of the life around you, rather than to project you into a vacuous, hypothetical future, or a vacuous, hypothetical elsewhere, in which certain conditions might prevail.

I would like to take a quotation here from Steven Marcus. In his book on *The Other Victorians* (1966), he says:

> To read a work of pornographic fiction is to rehearse the ineffably familiar; to locate that fancy anywhere apart from the infinite, barren, yet plastic space that exists within our skulls is to deflect it from one of its chief purposes.[299] [...] The transactions represented in this writing are difficult to follow because so little individuation has gone into them. In a world whose organization is directed by the omnipotence of thought, no such discriminations are necessary.[300]

This applies, so far as I can see from the science-fiction works that I have read, to the whole enterprise of science fiction. Even without having read the essential, *germinal* works of the genre, I would insist that the enterprise of science fiction is doomed at the root because it attempts to bring together two immiscible forms of imaginative enterprise. The creation of science-fiction springs, in one sense, from the belief that literature is in some way effete now. It is losing out. It has somehow failed and no longer has a true imaginative weight of its own. It also springs from a lack of confidence on the part of science, that in itself it hasn't got the imagination of literature. So, mutual heart transplants are performed in an attempt to revivify both of these enterprises, and it seems that the failure of this springs from a misunderstanding of the nature of both of these human activities. On the one hand, science is not this bereft spiritual enterprise which is commonly thought. It is not, as many of the intellectuals thought at the start of the nineteenth century, and indeed right into the 1850s, simply an accumulation of facts, a passive observation, and a miserly heaping up of information and data out of which theories emerge. If it were that, I think we might have some anxiety about the nature of science. Science in fact, as is now clearly realized, and has been expressed in many works of scientists writing on the philosophy of science, is the creation of self-sufficient conjectures. Imaginative leaps in which patterns and shapes and notions are projected – often on the basis of unrepresentative data, often on the basis of short runs of information – *into* the outside world, and then tested. Facts are then sought which might either refute or underwrite the proposal.

The essence of the scientific enterprise is in fact contained in this effort to project speculations into the outside world. It will be impossible, in fact, to have a science which proceeded on the basis of the famous induction of Bacon. Where would one start looking for facts? What facts would one look for? Which ones would one collect? How would one classify them? What order would they have? One needs some horizon of interest, and that horizon of interest is provided by the creative, speculative power of the scientific imagination, which roots it down, at the heart, to something which is closely in common with the literary imagination.

On the other hand, the literary imagination itself does not need to encase itself in scientific imagery or in the notions of technology or in the putative technologies of the future, in order to acquire relevance to the present day or in order to project hypotheses about how the future will be. That is acquired by honouring one's allegiance to the facts as they are, to the moral pressure of events as we experience them as moral creatures ourselves. This equipment of moral perception is not *improved* by science, nor is it undermined by science. It is something we create by encouraging the power of the moral imagination, something upon which science has *no* bearing, either for or against. The work of fiction acquires its dignity and its power by honouring the immediate experience of moral life.

Therefore, it is unnecessary to bring these two forms together. This doesn't mean that science need not feature in the work of fiction. I think that the scientific *idea*, and often scientific metaphors, have figured in perhaps the most successful piece of concealed science-fiction of all – in *À la recherche du temps perdu* (1913–27) by Proust, in which the greatest space journey of all times is taken by reconstructing the imagination and reconstructing the memory and reconstructing the experience by means,

309

often, of images drawn from science, from images taken from optics and from photography and from stereoscopy; but they are all *submerged* metaphors which do not predominate, which do not insist upon our acknowledging the work as a special genre of science fiction, but only a major work of the literary imagination. In the same way, Franz Kafka also created the world of today, the world of modernity, the world of the future, not by hauling in the equipment of science, not by hauling in capsules and ray-guns, nor by introducing computers, nor by introducing any of the equipment of science that was available at his time, but by simply consulting the power of his own dreams. By taking a journey inwards, into a meta-Prague, he was able, by calling it *Amerika*, to redeem his understanding and the importance of the experience of living in the first part of the twentieth century.

If you look at the last pages of Proust's great work, perhaps you see the return to the very point that we started this lecture with. At the end of his long journey, he says:

> If at least, time enough were allotted to me to accomplish my work, I would not fail to mark it with the seal of Time, the idea of which imposed itself upon me with so much force to-day, and I would therein describe men, if need be, as monsters occupying a place in Time infinitely more important than the restricted one reserved for them in space, a place, on the contrary, prolonged immeasurably since, simultaneously touching widely separated years and the distant periods they have lived through – between which so many days have ranged themselves – they stand like giants immersed in Time.[301]

Here perhaps, by redeeming the quiddity of things as they are – through the mysterious medium of the imagination, rather than through some mysterious medium of magnetism – we have perhaps reconstructed the true 'alternative world' which is the one which brings us to the most accurate and pressing sense of our own.

On rehearsing

Subsequent Performances, 1986[302]

Before rehearsals begin, I will have worked on a metaphorical level looking for similarities and affinities between the structures in the play and other works of art of the period. But these are very preliminary intimations of what might happen in the rehearsal period – sketches and suggestions about how things might proceed. They introduce guidance and limitations but not tyrannies. The director who approaches the work having apparently imagined everything has literally conceived everything but imagined nothing, thus missing the crucial point of directing: you must imagine very richly but you must also be capable of conceding, admitting and allowing to the same degree. It may be that actors regret, and resent, that they have not taken this initiative, and see themselves as *objets trouvés* assembled by the director in a collage of his making. But I do not think that this is a fair assessment because, although they are *objets trouvés* to the extent that the director identifies particular properties they have before the play starts, the actors show all sorts of completely unexpected features which develop in the course of rehearsal. It is nearly always the case that the director is surprised by what the actors bring to rehearsal. What follows is *adaptation* and *discussion*, and these two words describe the process of directing itself.

I like to let people start reading the play, and to wait for alternative inflexions to appear during the course of rehearsal, which I then edit, revise and emphasize. In this way salient features can emerge, or be introduced, as the production grows. I used to begin rehearsals with some long erudite lecture, but now I say less and less. I show the set, hand round the costume drawings and give thumbnail sketches of what I think the characters might be, and why I have chosen particular actors for the parts. People tend to believe in the pre-existence of the fictional characters, and mistakenly think of rehearsals as nothing more than the process of bringing these characters back to life. But I start out the rehearsals treating the speeches in the text as if they are premises-to-let that are to be occupied by persons as yet unknown. When casting, I may have advertised for a particular type of tenant but I cannot tell exactly how they will inhabit the role.

During rehearsals, the director and actors make visible something that is there but in some way obscured. The only point that I ever emphasize now is that the characters – Hamlet, Claudius, Troilus, Cleopatra, or whoever – are extremely indeterminate people. They are signposts pointing in a certain direction; indications of where there might be a character if the rehearsals go well and they come into existence. Another analogy, which I think of in order to describe rehearsals to myself, is that they are like séances. In the process of getting the actors to speak their lines, characters begin to take possession and to inhabit the speeches. By the time the rehearsals come to an end, the lines seem to be spoken by someone with whom the actor was unfamiliar at the outset but has come to know in the process of speaking the lines. As a director who is outside the play, for whom the lines have an objective existence, I have vague intimations as to what is in them but defer to and rely on the actors to bring characters out of those lines. It is only by inhabiting the lines, by being inside them, by speaking them and beginning to act through them that a direct knowledge of what they mean emerges in rehearsal.

The language we speak spontaneously, like the language that has been written down for someone else to speak artificially, has a double existence. The words have an objective existence for an outside hearer, who may infer something about what is meant by them, but they also have a subjective existence for anyone who speaks them. Obviously, their subjective existence is spontaneously created by the speaker because he or she knows what it is he or she wants to convey by speaking them. In the case of lines that pre-exist, because an author has left them behind him, their subjective identity has to be discovered by the conjectural process of speaking them. Merely reading a speech does not always tell you what is possible in the lines. Their full possibilities cannot become apparent until they are spoken.

An actor is someone whose imagination is galvanized and stimulated by taking the plunge and inhabiting the lines from within, not by reading them from the outside. Often the actor begins to make discoveries only by taking the risk of speaking the lines without having the faintest idea of what they mean. It is then the director's responsibility to notice and encourage consistent or interesting trends developing in the diction. In this way, confusing, conflicting or less interesting alternatives are gradually whittled away so that a cleft is made in the language. As the rehearsals continue, and the director encourages one implication rather than another, meaning opens out rather as if you have made fissures in the language itself.

From moment to moment in rehearsals all sorts of things happen that are not apparent when I read the text over to myself. When someone is up on their feet saying the words, I hear new intonations because of an intuitive inflexion introduced by the actor, and I point it out. This is where the analytic function of the director begins, and there is a kind of vigilant inactivity on the part of a good director by which he or she lets the rehearsals go on and simply records intonations as they occur from day to day. By gradually picking out and reintroducing often unconscious deliveries given by a particular actor, the rehearsal develops. This reminds me of an ambiguous pictorial figure where, by developing and shading in the interpretation that favours one particular configuration rather than another, a new image begins to emerge from the old format. As the other alternatives are minimized, the perspective alters, giving prominence to the one interpretation that gradually becomes visible. It is like the Necker cube (below): a skeletal outline of a cube in which no face is obviously nearer or farther than another so that the front and back faces appear to alternate, and perception tends to oscillate unstably between the two alternatives. It is up to the director to point out the alternatives in the text, and to observe which one is emerging in rehearsal. By providing the actors with extra information, one interpretation can be solidified and the visibility of the alternatives diminished.

I used to start off rehearsals with a formal reading, simply because I submitted to the tradition that you sat around on day one and read the play through from beginning to end. I have abandoned this approach because

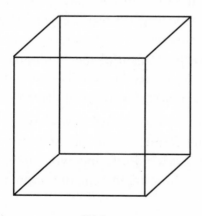

it exposes the cast to unnecessary risks of embarrassment and humiliation, which arise inevitably when one actor appears at the outset to have a more definitive reading than the others. This confidence may not be a good thing if it means that those who are still stumbling and finding their way are put off or paralyzed on the first day. Now I tend to split the reading into small sections and, with two or three actors, read scenes that are not necessarily at the start of the play. Often the most productive implications about a character emerge when you begin with scenes halfway through the play, as though you have dropped rather casually into the middle of an event. The ideas that develop as a result of that reading may extend backwards into the, as yet, unread beginning of the play. In other words, I am increasingly tempted to allow the play to develop gradually, so that from little buds or islands the ideas grow out as if from quite separate centres and eventually meet to form a continent of meanings which comprise the contours of the whole work.

At the start of rehearsal, the play has an existence rather like an objective continent that is waiting to be discovered, and it is terribly hard to decide where to start to put the boats ashore. I am less and less tempted to start with a frontal attack on a play because it is so daunting, and can defeat the imagination of everyone concerned. In a way, the problem is very similar to the one that philosophers such as Wittgenstein have raised. It was he who said, and here I paraphrase, that you get mental cramps if you attempt a frontal assault on a large philosophical question like the meaning of meaning. But if you can first tackle a smaller, manageable question, and ask 'What sort of meanings are there?' and 'What are the uses we put a particular word to?' then we become familiar with the fact that meaning is a cluster of concepts rather than one concept that can be penetrated. In the same way, the play seems to be a cluster of characters whose nature will be discovered by attempting an assault on some element that may, at first, seem to be peripheral to its larger meaning. Gradually, by allowing one or two actors the experience of inhabiting the lines from inside, the daunting, objective entirety of the work is broken down.

In an intelligent, well-conducted and convivial rehearsal the cast is improvising by simply acting a scene in a way that allows you to see that its outcome is not yet determined. Improvisation in itself does not benefit rehearsal. I cannot see how improvising in a vacuum can possibly increase our knowledge of the play, as we are still confronted with the problem of how to tackle and approach the script. In rehearsal, the unforeseen and unforeseeable implications of a scene will sometimes emerge as a result of solving an incidental, technical problem that seemed quite trivial at the time. For example, in the fourth act of Chekhov's *Three Sisters* there is a beguiling moment of bathos when Masha's cuckolded husband, Koolyghin, tries to console her grief at the forthcoming departure of her lover, Vershinin, by suddenly appearing in a woolly beard confiscated from one of his pupils. The actor playing Koolyghin wanted to know when he should take the beard off, and I found it difficult to say when exactly. 'Keep it on for a moment,' I told him, having nothing better in mind at that time. 'Brazen it out and we'll see what happens.' So, for a moment, he continued to wear the beard, not in his role as Koolyghin but as an actor who could think of nowhere else to put it. As we went on rehearsing, the prop reinstated itself as a feature in the play, and the actress playing Masha – in her role as Masha – suddenly took note of this woolly concealment, and, at the moment when she said it's time to go, she walked across to her husband and unhooked the beard from his ears, only to discover, beneath its absurdity, the serious concerned face of her hitherto neglected spouse.[303] It was as if by concealing himself under a deliberately assumed absurdity, he could reappear transfigured. In some mysterious way, the actor had gone into the beard as an insensitive clown and, because Masha had taken it off him, he emerged from its disguise appearing before her eyes as a man of dignity, kindness and patience. But all this happened as a result of solving an apparently trivial problem of when to take off a false beard.[304]

Another moment in rehearsal: Olga and Vershinin are standing together in the garden, studiously avoiding any reference to the dreadful moment when Masha will enter to bid Vershinin farewell. Janet Suzman had dreaded this moment almost as much as the character she was playing, and told me before we began rehearsing the scene that she would like to avoid the cliché of racing in distractedly. How to come in then? I suggested that the entrance might solve itself if she considered not so much her grief at his departure, or the distraction which that might provoke, but the embarrassment of farewells in general. She arrived, therefore, at the downstage corner of the scene, suddenly reluctant to draw attention to her own presence: wishing to be found, wishing to imply 'I know you care less about our parting than I do so I won't throw myself at you, and burden you with my insufferable misery. All the same, you should be able to tell by the abject self-effacement of my stance that I am grieving and that the rest is up to you.' Alternatively, it is as if Masha anticipates that there is no written script for farewells under these circumstances. No more than there is for Vershinin who dreads the farewell for reasons that are complementary to Masha's. As far as he is concerned another brief affair is over and presumably he would like to bring it to a conclusion as rapidly as possible. How tiresome if this were to involve a scene. Paradoxically, the effect of working all this through exerted a retrospective influence on the acting of the earlier relationship between the two of them. It was only by discovering the disparity of their emotions at the end of the relationship that we were able to go back to the beginning and discover aspects that had remained hidden when they were rehearsed in the chronological order of their occurrence in the play. In this respect, rehearsing a play is like constructing a novel, and in taking the events out of sequence the cast can enjoy the luxuries of analeptic conjecture.

I began by saying that as a director I do not have a secret method for rehearsals, but there is one strategy I find very useful, although it might be more aptly described as an abstention from strategy. Often, when an action or speech seems difficult or puzzling to an actor, the only way to resolve how it should be performed is to encourage him to find a way while pretending that you are not doing that at all. Let me give an example. At the end of a hard afternoon's work, when nothing seems to have happened, I will call the rehearsal to an end and then suggest that we simply run over the lines to help memory. A couple of us will then go and sit down in the stalls, with or without the books, and feed each other cues. By this inadvertent method you make discoveries, and glean meanings and intonations, rather than deliberately harvest them in performance. This process is analogous to the one I saw in a patient with Parkinson's disease, who very often found it difficult to make a deliberate assault on a task that he knew was hard for him to accomplish, but he could manage it if he pretended to do something else and literally caught himself unawares.[305] Sometimes you have to creep up on your intention by pretending to be unintentional. Polonius' words describe this circuitous approach:

And thus do we of wisdom and of reach,
With windlasses and with assays of bias,
By indirections find directions out
(II.i.61–63)[306]

In the process of rehearsal, it is often by the artful creation of apparent distractions that we discover direction. But it needs the vigilant attention of a director who, at the same time, pretends not to be looking out for such signs. At the end of rehearsal he must somehow resist the temptation to say: 'I wonder if you realize that you came up with some very interesting stuff then?' because the cast will then recognize this indirection for what it is. Perhaps three days later I might say, 'Incidentally, why don't you try it like that?' knowing perfectly well that the actor has already done so – whether he remembers it explicitly or not – as the little read-through will have made him familiar with a new intonation or delivery.

As I have grown older, and I hope more mature, I leave more and more of the discoveries to be made by the actors themselves. In a sense I am doing what so many actors criticize directors for not doing, as I leave it to the imaginative talent of the performers to make the discoveries, in the only way that really interesting discoveries are to be made in texts, by inhabiting the lines subjectively and not by looking at them from the outside.

Now, this may sound as if, with time, I have abdicated all interpretative responsibility, but the very reverse is the case. Despite the fact that I am confined to an objective relationship with the text, I do have very useful ideas, but these take effect only if I keep on handing out little fragmentary insights – like tiny pieces of mosaic – which I leave to the actors to realize in the performance. If the director's initiative were removed altogether, my role would be diminished to a consultative one and actors would come together, as they have done in the past, and form companies. The director would then be reduced to benevolently hovering over a bookshelf, checking the actors' queries, and knowing which shelf to go to in order to look up what Tudor underpants were like.

In contrast to this fact-finder of a director, I think it is essential that the director feels provoked by the text rather than responsible for it. I hope that when this happens I do not react eccentrically, or see things that it would be perverse to say existed in the text. I like to provide the cast with a series

317

of very approximate frames in which we can work. I am articulate but not, as it is often assumed, a terrifyingly intellectual director who daunts the cast. In fact, most of the people who have worked with me are struck by my permissiveness, in that my advice and recommendations are not dictations with regard to large-scale portraiture but little suggestions of gesture and nuance which, if acknowledged and possessed, the actors will find have implications beyond the play in question. The aim is that, without having to be further prompted, the cast will then continue to generate more performances that are consistent with these suggestions. The director is, in short, the creator of intuitive insights at moments where rehearsal might otherwise grind to a halt.

Complementary to the suggestion that only in the process of subjectively living the lines in performance will their full range of possible meanings come to light, there are certain aspects of the lines that can be brought to life *only* by some outside, objective judgement as to how the words sound when they are spoken in a particular way. The coexistence of the two – objective and subjective – is essential to the progress of the work as a whole. The lines must be lived actively and subjectively by the only person who is privileged to speak them – the actor – but, on the other hand, some of their meanings and implications are apparent only to someone who stands outside, and who will never enjoy the privilege of speaking them: the director. After all, this is what happens in our ordinary life. A person may speak the lines of their life without quite knowing what it is he or she means by them. Friends and bystanders are often in a better position to see what is meant than the person who is speaking to them.

In some ways the relationship of a director to an actor is, or should be, comparable to the relationship of any instructor to a learner. Obviously, learners can acquire a complex motor skill, like riding a bicycle, only if they take the risk of trying initially without adequate skill, and endure the possible humiliation and danger of falling before they succeed. A director can give broad instructions but cannot ensure success. Ultimately what must happen is that, like the child who has to taste the improbable experience of sitting upright on a machine whose base is not very easy to balance, the actor has to take a chance. In the end, no amount of explicit instruction will result in someone riding a bicycle. But discovering how to perform a play is much more complicated than riding a bicycle, and

I think that most actors would bear witness to the fact that a friendly, accommodating and tactful adviser is a useful presence.

As with learning a motor skill, there is an element of mystery. I often find that the skill is not acquired during the learning session and, when the day ends, both teacher and learner – or actor and director – go home tired and depressed by their failure to bring any skill to light. Then a day passes in which there is no rehearsal, no practice of any sort, and on their return the actors enter into the text and speak it like angels. So too a child, after a miserable day of falling off the bike in the park, despite instruction and encouragement, may find three days later that he or she simply rides off. How this happens I can only conjecture, but it is as if, in that interim without practice, all the results of practice are rehearsed in some internal representation. This mysterious process might be compared to a computer simulation based on all the information that has been garnered during the apparently futile practice period. The information has been fed into the database and, without having to go through the tiresome procedure of enactment, a simulated, diagrammatic practice is performed by the machine internally. When we then encounter the real apparatus it is as if the computer simulation has eliminated all the boshed shots, and nine-tenths of the work has been realized and become very familiar.

There is a great deal of sentimental dogma about the length of time necessary for rehearsal to allow the possibility of some kind of strange alchemy to take place. It can simply become self-indulgent, and an opportunity for all sorts of silliness. Rehearsal is rather like painting: you sketch things in rapidly, and can soon see what is acceptable. Then the director can erase and adjust in much the same way as an artist. My usual rehearsal period is four to five weeks. It becomes very boring if it stretches to six weeks. People could argue that this is because I have pre-empted the alternatives too early, and not allowed the play to be productively unstable for long enough. I can only say that I have never regretted any decision reached early on in rehearsal, and have often sent actors home after four or five weeks to rest for a couple of days rather than drag on with unnecessary rehearsal.

The uses of pain
Conway Hall, London, 20 November 1973[307]

I want to consider the uses of pain. Not the function of pain or its biological purpose, but its use. That is to say the ways in which we, as a species, exploit our own and other people's pain. The biological functions of pain are more or less self-evident and presumably we are all familiar with the harms that can befall anyone who has lost the sense of pain. Everyone knows for instance how easy it is to injure the tongue immediately after receiving a dental anaesthetic and, although it is not generally recognized, the horrifying mutilations of leprosy are a consequence of unnoticed injuries in a limb that has lost its sense of pain. So that although pain is, by definition, a more or less loathsome experience, our existence would be in jeopardy without it.

Nevertheless, in a natural context we seem to be equipped with a surplus sensitivity to pain. That is to say our capacity to feel pain is vastly in excess of any biological advantage that might be gained from it. There is an obvious advantage in being equipped with machinery which allows us to avoid injury, but it's hard to think of any natural advantages for some of the other agonies which we experience. Natural selection explains the existence of a sense which prevents the injuring overextension of joints or the prolonged contact of a limb with sharp edges. The pain of a blocked ureter, however, presents no natural advantage to the sufferer since there is no behaviour which the sufferer can adopt in order to cancel it out. Admittedly it would be hard to practise abdominal surgery in the absence of such pains, and surgeons derive so much information from what the patient says about his pain that he generally withholds analgesics until the agony has been accurately identified. However, it is hard to believe that natural selection actually anticipated the emergence of the medical profession, and inflicted years of functionless suffering with the expectation that a special profession would eventually emerge capable of taking appropriate action. For one reason or another, therefore, we seem to be equipped with a capacity for physical anguish somewhat larger than we need. Unfortunately, human ingenuity has been able to find a continuing use for the surplus and it is this use which I want to examine.

Before we examine the social uses of pain I would like to try and analyse the nature of pain itself and try to spell out some of the characteristics which distinguish it from all others. The most obvious feature of pain is of course its nastiness…that is, what makes it socially exploitable. It can be so unpleasant that men are willing to exchange all sorts of goods in order to avoid it. The threat of pain can persuade people to abstain from strong and immediate satisfactions. And conversely, the satisfaction of being relieved of pain can force a man to go against his strongest convictions, and so forth. The only other sensations which can produce behaviour of this sort are nausea, suffocation and perhaps extreme vertigo. All of these sensations belong in a class by themselves – not just because of their nastiness or because of the aversion associated with them, but on account of their relationship with events in the outside world. In order to make this point clear I would like to introduce a philosophical distinction between transitive sensations on the one hand and intransitive sensations on the other. To the first class belong sensations of warmth, pressure, motion, etc. The second class includes sensations like pain, ache, itch and possibly nausea. In making this distinction I am following the example of the philosopher Armstrong, who goes on to elucidate the distinction as follows. All sensation, he says,

> demands the existence of a sentient being who has the sensation. But in the case of the first class we can distinguish between warmth and a sensation of warmth, pressure and a sensation of pressure […] For warmth, pressure or motion can exist in the absence of sentient beings. However, we cannot make the same distinction between pain and a sensation of pain […] for pain *is* a sensation.[308]

Approaching the problem from the point of view of a clinician, Paul Schilder put the point as follows: 'In pain, the object becomes comparatively unimportant. When we suffer pain, we care less for the quality of the object than for the sensation.'[309] To all intents and purposes pain has no content apart from the fact that we wish it would stop. As Armstrong says, 'A violent pain is a pain that we have an intense desire to stop.'[310]

Of course pains can vary in many ways. They can be localized to one place or another, and they can vary in their actual quality, so that it makes sense to distinguish between aches, pains and soreness, for example. But when you subtract the aversive element from all of these there is nothing left to feel. The only distinctive property of pain, then, is the reaction which it produces in those who suffer it. As Armstrong puts it, 'It is [...] a mark of physical pain that we do not like it for itself. We have an immediate desire that it should stop; we think of it as bad as an end, bad for its own sake, and not simply bad as a means.'[311] In order to make clear what is meant by thinking something bad as a means, let us consider a case where serious injury is being done to our anaesthetized leg...not, as Armstrong points out, for a good reason. We would consider it a bad thing and would presumably want it to stop. But in this case our desire would be a judgement...a wish not to lose the leg. And if, as Armstrong says, we knew that the leg would renew itself like Prometheus's liver, we might even be indifferent to the operation. Whereas of course in Prometheus's case, the attentions of Zeus's eagle were not accompanied by anaesthetic, and the sole purpose of ensuring the regrowth of Prometheus's liver was to perpetuate a field of painful experience.[312] In fact, one of the problems which confronts the torturer is that his victim has limited resources of sensitive tissue and if the operation goes on too long, is conducted without care, the subject is no longer exploitable as a victim.

Of course, until recently pain and injury have been so closely associated that it is actually hard to inflict a severe pain upon someone without at the same time causing him such serious injury that his capacities to suffer any more pain are very limited. Conversely, serious injury is so closely associated with intolerable pain that until the invention of anaesthetics the penalty of losing a limb or an ear or a tongue was unavoidably compounded with the penalty of severe pain also. The fact that this is only a contingent association in the mind of those responsible for administering punishment is shown by the fact that when the Libyan authorities recently wished to reintroduce the traditional Muslim punishment for theft, Gaddafi insisted that the guilty hand should be removed under general anaesthetic.[313]

For those of us who are horrified by the idea of a judicial mutilation, the introduction of an anaesthetic seems like a pedantic refinement. What would we think though if experimental neurology made it possible to inflict all the pain of such an amputation without any of the injury? Would that horrify us also? As I say, until very recently this would have been an academic question since the only way to produce severe pain would have been through the equally severe injury and/or loss of tissues. Unhappily, electrophysiology opens up new vistas in the judicial use of pain. It's not possible at the moment, perhaps, but before very long we will be able to counterfeit the pain of injury by probing the nervous system itself. Once this has happened we shall have made a Promethean instrument with which to torment ourselves. In fact it goes one better than that. For if you recall, the eagle had to lay off every evening in order to allow time for Prometheus's liver to grow again. Electrophysiological techniques would make it quite unnecessary to injure the liver, since the pain of doing so could be reproduced ad infinitum by activating those areas of the brain responsible for appreciating such assaults. There were hints that this might be the case long before it became technically feasible.

For example, after the amputation of a limb the patient frequently continues to feel pain in what is no longer there – the so-called phantom limb phenomenon.[314] We all possess, it would seem, an internal model of our own physique. In fact, without such a model we would be unable to locate our own sensations or give any coherence to our own physical image. Unfortunately, this model appears to have a spontaneous life of its own and in some cases it is possible to rehearse this spontaneity in such a form that the subject continues to have experiences in what no longer exists. Who knows whether torturers in the future may not act as conscientious prompters to such phantom rehearsals, creating a cycle of torment which no longer has a natural end. I would suggest that the recent introduction of electric tortures represents a crude move in this direction.

With this alarming preamble I would like to chart some of the social uses of pain in the hope that we can clarify some of the more obscure issues. For a start I would like to distinguish between the active use of pain on the one hand and the passive use of pain on the other. The active use involves the deliberate infliction of pain or the threat of doing so for either legal, ceremonial or psychological purposes. The passive use of pain presupposes the spontaneous occurrence of pain is exploited in the practice of medicine.

Let me deal with the medical uses of pain first. Of all the complaints which bring people to their doctors, pain is the most frequent. Presenting itself as it does with unmediated nastiness, it is the symptom most likely to attract the patient's attention and needs no inference in order to wish

323

that it would cease. Someone who goes yellow all of a sudden, or who feels a lump, has to infer the nastiness by consulting a body of knowledge of superstition which places an unpleasant interpretation upon such changes. Pain, on the other hand, is experienced as an evil, in and of itself, and the patient often presents himself with the request that this particular experience be removed. Of course, the alarming inferences may complicate the picture, in the sense that a relatively mild pain may bring the patient sooner than a severe one if he has learnt certain unpleasant associations with that particular location. For instance, people who believe that heart pains occur over the left side of the chest may present themselves with such a pain much earlier than they would with, say, a comparatively more severe pain somewhere else. In the hand, say. Someone with quite a severe pain in the hand is apt to endure his suffering, although were he to know, as physicians do, that such a pain is sometimes more indicative of heart disease than pain over the left side of the chest, he might alter his attitude and come to the clinic much sooner. In fact, once this is known, the unmediated severity of the pain itself frequently increases. That is to say once the patient knows or else believes that a given type of pain has alarming significance, the actual quality of the pain itself changes accordingly. In this sense the quality of pains can change according to the uses to which they are put. In other words, the intrinsic self-evident nastiness of a pain can change as the result of certain known or believed implications.

It seems likely in fact that in the years since pain has acquired a subtle diagnostic significance, and patients have grown accustomed to being closely questioned as to the quality, location and timing of their pains, the subjective experience has also become much more refined and perhaps even more acute. In a culture which can ascribe no particular significance to the differences in abdominal pain, it seems unlikely that anyone would pay much attention to these varieties. A modern surgeon, for example, likes to know if an abdominal pain is continuous or intermittent, since his actions depend on making such a distinction. Eventually the culture becomes aware of such a distinction and the experience of pain diversifies accordingly. So, in this sense, the social uses of pain can affect the personal experience of it.

The physiological idiosyncrasies of pain also allow doctors to use it in order to distinguish between illnesses arising from an identifiable physical cause and those which spring from personal anxiety. The point is that patients can use pain in order to dramatize a personal misery – not in the crude sense of malingering, exactly, but by actually inflicting an anguish upon themselves in a part of the body which symbolizes their discontent. Fortunately, the human fantasy does not project its imaginary pains in a physiological pattern. So-called functional pains tend to be focused in regions where the patient believes his vital organs to be. Thus, the person who is anxious about his heart frequently complains, as I have said, of pain over the left side of the chest, for the simple reason that popular imagery places the heart there. Whereas of course pain which has its seat in the real heart projects to areas which the patient, in his ignorance, would never associate with cardiac disorder, i.e. the shoulder, the neck and the arm. This makes it relatively easy for the doctor to discriminate between a genuine heart pain and one which arises from the patient's anxiety about his heart. Of course this doesn't mean that symbolic pains are any less real than ones which spring from physiological causes. All pain is real.

Naturally, as the culture at large becomes familiar with facts of this sort, the subjective image of the organs concerned will change accordingly and anyone anxious about his heart, say, will no longer complain of pain over the left side of the chest but will now consolidate his complaints in the same place where actual pains in the heart present. And so, when this happens, as it already has to some extent in medically self-conscious countries like America, the physician will have to employ other criteria in order to distinguish hypochondriacal pains.

While I am on the subject of spontaneous pain, that is to say pain which arises without the help of others, let me throw out a few observations which might help to elucidate some of the problems associated with actively inflicted pain. It goes without saying that we all fear pain and do our best to avoid circumstances where pain might be a risk. And understandably we all, to some extent, fear the occurrence of spontaneous pain resulting from illness. Understandably, too, we have a dread of severe pain and, in the case of severe pain associated with final illnesses, most of us hope that we will be helped to a merciful end. However, except in the case of those who have a neurotic attitude to their own pain, the dread of spontaneous pain is small by comparison with the horror of actively inflicted pain. For some reason, which we must examine later, we have a peculiar attitude towards pains which result from the activity of others. We all dislike severe toothache, for instance, but many people will postpone relief if it means having to go through the ordeal of dentistry, even though the pain administered by the dentist is usually less than the one for which we seek relief. In the same way, most of us are distressed by the spectacle of someone else in pain, but our anxiety and horror is even greater when we have to witness anyone experiencing actively inflicted pain. Darwin, for instance, was driven out of medicine, not by the spectacle of spontaneous suffering, but by the cries of patients going through the ordeal of amputation. All this in spite of the fact that one knows that the pain is incidental to a merciful enterprise. And when it is a case of pain inflicted with the sole purpose of causing suffering, our horror and fascination is magnified into something out of all recognition. I mention fascination and even attraction in this context since horror and revulsion are part and parcel of the same peculiar process. In other words, we cannot begin to understand the role of torture without taking into consideration the fact that our hatred of it is underpinned by a complementary fascination. And that he who averts his eyes is always in company with others who cannot remove their gaze. And, in the long history of deliberate torment, the actual location of the deed reflects this reciprocity: the furtive privacy of an underground room and the ceremonial publicity of the market place. And yet, as I say, this muddle of violent feelings is uniquely associated with torture and execution. George Selwyn travelled to France to see Damiens torn to bits and yet we never hear reports of fashionable séances at eighteenth-century hospital bedsides. Lunacy was a popular spectacle but not a painful illness.

Having thrown out these half-conceived provocations, let me try and examine the active uses of pain. For the sake of argument I would like to distinguish two broad classes. The utilitarian group on the one hand, in which pain – either actual or threatened – is used in order to purchase some social advantage, i.e. the situation in which pain is used as a mechanical lever and therefore theoretically at least provides no satisfaction over and above the advantages which it supposedly purchases. On the other hand, there are those situations in which the pain is sought as an end in itself – either as a payment for some wrong, real or imagined, or else as a ceremonial incident in its own right, satisfying some deeply felt personal or social longing for the spectacle of another person's merciless suffering.

Let's take the utilitarian group first. This divides further into two groups. In one case, the threat of pain is used in order to secure conformity to certain agreed standards of behaviour, i.e. if you do this or fail to do that you will suffer a penalty. Whereas in the other case, what we call torture, the pain is actually employed with the promise of its remission or in return for services rendered – either the name of accomplices, or else a shaky signature on a document affirming one's guilt.

In the first case, where the pain is used as a deterrent, or supposedly so, the situation is complicated by a retributive element to the extent that we are logically unwilling to extend the title of punishment to any legally inflicted pain unless it falls upon those who are demonstratively responsible for the prohibited act. This, however, is a conceptual point about punishment rather than a moral point about the justification of inflicting pain. The point is this: one can imagine a system of allotting pains at random, in the hope that social order will be maintained in the face of such a threat; and, while we may regard it as an unjust manoeuvre, for reasons we shall examine later, it is not an example of unjust punishment. It is not punishment at all. On the other hand, individual instances of miscarriage – where a materially innocent person receives an inflicted pain, following a formally correct procedure – is an example of punishment, albeit unjust, since the formal requirements of his having been found guilty according to the accepted rules have been satisfied.

However, in spite of the fact that there is a logical objection to calling any other system of allotment 'punishment,' there is no such objection to inventing such an alternative, and in certain cases such systems have actually been adopted in order to secure social obedience of one sort or another. However, although these two alternative systems – punishment on the one hand and victimization on the other – are logically on a par with one another, in that they both represent utilitarian manoeuvres, the one is distinguished from the other by the fact that, in the case of punishment, a moral consideration forbids the random allocation of pain on the grounds that it is improper and unfair that the pain should be inflicted on someone innocent. So that, whether we further approve of the notion of retribution or not, there is no avoiding the fact that of the two alternative utilitarian systems of allocating pain, the one which we most consistently favour is the one which has a retributive justification – even if it only pre-establishes the minimum threshold required. I would like to suggest here that the requirement that *only* the guilty receive inflicted pain is the remnant of a much more extensive retributive theory that *all* the guilty should. In other words, our squeamishness about causing pain to the innocent is a residue of a much more ancient appetite for bringing agony to the guilty. And it seems to me that it's almost impossible to account for this wish. Nevertheless, it's there and it undoubtedly accounts for the anxiety which is now felt, as retribution progressively gives way to the notion of rational prevention and humane reform. Why should this be so? Because it is claimed the prisoner pays for his crime and must do so. However, the concept of payment is very odd in this context, since, in all other economic circumstances, obtaining an advantage of some sort is paid for by replacing what is taken with some equivalent advantage, either in goods or services. If retribution is, as is claimed, a reciprocal payment, what service is rendered to those who have sustained the loss? Now, it's simply a circular argument to insist that the repayment consists in the satisfaction of seeing justice done. The point is this: why is the spectacle or knowledge of another's agony regarded as just payment? It's easy to understand envy of another's great fortune, but it is hard to appreciate why he should gloat at his just suffering. And yet this image is deeply ingrained in the human imagination, raised to the level of what one authority has called an abominable fancy, in the patristic myth that the reward of the saved would consist in a ring-side seat at the torments of the damned.

What this boils down to, I think, is that at the heart of all our transactions in pain – even in those whose rationale is apparently utilitarian – there is a primeval appetite for witnessing or even causing the pain of someone who has been carefully rendered helpless. The notice of offence and its retribution then comes in later as a way of rationalizing and regulating the periodic satisfaction of this peculiar appetite. Nevertheless, we have become so conditioned to associate the idea of deliberately inflicted pain with that of punishable offence that even in the most sadistic fantasies the administration of the agony is pedantically preceded by sham tribunals… So much so that in the sadistic literature of the nineteenth century, the elaborate rituals of indictment and confession form an essential part of the fantasy – almost to the point where the rod itself never fails, postponed by an infinite train of humble confessions followed by endless entreaties for mercy. Agony *reservatus* as it were.

So far, Freudian psychology has offered the only plausible answer to the problem of this appetite, and even then the answer is too vague to satisfy all one's curiosity about this subject. I would like, however, to offer a complementary explanation for our interest in and horror of deliberately inflicted pain. In the normal run of events, pain and death are uncertain fixtures and, up to and including the end, the outcome remains uncertain but is partly determined by the subject's own efforts and struggles: the hypnotic interest shown in the condemned man. Formal execution, however, fixes the date and the moment of the end. By a single performative utterance on the part of a judge, the prisoner is converted into a unique individual – someone who actually knows the moment and the manner of his own end. Even the judge who issues the sentence is deprived of that knowledge and yet, by his fiat, the man standing before him is converted into a sacred person on account of the dreadful certainty surrounding him. It's no wonder, then, that the condemned prisoner acquires an almost hypnotic attention.

Psychoanalysts have spoken about the way in which small children will build models and toys of those situations over which they have no mastery, attempting as it were, by rehearsing a small scale version of something beyond their understanding, to bring that mystery within their control. Pain, mutilation and death are just such mysteries and I would like to suggest that one of our motives for rehearsing executions with such pedantic care, is that we are also operating a scale model of a mystery which surpasses all understanding. And that when a crowd watches with breathless fascination as someone is torn to bits with scholarly formality – as in the case of Damiens, for instance – they are tinkering at a magical level with the insoluble problem of life itself. I am not offering this as a substantial alternative to any Freudian interpretation of sadism...and it may be that the idea hardly holds water anyway, but it seems to be a plausible addition to psychoanalytic explanation. I do not believe, as so many people now seem to, that this form of human ferocity can be explained in terms of animal ethology. Obviously it has something to do with aggression, although it seems in many ways to be a complete contradiction of everything which the theologians have told us about that instinct. For instance, in the case of natural aggression, the activity is usually called off by the spectacle of one's opponent's submission. In the case of torture – submission, humility and cringeing – worse excesses than before appear to be called forth; and to say, therefore, that this is simply an example of perverted aggression merely begs the question. In any case, I am convinced that it is in the secret recesses of our humanity that we shall find the origins of what makes us bestial.

Whatever the origins of this appetite, it would be nice to say that the use of actively inflicted pain was on the way out. And, admittedly, since the Enlightenment its use in punishment seems to be vanishing. Certainly its effectiveness as a utilitarian instrument is now seriously in question and, in any case, we have developed much more elaborate and explicit scruples about pain itself and, even in cases of atrocious crime, our instinct for retributive punishment stops short of inflicting pain... It would be interesting, I think, to set this trend in a more general context of growing squeamishness and even to analyse what squeamishness *is* exactly. I think that the answer to questions of this sort will have to be postponed until we have looked more closely at the evolution of other manners, and attitudes towards pain, injury, blood, obscenity and filth of one sort or another.

Undoubtedly the rational interests of the Enlightenment played a large part in the abolition of actively inflicted pain. Unhappily, the very same movement was probably responsible for the peculiar reappearance of torture in recent years. This may sound perverse, but I think it is true. And paradoxically, the man whose writing was more directly responsible than any other for the abolition of torture was at the same time indirectly responsible for creating the conditions within which torture was almost bound to make its reappearance. I am thinking, of course, of Cesare Beccaria, the Milanese philosopher who in 1764 published a short tract on crimes and punishments in which he gave a completely convincing answer against the use of torture. Against its use as a retributive instrument he argued as follows:

> The belief is that pain, which is a sensation, purges infamy, which is a purely moral relationship. Is pain perhaps a crucible? And is infamy perhaps an impure, mixed substance? [...] Torture itself causes real

infamy for its victims. Thus, by this method, infamy is removed by inflicting infamy.[315]

As a utilitarian measure he argues thus: '[Torture] is a sure way to acquit the robust criminals and to convict the innocent who are weak.'[316] And as he also points out, the use of torture offends against basic principles of retributive justice since the pain falls on innocent and guilty alike until the torment has hopefully established which is which. In which case, the innocent has suffered the pains of the condemned in the very act of establishing his innocence, if indeed he ever does succeed in doing so. And so on.

In other respects, however, Baccaria was a precursor of nineteenth-century utilitarianism and was therefore committed to calculating the proper ration of whatever distress was needed to secure an even greater sum of satisfaction. Admittedly, he himself drew the line at pain for the reasons we have mentioned above – and, in any case, the magnitude of the various satisfactions which he and his contemporaries foresaw was such that the penalties needed to secure them were proportionately small and certainly wouldn't have included the extremes of judicial torture. But, with the emergence of millennial social theory – offering infinite satisfactions in some forthcoming social order – the utilitarian calculus could easily be used to justify proportionately large penalties to be used against anyone who threatened to frustrate the achievement of such infinite satisfactions. Arguing from Rousseau's tracts, for instance, the Jacobin theories of the French Revolution were able to justify almost any extreme of bloodshed, since the agony involved was dwarfed by the millennial possibilities of what was promised. The extremes of the revolutionary terror were only the start of what has now borne fruit today as the result of the fatal fertilization of utilitarian penal theory by millennial social programmes. In Russia, Nazi Germany, Greece, South America and elsewhere, the appearance of torture is an inevitable outcome of this dreadful marriage. Coupled with the as yet unextinguished appetite for inflicting pain as an entertainment in and for itself, the possibilities of controlling torture seem very faint indeed.

The awful irony is that the apparent success of the moral system which has seen fit to outlaw such practices creates a situation where it is now much harder to detect and control any examples of its violation. The success and esteem of rational humanitarianism is such that the regimes which wish and need to practise torture and terror now do so in secret, creating thereby a living hell, inaccessibly in the midst of ordinary life. This in turn creates a pathological blindness in those who have to live in such societies, although their imagination is haunted with the repressed knowledge of what is going on in the shuttered hotel over the street, or else just out of sight, beyond the skyline of Bavarian pines. Having abolished the fantasy of Hell, we have an alternative in reality. In the face of this knowledge, one is numbed with impotent lassitude. Of course, one applauds the noble conscientiousness of organizations like Amnesty, who will shortly publish a dreadful catalogue of what is growing all around us. With each revelation, however, our ability to do anything becomes less and, like the inhabitants of the countries where it is actually happening, we steadily grow indifferent – a banal sanity.

Foreword to *Voices of Victorian London*
2011

In February 1996, BBC2 transmitted a documentary about Henry Mayhew's exhaustive mid-Victorian study, London Labour and the London Poor *(1851–62).[317] For this programme, Miller brought his directorial skill to a selection of interviews from the book which were now rendered as acted monologues.[318] Several years later he was invited to provide the following introduction to an abridged volume of Mayhew.[319]*

In the inquiring mind of Henry Mayhew we are beginning to see the antecedents of social anthropology, the process of paying attention to the commonplace details of the lives of otherwise forgettable ordinary people, and particularly people below one's own social level, with whom one would not normally be acquainted. It is in the same way that in the late nineteenth century, anthropologists went off to the Torres Straits and actually engaged for the first time, face to face, with what were previously called 'savages.' And they began to ask for the first time, 'What do they do? How do they cook? How do they get up in the morning? Who is it they feel they can marry, and who is it they feel they can't?' and so on. So probably from the middle of the nineteenth century – when Mayhew did his pioneering interviews – and with accelerating frequency, you get an attention to 'The Other,' which epitomizes the neglected world of the previously inconsiderable.

Of course, we have to be careful about interpreting what Mayhew reports as being what people might have said to their own friends or relatives. The very nature of these interviews, with someone who is there to give a confession or a discourse about themselves to someone who is recognisably of a different class – and possibly superior – may in fact yield a different type of discourse from the one which Mayhew, instead of hearing, might merely have overheard. For example, there is a great difference between being a 'looker' and being an 'onlooker,' and in exactly the same way for speech there may be all the difference in the world between being a listener and an overhearer.

But the important thing is that this doesn't in any way compromise or vitiate the value, because these interviews are, in fact, straightforward descriptive accounts of what it is like to be *someone like that*. The philosopher Tom Nagel, in a famous paper, asks, "What is it like to be a bat?" (1974). Now, of course, when it comes to bats, as Nagel says, there is no way in which any interview will yield what it is like to be a bat, and for most people before Mayhew there was no interest in what it was like to be a crossing-sweeper. They may even have been assumed to be not all that different from bats.

What is noticeable about Mayhew, first of all, is that he addresses himself to people who are conspicuously unfortunate – in comparison with someone solvent and respectable like himself – and of a social class which is self-respecting. He addresses, and listens to, people who are quite clearly unfortunate, whose daily work would have been regarded by someone like himself as unconvivial and humiliating. Many of the occupations he explores and analyses are activities which someone of his class would have regarded as quite impossible to engage in, unless one dropped off the edge of one's social class due to drunkenness, or suffered a sudden misfortune which precipitated a slide into this subterranean world.

Indeed, there are a few interviews with such people who were from a social class nearer to Mayhew's own, such as the Seller of Fruity Drinks who was driven into poverty by illness. Such people maintain the language which they learnt of their previous class, and retain fluency and eloquence so that they talk with an accent conspicuously unlike the accents and idioms of the ordinary people with whom most literate people were unacquainted. It may be that the more elevated language they used – particularly when addressed by someone of their own previous class – helped to maintain their dignity by maintaining the diction of their previous occupation or previous level of occupation.

Mayhew described the London he explored as 'the undiscovered country of the poor,' and to our shame that country still exists today, and it is still undiscovered by many of us.[320]

When I go down into the nearby market every day to buy fruit or vegetables there are many people in the market with whom I have often quite lengthy conversations, which, if they were written down, would be not altogether different from Mayhew's. They are people from what would have been the same social class as his interviewees. They are none of them, with one or two exceptions, so unfortunate. Nevertheless, right around the corner from where I live there is a huge overcrowded residence for the homeless called Arlington House and many of the people there are in situations comparable to those that were reproduced by Mayhew 160 years ago.

But of course, in addition to the poverty endured by the people Mayhew spoke to, there was for some an additional burden of ill-health, and one of the interesting things about the representation of the disabled, or the sick, or the ill, is that it is very hard with hindsight – even with some sort of medical knowledge, which I still have – actually to make a retrospective diagnosis. I would hesitate to identify any of the disabilities, other than by their signs or symptoms, by saying they were blind or lame, or so forth. For example, the Blind Street-Reader refers to having had an aneurysm, but what would he know of aneurysms? I suspect that what happened is that he was probably given a diagnosis in the hospital, and hung on to that word 'aneurysm' without the faintest idea that an aneurysm is in fact a vascular disorder – a sudden dilatation, shortly perhaps to burst – with, perhaps, neurological consequences if it happened to occur inside the skull. Mind you, patients visiting a hospital today often don't have much more understanding of the terms used unless their doctor is a very good communicator. But at least today's doctor will know a lot more about aneurysms and how they cause illness than his Victorian predecessor would have.

For anyone looking at the history of illness through the Mayhew interviews, medical knowledge among doctors – let alone patients – at the time was so rudimentary that it is unlikely that anything the Londoners said to Mayhew about the nature or origins of their condition could be taken at face value. Take the Crippled Seller of Nutmeg-Graters, one of the most vivid and moving interviews in the book. As a best guess, he could have had cerebral palsy or some sort of disorder somewhere in the central nervous system that produced difficulties of locomotion, which then deteriorated with the effort and difficulty of walking or getting himself around. On the other hand, perhaps he had multiple sclerosis, a disease which itself progresses. But there's no way of knowing. The understanding of diagnostic entities in the middle of the nineteenth century was extremely primitive.

For a long time there had been some understanding of the organs in the body, based usually on post-mortems. Organs are identifiable because they are lumps which you can see when you open the chest or the abdomen. You can see a blocked intestine; you can see that the heart has undergone some sort of change of colouration, and so on. But it's only when you start doing microscopic analysis of sections of organs that you get to the next level down – what's called histology, the study of tissues. Aniline dyes enabled researchers to stain sections of organs and produce histological diagnoses. It's very interesting that the notion of tissue is derived from 'textile'; it means the same thing, a woven fabric. So, up to the eighteenth century you have the notion of 'organs,' then you get 'tissues' and then you get 'cells,' and you realize that tissues are themselves composed of different types of cells, which then combine in very complicated ways to make the various organs of the body.

Now, at the time when Mayhew is interviewing these people, while biological research was beginning the process of understanding how the body works, the practice of medicine had not yet reached the level of sophistication which enabled anyone to make a useful diagnosis.

Some of the street people give accounts of hospitals and doctors but it is sometimes difficult to tell from the interviews what purpose they served. The

Hot-Eel Man, for example, stayed in several hospitals for an unconscionably long time. He was in King's College Hospital, St Bartholomew's and the Middlesex for a total of 27 months, and I wonder why on earth he was there for so long, how was he treated, and indeed why was he eventually then kicked out? Was it because the doctors said 'We can't do anything more for you'? It's not as if they were doing anything for him anyway.

Of course, hospitals at least provided a sheltered residence, with, in some cases, the possibility of surgical interventions – amputations, for example, performed without anaesthetic. Even in the early days of anaesthesia there were no palliative measures – techniques which *reduced* pain, as opposed to eliminating it completely during an operation.

Nowadays, many of the most important disease prevention methods spring from an understanding of public health, but in Mayhew's time such understanding barely existed. The early Victorians were on the verge of developing the idea that something was wrong with sewage. There were intimations that ill-health might have been due to the bad arrangement of cities, and 'bad air' – what were called miasmas – and even malnutrition. But these causes were not visualized as disorders which you could systematize and classify. No one really thought about what constitutes a healthy diet. That idea developed towards the end of the nineteenth century when there arose an interest in the nature of diet, and the roles of proteins versus carbohydrates. Vitamins were not discovered until the early part of the twentieth century. No one really understood that vitamin deficiency might be the cause of several disorders.

As a result, many of the people Mayhew saw in the streets of London would have had problems of growth or development. They would have been wizened or shrunken. Children would have had various skeletal disorders as a result of inadequate calcium intake, and vitamin D deficiency as a result of poor exposure to sunlight. Scarcity of fruit and vegetables meant a lack of vitamin C. There was no idea of there being components which were necessary to supplement the diet, and which people now buy in supermarkets; none of those dietary supplements would have existed because there wasn't a natural history of diet. Mayhew was in no position to ask dietary questions because he himself knew nothing about dietary sufficiency; the biochemistry of diet was something with which he, and everyone else, was unacquainted.

That lack of knowledge of practical measures to prevent or treat disease meant that some of the people Mayhew met had to endure much more advanced stages of illness and disability than any modern patient, while still trying to earn a living.

Someone today who had become afflicted in childhood by whatever the Nutmeg-Grater Seller had, for example, would probably never have got to the stage of locomotor disorder of Mayhew's interviewee. Many of the cases of profound, almost unintelligible, disorders which figure in Mayhew would not now occur at all. They can be pre-empted by antenatal care, for example, which did not actually appear as a systematic format until the establishment of the National Health Service; or by pre-natal diagnosis, or intra-uterine surgery, or methods of treatment of babies and young children that were not available in Mayhew's time.

There is a very interesting study of the types of birth disorders that occurred in Scotland among working-class women of the 1940s as the result of an increased frequency of bad deliveries. It turned out that poor women giving birth had had their pelvises affected by malnutrition in *their* infancy, which produced pelvic narrowing, meaning that the birth of their foetuses was compromised. This was not discovered until 1948.

In the absence of such knowledge of cause and effect, people accepted that life was little more than a gamble in which the poor suffered more than did the affluent. Nevertheless, the affluent realized that they would lose many of their children in the first eight years of life. If you look at gravestones from the eighteenth and early nineteenth centuries, you will see how many of those buried are less than four weeks old. Many of them died of diseases for which they would now merely be excused PE.

Judging from the number of blind people Mayhew spoke to, there was a lot more blindness around – or at least, more blind people were forced to work in some capacity. For many, such disability would have been the result of serious infection – preventable today – which would have produced severe scarring on the anterior part of the eyeball, causing opacity of the cornea, preventing the retina from receiving a projected image. Few of them wonder about what it would be like to see; perhaps expectations of good fortune are so low that they settle for the misfortunes they have been dealt, and are therefore disinclined to wonder about what it is they have lost, and consider this loss as part of the risk of being alive. One might consider this is a kind of stoicism, but I do not think that is accurate in this context. Stoicism is a word you might use of someone who has high expectations of a long and healthy life and is then struck by misfortune, but in a world before effective medical intervention, people accepted unaccountable biological misfortunes. There might have been grief, but people settled for their lot. Indeed, they even thanked God that things were not worse.

It may well be that in that period mere survival of self, albeit a reduced form of selfhood, would itself be a privilege, which you would assign to the benevolence of the Creator, notwithstanding the idea that the misfortune itself was the result of the Creator. They saw the Creator as the source of good fortune and not of bad fortune, and offered praise for the extent to which they survived.

Perhaps this was peculiar to the class to which Mayhew addressed himself. The people he met don't seem to ask the more general question, 'Why am I socially unfortunate?', in addition to 'Why am I medically unfortunate?' There is some sort of acceptance because social structure had not yet been called into question in England. If you read the conversations Mayhew had with the crossing-sweepers, there seems to be no question of resentment of their social position as they make a path for the affluent, stepping delicately through the mud and the shit. They don't ask, 'Why is it that I am sweeping for them, and that no one is sweeping for me? Why is the social structure organized such that I have, in addition to my medical disorder, a social disorder which assigns me to a job which I know these gentry would regard as an impossible humiliation?'

They may have seen what the gentry looked like when they crossed the road, but could not conceive of the gentry's lives when they had crossed the road and returned to their homes, and what their occupations were which made them relatively immune to injuries suffered by those on a lower social level.

One of the things that is most conspicuous about these interviews is that there is little social indignation, and, as a consequence, little sense of social injustice. There is no apparent expression of 'It is unfair.' Social discrepancy was not yet articulated and visualized in ways which gave rise to socially organized discontent. Only then would revolutions begin to occur, or at least social organizations arise which – through unions and other organizations – could express the notion of injustice.

This is partly lack of information, but also lack of rhetoric. Where does the rhetoric start to spread which gives the working class the sense that there is an articulated justification for discontent? And it isn't just that they are quietly forbearing – there is not yet a language in which the notion of injustice and discontent come together and express themselves in some sort of social arrangement of outrage.

It may of course be that Mayhew avoided raising those issues, because in fact, being of the class that he was, he did not wish to open the lid to the notion of unfairness – either the unfairness on the part of the Creator, or the unfairness on the part of 'my betters.'

It is one result of the neutrality with which Mayhew went about his task that *we* can ask these questions, and many others, on behalf of his interviewees when, on the whole, he does not. He was the earliest 'fly on the wall' journalist, and it is thanks to the fact that he provides such a wealth of raw data about poor people's working lives that his interviews are such a fertile stimulus for speculation, curiosity and wonder.

Plays and players
Non-Verbal Communication, 1972[321]

Between 1965 and 1970, a study group of the Royal Society investigated the 'ritualization of behaviour in man and animals.'[322] Miller's contribution to the resulting collection of essays is an early example of his interest in non-verbal communication and its value as a component of acting.

In this essay I intend to deal exclusively with the non-verbal aspects of those types of performance which are specifically associated with speech. This is because I assume that verbal communication takes precedence in human discourse and that non-verbal behaviour achieves most of its communicative significance in the context of syntactically organized utterances. For this reason I intend to overlook the *deliberately* non-verbal types of theatrical performance – mime, ballet and ritual dance – on the understanding that these displays are highly specialized acts comprising a deliberate abstention from spoken language. In ballet and mime, speech is conspicuous by its absence, and the audience is required to adjust its expectations in such a way that it does not experience the performance as merely impoverished versions of spoken language.

The essential feature of Western theatre therefore is a script or verbal recipe, in minimal accordance with which the actors must reproduce the propositional assertions created by the author. In other words, the central ingredient of a play consists of a series of utterances which express, as Wittgenstein points out, *the way things are*. These expressions are designed to allow the various characters to mention or refer to some state of affairs, either in the outside world or in their own minds.

Of course this script may be extremely attenuated – in the case of certain plays by Beckett it is reduced to alarming thinness – but such as it is, the verbal recipe is the essential core giving meaning to all the silences which intervene. The gestures and grimaces which succeed one another during these silences only acquire full significance in the context of the verbal expressions which they either precede or follow. They represent changes of mood following something that *has* been said, or else states of vigilance and expectation with regard to something that *might* be said. In the absence of an utterance which asserts something or other, these non-verbal passages fall off into a state of frustrated restlessness.

The different signals which jointly comprise such 'interstitial communiqués' are similar in some ways to the non-verbal acoustic cues which precede the making of either a successful or an unsuccessful telephone call. A ringing tone shows that a putatively successful bid for attention has been made, but if the tone continues for a certain time without being interrupted, one begins to doubt that the person is in. A high-pitched buzz shows, but does not assert, that although the bid has been correctly formulated at the caller's end, it has failed to even compete for attention at the other end. A sequence of familiar double-tones, also high-pitched, signifies that the call is correct in all respects and would have gained attention but for the fact that the subscriber at the other end is already engaged in conversation. And so on. Now, although these signals have an agreed significance, they only acquire it within the context of an intended exchange of verbal utterances. None of these cues would have any meaning outside the context of a possible conversation. Within this context, however, they help to eliminate certain ambiguities which arise in the course of trying to set up such an exchange. It is easy to imagine the doubts which would be created if there was a silence every time one dialled, since there would be no way for the caller to distinguish between a misdial, a line out of order, an engaged number, or no one at home. In the same way, the gaps which intervene between the utterances of a theatrical scene are filled with non-verbal signals, one of whose functions is to inform the various participants of the chances of their respective forthcoming utterances receiving attention. One character, say, will clear his throat, thereby inducing his putative communicant to register his willingness to receive the message by turning his head with an expectant raise of the eyebrows. Neither the cough nor the raising of the eyebrows have much significance on their own, but in the context of a conversation *about* to occur, they considerably facilitate the chances of it bearing fruit. If character A did *not* clear his throat before speaking, and if his partner was otherwise engaged at the time, the significance of the first few sentences might be lost on thin air. The cough is an attempt to ensure that what follows will be attended to, right from the outset. On the other hand, if character B did not respond to the cough by turning his head and raising his eyebrows, character A would remain in doubt as to the success of his cough in gaining attention.

Actors who wish to reproduce an accurate version of two people trying to hold a conversation with one another must therefore take care to include imitations of these interstitial communiqués. One of the most vivid illustrations of the difference between professional and amateur actors is the failure of the amateur to come up with convincing versions of these non-verbal 'attention' signals. Not that they are as simple as I have made out. Unlike the phone example, the interstitial signals which are used for registering the various states of listeners' attention are not compiled in accordance to a strict convention. A man may bid for attention in any one of a hundred non-verbal ways; likewise, a putative listener may signify his willingness to attend by choosing from a large repertoire of facial or vocal acts. Moreover, each one of these acts may also indicate the *quality* of the attention which is being given. By rolling the eyes upwards and closing the lids for a moment, the listener may announce that, while he is prepared to listen, he is doing so with great reluctance and that he will attend to the forthcoming message in a mood of sceptical resignation. The speaker who appreciates this preliminary response to what he is about to say will often be forced to rephrase his utterance, to make it more convincing. Not to mention the immediate modulation of the non-verbal accompaniments of the speech itself, with which the speaker will invest his remarks in the knowledge that he is about to deliver his message into a hostile ear.

This last consideration brings us to a realization of the fact that, while speech assumes priority in the flux of messages that pass between members of a given community, it is only when they are fully invested with non-verbal signals that spoken utterances can succeed in rising above the bare grammatical meaning of their constituent expressions. When, for instance, at the start of *The Seagull*, Masha announces that she is in mourning for her life, there is a sense in which it could be said that anyone who speaks English is bound to understand what Masha means by that particular expression.[323] But at the same time there is clearly another level at which the mere knowledge of English grammar and vocabulary does *not* exhaust the significance of what the character is saying. The actress who is charged with the task of uttering this statement must therefore use it in such a way that it will 'mean' something over and above the significance which may be derived from a mere paraphrase of its component words. In order to do this, she has at her disposal the following parameters within which variations may be introduced to modulate the full meaning.

a. *Vocal.* (i) Overall volume.
   (ii) Differential volume within the phrase.
   (iii) Pitch and tone variants.
   (iv) Use of accents.
b. *Facial.* Smiles, sneers, set of jaws. Elevation of eyebrows, etc.
c. *Posture.* Set of head on shoulders. Spinal posture. Stance.
d. *Manual gestures.*

By simultaneously modulating all these parameters, the bare grammatical phrase 'I am in mourning for my life' can finally be made to render a plenum of meaning which has coherent significance within the ongoing life of the character portrayed.

However this does not mean that the full 'meaning' of the utterance is finally specified when all the non-verbal variables are fixed. Even when it is fleshed out with inflections and gestures, the phrase cannot be relied upon to deliver its 'full' complement of intended meaning. For the phrase, as conceived, *has* no fixed complement of antecedent meaning – but is instead a shot in the direction of some altogether hypothetical limit of 'meaning.' Added to which, the non-verbal cues, which are used to inflect any given phrase towards this hypothetical limit, are so vague and equivocal that no two listeners will ever quite agree as to the precise significance of the accents, tones, emphases, expressions and gestures which jointly make up its concrete performance.

Of course in real life, whilst speaking spontaneously, no one is ever aware of the distinction that exists between the bare grammatical meaning or reference of a phrase and the swarm of non-verbal elements that help to inflect that phrase towards the meaning which the speaker intends it to convey. The phrase and its performance are conceived as one, and it would, I think, be a serious mistake to imagine the production of speech in the same terms as the manufacture of a motor car on an assembly line, with a chassis of syntax rolling up to a section of the brain which then clothes it in a coachwork of non-verbal signs.

When we come to dramatic performance, however, the metaphor of the automobile assembly line becomes awkwardly relevant. For the script exists as a grammatical entity long before it assumes life as an actual utterance, so that when the actor undertakes to perform the lines, he is confronted by the peculiar task of investing them with a suitable accompaniment of non-verbal cues; and to do so, moreover, as if the whole act had taken place simultaneously. This would offer no particular problems if one could read into the lines a set of specifications that automatically insisted upon the way in which they should be spoken; but as everyone knows, it is possible to perform the lines assigned to Hamlet, say, in a hundred different ways, all of which are at least *compatible* with the basic semantic references of the script. Of course, it would be foolish to expect each phrase taken in isolation to specify its own 'correct' performance. It is essential to consider all the speeches as a whole and, from this conspectus, to arrive at some instructive generalization as to the appropriate mode of uttering any one of the constituent lines. But no two actors will arrive at the same generalization and, although the resulting performances may each, respectively, be compatible with the text, the different characters who utter this text may be quite incompatible with one another. Which only goes to highlight what Professor Strawson pointed out 20 years ago, that it is *people* who mean and not *expressions*; so that it is quite possible for two people to mean different things *by* the same expression.[324]

The task of rehearsal therefore consists of an effort to discover a 'person' who could mean something by the sum of the expressions which comprise his part.

What is surprising perhaps is that playwrights seem to take so little trouble to specify, by means of collateral evidence, what sort of person *they* have in mind. Presumably they *do* have someone in mind, for strings of dialogue do not normally suggest themselves to the mind's ear without being set in the mouths of someone who 'means' something by them. When a writer creates speeches, he must, to some extent, conceive them in the mouths of a more or less distinct individual person; which means, in turn, that he cannot really *avoid* entertaining an image of how the characters are standing when they speak – what they are doing with their faces, hands, tones and inflections, through the collective medium of which the character tells us what he means by the expressions he is using. And yet, more often than not, the only thing that survives in the written script is the lines themselves – like the skeleton of a prehistoric creature – leaving the actors and directors free to reconstruct the soft parts of the role, in a way that may be at odds with the creature that once lived as a whole within the writer's imagination. It has always seemed rather puzzling to me that authors who are so jealous of their conceptions should leave so much to chance in their subsequent re-creation; and I can only suggest that their almost consistent failure in this respect arises from the lack of a satisfactory notation within which the non-verbal parameters of human expression might be registered. Whatever the reason, the brute fact stands that the scripts of plays impose upon the actor the peculiar task of manufacturing a personal identity that can significantly include the lines written opposite his name in the script.

Now, the way in which this synthesis is carried out depends to a very large extent upon the significance which any given actor attaches to the notion of 'a person.' In other words, whether he explicitly realizes it or not, the actor compiles his performance of the lines in accordance with a philosophical assumption as to the correct definition of an individual. For in undertaking to portray the character whose name appears opposite certain lines in the text, he is accepting the tacit assumption that there is a continuous identity which spans the interval between successive exits and entrances of the character thus named. Now, although he may not openly confront the logical problems that are raised by such an assumption, the actor must make a decision, at some mental level or other, as to the criteria which convince him that he is entering as the same person as whom he exited half an hour ago. More often than not he will go and sit in the green room and read a newspaper until the cue for his next entrance; which means, in effect, that he has to reassemble the impersonation which he shed on stepping into the wings. Now, the point is this: in the act of assembling himself for re-entry, he must refer to certain criteria that will define for him, no matter how vaguely, what it *means* to come back as the same person who previously exited. He must know, in some way or other, the sort of features that would count either for or against this putative continuity. It is my contention that there are two criterial extremes which might underlie this decision. At one end there is the assumption that personal identity is a self-evident sense of subjective continuity, and that a person is a sum of private experiences to which he and no one else has access. At the other extreme lies the belief that a person is nothing more than a physique, whose uniqueness and identifiability are associated with a set of behavioural dispositions which mark them off from any other claimant. Gilbert Ryle has characterized the last position in *The Concept of Mind* (1949), and many actors implicitly endorse it by approaching their parts as if identity *was* defined by behavioural features alone. Within the profession such actors are often referred to as 'physical' performers, and while their colleagues may marvel at the sparkling idiosyncrasy of their performances, they often express anxiety at the so-called lack of feeling involved. However, since no other person has access to anyone else's state of mind, the accusation of lack of feeling must depend upon the observer having detected a gap in the outward display of non-verbal behaviour. In talking to actors about this, however, I have never succeeded in getting them to describe what these missing cues consist of. They can never say how to distinguish between a portrayal which is subjectively well understood but badly executed, and one in which there is no subjective sympathy but a great deal of outward accomplishment. 'I can't put my finger on it,' they will say. 'I just feel it in my bones.' 'There's no heart there.' And so on.

At the other extreme there are actors who actually refuse to 'perform' during rehearsal and who prefer to mumble their lines without expression until, by some collateral route, they have arrived at a sympathy for the *state of mind* which would have led the character to say the lines assigned to him. Then, often quite suddenly, the performance will materialize, fully inflected, the whole utterance fledged with gestures and expressions.

It would be a mistake to leave the impression that actors segregate themselves sharply into one or other of these two extremes and that you could, by questioning members of the profession, get them to admit their respective allegiance to the alternative criteria of a person. An otherwise behavioural actor will often resort to a subjective justification for certain types of expression he is using, whilst an introspective performer will frequently admit that he has introduced a certain idiosyncratic inflection or gesture because he likes doing it, or simply because it helps to point up the distinctiveness of the personality he is portraying.

Besides, a considerable percentage of the ongoing stream of non-verbal behaviour takes place without it necessarily signifying *anything*; and while, without it, one would be tempted to deem a given performance as expressionless, in its presence one would almost certainly be at a loss to say *what* it actually expressed. This holds even in the case of a meticulously subjective performance. Stopped in mid-stream and asked to justify a given twist of the lips or drop in tone, the actor may not be able to say *why* he did it and in many cases he may be unaware of the fact that he has done it at all. In fact, one can often recognize the really accomplished performance by the degree to which the performer is able to realize a proportion of *contentless* expression, in terms of which a sense of human vitality is conveyed without its laying an obligation upon the audience to try and decode its semantic significance. And in those performances where the actor seems hell-bent on inflicting a clearly visualized meaning into every gesture, we say that he is overacting.

Given the fact, then, that a significant proportion of facial movement and vocal intonation carries no intentional meaning anyway and that the rest is so variable in its significance, one can see how easy it is for an audience to read a performance as if it were, to some extent, a Rorschach blot. Even a group of perceptive critics can witness the same performance and disagree widely amongst themselves as to the meaning of what was being acted. This may assume absurd proportions, as for example on the occasion when I heard a critic give high praise for certain pauses which I, as the director of the show, was privately deploring in the knowledge that the actor was merely forgetting his lines. Conversely, in a production of *King Lear* for which I was also responsible, the actor playing the lead was widely condemned for failing to convey, presumably by non-verbal signs, the majesty which is conventionally expected of the role.[325] Now, it so happens that, for what it was worth, we had deliberately erased from the performance all gestures and facial mannerisms that might have conveyed a sense of majesty. What I would still like to know is whether the critics, on witnessing this performance, detected *formes frustes* of majestic expression and were then criticizing the failure of the actor to develop these to their appropriate level – through lack of technical ability – or whether they acknowledged that a decision had been made to eliminate such expressions altogether and were condemning *this decision*.

This problem recurs with monotonous regularity without anyone ever having published the principles according to which dramatic perception is organized. What I do know is that circumstantial evidence, often quite irrelevant to the performance in question, plays a crucial part in the final judgement that is passed. For example, a celebrated actor is almost invariably credited with total deliberation, with the often absurd result that both critics and audiences are led to over-interpret his gestures and expressions and read meanings into movements that had no significance whatsoever. In the same way, if a well-known comedian takes on a serious role, audiences who have grown accustomed to the comic use to which he has previously put his face and voice will inadvertently read humorous or even satirical intentions into his performance. The point is, to go one step further than Strawson's analysis, not only is it true to assert that *people* mean and not expressions, but it is often audiences who decide what people mean; using, in order to arrive at this decision, evidence which is not actually given in the performance itself.

For this reason I often think it is important to talk to critics before they see a play, in spite of the fact that convention insists upon the notion that the performance should stand or fall on its own merits and that critical vision is blurred by such tendentious information. For, as I see it, the dogma of critical impartiality rests upon a psychological fallacy, according to which it is assumed that perception is derived solely from what is given to the senses. Whereas modern cognitive psychology has shown quite clearly that perception is a conjectural enterprise, in which antecedent introductions are essential prerequisites for distinguishing the figure from its ground. Far from being an unprincipled act of collusion, preliminary advice from the director may be an important contribution towards ensuring that the critic properly adjusts his perceptual horizon for the best chance of his seeing the distinctive inflection that has now been given to an otherwise familiar text. Otherwise, theatrical innovation is repeatedly seen as a failed example of what the critic expects rather than as an achieved instance of something altogether new.

This argument assumes importance in the context of Western theatre due to the fact that we follow a more or less naturalistic tradition. That is to say, the face, hands and voice are not used to inflect meaning in accordance to a rigidly formalized code, but are, as in real life, moved in an irregular and often unreliable relationship to the underlying, expressive intention of the utterer. Which leaves of course a large leeway for equivocal guesses. In more traditional forms of theatre, the variations of non-verbal behaviour are artificially constrained within a closed series of mutually distinct, expressive morphemes, and, in order to reinforce the formal clarity of this paradigmatic system, every effort is made to minimize the visibility – or audibility – of intervening states which might otherwise blur the issue. For example, lest irrelevant physiognomic perceptions be derived from small variations of expression that intervene between the agreed paradigms of facial movement, the features are carefully painted in order to give exclusive priority to the elements that *do* have significance within the code. Or, to put it in the words of Erving Goffman, 'Messages that are not part of the officially accredited flow are modulated so as not to interfere seriously with the accredited messages.'[326] Whereas in a dramatic tradition that reflects a culture where peculiar emphasis is put upon the uniqueness of individuals, physiognomic attention spills over and applies itself to those very features which lie outside the accredited system.

During this century, however, there have been several backlashes against the sort of dramatic tradition which confers such loving emphasis upon idiosyncratic personal expression. Playwrights like Brecht, for example, have explicitly repudiated the sort of emotional sympathy which such naturalistic portrayal almost inevitably elicits from a Western audience, and by reverting to a codified and largely demonstrative type of non-verbal expression have forced their actors to *quote* the characters they represent instead of actually *inhabiting* them. It is therefore not an accident that when Brecht wrote theoretical commentaries upon his method he reverted frequently to the artistic credentials of the Chinese theatre.

> The Chinese artists' performance often strikes the Western actor as cold. That does not mean that the Chinese theatre rejects all representation of feelings. The performer portrays incidents of the utmost passion, but without his delivery becoming heated. At those points where the character portrayed is deeply excited the performer takes a lock of hair between his lips and chews it. But this is like a ritual, there is nothing eruptive about it. It is quite clearly someone else's repetition of the incident: a representation, even though an artistic one. The performer shows that this man is not in control of himself, and he points to the outward signs... Among all the possible signs certain particular ones are picked out with careful and deliberate consideration.[327]

It is self-evident, I think, that an audience which was otherwise accustomed to inferring the character's state of mind from the continuous flux of facial and vocal expression, would be made very uneasy by being made to focus its attention upon a discontinuous succession of discretely coded gestures.

In fact, until the audience has successfully and unselfconsciously incorporated the paradigm which confers distinctive meaning upon the various gestures and inflections that are raised to the status of signs under its aegis, they will witness the new performance with reference to the old semantic paradigms and will therefore almost inevitably condemn what they see and hear as nothing more than a stilted version of the familiar idiom.

The same problem arises in the visual arts, of course, when a new paradigm of representation is introduced. Accustomed to the psychological regime that gives significance to the so-called naturalistic representation of faces and objects, the naive spectator, confronting Cubism for the first time, will dismiss what he sees as a clumsy travesty of the pictorial reality he is used to. What he has failed to understand, though, is that the self-evident immediacy of the idiom which he favours is itself organized in obedience to a representational grammar which has to be learnt in the first place. The difficulty being that once a grammatical paradigm has been incorporated, it works without its user being directly aware of the fact that he is referring to it, so that he is deluded into thinking that he is experiencing a direct and unmediated meaning.

A further example taken from linguistics may help to make this point even clearer. A native English listener understands everything that is said to him in this tongue, and although it is possible to write out the rules that define the meaningful use of English, it is part of the definition of knowing English that any utterance phrased in it can be understood without explicit reference to this set of rules.

In other words, although it is true to say that a native listener does not know two things – English grammar and English language – his single competence in English depends on the fact that he has, at some time or other, incorporated a set of rules which defines the way in which meaning is assigned to the linguistic moves initiated under its legislation. We are all familiar with the semantic inaudibility of an unfamiliar language and no one expects to overcome this without consulting the rules of the new grammar. Furthermore, no one except the most rabid linguistic chauvinist conceives this new system as an incompetent foreign bosh-shot at English. In the same way, unfamiliar modes of dramatic non-verbal expression are organized with reference to a grammar that has to be learned before it can be forgotten.

It remains to consider some other influences upon the use of non-verbal signs in the theatre. I would like to speculate about the influence of fiction on the one hand and that of cinema and TV on the other.

Take fiction first. Although it would be difficult to verify, it seems probable that the rise of the art of fiction caused a subtle change in the emphasis that was given to naturalistic facial expression on the stage. For whilst, as we have already noted, the text of a play is limited to bare dialogue, coupled perhaps with enough stage directions to show how the action goes forward, the novelist is free to suspend both action and dialogue and tell the reader not just about the mood of the characters but about the way in which these moods were betrayed or concealed in terms of gesture, expression and intonation. An expression, for example, which might have been misinterpreted when described from outside only, could be properly placed by saying what the character actually meant by it. Here for instance is Tolstoy explaining just such a situation in *Anna Karenina* (1873–77).

> The Englishman puckered his lips, intending to indicate a smile that anyone should wish to check on his skill at saddling.[328]

This short sentence contains an enormous amount of complicated psychological information. For in addition to telling us that Vronsky's groom was proud of his skill and that he tended to show his amusement when someone called it into question, Tolstoy has also indicated that a servant is not altogether free to show his amusement blatantly, but must confine his expression to a form that is sufficiently equivocal for an aristocratic employer not to take immediate offence at it. A less careful writer might simply have said 'The Englishman smiled contemptuously that anyone should cast doubts upon his skill at saddling,' which would leave the reader, knowing Vronsky's temperament, to wonder why he had not reprimanded the man for dumb insolence – an offence which would, in the eyes of a cavalry officer, stand high amongst the punishable sins. The idiom of the novel allows the writer to convey all these nuances of dissimulation and to show the complex relationship that exists between a state of mind and the expressions which might or might not bear witness to it. It is my contention that a readership which had been conditioned to such descriptive subtlety would approach theatrical performance with an eye and an ear curiously sensitized to the tell-tale variations of non-verbal expression. They would become intolerant of gross formality and by a process of natural selection would encourage the growth of physiognomic naturalism in the theatre. As I say, it would be hard to verify the assertion, and it could always be said that naturalism arose simultaneously in the novel and drama from a common origin in social and political individualism. Nevertheless, art forms do influence one another and it is, I think, a plausible hypothesis to suggest that this influence played a part in the development of twentieth-century dramatic style.

Finally, I would like to consider the effects of certain artificial media – principally film and TV. And in spite of Marshall McLuhan's assertions to the contrary, most of the claims that might be made for film hold for TV too since both are variations of moving photography.[329]

Perhaps the most dramatic effect of film arises from the fact that the audience is no longer obliged to view the action from a fixed distance, but can, through the medium of the close-up, pay special attention to the subtle and above all continuous flux of facial expression. And although the size constancy phenomenon ensures that the spectator is not actually conscious of the vast bulk of a 20-foot face on the screen, he cannot fail to take advantage of the enormous magnification of expressive detail which is thus offered. The psychological consequences of this now almost hackneyed innovation must have been enormous, for it introduces the audience to an almost entirely new vision of the relationship that exists between mental states and the expressions by which they are registered. In the days before the movie, the large fixed distance between the performer and the auditorium made it very unlikely that a spectator would see, let alone pay much attention to, the movements of the face that intervened between relatively large-scale gestures. In fact, for someone sitting in the gallery, there is nothing much between a broad smile and a deep scowl, with the result that non-verbal expressions almost inevitably assume a discontinuous, quasi-atomic form. Recognizing which, the actor would quite naturally put particular emphasis on those expressions which he knew could be seen, and let all others go by the board.

Under such a regime of limited visibility, actors and audience unconsciously cooperate to maintain the 'atomic' idiom of emotional representation. The introduction of the close-up, however, swings a high-power microscopic objective on to the scene, and, by magnifying the muscular activity that intervenes between the traditionally significant postures of the face, succeeds in disestablishing their mutually exclusive physiognomic integrity. Once the audience had been exposed to this transformation they would return to the theatre with eyes skinned for small-scale variations of expression, and although they would still have difficulty in seeing them all, there is no doubt that – having had their attention retrained – they would still succeed in detecting much more than they had before. Conversely, the actors would soon become aware of the fact that the vision of the audience had become more sophisticated, and they would soon feel obliged to satisfy this sophistication by modulating their performance in the direction of greater naturalistic subtlety.

If the close-up on its own could produce these effects, it is easy to imagine the added power that such an innovation would acquire by being integrated with the techniques of montage and editing. Eisenstein, for example, showed very neatly how a relatively equivocal facial expression shown in close-up could acquire strong emotional significance if it was juxtaposed in sequence with a strongly evocative frame. A fixed gaze surmounted by a frown might be taken to show horror, love or mere concentration, respectively, all according to whether it was followed by a corpse, a baby or a milking machine. The point is that by putting the face to work in a dialectical context like this, Eisenstein and the directors who followed him raised the audience's interest in the subtleties of facial expression. And within the acting profession the artificial large-scale gesture lost its respectability, and performers began to judge their colleagues by the extent to which they could minimize their expressions and still convey an emotional meaning.

The film, I think, has also brought about a radical change in the way in which the voice is used. By hanging the microphone just above the frame-line, it is possible for the actor to drop his volume and to signal minute changes of mood with relatively minor alterations of inflection. Just as in real life, in fact. And while it is not possible to reproduce such quiet modulations in the theatre, stage actors have now become very adept at giving a scaled-up version of such acoustic naturalism; with the result that dramatists are encouraged to write their dialogue to fit, and to produce plays which could not have been spoken by traditional performers. In his book on Shakespeare, the critic John Wain has pointed out that the prosodic technique of blank verse was partly introduced to overcome the acoustic difficulties of the Elizabethan theatre, and that the resounding periods of Shakespearean diction were a primitive form of public address system designed to compel attention in an open-air auditorium.[330] It is interesting to note, however, that the declamatory style outlasted the acoustic obstacles it was designed to overcome, and that artificial, demonstrative verse-speaking continued to dominate the production of Shakespeare's plays until the later years of this century. And although experiments in naturalistic diction were being made in the 1920s, it is only in the last 20 years that it is widely possible to hear Shakespeare's speeches uttered in something like the tones of voice that we are accustomed to in everyday life. The remarkable thing is that Shakespeare's text is so semantically elastic that it can be naturalistically inflected without apparently seeming to undergo poetic deterioration.

This does not mean however that the effort to detumesce classical diction has not met serious critical opposition. Older members of the theatrical audience still object to the vernacularization of their Shakespeare and expect the dignity of the Bard to be upheld in terms of grand gesture and orotund vocal delivery. According to them, anything else cheapens the great poet's imagination; and because they have not yet familiarized themselves with the new code, they find it impossible to discern the moral seriousness which the new techniques try to embody. And of course by the time they *have* accustomed themselves to the new idioms of non-verbal expression, the stage will have moved on again, possibly, as I have already indicated, in the direction of *heightened* artificiality. Directors like Peter Brook are already experimenting with the hieratic techniques of Persian theatre, and we can, I think, expect to see in the next ten years some extremely complicated negotiations with the various resources of non-verbal sign behaviour. Awkwardly enough, however, such dramatic experiments now tend to succeed one another with such speed that an innovation does not have time to catch on before it is overthrown by a new one. With the immediate result that no single innovation has time to establish itself within a community of understanding. Now this may or may not be a bad thing. On the one hand, there is the obvious danger that the mass audience will become altogether alienated from a theatre which gives it no time to catch on, with the obvious consequence that the drama will die for lack of support; but, on the other hand, it is possible that the dramatic – like the visual arts – will gain attention not by virtue of the reality which is depicted by it, but as a structure of formal relationships which is of interest as a thing in itself. In the same way as a painting by Mondrian achieves acceptance through the contemplation of its own internal relationships, dramatic performances in the future could be sponsored by audiences who may be satisfied by the formal patterning of facial and manual gestures. In other words, the progressive 'dehumanization of art' as predicted many years ago by the Spanish critic Ortega y Gasset.[331]

As it happens, though, I believe that this tendency towards purely aesthetic dramatic structuralism will be comparatively short-lived, and while it may survive as a thin parallel stream – notably in ballet – it is extremely unlikely that the theatre will ever succeed in exorcizing from its developing practices the attempt to depict meaningful states of mind. Which means, moreover, that propositional dialogue will continue to assume its peculiar precedence in all-out dramatic performances and that non-verbal behaviour will remain, as it has always been, a subtle and all-pervading context, through the medium of which human beings will attempt to make clear to one another what it is they *mean*.

Onwards and upwards?

Vogue, 15 October 1966[332]

There's a great risk in writing too freely about the future. The imagination overreaches itself and you can easily end up with stuff which reads like hardcore pornography. Both pornography and prophecy take place in a dateless nowhere, full of extravagant and rather dubious fulfilment. Development is limited to a spiral of ever-increasing enormity. In literature, the future, like sex, has to be measured out in small doses. Otherwise fear and hope go haywire and the whole thing degenerates into a boring fantasy of wristwatch telly, moon buses, thought police and the wilder excesses of McLuhanacy.

Anyway, the future is here already. We're just too hell-bent on prophecy to recognize it, and like science-fiction writers, we're so intrigued by the pornotopian possibilities of a hypothetical future that we fail to see how much our lives have already taken on the outlines of tomorrow. That's because the real future, the future as it is actually experienced, is a mixed condition, half in and half out of the past. It's difficult for anyone living in the middle of it to make out the details of what is really new. After all, human history is quite continuous, forwards and backwards, so that the future often starts much earlier than anyone realizes. And the past can often survive the most violent change. Because, for all their adventurous ingenuity, human beings are nostalgic, lazy creatures who hang on to outdated habits through cataclysms of technical progress. But, on the other hand, they're very adaptable too, carelessly assuming novelty without a second thought. This paradoxical combination of inert conservatism and fickle adaptability sometimes makes it very hard for us to know where we are on the line of human progress.

It's never been harder than now of course. In the last 20 years, since the war, and largely as a result of a technical skill which grew out of it, knowledge and power have developed faster and more comprehensively than in the rest of the history of our race. And it's not just a matter of *quantity*. There is something peculiar about the *quality* of modern knowledge. It grows in a totally different way to anything we've known before. Each increment, instead of simply adding to the bulk of what is known, sets off an explosion of fresh discovery which then detonates something even bigger. The growth transcends itself from moment to moment like some enormous Domesday device working out of control.

It's all happening so fast that it's hardly possible to store all the information. It's certainly not possible for any individual to keep tabs on anything but a small fraction of even a single subject. And quite apart from the bulk of it all, there's the complexity too. Modern knowledge has become so abstruse that a vicious process of intellectual natural selection is beginning to work. It's not just manual workers who feel the wind of change too. Progress in many fields, from economics to pure physics, is so fast that only the most excellent minds can keep up. There was a time, not so long ago, when an ordinary university degree automatically qualified one for membership in the social elite. Degrees of this sort are little better than platform tickets now, and of the intellectuals who travel, few arrive.

I can vouch for this from personal experience. I went into medicine 15 years ago in the hope of becoming a neurologist. It now turns out that I have misread the time. Neurology, like all the other hard biological sciences, was just on the point of taking off into the future. I had joined up as a result of reading the copy from the old recruiting campaign – dignified ward round, philosophical speculation, observation and so on. Most medical students of my generation went into the profession because it was the only science where good maths was not needed. Then all of a sudden they changed all that. Neurology was taken over by the physicists and became a subsidiary company in the gigantic cartel of maths and cybernetics. People like myself, who would have been bowled over by anything worse than a quadratic equation, found themselves consigned to a timber outhouse of the new glass-and-steel establishment where the computer and micro-electrode held sway. At the time I was qualified I could see that I would be pensioned out of service if I stayed longer than ten years. It seemed more and more unlikely that I would ever make a significant contribution to a subject whose growing points were already way beyond my reach. I could read the digests in *Scientific American*, but I was usually too dull to understand the original papers from which these popular summaries had been made. I was certainly too dim to stand a chance of making any contribution myself. So, rather than hang around as a juvenile pensioner on this renovated estate, I decided to get out while the going was good. There must be thousands of people in the same position, and there'll be many more before the century is much older. We are a new social species. A large intellectual middle class threatened by progressive disinheritance. What's to become of us?

But the knowledge explosion has created another sort of social refugee. These are the people who have no share whatsoever in the new knowledge – the main bulk of the population, working class and white-collar folk, who ride on the swell of the future without having the foggiest idea of what it means. This is not just a matter of nuclear physics or solid state theory. It's something much nearer home. Their personal, political and economic destiny is determined more and more by the manipulation of knowledge to which they have no access. To some extent this has always been the case. It's unlikely that many people below the upper-middle-class of Victorian England really grasped the issues of the Corn Law debates. But the complexity of modern economic and social wisdom makes it quite impossible for anyone except the professionals to understand the subtleties of the forces which determine their individual fates. So that both in England and in America the common people are suffering from a tremendous sense of intellectual exclusion. They feel more and more isolated from the information which, it is said, affects their future. And in both countries this has produced a rising tide of reactionary irrationalism. This may come out, as it does in America, in the form of anti-communism, John Birch movements and voting for Goldwater.[333] But most of the people who hold these views are really not interested in communism one way or the other. And, in fact, in the course of the witch hunts, it was

357

East Coast intellectuals as much as old guard Stalinists who got it in the neck. Communism simply spelled modernism; a name with which to label the vague fear of everything which threatened to overthrow the old values of common sense, hard work and traditional virtue. In England, where there is as yet no formally constituted party around which to crystallize such anxieties, the sense of intellectual impotence comes out that rather more patchily; say, in campaigns to clean up television. In fact, the Mary Whitehouse mission illustrates this rather well. On the face of it, Mrs Whitehouse and her horde of Bacchae are out to get dirt off the air. They think that television has become filthy and dangerous. But in fact they are really voicing a popular outcry against centralized sophistication. For if television is dirtier, that's to say franker than it was before, it's not because the controllers have lost their sense of decency, but simply because everyone concerned with modern communications has developed complicated attitudes about *everything*, sex included. More and more people coming into television are drawn from the universities, or at least from places where the new knowledge is available. They're not satisfied with pedalling the old simplicities anymore, so that their programmes reflect all the complexities of modern doubt. People like Mary Whitehouse, meeting this new output head-on, completely ignorant of the sources of what they see and hear, simply put the whole thing down to moral degeneration.

And exactly the same thing goes for the modern controversy over crime and punishment. Here also is an area where special knowledge has grown out of all recognition since Beccaria first proposed a rational procedure for dealing with crime at the end of the eighteenth century. But it's a subject upon which ordinary people, without special knowledge, also hold very strong views. And since these views arise from feeling rather than informed thought, the gap between popular and professional opinion grows wider and more painful by the moment. In becoming scientific, criminology has become very deterministic, talking of causes rather than faults, all of which tends to blur the traditional firmness of morals. Since the idea of fault is a much simpler way of understanding crime than that of cause, it's much easier to blame than it is to explain. Faults, after all, belong to the wrongdoer. They live in him and can be eradicated, or so the belief goes, by punishing the owner. Causes, on the other hand, are much vaguer. Instead of owning the causes of his crime, the criminal is possessed *by* them. They are outside his personal control since they are said to be lodged in his childhood, or, even more remotely, in the cruel eccentricities of the society which surrounds him. It's quite obvious that this sort of deterministic view makes it very much harder to come to any quick, practical conclusion about individual responsibility, and therefore culpability. It means, once again, that the professionals seem to have usurped the ordinary man's right to judge for himself the rights or wrongs of the criminal case.

As it turns out, the uncertainty which arises from such a view of human nature comes at an unfortunate moment in the history of crime. Just when crime seems to have taken a dramatic upswing, the public is maddened to find that those responsible for dealing with it seem to have been seduced away from strong common-sense action in favour of obscure 'pseudointellectual' regimes which seem downright soft. And besides, all this talk of antecedent causes, rather than plain, straightforward blame, appears to threaten the idea of personal free-will on every *other* front, not just crime. For if blame is dissolved by determinism, praise must suffer by the same token. Virtue vanishes with the violation of vice. And to a public unfamiliar with the new knowledge it must seem that their lives are being taken over, lock, stock and barrel, by stuck-up boffins who claim to be in the know. The feeling is quite understandable and in some senses even legitimate. But it is intolerable when journalists find it expedient to whip up the feeling even further by all sorts of calculated campaigns. People, that is, who actually do know better but feign a plain man's ignorance just in order to curry favour with the resentful mass audience. One has become very familiar with the peculiar lingo of this *trahison des clercs* since the gap between common sense and special knowledge makes a happy hunting-ground for thwarted intellectuals on the make – what one might call the Moseleys of modern communication. For unlike the betas and gammas of Aldous Huxley's *Brave New World* (1932), the intellectually underprivileged of the future are *not* going to be satisfied with their status. When they find that modern knowledge is becoming absurdly inaccessible, they will fall back, not into a complacent recitation of their own virtues but into a fierce and irrational hatred of the new wisdom. This protest will take many forms, most of which already exist in seedling form today. Some of these will take the form of violent bouts of intellectual machine-breaking, or sociological Luddism. Others will be less violent and more escapist – journeys into inner space on rafts of LSD. In fact, in California, where the new knowledge has already developed beyond the reaches of science fiction, psychedelic flight is rife, as are the wilder excesses of Birchism.

Surprisingly enough, it's very rarely the science-fiction writers who accurately anticipate these social consequences of the future. It is generally left to the literary artists – people with a keen social eye for what's going on at the moment – to make successful predictions about the way our community is going to turn out. For example, Samuel Butler anticipated modern criminology nearly a hundred years ago. In his Utopian novel *Erewhon* (1872) he had criminals treated as if they were sick, and patients punished as if they had committed a crime. Similarly, the wilder forms of political irrationalism were anticipated in the novels of *fin de siècle* American populists like Hamlin Garland and Ignatius Donnelly. So, also, it was Wells who had some of the shrewdest guesses about the madness of the future. In *The Time Machine* (1895) his hero discovered a tribe of blond, lotus-eating teenagers who floated vapidly around the world, bent only on pleasure, completely indifferent to the pain or misfortune of their fellows. Bernard Shaw also saw the footling hedonism in store for modern youth, though he saw by contrast with the dignified senility of his ancients in *Back to Methuselah* (1922).

The whole question of age, of course, may well be the crux of the future. We have always dickered with the idea of immortality, but until modern science made the astonishing advances that it has in the last 20 years, it remained a utopian fantasy. Even now, there seems no immediate possibility of our living for ever, though there has been a remarkable change in the length of human life; not in the overall length, but in the way that more and more people are given a chance of at least completing the Biblican span. Medical progress in the last 50 years has simply cleared the obstacles off the human racetrack. The lethal hedges of infancy, youth and maternity have been chopped down to size so that nearly everyone has the same chance of reaching the winning post, but the course itself remains the same length. But if medicine really can dissolve the deadline of old age, there will be a dramatic change in the whole quality of human life. Up till now, the Biblical span has been the metrical unit by which we measure the course of history. It's a fixed value and gives some sort of scale to our sense of time, just as the fixed values of height and breadth yield the cubits, inches and feet with which we measure space.

For the first time in the history of biology it begins to look as if the fixed limits of this span may be on the edge of yielding. Organ replacements grafts and tissue transplants begin to look like practical possibilities. And at a much subtler level, our sudden increase in the understanding of biochemical codes suggest that, within the conceivable future, we may have control over the actual cellular process of ageing and degeneration. Once this becomes a reality it's hard to calculate the effects it will have upon a species whose spiritual values have been firmly based upon the conviction that its days are but grass. What would we think of ourselves if the dawn redwood becomes the measure of our mortality? How much human folly would evaporate in the bright light of eternity? Right now the indecent haste of our short span makes us all into clowns. Hope and ambition are ridiculously distorted by the deadline we all work to at the moment. Given a century or more of vigorous life we could presumably plan our individual futures with much more leisure. Failure would cease to be the tragedy it has always been, since the whole idea of single careers would give way to successive seasons of endeavour in which the failure of one would be offset by the success of another. Or, as one of Hemingway's heroes once said: 'Wouldn't it be pretty to think so?'[334]

Q&A
Various dates and venues

MICHAEL PARKINSON (1980)[335]: You have an extraordinary range of interests and you move between theatre and opera and films and television; you range from documentaries about the human body, to this new venture of yours – the [BBC] Shakespeare thing.[336] It seems to me not to have a unifying theme, but is there one, to yourself?

MILLER: Yes, and there always has been, in that I've always been interested just simply in the way in which – it sounds very pompous, this, but I really mean it very strongly – I'm interested in the way in which this peculiar part of nature has come together with the nervous system and is capable of understanding the rest of nature, and of acting inside nature, and the thing that's always interested me is the way in which the nervous system actually *performs*, and how we get around, how we understand and how we act – acting in real life or acting on the stage – and all of these things intrigue me, and I'm just simply interested in performance of every sort, whether it's performance in real life or performance on the stage, and the representation of behaviour and the details of human natural history.

ROBERT BOOTH (1988)[337]: How do you feel about first nights? What happens to you? The cast is on the stage, who are suffering first night nerves and so on, but you're responsible for the production, aren't you?

MILLER: I get nervous on the first night, partly because my tension doesn't have the opportunity of being discharged in action, which of course is what happens to the performer. The performer may be juddering with fear before they go on and it may even last for the first half of the first scene, but once they're performing, their nerves usually go because they are somehow relieved by the action of simply doing it. All I can do is pace around at the back. I've never actually attended one of my own first nights.

BOOTH: Why not?

MILLER: Partly out of terror and partly out of boredom. The funny thing is that, by the time you've rehearsed the play over and over again, the frustration, the tension and the boredom of having seen it so many times without having had the advantages of performing it, make it really almost impossible for me to attend the performance. I'll hang around at the back. I'll even go to the cinema, or out to dinner. But what I won't do is sit in the auditorium, hypersensitive to the slightest rustle, the slightest restlessness, and feel 'Oh God, they're not liking it.'

BOOTH: Will you come back for the last five minutes?

MILLER: I will sometimes come back for the last five minutes, but I don't really even like that, because I don't like to hear the amount of applause. It never seems to me to be quite enough.

RICHARD BLACK (2001)[338]: Does it bother you as an opera director that 'bums on seats' – getting the public in – is as important as doing what you want to do with a work?

MILLER: That's always been a problem when you make things. You have to get people to pay for it. You have to get people to pay you and you have to get people to pay for the paint or whatever you're doing. That's *always* been a difficulty. In fact, in some respects it's easier now than it was, say, 150 years ago, when the state felt no responsibility to pay for these things. There might have been the benevolence of a German prince or graf or duke, who would, as it were, pay for it as an ornament of his court – or when the Medicis paid for it as an ornament of their life and their world.

BLACK: But surely you like the idea that your work is universally appealing? I remember that production of *Rigoletto*.[339] "La donna è mobile", the famous aria, began with someone putting a dime into a slot machine.

MILLER: I was pleased that the audience liked it.

BLACK: But it was *popular* and it seemed self-consciously popular, in a wonderful way.

MILLER: It's just that that seemed to me to be a nice way of doing it. I didn't do it because I felt it would be popular. I was doing it because I was a creature of my times who had been soaked in movies and gangster films of that sort, so it was inevitable that I would do it since I was not hidebound by the normal restraints and resistances that a traditional producer might have. He or she might have felt themselves briefly, 'wouldn't that be nice to do…but one couldn't *possibly* do that.' Whereas, because I came from outside the operatic world, I was much less restrained and held in by those sorts of compunctions. I felt I could do what I damn well liked!

PARKINSON (2007)[340]: Did you ever have a chance to go to Hollywood, Jonathan?

MILLER: No. No, I… I was once asked by Peter Sellers to go and meet him while he was making a film, in order to talk about something, and I went on to the set while he was doing the thing and it was about three days after I'd arrived, and there he was, and he suddenly saw me through the lights. *(Waves.)* 'Oh, hi! What are you doing here?' He'd completely forgotten that he'd asked me to come. He was completely potty.

PARKINSON: He was mad, yes.

MILLER: I directed him once when I did the film of *Alice in Wonderland*. He played the King of Hearts, and he was absolutely mad then. It was very hard to get him on to the set because on one occasion, for example, he'd arrived, and a black cat had gone across the road in front of his Rolls Royce, and therefore he'd consulted his astrologer, who said that he ought to spend at least three hours readjusting himself to the possible tragic outcomes of this encounter between the Rolls and the cat. It was very hard to get him back on to the set to film with him.

He was barmy but brilliantly talented. He improvised wonderful stuff in *Alice in Wonderland*. We had one wonderful moment when we were doing the trial scene and Wilfrid Brambell was playing the White Rabbit – we got rid of all the animal masks, you see – and Wilfrid Brambell said, '*Oh*, this letter's just been picked up.' (Played it very gay, you see.) And Sellers said, 'Who's it from?' 'It's not addressed to anyone.' That was in Lewis Carroll. And Sellers then said, 'Well it must be addressed to *somebody*.' He said, 'I mean, you can't just write to nobody. If everyone did that all the time, well, I mean, the Post Office would come to a standstill.' That was absolutely off the top of his head. Wonderful.

DICK CAVETT (1980)[341]: You have as far as I know never directed movies, and that's supposed to be the hot medium that everyone finally wants to get into: cinema and celluloid.

MILLER: Well, I've got into celluloid several times but only as it were for the BBC. I've never 'worked for the majors,' mainly because one has to encounter these awful sort of weight-reducing figures in the front office who always say *(leans forward, fixed stare)* 'We're very excited by your project,' and this huge sort of Easter Island face confronts you with its excitement. I remember once having to go to see some extraordinary figure once in London, because I was trying to make a film of *Alice in Wonderland*, and I was ambitious to make it on the big screen so I thought that I would have to go and try to get the money from a big American company. My agent said 'they'd like you to take a meeting with…' – agents always want you to 'take meetings with' people, rather than have meetings… 'I'd like you to meet with Mill Frankenstein who's just taken over Europe for United Artists.' This sort of Attila-like figure 'taking it over'! I had to wait in the outer office for a long time and there was this secretary filing her nails, sitting at a strip-pine flower bin converted into a desk. 'Mr Frankenstein will see you now.' And I went in to see Mill Frankenstein, who had that terrible thing that those big, big American producers have: they don't just shake your hand, they *incubate* it. Have you noticed they do his? *(Miller wraps Cavett's hand with both of his.)* In the hope that your hand will hatch in some way. And he gives you a level, sincere stare and a slight head-rock as if it's on gimbals: 'We're very excited by this whole project over at UA.' And then they said, 'We're very concerned to get into the whole zany area. We see Jane Fonda as Alice.' And then I realized that I had to go to the BBC and try and reconstruct some version of what I had in mind when I thought of the thing.

CAVETT: You did a movie once, I'm told, called *Take a Girl Like You.*

MILLER: Oh, I knew it would come up! *(Writhes in pain.)* Well, yes, I did have one brush with the majors. I did a film of a Kingsley Amis novel and it was an absolute disaster, I'm afraid. It was very heavily pressed on by the front office and there was a producer who wanted certain things… I mean, the terrible scenes I had to do… I had to do a kissing scene, shall we say, in which Hayley Mills and Oliver Reed had to get into some sort of carnal contact with one another. And I directed it, I thought, rather delicately. It wasn't a chaste scene, by any means, but nevertheless there was a certain amount of hand-lightly-on-breast at one point. My producer said *(coarse, booming American)* 'No! Get in *close* on that hand!' And I said, 'No, there's no need to do that at all. I think the audience can see even on a wide-angle lens that what he's doing is what he's doing.' 'No, you're not making television! Get it right in there and show it.' And I said, 'I am not going to do a close-up of that hand on that breast.' 'I'll take them away and do it myself!' (In a side room, a hand-on-breast room…) Fortunately, my actors were very loyal to me and Hayley Mills was not going to lend her breast to this cutaway, and Oliver Reed wasn't going to lend his hand to it either. So I thought for a moment that I'd got away with it until I was seeing the rushes the next day. Suddenly, in the middle of the rushes which I'd shot of this wide-angle scene, quite suddenly, there was an enormous hand clawing a breast. And indeed it was Oliver Reed's hand, and, from what I could tell, Hayley Mills. But I noticed that... 'I didn't shoot that, and I know they hadn't shot it...' Then I suddenly realized from the grain of the thing that, actually, what the producer had done was he'd taken a frame from my wide-angle shot and blown up the section where the hand was on the breast. So it looked like captured Nazi atrocity film, you know. And I believe it's still in the film; the whole film suddenly changes its optical quality, and there's this extraordinary hand with grain dancing across it. I realized then that there was really no point in being in the movie industry.

DR KEVIN PATRICK (1987)[342]: Norman Cousins has stated that medical students typically arrive at medical school in a state of what he calls educational disequilibrium. They have emphasized, much to their detriment, science over the humanities. They have had little training in human behaviours. Would you care to comment on this, and if you could design a medical educational process, how would you do that in ways that would perhaps deal with this problem?

MILLER: It's very easy to start designing medical programmes from a distance when you haven't really got to make it stick, so that most of the ideas that I might have are sort of utopian transfers, really. I do think there are problems about people coming into medicine the way that they do, perhaps because they're trained in science first. I'm not certain that a training in the humanities actually makes them into better doctors. I think that reading *Middlemarch* doesn't actually make you into a better person, and science may not actually pre-empt the possibility of being a sympathetic person either. I actually think the problem is that you get people too young. Not that they're ignorant by being scientists, but probably people start too young. I know that they start later in the United States and that they have to be graduates before they can become MDs. Even so, I think probably it's too early. I wouldn't let anyone really lay hands on patients until they were 30. I just think that the most important experience you have to have is just simply living life. I don't think a course in the humanities necessarily helps you. I think there's a prevailing belief, perhaps stronger in the United States than it is in England, that you could actually legislate for improvements in personality. You could just set up ideal conditions to make people warm, relating, nice people who would be naturally good at the bedside.

I remember once seeing an example of this when I was doing *Così Fan Tutte* in St Louis. I went to Barnes Hospital on a grand round on the maximum patients' surgical floor, where people were suffering and undergoing really the most appalling and mutilative operations for carcinomas of the upper respiratory tract. There were also problems with the young interns and the young residents having to confront these things. There were plans to have psychiatric sessions for the benefit of the residents and the interns. I really found myself objecting very much to the scheme. It seemed to me to be typical of what I think is happening today, that you can actually set up programmes to fix things, to get people to be less disturbed by, or more responsive to, say, mutilating operations. I don't think it's a matter of psychiatry. It's actually a matter of encouraging the imagination in some ways, and that's not necessarily done best by expert systems. I would dread having a psychiatrist tell me how to adjust myself to the idea that half of someone's face was going to be taken away. I think that the way you do this is by using plain English very clearly and saying, 'What you're going to see is someone with half of their face not there. Try and imagine what it's like having a skin graft which results in your nipple growing out of your tongue.' This is what I saw in the ward there. But instead there are these elaborate expert-system circumlocutions to remove, which are supposed to actually train these kids into sensitive human beings. Actually, I don't think there is any way of legislating for it. I don't think programmes in humanities do it either. You can read *Middlemarch* until you are blue in the face, but I don't think you'll do better at the bedside. I think actually what does make people better at the bedside is just simply living out some other form of existence before you are allowed the privilege of laying hands on someone else's body. I think people come to it too early. I just think that a whippersnapper of 22 who is allowed to ask someone whether their sex life is very good…it's an impudence. I think that these are intimate questions. I think people ought to be qualified to ask people the questions. It's a great privilege to have access to someone else's body and someone else's privacy, and I don't like the idea of a young punk being allowed to do that simply because he's wearing a white coat. We robe people in white coats and stethoscopes and give them reins of office. This licenses them to intrude in ways in which we normally would hit them in the face for asking such questions if they weren't wearing white coats. I really think that we ought to start later.

ELEANOR WACHTEL (2000)[343]: I get the sense that you're mocked for being brainy and then you're disdained by the pure scientists.

MILLER: I do feel caught between two fires. In theatre or in journalism – where you are criticized by people who, in fact, are not your peers – you are either envied or despised for being what they call 'brainy.' So I can read without moving my lips and make references to things that are outside my field of expertise, and I'm called a polymath – which is really another way of saying jack of all trades and master of none. But I'm usually accused of that by people who are barely jacks of one trade.

WACHTEL: You said that to lay claim to being an intellectual is stating an occupation, but in England there's an uneasiness with intellectuals and it's regarded as a boast. Why do you think that is?

MILLER: I don't know why there's such suspicion of organized and often difficult thought. One can become quite fascinated by things which actually defeat all analysis, like being able to speak fluently and grammatically. What goes into speech is much more complicated than it seems to us as performers. That's one of the things that Chomsky drew our attention to. Now, you start to invoke a name like Chomsky amongst English journalists, and they say, 'Yeah, yeah, Chomsky, Chimsky… Just a blabbermouth.' The people who say that are not clever enough to understand what Chomsky did – that he actually drew attention to the fact that we can do things which seem second nature, which seem dead simple, but are actually very complicated. That what allows us to do them is something that currently defeats analysis. We may be able to invent computers that can play games of chess, but we're not very smart at inventing computers which can see that this sentence might mean at least five things. If it's as difficult as it turns out to be, then it's worth being difficult about it. But that's thought to be pretentious and stuck-up in England; a way of just strutting around. A bit of strutting around is quite useful, really. A lot of interesting things have happened by strutting around.

WACHTEL: Is there a place for public intellectuals?

MILLER: In England, yes, but they have to have a certain sort of form. On the whole, people who cross boundaries and see connections between more than two things are thought to be pretentious. It's regrettable and it's rather sad. It's quite hard to live in a country where most journalists think it's acceptable to use the word *pseud*, from that ghastly magazine *Private Eye*. What do they mean if they call something *pseud*? What do they mean by pseudointellectual? Presumably they have some standard of what being intellectual is, by which you can judge whether something is pseudointellectual. Well, most of the people who invoke the notion of the pseud have a very marginal acquaintance with what it's like to be an intellectual at all, or they think it's just as simple as being able to read Anthony Trollope.

WACHTEL: Is it any better in North America? Here we would probably think it's better in England.

MILLER: In North America there's a much more generous accommodation to the idea of cross-disciplinary interests, to moving from one field to another and seeing that they are closely related to one another – that thoughtfulness, in fact, is valuable and interesting and productive. This is not necessarily because it's materially productive – producing laptops, for example – but because what goes into making laptops helps us to think about what it's like to have a mind. On the whole, North Americans are much more hospitable to these sorts of cross-references, and they don't think it's pretentious. They delight in it and they like to see people making smart moves. I like that. I think that it's one of the reasons why America has been as explosively successful, intellectually and technically, as it has been. If you're bending over backwards to appear reticent, modest and a decent English gent, the result of it is that you don't actually do anything.

PARKINSON (1977)[344]: When did you get your first opportunity to be a director?

MILLER: It was by accident. George Devine, who was directing the Royal Court at that time, was looking for someone to direct one half of a double bill of John Osborne plays, and I believe that they had hawked it around and hadn't been able to find a director.[345] So, finally, scraping the bottom of the barrel, they said: 'Why don't we try one of those *Fringe* fellows?' and the script was sent to me through the post.

I hadn't even directed a play before, and I had no idea of what one did; there were all sorts of anxieties about words, and so forth. 'Blocking.' People kept on using the word 'blocking' to me. I met John Dexter – who was directing the other half – after about the third week, and he said, 'Well, I've finished the blocking now. How about you?' I said, 'Ah, well. Um – ah, yes…ah, yes. Re the blocking – I'm hoping to get round to that, perhaps, just before we open…' And I began to be very anxious that, if I asked the actors about the blocking – 'Are you missing the blocking here?' – they would wonder about my competence. Then I still hadn't blocked anything, whatever it was, and so I would just have to wait for those frightful reviews saying: 'This brilliant play of Osborne's was marred by an incompetent sense of blocking.' It seemed to go all right, so, from that day on, I've never blocked a thing – not knowingly.

SUE LAWLEY (2005)[346]: Trivia is what you're concentrating on artistically, isn't it? You do collages and sculptures made up of bits of old rubbish, detritus.

MILLER: Well, I wouldn't think of it as art, really. I like pieces of faded, coloured typography, and I began putting them together again in geometrical assemblies.[347] I'm deeply influenced in some ways by something which is completely out of date now. (Everything about me, I suppose, is out of date.) I'm an early-twentieth-century modernist, in the sense that those are the people that excite me, and I think I'm still under the influence when I start making my own compositions, and I do things out of wood and I do things out of paper, and metal now.

NORMAN LEBRECHT (2009)[348] You direct, you write, you sculpt, you paint. It sounds almost too much for one life, but you don't believe in that any more?

MILLER: No – I do them all one after another. In a way I'm a sort of grasshopper. A much better title than polymath. It's just that I get taken up by something which intrigues me, or accept an invitation to do something. And I simply say, 'Well, why not?' I think perhaps if I'd concentrated more on one or two things I might have done them better, though I'm quite proud of some of the things I've done in the theatre, in the opera. I do think they're actually rather good; though, or if not *because* I say it myself!

BISHOP RICHARD HOLLOWAY (1987)[349]: One of the ways that we handle [death] is to act out our grief in appropriate ceremonies: funeral services and memorials. Do you have any ideas about how you want to be memorialized in that way?

MILLER: I'm very glad you've raised that question because I do think that funerals for the godless are dreadful affairs. I do deplore these increasingly frequent visits which I make to crematoria around London to see my godless friends off the map. We are at a loss for words and ceremonies and ways of somehow dignifying it. We collect scraps and anthologies of poems that he or she might have liked. Bits of music which he or she might have liked. And they sound like benefits for a theatrical charity, and we climb on buses and go away and feel that something was missing, and yet I cannot subscribe to the ceremonies which in fact are wholeheartedly undertaken by those who believe. I sit enviously at the back of funerals conducted in churches or in synagogues or in cemeteries where there is a minister and feel, how nice it would be if I could subscribe to all that. But I know that for people like myself, one must just endure one's going hence and know that it's going to be a scrappy, suburban business.

HOLLOWAY: You're not going to leave any directions then?

MILLER: Well, in one's wilder moments, like these desert island disc[350] ideas of heaven, of course one does – as a parlour game, like Trivial Pursuits, it is the most trivial of all pursuits inventing one's own secular funeral service in which one says, 'I'd like very much to hear...' but since I won't be there, 'I'd like them to hear...' the wedding canon from *Così Fan Tutte*, the quartet from the first act of *Fidelio*. But in fact, as one goes on, one realizes what one's doing in concocting this posthumous event is actually, really, putting on costume jewellery. It's a species of vanity. It's a way of saying 'My *word*, this was a sensitive fellow that is now being conducted to the grave!'

HOLLOWAY: No, people love you and they will want to affirm your life and their grief and take leave of you and that there is a way of doing that in dignity.

MILLER: In which case, then, I hope that it's up to them. But the idea of someone before death compiling their own exequies and putting together an anthology is, I think, a species of vanity. It's a way of combing one's hair and adjusting one's parting and putting on a really *nice* tie and something which shows off the colour of one's eyes. It's a way of showing how smart, how clever, how sensitive one was, and might continue to be in this afterlife which you've invited me to believe in. But it's a good parlour game. It's a good trivial pursuit. It's a good after-dinner conversation.

MARK LAWSON (2007)[351]: I wasn't sure what to call you, because since 2002 you could be Sir Jonathan. I think of you as Dr Miller. When they offer you, on those websites, the little drop-down menu, what do you take?

MILLER: Well I usually just have my name, Jonathan, and sometimes – because I'm proud of being a doctor – I quite like...because it was a qualification which I earned by exam. The other thing...one doesn't know how one earns it, or indeed if one ever did! And therefore I never use it at all.

LAWSON: Some people don't *take* them at all. I think it's known that Michael Frayn the playwright said 'no,' as others have, but you took the knighthood.

MILLER: Yes. It's very interesting the people who didn't, but nevertheless it's *known* that they refused, so that they have the advantage of the honour and also the reputation of a sort of social chastity of refusing. It seemed to me to be reasonable to accept and it was quite nice going to the Palace and having all that...dubbing going on, and seeing people being called in one by one. 'Miss Elaine Shilders for services to the hard of hearing in Cumbria: an OBE.' So it was quite a good thing to watch.

LAWSON: And at the moment of dubbing, what was said to you?

MILLER: Well there was rather a marvellous moment. Perhaps I'm going to be executed for saying this, but, as I rose unsteadily to my feet, at the age that I am, and one shakes hands with Prince Charles, he said 'I gather you're not working that much in the United Kingdom at the moment?' I said 'No.' And then he turned to one side and said, 'I wish I was in *your* shoes.'

CAVETT (1980)[352]: Were you brought up religious?

MILLER: It was a Jewish family that I was born into, and I say that as if to say I'm not Jewish, and in a sense I am trying to say that because although my family were Jewish and I am genetically Jewish, I have absolutely no subscription to the creed and no interest in the race. I don't believe in race and I find racial notions objectionable but I can't think of myself as being Jewish in that way. I'm Jewish for the purpose of admitting it to anti-Semites, and that's all. It's something that, if it matters to someone else that I am, then yes, all right, 'Do you want to do something about it?' But I'm not prepared to be Jewish in the face of other Jews.

CAVETT: Have you ever been in that position that was in Raphael's *The Glittering Prizes* in which he was at a wealthy country home...

MILLER: And people makes anti-Semitic remarks? Yes, I've heard people make anti-Semitic remarks in my presence, because I don't look like what people who are anti-Semitic tend to think Jews look like, and therefore they tend to tell me all sorts. I remember one marvellous episode once, when I went to my bank manager to ask for some sort of investment advice – a vacuous thing for me to ask for – and he said, 'Well, look. I'll tell you what I'll do. I'll get you some fellow down from the City who will give you some chat about this.' And so a strange, flushed, blue-eyed sea-captain-like figure appeared who was a big investment figure from the City, and he said, 'Have you had any advice up to now on your investments?' I said, 'No. Well, I did know someone...' and

I mentioned the name of a well-known Jewish commodity merchant, and I said, 'Well, I've had some advice from him.' 'Oh yes, well that's a very sound opinion. A very sound opinion. A bit of a hook-nose, but a very sound opinion.' Well, now. I didn't find that I was *personally* offended by that remark. I didn't feel he was getting at my race. I found it offensive as just simply a human being to hear people discriminating on those grounds. Anti-Semitic remarks don't offend me *vis-à-vis* my Jewishness, but *vis-à-vis* my humanity.

CAVETT: You didn't feel obliged to say, 'What did you say?'

MILLER: 'Now, look here! I'm Jewish. I'm as Jewish as you are…I'm sorry, I'll put it another way. I'm as Jewish as you're *not*, let's put it that way.' But I do find it very paradoxical, the idea of being Jewish in England if in fact one doesn't actually participate in Jewish life or have an interest in Israel or do all the things, in fact, which your interested Jewish friends – one's committedly Jewish friends – think one ought to do. And often I find myself in great conflict with my relatives over the fact that I don't stand up and count as a Jew. As I say, I will only stand up and count myself as a Jew for the purpose of putting down anti-Semites. But it doesn't interest me to join the Jews for the purpose of any solidarity. I don't think the solidarity is important. I don't think it *prevents* holocausts, for example. And I think that one of the things which I find objectionable about holocausts was the moment when one of the characters in the Holocaust found, when execution was going on on the other side of the wall, that he couldn't say the Mourner's Prayer. 'I've forgotten the words,' he said, and his friends looked pityingly at him, as if somehow, if only he had kept up his Jewish commitment, he would have known the prayers and could have kept his solidarity. I think that's an invidious idea, that somehow his humanity was vitiated by the fact that he hadn't kept up his subscriptions to the Jewish race. You keep up your humanity by keeping up your subscriptions to the human race, and if you don't feel an immediate allegiance to your own racial group for religious reasons, I don't think it's any reason to feel guilty that you've actually assimilated into the group where you live, which is what I have done in England. And it may well be that I shall learn at some future date that I will be dug out and identified as a Jew and burnt for it, but that's their problem not mine. And in a way anti-Semitism is the problem of anti-Semites, rather than Jews.

PARKINSON (1977)[353]: Was your stammer very bad as a child, Jonathan?

MILLER: It always got troublesome when I was on trains or on buses, having to ask for my fare; and then there were all these stammerers' circumlocutions that I had to go through.

The awful thing about stammering is that you never know which consonants are going to be the fatal ones. You think that you've got it all taped – avoid T-s and D-s today, and it'll be all right. Then, suddenly, you find that you'd be tripping up over an N. I remember once having a very bad time with initial M-s, which made the noise that tube trains make when they're waiting – a sort of Westinghouse stammer – and, very foolishly under the circumstances, travelling to Marble Arch. I could see the conductor coming down the corridor towards me and I knew that I would have to say 'M-M-M-', and, finally, as often happens with stammerers, a fantastic act of creation took place. I said 'One to the arch that is made of marble, please.'

I used to have to go to Swiss Cottage, which was all right on M days, but there were times when – 'Sw-Sw-Sw-' – you produced this sound of a bath house. So what I had to do was either to get off unnecessarily soon and walk the rest of the way, or else find that the only station I could possibly get to was somewhere like Wembley Park. So I was given extra fare money by my parents to cover this. I would simply take a long journey out to Wembley Park and then aim as near as I could for Swiss Cottage or Finchley Road. But then, by the time I got out at Wembley Park, my stammer had changed to initial F, and I would have to go out to Dollis Hill again. Now I have a Red Rover, fortunately.

KIRSTY WARK (2004)[354]: Are you terrified of boredom?

MILLER: No, I'm not terrified of it. I'm frequently a victim of it. I descend into these things which the medieval theologians refer to as acedia – long periods of staring sightlessly at nothing and wondering what on earth is worth doing, and then something would get me going again. Acedia and activity are alternating forms of my own existence. I don't dread one and relish the other. It's just that I find myself alternating between acedia and activity.

PARKINSON (1977)[355]: You went to America for the first time with *Beyond the Fringe*. How much of a culture shock was New York for you?

MILLER: The real shock was comparing the fantasy of America, always seen on films through the back window of Yellow Cabs, with the reality. I remember being amazed by the strange antiquity of New York. It wasn't the modern, bristling, pristine, clear place that I'd thought. It was actually a rather grimy, nineteenth-century city and, in a way, almost like H. G. Wells's fantasies about the shape of things to come.

Going to Los Angeles was a fantastic shock. You get this extraordinary distortion of all four dimensions, because the city seems to extend infinitely – for thousands of miles, apparently; it seems to have no limits at all. But, on the other hand, everything is only about five years old. You get this squashing of time and extending of space, so that one is sometimes overwhelmed with the antiquity of something which was built in the 1920s. You go to visit somewhere like Venice, in California, and you feel as if you're visiting Herculaneum.

PARKINSON: Did you go to any of the sexy, showbiz parties in America that you hear of?

MILLER: There were occasional, rather disreputable parties, set up for entirely sexual purposes. I was once invited to one of those and sat, rather anxiously, on the edge of a bed, in total darkness, while all sorts of grunting and strainings went on. While there were these heaving things one could see occasionally against the slatted blinds, there was this very decorous man, in a white coat, walking around with a silver tray, offering whisky to people who were... And that was all very odd. We started off in perfectly normal light, everyone was talking and chatting about shows, and then suddenly the light went out. There was total silence for about five minutes and then there was this faint rasp and noises and giggles. I sat on the edge of the bed, hoping that I would be seriously interfered with. I hoped I was relaying my desire to those nearest to me, but nothing happened at all.

DR ANTHONY CLARE (1999)[356]: Seeing what you know about a condition like Alzheimer's, do you worry about it affecting you, since you so represent in a sense a certain kind of intellectual vitality?

MILLER: Yes. Of course. I think that anyone who has had it in the family thinks, 'My God, am I…?' as I forget names or forget telephone numbers or find that I've forgotten the name of a painter. I think, 'A-ha. This is it. I'm on the same slippery slope.' But I think everyone thinks about that now, and I think anyone who's had it in the family always, always dreads that. I don't dread it because I think it's going to be the fall of a fine mind! Anyone who's got a mind at all, who could find his way to the front door without advice, dreads the thought that they might in fact fall victim to this.

CLARE: Do you feel any better than you did a few years ago about getting old?

MILLER: Oh, I've never been worried about getting old.

CLARE: You were pretty critical of it?

MILLER: Well, I mean, I don't want to get feeble. I'm not worried about the fact that I have less time left than I once had. I don't want to go home from the party before the jellies and the musical chairs, and that's what I always feel about death. But then, looking at so many people who I know who have died recently, you see that on the whole they get to a point where they don't *want* the musical chairs. They are prepared to go home before the jellies and the presents are unwrapped.

CLARE: They're tired.

MILLER: They're tired, and I hope what happens is that I remain intellectually and physically vigorous and surrounded by my family until the moment when in fact something occurs which makes me think, 'Well. Bye-bye. Time to get off the bus. This is a request stop.'

LAURIE TAYLOR (2010)[357]: Do you sometimes think that you might wish that you were a national treasure, like Alan Bennett?

MILLER: I'm rather glad I'm not. I'm quite pleased to be what I think I am, which is a sort of national liability.

Notes

1   This television adaptation of M. R. James's 1904 short story "Oh, Whistle, and I'll Come To You, My Lad" was written and directed by Miller, and transmitted as part of the arts strand *Omnibus* (BBC1, 1967–2003). The Colonel was played by Ambrose Coghill and the Professor by Michael Hordern.

   The script extract – which includes cut material – was first published as "Death and destruction", *Listener*, 16 May 1968, pp. 635–636. For further discussion of the story, as well as details of how Miller achieved certain visual effects in the film, see "The horror story" on pp. 260–265 of this volume.

2   "My day" appeared in the London edition only, pp. 25, 43, 44.

3   William Hazlitt, *The Spirit of the Age, or Contemporary Portraits* (London: Henry Colburn, 1825), pp. 65–66.

4   Here, Miller is directing John Wells' adaptation of Georg Büchner's *Danton's Death* for the National Theatre. The production opened at the New Theatre on 3 August 1971.

5   Sir Laurence Olivier was the founding artistic director (1963–73) of the National Theatre. Miller had recently directed him in *The Merchant of Venice* (1970). (See note 116 on p. 388.) For his memories of working with Olivier, see "Aboard the Victory O" on pp. 81–85 of this volume.

6   *Julius Caesar* opened at the Arts Theatre, Cambridge, on 4 October 1971, before heading out on a US tour. It then arrived at the New Theatre, London, for its 13 March 1972 opening. This was the Oxford and Cambridge Shakespeare Company (OCSC)'s third collaboration with Miller, following *Twelfth Night* (1969) and *Hamlet* (1970).

7   Culshaw was a frequent collaborator of Miller's over the course of several decades, including a long run of shows for Kent Opera. *Julius Caesar* was their second encounter, following the OCSC *Hamlet* of 1970. For an interview about their working relationship, see "Conversations: Bernard Culshaw" (pp. 105–110) in Michael Romain, *A Profile of Jonathan Miller* (Cambridge: Cambridge University Press, 1992).

8   Schofield, Robert E., *Mechanism and Materialism: British Natural Philosophy in An Age of Reason* (Princeton: Princeton University Press, 1969).

9   The Darwin College Lectures is an annual programme of talks first established in 1986. In its fourth year the theme was communication. The speakers were Noam Chomsky (13 January 1989), D. H. Mellor (20 January), Horace Barlow (27 January), Patrick

Bateson (3 February), David Lodge (10 February), Jonathan Miller (17 February), Alexander Goehr (24 February) and John Alvey (3 March). Revised versions of these lectures were collected as D. H. Mellor (ed.), *Ways of Communicating* (Cambridge: Cambridge University, Press, 1990), with Miller's text on pp. 113–124.

10 Betty Edwards, *Drawing on the Right Side of the Brain* (London: Souvenir Press, 1981), pp. 100–101. First published in the US by J. P. Tarcher of Los Angeles, 1979.

11 J. L. Austin, *How to do Things with Words: The William James Lectures delivered at Harvard University in 1955*. Ed. J. O. Urmson. (London: Clarendon Press, 1962).

12 Charles Dickens, *Barnaby Rudge: A Tale of the Riots of 'Eighty* (London: Chapman and Hall, 1841), p. 274.

13 "Pretending" was first delivered as part of a symposia at the University of Southampton on 13 July 1958. These talks were collected as *Proceedings of the Aristotelian Society*, v.32 (1958), with Austin's essay appearing on pp. 261–278. "Pretending" was later collected in J. L. Austin, *The Philosophical Papers*. Eds J. O. Urmson and G. J. Warnock. (London: Clarendon Press, 1961), pp. 201–219. In the second edition (1970) it moved to pp. 253–271. Those page numbers remained the same for the third and final edition in 1979.

14 Erving Goffman, *Relations in Public: Microstudies of the Public Order* (London: Allen Lane, 1971).

15 "A plea for excuses" was Austin's presidential address at a gathering of the Aristotelian Society on 29 October 1956. It featured in the subsequent *Proceedings of the Aristotelian Society*, New Series v.57 (1956–57), pp. 1–30, and was later collected in J. L. Austin, *The Philosophical Papers*. Eds. J. O. Urmson and G. J. Warnock. (London: Clarendon Press, 1961), pp. 123–152. In the second edition (1970) it moved to pp. 175–204. Those page numbers remained the same for the third and final edition in 1979.

16 Goffman, *Relations in Public*, pp. 184–185.

17 B. S. Johnson (ed.), *The Evacuees* (London: Victor Gollancz, 1968). This volume was an anthology of wartime reminiscences from 32 writers, with Miller's untitled essay appearing on pp. 199–204. Miller also featured in Johnson's accompanying documentary for the BBC2 arts magazine *Release*. This was transmitted on 24 October 1968, then as a stand-alone revised repeat on 31 August 1969.

18 The story originally appeared in *Pall Mall Magazine*, v.7 n.32 (December 1895), pp. 639–647. It was later included in M. R. James, *Ghost-Stories of an Antiquary* (London: Edward Arnold, 1904), pp. 31–52. The scene in question appears on pp. 642–643 and pp. 39–40 respectively.

19 "Views" appeared on p. 814 of this issue.

20 "Church going" (lines 55–57) in Philip Larkin, *The Complete Poems*. Ed. Archie Burnett. (London: Faber and Faber, 2012), p. 37.

21 The production he is likely referring to is of Chekhov's *The Seagull*, which opened at the Nottingham Playhouse on 27 November 1968 as part of Stuart Burge's first season as artistic director. Miller had earlier taken on Sheridan's *The School for Scandal*, which opened there on 2 October 1968. He returned to the venue for *King Lear* (1969) and *The Malcontent* (1973). For more on *The Seagull*, see "On Chekhov" on pp. 250–260 of this volume, as well as note 133 on p. 390 and note 236 on p. 397.

22   This talk was recorded on 6 March 1970. Sadly no script survives at the BBC archives and it was not possible to access a reference recording. The version used here was published as "In praise of fear: Jonathan Miller on Dickens", *Listener*, 28 May 1970, pp. 704–705.

23   Charles Dickens, *The Personal History of David Copperfield* (London: Bradbury and Evans, 1850), p. 10.

24   'They passed on to the monster, roaring in the distance, and were lost.' – Charles Dickens, *Dealings with the Firm of Dombey and Son: Wholesale, Retail and for Exportation* (London: Bradbury and Evans, 1848), p. 341.

25   Charles Dickens, *Little Dorrit* (London: Bradbury and Evans, 1870). The spread of rumour is described on pp. 536–537. The house of Clennam collapses on p. 600.

26   'Smears like black fat', 'stagnant, sickening oil' – Charles Dickens, *Bleak House* (London: Bradbury and Evans, 1853), pp. 311–320.

27   "A bit of a giggle" appeared on pp. 39–45 of this issue.

28   The Crazy Gang were presenting their 'farewell show' *Young in Heart*, which opened at the Victoria Palace on 21 December 1960. The final performance was on 19 May 1962.

29   The Licensing Act of 1737 granted such powers to the Lord Chamberlain – an office of the Royal Household – that he could veto or modify any new stage play, and without his script approval a play could not be performed. These powers were modified by the Theatres Act 1943 and, finally, the Theatres Act 1968, which abolished this interventionary role altogether. For a primer, see Dominic Shellard and Steve Nicholson with Miriam Handley (eds), *The Lord Chamberlain Regrets: A History of British Theatre Censorship* (London: British Library, 2004). Nicholson's four-volume *The Censorship of British Drama 1900–1968* (Exeter: University of Exeter Press, 2003–15) expands greatly on the Office's later years.

30   Geoffrey Chaucer, *The Canterbury Tales of Chaucer, Volume 2*. Ed. Thomas Tyrwhitt. Second edition. (Oxford: Clarendon Press, 1798). "The Miller's Tale" appears on pp. 123–151.

31   *It's That Man Again*, commonly abbreviated to *ITMA*, was first a BBC Radio series (1939–49), then a film (1943). It was written by Ted Kavanagh and provided a vehicle for comic Tommy Handley, who each week encountered a wide variety of characters which were brought to life by his supporting cast. See Asa Briggs, *The History of Broadcasting in the United Kingdom, Volume III: The War of Words* (Oxford: Oxford University Press, 1970), pp. 564–567.

32   The aggressively anti-communist Dulles (1888–1959) was appointed United States Secretary of State soon after President Eisenhower took office in 1953.

33   Miller expanded on his views about Lenny Bruce for a memorial piece following the comedian's death – "On Lenny Bruce (1926–1966)", *New York Review of Books*, 6 October 1966, pp. 10, 12. This was reprinted in Jonathan Miller, *On Further Reflection: 60 Years of Writing* (Newbold on Stour: Skyscraper Publications, 2014), pp. 28–36.

34   Translated as 'world pain,' this term encapsulates the ennui felt about the gulf between the way the world is and how the mind imagines the world could be. The expression was popularized by the Romantics in the nineteenth century.

35   "Intestinal ethics" appeared on p.88 of this issue. It was the second of eight "Mind and Body" medical columns penned by Miller for the *Spectator* in the guise of John Lydgate. This was a nod to the lead character in George Eliot, *Middlemarch: A Study of Provincial Life* (Edinburgh and London: William Blackwood and Sons, 1871–2). Miller's columns were published fortnightly between 6 January–28 April 1961.

       The cover date for the final column happens to coincide with the *Beyond the Fringe* previews in Cambridge ahead of its arrival in the West End. Miller at this point gave up his place at Addenbrooke's Hospital in Cambridge, but would continue to keep a foot in the world of medicine during the revue's Fortune Theatre run, via posts at London Hospital and the Royal Marsden. For more on his reluctance to leave medicine during this period, and his frustrations with the posts obtained, see Kate Bassett, *Jonathan Miller: In Two Minds* (London: Oberon Books, 2012), pp. 102–105.

36   Sir William Arbuthnot Lane (1856–1943) was a pioneering British surgeon.

37   The Michelin Distinguished Visiting Lecture was first published as "Jonathan Miller Reflects (on damaged brains, acting, the afterlife of artworks, etc.)" in *Engineering and Science*, v.62 n.3 (1999), pp. 28–37.

38   The exhibition *Mirror Image: Jonathan Miller on Reflection* ran from 16 September–13 December 1998. It spawned a book, *On Reflection* (London: National Gallery Publications, 1998), as well as a four-part television series, *Jonathan Miller on Reflection* (BBC2, 16 September–7 October 1998). An extract from the book – "Self-recognition" – can be found on pp. 222–230 of this present volume.

39   Miller became engaged to Helen Rachel Collet in June 1954. They married on 27 July 1956. See Bassett, pp. 78, 84.

40   David Chalmers, *The Conscious Mind: In Search of a Fundamental Theory* (New York: Oxford University Press, 1996), pp. 24–25.

41   Originally published as "What is it like to be a bat?", *Philosophical Review*, v.83 (October 1974), pp. 435-450, the essay became more widely available as part of Thomas Nagel, *Mortal Questions* (Cambridge: Cambridge University Press, 1979), pp. 165–180.

42   John R. Searle, *The Rediscovery of the Mind* (Cambridge, Mass.: The MIT Press, 1992), pp. 111–126.

43   The Churchlands had recently published a collection of their respective writing: *On the Contrary: Critical Essays, 1987–1997* (Cambridge, Mass.: The MIT Press, 1998). This included a reprint of the co-authored "Recent work on consciousness: philosophical, theoretical, and emperical", *Seminars in Neurology*, v.17 n.2 (June 1997), pp. 179–186.

44   The 1903 paper "Om arvelighed i samfund og i rene linier" was later revised as part of Wilhelm Johannsen, *Elemente der exakten Erblichkeitslehre* (Jena: Gustav Fischer, 1909).

45   Nelson Goodman, *The Languages of Art: An Approach to a Theory of Symbols* (London: Oxford University Press, 1969), pp. 52–57. First published in the US in 1968.

46   Ibid, pp. 110–111.

47   Ernst Mayr, *Populations, Species and Evolution: An Abridgment of 'Animal Species and Evolution'* (Cambridge, Mass.: The Belknap Press, 1970), p. 30. Mayr is referring to H. S. Barber, "North American fireflies of the genus Photuris", *Smithsonian Miscellaneous Collections*, v.117 (1953), pp. 1–58.

48   In actual fact, White distinguished three types of willow-wren, commonly known as the chiff-chaff, willow warbler and wood warbler. This was related in a letter to Thomas Pennant dated 18 April 1768, published as part of Gilbert White, *The Natural History and Antiquities of Selborne, in the Country of Southampton* (London: B. White and Son, 1789), pp. 44–45.

49   Ibid, pp. 112–122.

50   This is likely a reference to T. S. Eliot's essay "Tradition and the individual talent", published in two parts in *Egoist*: September 1919, pp. 54–55; December 1919, pp. 72–73. It was later included in T. S. Eliot, *The Sacred Wood: Essays on Poetry and Criticism* (London: Methuen and Co., 1920), pp. 42–53.

51   In 1999, retirement was still some way off for Miller. At the time of compiling this volume, Miller's most recent stage project – revivals apart – was the Northern Broadside touring production of *King Lear* (27 February–13 June 2015).

52   "Trailing clouds of glory" appeared on pp. 56, 59–60 of this issue. Miller had a brief stint as film critic for the *New Yorker*, filing four pieces in August 1963, of which this was the last. He returned with television commentary on 16 November and 28 December.

53   C. B. Macpherson, *The Political Theory of Possessive Individualism: Hobbes to Locke* (Oxford: Clarendon Press, 1962), p. 29.

54   A contested quote which has been corrected for this edition. It was given to the journalist Robert Sherman and derives from a press conference held by Bush on 27 August 1987 during his time as Vice-President.

55   These quotes, though in common circulation, are disputed.

56   Havelock Ellis, *Impressions & Comments*. New Edition. (London: Constable and Co., 1930), p. 130. First published in 1924.

57   Aristophanes, *A Metrical Version of The Archanians, The Knights and The Birds with Occasional Comment*. Trans. John Hookham Frere. Second edition. (London: George Routledge and Sons, 1887), p. 89.

58   Disputed.

59   In paraphrase, see Epicurus, *The Art of Happiness*. Trans. George K. Strodach (New York: Penguin, 2012), pp. 156–157. Originally published in 1963 by the Northwestern University Press.

60   Book I, lines 84–85, 88–89 of Titus Lucretius Carus, *Of the Nature of Things*. Trans. Thomas Creech. (London: G. Sawbridge, 1714), p. 130.

61   Unknown translation. Corresponds with Book II, lines 557–564 of Lucretius Carus, *Of the Nature of Things*, pp. 138–139.

62   Unknown translation of *Politics* Book V. Corresponds with line 1314 b39 of Aristotle, *The Complete Works of Aristotle: The Revised Oxford Translation, Volume 2*. Ed. Jonathan Barnes. (Princeton: Princeton University Press, 1984), p. 2087.

63   Marcus Tullius Cicero, *The Nature of the Gods*. Trans. Horace C. P. McGregor. (Harmondsworth: Penguin, 1972), p. 94.

64   Disputed.

65   "Views and reviews" appeared in the London edition only, p. 10.

66   The exhibition opened on 9 June 1967.

67   The career retrospective of Tim Scott was at the Whitechapel Gallery from 8 June–9 July 1967.

68   The production opened on 13 June 1967.

69   Garry O'Connor (ed.), *Olivier: In Celebration* (London: Hodder and Stoughton, 1987). Miller's contribution appeared on pp. 125–129.

70   George Lascelles (1923–2011) was the seventh Earl of Harewood. He was notable for succeeding Robert Ponsonby as director of the Edinburgh Festival in 1961, one year after the debut of *Beyond the Fringe* (see note 98 on p. 386). Lord Harewood was also highly active in the world of opera and made Miller an associate director of the English National Opera in 1979. – see Bassett, p. 387.

71   The 'catastrophe' was *Take a Girl Like You*, a Columbia film based on the Kingsley Amis novel, which was completed in 1969 and released in 1970. The trauma of its making became something of a party piece for Miller. – see "Q&A" on pp. 365–366 of this volume.

72   'Joanie' is a reference to Dame Joan Plowright (1929–), who married Olivier in 1961. For details of the production, see note 116 on p. 388.

73   Arliss (1868–1946) was a stage actor celebrated for his titular role in the film *Disraeli* (1929).

74   Olivier starred in Michael Blakemore's National Theatre production, which opened at the New Theatre on 21 December 1971. A television recording, directed by Blakemore and Peter Wood, was transmitted by ABC in America on 10 March 1973 and on ITV's *Sunday Night Theatre* in the UK on 22 April 1973. For this, Olivier won an Emmy Award for Outstanding Single Performance by an Actor in a Leading Role. For a detailed account of the production, see Michael Blakemore, *Stage Blood* (London: Faber and Faber, 2013), pp. 62–98 (stage), 161–167 (television).

75   Archie Rice is the lead role in *The Entertainer* by John Osborne, which opened at the Royal Court on 10 April 1957. Olivier repeated his performance for a 1960 film adaptation, which was also directed by Tony Richardson.

76   "In cold print" appeared on p. 395 of this issue.

77   Miller wrote at length about Norman Mailer in "Black-mailer", *Partisan Review*, Winter 1964, pp. 103–107.

78   Marion Crawford (1909–88) was governess to the children of King George VI, namely Elizabeth and Margaret, from 1933. Her affectionate nickname during the time of her Royal employ was Crawfie, but a subsequent column for *Woman's Own* – later collected as *The Little Princesses* (London: Cassell and Co., 1950) – was badly received by Buckingham Palace and caused her to be ostracized.

79   Hannah Arendt, *Eichmann in Jerusalem: A Report on the Banality of Evil* (London: Faber and Faber, 1963).

80   This lecture was first published as *"King Lear* in rehearsal: a talk" (pp. 17–38) in B. J. Sokol (ed.), *The Undiscover'd Country: New Essays on Psychoanalysis and Shakespeare* (London: Free Association Books, 1993). Miller's talk was transcribed from a recording by Barbara Wells (p. vii). Quotations and text references were originally from William

Shakespeare, *King Lear*. Arden Shakespeare. Second Series. Ed. Kenneth Muir. (London: Methuen, 1955). However, for this new edition of "*King Lear* in rehearsal", the text corresponds with William Shakespeare, *King Lear*. Arden Shakespeare. Third Series. Ed. R. A. Foakes. (London: Methuen, 1997).

81   Miller's first *King Lear* was at Nottingham Playhouse, opening 29 October 1969. The next two were for BBC Television: an abridged *Play of the Month* transmitted 23 March 1975, and an entry in the *Television Shakespeare* on 19 September 1982. All three productions starred Michael Hordern. At the time of this talk Miller was rehearsing a fourth *Lear*, with Eric Porter in the title role. The production opened at the Old Vic on 29 March 1989.

82   "Fool in Lear" (pp. 125–157) in William Empson, *The Structure of Complex Words* (London: Chatto and Windus, 1951).

83   Victor W. Turner, *Schism and Continuity in an African Society: A Study of Ndembu Village Life* (Manchester: Manchester University Press, 1957); *The Ritual Process: Structure and Anti-Structure* (London: Routledge and Kegan Paul, 1969); *Dramas, Fields, and Metaphors: Symbolic Action in Human Society* (London: Cornell University Press, 1974).

84   Miller expanded on the notion of a royal touch in *The Body in Question* (London: Jonathan Cape, 1978), pp. 59–62.

85   Aribert Reimann's *Lear* premiered at the National Theatre Munich on 9 July 1978.

86   Hannah Arendt, *Eichmann in Jerusalem*, p. 253.

87   Widely quoted, this actually originates from an interview: "'The secret of happiness is to face the fact that the world is horrible, horrible, *horrible*... You must feel it deeply, and not brush it aside... You must feel it right in here" – hitting his breast – "and then you can start being happy again.'" – Alan Wood, *Bertrand Russell: The Passionate Sceptic* (London: Allen and Unwin, 1957), p. 237.

88   Ivan Vaughan, *Ivan: Living with Parkinson's Disease* (London: Macmillan, 1986). Miller's foreword is dated May 1986 and appears on pp. xiii–xvi.

89   James Parkinson, *An Essay on the Shaking Palsy* (London: Sherwood, Neely and Jones, 1817). This monograph was reprinted in facsimile as part of Macdonald Critchley (ed.), *James Parkinson (1755–1824)* (London: Macmillan and Co., 1955), pp. 145–218.

90   Édouard Brissaud, *Leçons sur les Maladies du Système Nerveux* (Paris: Masson, 1895). Quoted in English translation in C. David Marsden and Stanley Fahn (eds), *Movement Disorders* (London: Butterworth Scientific, 1982), p. 8.

91   *Ivan* (BBC2, 3 December 1984) was transmitted as part of the long-running science strand *Horizon* (1964–). For a full account of its making, see Vaughan, *Ivan*, pp. 119–137, 142–147, 152–159.

92   Carlo Ginzburg, *The Cheese and the Worms: The Cosmos of a Sixteenth-Century Miller*. Trans. John and Anne Tedeschi. (London and Henley: Routledge and Kegan Paul, 1980), p.xiii. First published in Italy as *Il Formaggio e i Vermi: Il Cosmo di un Mugnaio del '500* in 1976.

93   Publication date for the New York edition, where "I won't pay for the trip" appeared on pp. 286, 287, 350. The article later surfaced in the London edition of *Vogue*, 15 October 1967, pp. 98–99, where sentences were dropped and two final paragraphs added. The text in this present edition is a merger of the two.

94   'Now, there is a law written in the darkest of the Books of Life, and it is this: If you look at a thing nine hundred and ninety-nine times, you are perfectly safe; if you look at it the thousandth time, you are in frightful danger of seeing it for the first time.' – Gilbert K. Chesterton, *The Napoleon of Notting Hill* (London and New York: John Lane, 1904), pp. 23–24.

95   This was the North London overground journey from Broad Street to Kew. Miller took viewers on this journey as part of his contribution to the documentary film series *Cities*. The episode "Jonathan Miller's London" was produced in 1979 and transmitted by ITV on 3 September 1981. The series was a co-production between John McGreevy Productions and Nelsen-Ferns International Ltd, and the 13 talks that formed it were also compiled as John McGreevy (ed.), *Cities* (London: Angus and Robertson, 1981). See pp. 108–127 for Miller's contribution.

96   This talk was recorded on 23 May 1975. Sadly, no tape or script survives at the BBC archives. The version used here – which may not be complete – was published as "Before the Fringe", *Listener*, 17 July 1975, pp. 80–81.

97   Tripos is a course structure at Cambridge University. The natural sciences version – as studied by Miller – comprises a diverse range of subjects in the two-year Part I and a single specialism in Part II, which is the third year of the course.

98   *Beyond the Fringe* opened as part of the Edinburgh Festival on 22 August 1960. It transferred to the Fortune Theatre, London on 10 May 1961 and then the John Golden Theatre, Broadway on 27 October 1962. The earliest known performance of Miller's monologue, however, was as part of *Bright Periods*, a Fallopians revue at University College Hospital in 1957. – R. J. M. Gold, "Fallopians – 1957", *UCH Magazine*, v.42 n.2 (December 1957), pp. 51–52.

    The version of the script in this present volume is the 1987 revision, first published as part of Alan Bennett, Peter Cook, Jonathan Miller, Dudley Moore, *Beyond the Fringe* (London: Methuen, 1987), pp. 31–32. This was a corrected text derived from various sources and edited by Roger Wilmut.

99   Betty Miller, *On the Side of the Angels* (London: Capuchin Classics, 2012), pp. 9–10. The novel was first published in 1945.

100   Betty Miller died in November 1965, at the age of 55. Jonathan Miller subsequently became President of the Alzheimer's Society in 1988, and later its President Emeritus. His broadcasts on the subject include *Life File* (BBC2, 5 April 1988), *Who Cares?* (BBC2, 11 May 1989) and *Lifeline* (BBC1, 15 April 1990).

101   *Così* has been a staple of Miller's working life for over 30 years. Further to the 1974 and 1982 productions detailed in note 209 on p. 395 and note 285 on p. 400, there was a television studio recording co-produced by the BBC and the Arts and Entertainment Network, which was transmitted by BBC2 on 31 March 1986 with a stereo simulcast on BBC Radio 3. A documentary, *Miller on Mozart*, had aired on BBC2 four days prior.

    The director created a fresh production for Maggio Musicale at Teatro della Pergola, Florence, opening 21 June 1991. This too was the subject of a documentary: *Kaleidoscope: Bring on the Albanians!*, BBC Radio 4, 20 July 1991.

    Later, he delivered an Armani-costumed production at the Royal Opera House on 18 January 1995. This was his Covent Garden debut and has since been revived many times, as well as screened live into cinemas in 2010. The original run was twinned with Teatro dell'Opera di Roma, where it opened on 18 February 1995. Covent Garden rehearsals were filmed for a Miller profile on *The South Bank Show*, LWT/ITV, 12 February 1995.

The 1995 modern-dress production has been adapted by Miller several times internationally: for Opera Island in Scandinavia in 2002 (subject of the television documentary *The Opera Island: Bornholm*); at Brooklyn Academy of Music from 24 April 2003; for the Mostly Mozart Festival at the Lincoln Centre, New York on 10 August 2004; at Seattle Opera from 25 February 2006; and for Washington National Opera at the Kennedy Center Opera House from 8 March 2012.

102 "3 ½" appeared on pp. 11–12 of this issue.

103 'Opportunity State' was a phrase popularised by the Conservative Party of Great Britain during the 1950s to express its economic aims. An early use was by Sir David Maxwell Fyfe, the Home Secretary in Winston Churchill's second Government, in a speech which was delivered a few weeks after the party came to power in the 1951 General Election: 'We dislike our present austerities. It is not our conception of society. But we believe that the Opportunity State, in which the creative element in our people is given the chance to harness scientific advance to popular needs, is not far off once we have completed our first-aid job.' – Unsigned, "The 'Opportunity State'", *Times*, 5 January 1952, p. 3. Later, Harold Macmillan defined the Opportunity State as a balanced alternative both to the 'destruction of all private rights of the individual' represented by socialism, and the 'extreme individualism of the nineteenth century.' The Opportunity State was described as a 'match' for the Welfare State, augmenting it with the state's ability to generate opportunities for individual advancement and personal fulfilment. In a speech delivered in Leicester on 18 March 1957, Macmillan said: 'This Britain of ours cannot live on a kind of sloppy, socialized basis. It can only live if opportunity is given to the bold, the strong, the adventurous, to make their way in the world and are not ashamed of it.' – The National Archives CAB 21/4767.

104 Alfred, Lord Tennyson, "Tithonus", *Cornhill Magazine*, v.1 n.2 (February 1860), p. 175.

105 Originally published as Ann Pasternak Slater, "Jonathan Miller: An Interview", *Quarto*, n.10 (September 1980), pp. 9–12. Slater shared the following memories in an email to the editor of the present volume:

There were a lot of difficulties with the interview, which was done three times. Originally I came to the BBC's White City studios, only to find that the square-pin plug of my tape recorder didn't fit their out-of-date round-pin sockets and I didn't have an adaptor. So Jonathan kindly invited me to come and watch him rehearsing *The Taming of the Shrew* and talk to him afterwards. When I tried to transcribe that at home, I found the tape lost power half way through and became untranscribable. So poor Jonathan had to invite me to lunch at his house and do it all over again. That's why the interview gets increasingly comfortable and expansive as it goes on.

My only regret is that Jonathan's voice doesn't come across in its entirety. I can still remember the sardonic richness with which he emphasised the 'rostrums' he associated with Gordon Craig's productions. And his irreverent, quavering warble, when imitating Robert Lowell's dotty theatrical brainwaves.

I enjoyed interviewing him, and watching him rehearse, immensely. He was unstintingly generous with his time and his ideas.

Email from Ann Pasternak Slater, 1 July 2016.

106 *The Taming of the Shrew*, BBC2, 23 October 1980.

107 *Timon of Athens*, BBC2, 16 April 1981.

108 *Antony and Cleopatra*, BBC2, 8 May 1981. US transmission was earlier, on 20 April 1981. An accompanying BBC2 documentary, *Jonathan Miller Directs*, covered rehearsals and was transmitted on 7 May 1981.

109 *Othello*, BBC2, 4 October 1981.

110 *Troilus and Cressida*, BBC2, 7 November 1981.

111 *The Merchant of Venice*, BBC2, 17 December 1980.

112 *The Winter's Tale*, BBC2, 8 February 1981, and the three-part *Henry VI*, BBC2, 2–16 January 1983. The third part was produced by Shaun Sutton.

113 *All's Well That Ends Well*, BBC2, 4 January 1981, and *A Midsummer Night's Dream*, BBC2, 13 December 1981.

114 *King Lear*, BBC2, 19 September 1982.

115 The National Theatre touring production of *Measure for Measure* opened at Harlow Playhouse on 15 October 1973. This version, set in interwar Vienna, was revived as part of *Bed Tricks* at Greenwich on 13 August 1975, the companion play *All's Well That Ends Well* having opened on 10 July.

116 The National Theatre production of *The Merchant of Venice* opened at the Old Vic on 28 April 1970. Although a film production fell through, a studio recording for television, directed by John Sichel, was completed (ATV/ITV, 10 February 1974).

There is some dispute over who conceived of the late-Victorian setting, with suggestions that it was Sir Laurence Olivier's own idea. Miller was happy to accept this version of events when writing in 1987 – see "Aboard the Victory O" on pp. 81–85 of this volume. For more on the 'puzzling collage' of memories, see Bassett, p. 372, and, for a further account of the production, Daniel Rosenthal, *The National Theatre Story* (London: Oberon Books, 2013), pp. 156–158.

117 This production of *The Tempest* opened at the Mermaid on 15 June 1970. A later reworking opened at the Old Vic on 11 October 1988.

118 See "My Day" on pp. 3–8 of this volume, and, for production information, note 6 on p. 379.

119 *Saturday Night at the Mill* (BBC1, 1976–81) was a chat show. Slater is paraphrasing Miller's appearance on *Boxing Night at the Mill*, a special recorded on 15 December 1979 for transmission 11 days later. As he told presenter Bob Langley:

If we were to see a performance of the way in which Shakespeare first saw his own plays put on, I think we'd probably find it quite hard to understand. And we may even find it, quite frankly, *absurd* because there were all sorts of gestures and extravagant forms of presentation which I think we would find very ludicrous indeed. We have got used to a subtlety and a naturalistic expression from watching the screen on television, and we've got used to seeing things done in a very much more subtle way. In those days, for one thing it was performed for audiences who were comparatively crude. They also saw it at a great distance and people had to make very large, rhetorical gestures in order to convey the effect to the back of the hall.

120   Anne Hollander, *Seeing Through Clothes* (New York: Viking Press, 1978), pp. 296–301.

121   *A Midsummer Night's Dream* for Vienna Burgtheater, from which Miller was sacked in 1979. It was during this period that he was offered the BBC Shakespeare project. See Bassett, p. 230.

122   Elijah Moshinsky took the directorial reins on *The Tragedy of Coriolanus*, transmitted in the US on 26 March 1984 and on BBC2 in the UK on 21 April. Shaun Sutton – a highly-experienced television director and Head of Drama at the BBC – took over from Miller as series producer in late 1981, through to the conclusion of the project in 1985. The complete history is told in Susan Willis, *The BBC Shakespeare Plays: Making the Televised Canon* (Chapel Hill: University of North Carolina Press, 1991).

123   This is perhaps a misdating by Slater of Michael Billington, "Doctor's dilemma", *Guardian*, 17 April 1974, p. 12. In an otherwise positive assessment of *Family Romances* at Greenwich, Billington wrote: 'Miller's greatest weakness is that he often underestimates the importance of specific physical images. [...] Miller's distaste for theatrical vulgarity also leads him to acts of ruthless depopulation: in any of his productions, three is literally a crowd. [...] In Miller's productions it looked as if the plague had suddenly struck.'

124   The English National Opera production of Mozart's *The Marriage of Figaro* opened at the Coliseum on 22 November 1978. An accompanying documentary – *Anatomy of an Opera* – aired as part of *The South Bank Show* (LWT/ITV, 17 December 1978). See Bassett (p. 386) and Romain (pp. 63–64, 116–117) for further details of the production design.

125   There were nods to Gillray also. The Nottingham Playhouse production opened on 2 October 1968 and was revisited by Miller for the National Theatre at the Old Vic from 11 May 1972, and again at Harvard in 1983. The designers discussed all three productions during "Conversations: Patrick Robertson and Rosemary Vercoe" in Romain, pp. 113–121.

126   The Centre Theatre Group's production of *Richard II*, starring Richard Chamberlain, opened at the Ahmanson Theatre, Los Angeles on 7 March 1972. Miller's commission was originally announced to the press as a production of Jean Anouilh's *Becket*, which would also have starred Chamberlain.

127   In the event, *A Midsummer Night's Dream* was instead directed by Elijah Moshinsky.

128   For the eventual production, Anthony Hopkins was cast as Othello with Bob Hoskins in the role of Iago.

129   *The Old Glory* opened at the American Palace Theater on 28 October 1964. The production had been announced more than a year prior, but renovations at the venue caused a six-month delay to the planned April opening. Two readings were held, for subscribers only, on 1 March and 2 March.

       For details of Miller and Lowell's later collaboration on *Prometheus Bound*, see note 312 on p. 401.

130   This ambition was fulfilled during Miller's tenure as artistic director of the Old Vic. The production opened on 23 August 1988.

131   The Nottingham Playhouse production of *The Malcontent* opened on 11 April 1973. Previous stagings include a London revival in 1850 and two student productions in the 1960s.

132   In fact, Miller's first production whilst artistic director of the Old Vic was Racine's *Andromache*, opening 19 January 1988. A translation by Craig Raine had been commissioned, but was rejected; Miller's school friend Eric Korn then stepped in. For the director's remarks about the two translations, see Romain, pp. 73–74. Korn's script was published as *Jean Racine's Andromache* (London: Applause, 1988) with an introduction by Miller (pp. v–vi). Raine's was published as *'1953': A Version of Racine's Andromaque* (London: Faber and Faber, 1990) and eventually surfaced at Glasgow's Citizens Theatre in 1992, with a further staging at the Almeida, London in 1996.

133   This was as part of Miller's *Family Romances* season at Greenwich, which brought together *Ghosts*, *The Seagull* and *Hamlet* in order to highlight similarities between their internal structures. *Ghosts* opened the season on 17 January 1974.

134   Miller directed two films based on Plato for *Sunday Night* (1965–66). This was a short-lived BBC1 arts strand which had succeeded *Monitor* (1958–65). The first film was *The Drinking Party* (14 November 1965), 'a modern recreation' of the *Symposium* written by Leo Aylen and Miller. The follow-up film *The Death of Socrates* (3 July 1966) – script by Aylen – focused on the *Crito* and *Phaedo* dialogues and was set in a nameless twentieth-century jail.

135   Bassett notes there were efforts to adapt *The Drinking Party* for the National Theatre, but it is speculated that rights issues with Leo Aylen hampered the project (p. 377).

136   See note 15 on p. 380.

137   Goffman, *Relations in Public*, pp. 187, 128.

138   Charles Dickens, *Great Expectations* (London: Chapman and Hall, 1861), v.1, pp. 211–216.

139   Recorded 13 January 1972. The talk was shortened for publication as "The dog beneath the skin", *Listener*, 20 July 1972, pp. 74–76, which is the version used in this present volume.

140   Their findings were published as W. H. R. Rivers and Henry Head, "A human experiment in nerve division", *Brain: A Journal of Neurology*, v.31 n.3 (November 1908), pp. 323–450.

141   Wilfred Trotter and H. Morriston Davies, "Experimental studies in the innervation of the skin", *Journal of Physiology*, v.38 n.2/3 (9 February 1909), pp. 134–246; Wilfred Trotter and J. Davies, "The peculiarities of sensibility founds in cutaneous areas supplied by regenerating nerves", *Journal of Psychology and Neurology*, v.20 (1913), pp. 102–150.

142   "There is, I think, a duplex condition: *1.* negatively, loss of control; *2.* positively, increased activity of healthy lower centres." – John Hughlings Jackson, "On epilepsies and on the after effects of epileptic discharges (Todd and Robertson's hypothesis)", *West Riding Asylum Medical Reports*, v.6 (1876), p. 271. Later published in John Hughlings Jackson, *Selected Writings of John Hughlings Jackson, Volume 1: On Epilepsy and Epileptiform Convulsions*. Ed. James Taylor. (London: Hodder and Stoughton, 1931), pp. 135–161. The quoted text appears on p. 138.

143   Herbert Spencer, "Progress: Its Law and Cause", *Westminster Review*, New Series n.22 (April 1857), pp. 445–485.

144 See "A study of convulsions" (pp. 8–36) in Jackson, *Selected Writings, Volume 1*. The paper was first published as part of *Transactions of the St Andrews Medical Graduates*, v.3 (1870), pp. 162–204.

145 Francis E. Anstie, *Stimulants and Narcotics, Their Mutual Relations: With Special Researches on the Action of Alcohol, Æther, and Choloroform, on the Vital Organism* (London: Macmillan and Co., 1864).

146 Letter from Byron to Annabella Milbanke, 29 November 1813 – Leslie A. Marchand (ed.), *Byron's Letters and Journals, Volume 3: 1813–1814 – 'Alas! The love of women!'* (London: John Murray, 1974), p. 179.

147 Charles Darwin, *On the Origin of the Species, By Means of a Natural Selection, or the Preservation of Favoured Races in the Struggle for Life*. Third Edition. (London: John Murray, 1861).

148 F. M. R. Walshe, "The anatomy and physiology of cutaneous sensibility: a critical view", *Brain: A Journal of Neurology*, v.65 (1942), pp. 64–66. Reprinted as "The anatomy and physiology of cutaneous sensibility" (pp. 3–79) in F. M. R. Walshe, *Critical Studies in Neurology* (Edinburgh: E. and S. Livingstone, 1948).

149 John Hughlings Jackson, "Evolution and Dissolution of the Nervous System: Lecture II", *Lancet*, n.3163 (12 April 1884), p. 651. This was the second of three Croonian Lectures delivered at the Royal College of Physicians in March 1844, later collected in John Hughlings Jackson, *Selected Writings of John Hughlings Jackson, Volume 2: Evolution and Dissolution of the Nervous System, Speech, Various Papers, Addresses and Lectures*. Ed. James Taylor. (London: Hodder and Stoughton, 1932), pp. 45–73. Lecture II appears on pp. 53–63 and the quoted text on p. 58.

150 Walter Bagehot, *Physics and Politics, or Thoughts on the Application of the Principles of 'Natural Selection' and 'Inheritance' to Political Society* (London: Henry S. King and Co., 1872), pp. 154–155. This chapter first appeared as "Physics and Politics No. IV – Nation-making" in *Fortnightly Review*, New Series v.10 n.60 (1 December 1871), pp. 696–717, with the quoted text appearing on the final page. The same passage is quoted in Miller, *The Body in Question*, pp. 323–324.

151 W. H. R. Rivers, *Instinct and the Unconscious: A Contribution to a Biological Theory of the Psycho-Neuroses*. Second Edition. (London: Cambridge University Press, 1922), pp. 131–132. First published in 1920.

152 Ibid, p. 149.

153 William McDougall, *The Group Mind: A Sketch of the Principles of Collective Psychology with Some Attempt to Apply Them to the Interpretation of National Life and Character* (Cambridge: Cambridge University Press, 1920), p. 45.

154 "Beyond dispute" appeared on p. 652 of this issue.

155 Miller would later act as editor of an essays collection, *Freud: The Man, His World, His Influence* (London: Weidenfeld and Nicolson, 1972).

156 "West side stories" appeared on pp. 213–214 of this issue.

157 "Where is thy sting?" appeared on p. 308 of this issue. This column was the fifth in a series of eight for the *Spectator* written under the pen-name John Lydgate. See note 35 on p. 382.

158   Recorded 18 October 1973. The talk was later published as "Mesmerism", *Listener*, 22 November 1973, pp. 685–690.

159   George Herbert Palmer (ed.), *The English Works of George Herbert, Volume 1: Essays* (Boston and New York: Houghton Mifflin and Company, 1905), p. xii.

160   Published in five volumes between 1966 and 1989. Miller here refers to the first two volumes of the *Wellesley Index*, which were edited by Walter E. Houghton and published by the University of Toronto Press in 1966 and 1972 respectively.

161   James F. Palmer (ed.), *The Works of John Hunter with Notes, Volume 1* (London: Longman, Rees, Orme, Brown, Green, and Longman, 1835), p. 337.

162   Letter to Rev. J. Bretland, 26 June 1791. – John Towill Rutt (ed.), *Life and Correspondence of Joseph Priestley, Volume 2* (London: R. Hunter, M. Eaton and C. Fox, 1832), p. 111.

163   William Falconer, *A Dissertation on the Influence of the Passions Upon Disorders of the Body*. Third Edition. (London: 1796).

164   John Haygarth, *Of the Imagination, as a Cause and as a Cure of Disorders of the Body; Exemplified by Fictitious Tractors, and Epidemical Convulsions* (Bath: Cadell and Davies, 1800).

165   William Falconer, *A Brief Account of the Qualities of the Newly-Discovered Mineral Water at Middle-Hill, near Box, in Wiltshire*. Second Edition. (Bath: 1789).

166   Thomas Young, *A Course of Lectures on Natural Philosophy and the Mechanical Arts, Volume 1* (London: Joseph Johnson, 1807), p. 740.

167   D. P. Walker, *Spiritual and Demonic Magic From Ficino to Campanella* (London: Warburg Institute, 1958), p. 13. This, according to citations, is translated from Ficino's *Opera Omnia* (Basileae: 1576), p. 535.

168   Donald Robertson (ed.), *The Discovery of Hypnosis: The Complete Writings of James Braid, the Father of Hypnotherapy* (Studley: National Council for Hypnotherapy, 2008), p. 384.

169   J. C. Colquhoun, *Isis Revelata: An Inquiry into the Origin, Progress, and Present State of Animal Magnetism, Volume 2* (Edinburgh: Maclachlan and Stewart, 1836), p. 167.

170   Ibid, p. 150.

171   Chauncy Hare Townshend, *Facts in Mesmerism, with Reasons for a Dispassionate Inquiry Into It* (London: Longman, Orme, Brown, Green, and Longmans, 1840), p. 337.

172   Ibid, p. 339.

173   Ibid, p. 165.

174   Ibid, p. 165.

175   Θυος Μαθος [Mary Anne South], *Early Magnetism in its Higher Relations to Humanity, as Veiled in the Poets and Prophets* (London: H. Bailliere, 1846), pp. 9–10.

176   William Wordsworth, "Lines written a few miles above Tintern Abbey, on revisiting the banks of the Wye during a tour, July 13, 1798" in *Lyrical Ballads, with A Few Other Poems* (London: J. and A. Arch, 1798), p. 204.

177   All Richard Chenevix: "Animal magnetism: on mesmerism, improperly denominated animal magnetism", *London Medical and Physical Journal*, New Series v.6 n.33 (March 1829), pp. 219–230; "Mesmerism: observations and experiments on mesmerism", *London*

Medical and Physical Journal, New Series v.6 n.36 (June 1829), pp. 491–501; "Mesmerism: experiments and observations on mesmerism", *London Medical and Physical Journal*, New Series v.7 n.38 (August 1829), pp. 114–125; "Mesmerism: experiments and observations on mesmerism", *London Medical and Physical Journal*, New Series v.7 n.39 (September 1829), pp. 210–220; "Mesmerism: experiments and observations on mesmerism", *London Medical and Physical Journal*. New Series v.7 n.40 (October 1829), pp. 315–324.

178   Chenevix, *London Medical and Physical Journal*, March 1829, pp. 228–229.

179   *The Elements of Physiology* by Johann Friedrich Blumenbach was translated from the Latin by John Elliotson. In all, four editions were published – in 1815, 1817, 1820 and 1828.

180   Unsigned, "University College and Hospital: Expulsion of Elizabeth O'Key – Resignation of Dr Elliotson – Meeting of Students", *Lancet*, v.1 (5 January 1839), pp. 561–562.

181   Unsigned, "The faculties of Elizabeth O'Key", *Lancet*, v.2 (15 September 1838), p. 873.

182   I. M. Lewis, *Ecstatic Religion: An Anthropological Study of Spirit Possession and Shamanism* (Harmondsworth: Penguin, 1971), p. 70.

183   Unsigned, "'Animal magnetism'; or, 'Mesmerism' – Experiments performed on Elizabeth and Jane O'Key at the House of Mr Wakley, Bedford Square, in August 1838", *Lancet*, v.2 (1 September 1838), pp. 805–814.

184   Unsigned, "University College and Hospital: Meetings of students to discuss the resignation of Dr Elliotson", *Lancet*, v.1 (12 January 1839), p. 590–597.

185   Unsigned, "The faculties of Elizabeth O'Key", *Lancet*, v.2 (15 September 1838), p. 873. Wakley also published an anonymous pamphlet in 1842, titled *Undeniable Facts Concerning the Strange Practices of Dr. Elliotson, with his Female Patients; and his Medical Experiments Upon the Bodies of E. & J. Okey, etc.*

186   'I like to recal your great goodness and kindness' – William Makepeace Thackeray, *The History of Pendennis; His Fortunes and Misfortunes, His Friends and His Greatest Enemy, Volume 2* (London: Bardbury and Evans, 1850), p. iii. Elliotson is also considered the inspiration for Dr Goodenough in William Makepeace Thackeray, *The Adventures of Philip on His Way Through the World; Shewing Who Robbed Him, Who Helped Him, and Who Passed Him By* (London: Smith, Elder and Co., 1862).

187   David Brewster, "Connexion of intellectual operations", *Quarterly Review*, v.45 (1831), p. 342.

188   John Elliotson, "Prospectus", *Zoist*, v.1 (March 1843), p. 3.

189   Ibid, p. 3.

190   Auguste Comte, *The Positive Philosophy of Auguste Comte*. Trans. Harriet Martineau. (London: John Chapman, 1853). Two volumes.

191   Harriet Martineau, *Letters on Mesmerism* (London: Edward Moxon, 1845), p. 4.

192   Ibid, pp. 7–8.

193   Ibid, p.10.

194   All Harriet Martineau, "Miss Martineau on mesmerism", *Athenaeum*: 23 November 1844, pp. 1070–1072; 30 November 1844, pp. 1093–1094; 7 December 1844, pp. 1117–1118; 14 December 1844, pp. 1144–1145; 21 December 1844, pp. 1173–1174.

195   Ibid, p. 63.

196   "Valete" was first published in the festival magazine *The Edinburgh International Television Festival*, n.9 (1984), pp. 84–87.

197   *Did You See..?* (BBC2, 1980–88; 1991–93) was a magazine and review show about television. In its first incarnation it was hosted by Ludovic Kennedy, and for its revival by Jeremy Paxman. An interview with Miller, in which he discussed the themes of his MacTaggart Lecture, was transmitted as part of the 16 October 1983 edition.

198   Dickens, *Bleak House*, p. 319.

299   *Macbeth* (Thames/ITV, 4 January 1979).

200   Miller had accepted a three-year research fellowship in the cognitive sciences department of the University of Sussex. This proved an unsatisfying experience, however, as he explained to Lewis Wolpert:

> I didn't stay in the end for several reasons. First of all, I think it was just simply a misfortune in that I chose that particular place. Not because Sussex isn't an excellent university, but it was not a good choice for the subject I was interested in. It didn't have a clinical centre. I didn't have access to the patients that I would have had to have in order to really follow through my interests, and I really didn't like the long journeys backwards and forwards on the Southern Region. [...] I found science very hard as well. I think what I also found was that an ageing figure lumbering back to this university, where there were young research students who were...first of all, wondered what this sort of tatty figure was doing around the laboratories. It was rather humiliating to find that I couldn't do the maths. That there they were, you know, tapping out on computers and even laughing at the results that came up on the screen. And I felt myself to be a disabled old fart, really.

> *Third Ear*, BBC Radio 3, 29 January 1988.

He expanded on this point to Robert Booth:

> Unless you understand logical processes you haven't a hope in hell of understanding how computers work, and if you don't understand how computers work you haven't a hope in hell of being a creative neurological thinker. Now, I don't want to be brilliant at [maths] but I do want to be competent at it, and I think my competence was stifled rather early by simply being badly taught. [...] I think it was possible for a duffer to do medicine when I first got into it. Certainly, it didn't recruit the brightest students when I was at Cambridge. On the whole, the duller students were the medical students and the people in estate management.

> *Three Wishes*, BBC World Service, 7 July 1988.

In conversation with Eleanor Wachtel, Miller described how a loss of discipline had also contributed to his failure at Sussex:

> By that time my moral fibre had rotted. I couldn't stick with it in the same way that I might have done earlier. The whole point about being a scientist is that you've got to get up in the morning very early and stay in the lab till very late at night, and you often have to perform very dreary routines in order to have any achievement of any sort at all. Well, spending time in rehearsals and dressing people in other people's clothes distracts you from that sort of regime. [...] If you do it for long enough, after

a while your moral fibre softens. But I do constantly regret it and try, often rather fruitlessly, to make a return. It doesn't work. I've become too frivolous and silly.

Writers & Company, CBC, July 2000; transcribed in Eleanor Wachtel, *Original Minds: Conversations with CBC Radio's Eleanor Wachtel* (Toronto: HarperFlamingoCanada 2003), pp. 36–37.

In the interests of balance, Bassett notes that time spent at Sussex helped Miller generate a co-written paper for the medical journal *Cortex* (December 1987) as well as documentaries for BBC2's *Horizon* (see "Foreword to *Ivan*" on pp. 108–112 of this volume and note 91 on p. 385) and Channel 4's *Equinox* (*Prisoners of Consciousness*, 14 August 1986).

201   Published in edited form as "Native medicine", *Listener*, 18 January 1979, pp. 74–75. This was the ninth in a 13-part series of weekly transcripts from BBC2's *The Body in Question*. For the book of the series, published by Jonathan Cape in 1978, the scripts were radically revised and reconceived as eight new essays; the content of episodes two and 13, for instance, scarcely features at all. Passages in chapter two of the book, "Healing and helping" (pp. 54–103), cover similar ground to the original "Native medicine" script.

202   The anthropological trip to the Azande lasted 20 months between 1926–30. – Mary Douglas, *Evans-Pritchard* (Glasgow: Fontana, 1980), p. 9.

203   E. E. Evans-Pritchard, *Witchcraft Oracles and Magic Among the Azande*. Abridged. (Oxford: Clarendon Press, 1976), p. 244. This passage did not feature in the first edition of 1937.

204   Originally published in two parts: Harold Rosenthal, "Miller on producing opera: extracts from a conversation between Jonathan Miller and the Editor", *Opera*, October 1977, pp. 932–938; Harold Rosenthal, "Miller on producing opera: Part 2 – Extracts from a conversation between Jonathan Miller and the Editor", *Opera*, November 1977, pp. 1030–1034. For ease of citation, a line of five asterisks has been added to denote the break between issues.

205   Miller's production of Benjamin Britten's *Noye's Fludde* was performed at the Roundhouse, Camden Town, from 21–23 December 1972. For an account, see Bassett, p. 212.

206   *Arden Must Die*, Sadler's Wells, 17–19 April 1974. BBC Radio 3 relayed it live on the final night.

207   The term *Gesamtkunstwerk* translates as 'total work of art,' and is strongly associated with ideas put forward in Richard Wagner's 1849 essay "The Artwork of the Future". Here it was argued that all elements of art – dance, music, poetry, etc. – should be fully integrated in a theatrical work. Wagner's *Ring* reflects this philosophy.

208   The Kent Opera production of Monteverdi's *Orfeo* opened at the Theatre Royal, Bath on 3 June 1976. The 5 June performance was relayed live on BBC Radio 3. A studio recording for television was later transmitted on BBC2, 13 January 1979.

209   The first of many Miller productions of the Mozart opera, this version for Kent Opera opened at the Congress Theatre, Eastbourne on 6 November 1974. The production was revived at Sadler's Wells on 29 April 1981.

210   Miller's 1850s *Rigoletto* was produced by Kent Opera and opened at the Congress Theatre, Eastbourne on 4 November 1975.

211   *The Cunning Little Vixen* opened Glyndebourne Festival on 22 May 1975.

212 *Arden Must Die*. See note 206 on p. 395.

213 A Kent Opera production of *La Traviata* emerged within two years of this interview, opening at King's Theatre as part of the Edinburgh International Festival on 21 August 1979.

214 Originally published in Miller, *On Reflection*, pp. 134–150. For details of both this book and the associated exhibition and television series, see note 38 on p. 382.

215 A reference to the kinetic sculptures of Alexander Calder (1898–1976).

216 A. N. Meltzoff and M. K. Moore, "Imitation of facial and manual gestures by human neonates", *Science*, New Series v.198 n.4312 (7 October 1977), pp. 75–78.

217 Gordon G. Gallup Jr, "Chimpanzees: Self-recognition", *Science*, v.167 n.3194 (2 January 1970), pp. 86–87.

218 Gordon G. Gallup Jr, "Self-recognition: research strategies and experimental design" (pp. 35–50) in Sue Taylor Parker, Robert W. Mitchell and Maria L. Boccia (eds), *Self-awareness in Animals and Humans: Developmental Perspectives* (Cambridge: Cambridge University Press, 1994). The quoted text appears on pp. 35–36.

219 David Premack and Guy Woodruff, "Does the chimpanzee have a theory of mind?", *Behavioral and Brain Sciences*, v.1 n.4 (December 1978), pp. 515–526.

220 Anne Hollander, *Seeing Through Clothes*, p. 396.

221 Although the majority of film inserts for *Monitor* (BBC TV, 1958–65) still exist, a great deal of videotaped or live studio material is now lost. Unusually, all of Miller's first edition as series editor (transmitted 17 November 1964) is missing from the archive. However, a rough transcript of the complete Susan Sontag recording session exists, from which the editor of this present volume has created a new cut of the interview.

222 The New Yorker Theatre was a cinema at 2409 Broadway which specialized in revivals. The lobby scene in Woody Allen's *Annie Hall* (1977), featuring Marshall McLuhan, was shot there. The building was demolished in the mid-Eighties.

223 Jonathan Miller, "Jokers in the pack", *Times Literary Supplement*, 6 August 1964, p. 703.

224 Penelope Gilliatt, "In praise of Carrying On", *Observer*, 9 August 1964, p. 20.

225 Jonathan Miller, "The sick white negro", *Partisan Review*, Spring 1963, pp. 149–155.

226 A programme of lectures was held at Queen's University between 24–28 August 1987 to mark the Annual Meeting of Section X (General) of the British Association for the Advancement of Science. The talks were later compiled in Jonathan Miller and John Durant (eds), *Laughing Matters: A Serious Look at Humour* (Harlow: Longman Scientific and Technical, 1988). Miller's "Jokes and joking: a serious laughing matter" appears on pp. 5–16.

227 Primo Levi, *If This Is A Man*. Trans. Stuart Woolf. (London: The Orion Press, 1960), pp. 22–23. First published in Italy in 1958 as *Se Questo è un Uomo*.

228 See Michael Neve, "Freud's theory of humour, wit and jokes" (pp. 35–43), chapter three in Miller and Durant (eds), *Laughing Matters*.

229 Henri Bergson, *Laughter: An Essay on the Meaning of the Comic*. Trans. Cloudesley Brereton and Fred Rothwell. (London: Macmillan and Co., 1911). The book is based on three articles published in the *Revue de Paris* in 1900. Miller's mother Betty was great-niece to Bergson.

230 Bennett et al, *Beyond the Fringe* (London: Methuen, 1987), p. 81.

231 See Edmund Leach, "Sermons from a man on a ladder", *New York Review of Books*, 20 October 1966, pp. 28–31, later reprinted in Bryan Rennie (ed.), *Mircea Eliade: A Critical Reader* (London: Equinox, 2006), pp. 278–285. For further reading, see Stephen Hugh-Jones and James Laidlaw (eds), *The Essential Edmund Leach, Volume 2: Culture and Human Nature* (New Haven and London: Yale University Press, 2000), p. 230.

232 Christopher Hill, *The World Turned Upside Down: Radical Ideas During the English Revolution* (London: Maurice Temple Smith, 1972).

233 Originally in Jonathan Miller, *Subsequent Performances* (London: Faber and Faber, 1986), pp. 164–171. This section was also extracted as "Subsequent Performances: Chekhov" (pp. 136–146) in Patrick Miles (ed.), *Chekhov on the British Stage* (Cambridge: Cambridge University Press, 1993).

234 Constantin Stanislavsky, *My Life in Art*. Trans. J. J. Robbins. (London: Geoffrey Bles, 1962), pp. 370–371. The first English edition was in 1924.

235 Ibid, p. 371.

236 Miller's first production of *The Seagull* opened at Nottingham Playhouse on 27 November 1968. This was remounted at the Chichester Festival Theatre on 23 May 1973. Chekhov's play also formed part of *Family Romances* in 1974 – see note 133 on p. 390.

237 Miller's production of *Three Sisters* commenced a six-week tour at the Yvonne Arnaud Theatre, Guildford on 20 April 1976. Its West End opening was at the Cambridge Theatre on 23 June, where it ran for 100 performances through to 18 September 1976. The director revisited the play at RADA in 2008.

238 An intriguing claim, as Miller did not direct a professional production of *The Cherry Orchard* until that which opened at the Sheffield Crucible on 20 March 2007.

239 Anton Chekhov, *Chekhov Plays*. Trans. Elisaveta Fen (Harmondsworth: Penguin Classics, 1960), p. 249.

240 Ibid, p. 250.

241 Ibid, pp. 257–258.

242 Ibid, p. 257.

243 Ibid, p. 258.

244 Ibid, p. 249.

245 Ibid, p. 259.

246 Ibid, p. 280.

247 Ibid, p. 170.

248 Ibid, p. 162.

249 Ibid, p. 329. Miller's emphasis.

250 Although Miller had first experimented with overlapped dialogue in the Nottingham Playhouse productions of *The Seagull* and *The School for Scandal* (both 1968), it was his 1986 Broadway production of Eugene O'Neill's *Long Day's Journey into Night* which gave the director a notoriety for making use of this technique, shearing over an hour from the

play's usual running time. See Bassett, pp. 264–265, for details of the production as well as its relationship to the 1976 *Three Sisters*.

251   The lecture "Replies and responses" was first delivered by Goffman at NWAVE III, Georgetown University on 25 October 1974, and published in *Language in Society*, v.5 n.3 (1976), pp. 257–313. It was reprinted in Erving Goffman, *Forms of Talk* (Oxford: Basil Blackwell, 1981), pp. 5–77.

252   H. Paul Grice first delivered "Logic and conversation" as part of his William James Lectures at Harvard in 1967. It was later published in Donald Davidson and Gilbert Harman (eds), *The Logic of Grammar* (Encino: Dickenson Publishing, 1975), pp. 64–73. See also H. Paul Grice, "Further notes on logic and conversation" (pp. 113–127) in Peter Cole (ed.), *Syntax and Semantics, Volume 9: Pragmatics* (New York: Academic Press, 1978); and H. Paul Grice, "Presupposition and conversational implicature" (pp. 183–198) in Peter Cole (ed.), *Radical Pragmatics* (New York: Academic Press, 1981).

253   Dickens, *Great Expectations*, v.2, pp. 65, 69.

254   Ibid, p. 282.

255   Irene Worth starred in Miller's remount at Chichester in 1973. Fenella Fielding's turn was at Nottingham Playhouse in 1968. See note 236 on p. 397.

256   Miller's *Omnibus* film *Whistle and I'll Come To You* (BBC1, 7 May 1968) is often regarded as a precursor to the television plays transmitted on BBC2 during the 1970s under the *Ghost Story for Christmas* banner. These were largely derived from the works of M. R. James. The first production – *The Stalls of Barchester* – aired just one day after the radio interview presented here.

257   James, *Ghost-Stories of an Antiquary*, pp. 204–205.

258   Ibid, pp. 216–217.

259   Ibid, pp. 47–48.

260   Ibid, p. 75.

261   Ibid, pp. 229–270.

262   "Can English satire draw blood?" appeared on p. 21 of this issue.

263   N. F. Simpson's play *A Resounding Tinkle* was first performed at the Royal Court on 1 December 1957 in an 'alternative two-act version' which was forced upon the writer, then in an abbreviated one-act form at the same venue from 2 April 1958. Simpson's original two-act version had been thus far unperformed. It was however embraced by John Bird and the Cambridge University Actors, who staged the first complete production at the ADC Theatre, Cambridge on 20 January 1959. This starred Peter Cook as Bro Paradock. The production visited the Royal Court on 15 March 1959. – N. F. Simpson, *Collected Plays* (London: Faber and Faber, 2013), pp. 2–6.

264   Sinclair Lewis, *Elmer Gantry* (New York: Harcourt, Brace and Co., 1927).

265   Talbot Baines Reed, *The Fifth Form at St Dominic's* (London: Thames Publishing, 1951).

266   "Satire's brightest star: Peter Cook" appeared on p. 14 of this issue.

267   *Clive Anderson Talks Back*, Hat Trick for Channel 4, 17 December 1993.

268   "The call of the wild" appeared on pp. 10, 12, 13 of this issue.

269   Letter from L. F. Jauffret, quoted in Harlan Lane, *The Wild Boy of Aveyron* (Cambridge, Mass.: Harvard University Press, 1976), pp. 13–14.

270   Bruno Bettelheim, *The Empty Fortress: Infantile Autism and the Birth of the Self* (New York: The Free Press, 1967).

271   Richard Bernheimer, *Wild Men in the Middle Ages: A Study in Art, Sentiment, and Demonology* (Cambridge, Mass.: Harvard University Press, 1952), p. 3.

272   'Four-footed, mute, hairy.' – Charles Linnè, *A System of Nature, Through the Three Grand Kingdoms of Animals, Vegetables, and Minerals, Systematically Divided Into their Several Classes, Orders, Genera, Species, and Varieties, with their Habitations, Manners, Economy, Structure, and Peculiarities*. Trans. William Turton (London: Lackington, Allen and Co., 1806), v.1, p. 9.

273   Charles Coulston Gillispie, *The Edge of Objectivity: An Essay in the History of Scientific Ideas* (Princeton: Princeton University Press, 1960).

274   Bettelheim, *The Empty Fortress*, pp. 351–356.

275   Maria Montessori, *The Montessori Method: Scientific Pedagogy as Applied to Child Education in 'The Children's Houses' with Additions and Revisions by the Author*. Trans. Anne E. George. (London: William Heinemann, 1915). First published in Italy in 1909.

276   William Petty, *The Advice of W. P. to Mr Samuel Hartlib for the Advancement of Some Particular Parts of Learning* (London: 1647), p. 24 (erroneously marked as p. 12).

277   John Stuart Mill, *Autobiography* (London: Longmans, Green, Reader, and Dyer, 1873), p. 5.

278   Peter Handke, *Kaspar*. Trans. Michael Roloff (London: Eyre Methuen, 1972). First published in Frankfurt in 1968.

279   Jacques Barzun, *The House of Intellect* (London: Secker and Warburg, 1959), p. 29. This same passage was quoted by Miller in his sixth 'John Lydgate' column, "It's all in the Mind, y'know", *Spectator*, 17 March 1961, p. 381.

280   The version of "Alice in wonderland" presented here is from the New York edition, where it appeared on pp. 240–247, 261. The article had originally appeared in truncated form as "Tiny Alice", for the London edition of *Vogue*, 15 October 1966, pp. 144–145, 171.

281   The advert read: 'a ten-year-old girl with no stage experience, not very pretty but curiously plain, sallow and a bit priggish, Rossetti-like rather than Tenniel.' – David Leitch, "Atticus: Miller in Wonderland", *Sunday Times*, 27 February 1966, p. 11. Seven weeks later the production office had received 600 responses (Sally Harvey to Marie Deans, 18 April 1966, BBC Written Archives Centre T51/9/1 *Alice in Wonderland* – File I). Anne-Marie Mallik was cast by early May and her camera test was on 15 June (J. P. Mallik to Jonathan Miller, 8 June 1966, BBC Written Archives Centre T51/9/1 *Alice in Wonderland* – File I).

       The eventual production was transmitted as *Alice in Wonderland* (BBC1, 28 December 1966). Due to the press controversy ahead of broadcast, the BBC took the unusual step of arranging an extended radio interview with Miller in order to prepare viewers for the 'adult' nature of the production. This aired as *The Anxieties of Growing Up* (BBC Network Three, 20 December 1966).

282   "Breaking out of the box: An interview with Jonathan Miller" appeared on pp. 41–49 of this issue.

283   Miller co-directed *The Emperor* with Michael Hastings. The production opened in the Theatre Upstairs on 16 March 1987 and transferred to the main room at the Royal Court on 8 September 1987. A version for television was transmitted as part of BBC2's arts strand *Arena* on 5 February 1988.

        The book on which it was based was first published as Ryszard Kapuściński, *Cesarz* (Warsaw: Czytelnik, 1978). It appeared in English as Ryszard Kapuściński, *The Emperor: Downfall of an Autocrat*. Trans. William R. Brand and Katarzyna Mroczkowska-Brand. (London: Quartet, 1983).

284   Penelope Gilliatt, "Doctor in spite of himself", *New Yorker*, 17 April 1989, pp. 52–56, 79–84, 86–89. Miller discusses the Sprecher on p. 80.

285   *Così fan Tutte* opened at the Opera Theatre on 16 June 1982. This production marked Miller's US opera debut.

286   Nunn's *Othello* opened at The Other Place in Stratford on 24 August 1989, and transferred to the Young Vic on 20 September 1989.

287   *Hamlet* opened at the Donmar Warehouse on 17 August 1982, and transferred to the Piccadilly Theatre on 22 September 1982.

288   The Scottish Opera production of *Candide* opened at the Theatre Royal, Glasgow on 19 May 1988. It arrived at the Old Vic on 1 December 1988.

289   Miller's production of *The Trial* did not come to fruition. Indeed, his tenure at the Old Vic was supposed to run until March 1991 but instead ended abruptly in October 1990. See Bassett, pp. 270–271.

290   *The Tempest* opened at the Old Vic on 11 October 1988.

291   Miller never gained control of the National Theatre Studio's site, which had been leased in 1984. For details of its setting up, see Rosenthal, pp. 379–382. Gill was sacked on 1 October 1990, almost to the day of Miller's resignation next door. – Richard Eyre, *National Service: Diary of a Decade* (London: Bloomsbury, 2003), pp. 123–124; see also Rosenthal, pp. 462–464.

        When the Old Vic went up for sale in late 1997, the NT bought the annex outright for £1.1m. – Robin Stringer, "£1.5m pledge may save the Old Vic for the nation", *Evening Standard*, 29 June 1998, p. 14.

292   "Cambridge diary" appeared on p.6 of this issue. For one university term Miller wrote and illustrated this column for the student newspaper *Varsity*, comprising eight weekly columns, from 9 October–27 November 1954. The preceding term's diary was by Frederic Raphael, and Miller's successor on 15 January 1955 was James Ferman.

293   From "The Good-morrow" by John Donne. See *The Songs and Sonets of John Donne* (London: Methuen and Co., 1956), p. 2. First published in 1633.

294   This formed part of a series of lectures at the Royal Institution. Six were transmitted on BBC1 under the banner *Writers in Society*: Richard Hoggart (3 November 1971), Jonathan Miller (11 November), George Steiner (17 November), Mary McCarthy (24 November), Lord David Cecil (1 December) and Conor Cruise O'Brien (8 December).

295   Michel Foucault, *The Order of Things: An Archaeology of the Human Sciences* (London: Tavistock Publications, 1970), p. xv. First published as *Le Mots et le Choses* in 1966.

296   Letter to Thomas Poole, 23 March 1801. – Samuel Taylor Coleridge, *Letters of Samuel Taylor Coleridge, In Two Volumes.* Ed. Ernest Hartley Coleridge. (London: William Heinemann, 1895), v.1, p. 352.

297   Letter to Robert Southey, 7 August 1803. – Coleridge, *Letters*, v.1, p. 428.

298   In the original talk, the location of the Martians' landing in *The War of the Worlds* was erroneously given as Bagshot Heath.

299   Steven Marcus, *The Other Victorians: A Study of Sexuality and Pornography in Mid-Nineteenth Century England* (London: Weidenfeld and Nicolson, 1966), p. 268. Miller recorded a conversation with Steven Marcus on 30 July 1964, with the intention of using it as part of *Monitor*. Although a transcript survives at the BBC Written Archives Centre, the interview is thought not to have been transmitted.

300   Ibid, p. 277.

301   Marcel Proust, *Time Regained.* Trans. Stephen Hudson. (London: Chatto and Windus, 1931), pp. 433–434.

302   Originally in Miller, *Subsequent Performances*, pp. 96–102.

303   Chekhov, *Chekhov Plays*, pp. 327–328.

304   See note 237 on p. 397 for details of this production.

305   A reference to Ivan Vaughan. See "Foreword to *Ivan*" on pp. 108–112 of this volume and note 91 on p. 385.

306   William Shakespeare, *Hamlet.*

307   The 55th Conway Memorial Lecture was published as a pamphlet by the South Place Ethical Society in 1974, with Miller's text appearing on pp. 4–15.

308   David Malet Armstrong, *Bodily Sensations* (London: Routledge and Kegan Paul, 1962), p. 1.

309   Paul Schilder, *The Image and Appearance of the Human Body: Studies in the Constructive Energies of the Psyche* (New York: International Universities Press, 1950), p. 99.

310   Ibid, p. 90.

311   Ibid, p. 92.

312   Miller collaborated with the poet Robert Lowell on a free adaptation of Aeschylus' *Prometheus Bound.* This production enjoyed three stagings: at Yale Repertory Theatre, New Haven, from 8 May 1967; on BBC Radio 3, airing 3 January 1971; and at the Mermaid Theatre, London, opening 24 June 1971.

313   On 11 October 1972, the Law on Offences Against Property was enacted. This was one of several pieces of legislation which approximated sharia law within existing Libyan law. As a result of these limitations there were concessions, as Ann Elizabeth Mayer explains:

> The amputation must be preceded by a medical examination. It must be delayed where it could prove dangerous to the health of the prisoner by reason of an ailment or pregnancy. It must be carried out as a regular surgical procedure under anaesthetic in a hospital, and all precautions must be taken during the recuperative stages to ensure recovery. Clearly the intention is that this procedure should be carried out in private with minimum physical impairment to the

criminal. The law altogether dispenses with the further amputations that were called for in the tradition rules for successive convictions of the same offense.

> Ann Elizabeth Mayer, "Reinstating Islamic criminal law in Libya" in Daisy Hilse Dwyer (ed.), *Law and Islam in the Middle East* (New York: Bergin and Garvey Publishers, 1990), p. 105.

This was part of a wider programme of hadd law introduced by Gaddafi. However, according to Mayer, on 15 April 1973 the Libyan leader decreed that 'all legislation was suspended in order to remove legal impediments to the revolutionary surge. While existing legislation was in abeyance, the law of the land would be sharia law' (p. 102).

For the full content of the 1972 Law, see Tahir Mahmood, "Legal system of modern Libya: Enforcement of Islamic Penal Laws" (pp. 375–388) in Mahmood et al, *Criminal Law in Islam and the Muslim World: A Comparative Perspective* (Delhi: Institute of Objective Studies, 1996). This chapter was written in 1974 and details criminal legislation in Libya since it achieved independence in 1951.

314   See also Miller, *The Body in Question*, pp. 20–21.

315   Cesare Beccaria, *On Crimes and Punishments and Other Writings*. Ed. Aaron Thomas. Trans. Aaron Thomas and Jeremy Parzen. (Toronto: University of Toronto Press, 2008), pp. 33–34.

316   Ibid, p. 29.

317   All Henry Mayhew: *London Labour and the London Poor, Volume 1* (London: 1851); *London Labour and the London Poor, Volume 2* (London: 1851); *London Labour and the London Poor, Volume 3* (London: 1851); *London Labour and the London Poor, Volume 4* (London: Charles Griffin and Co., 1862).

318   *Voices of Victorian London,* BBC2, 11 February 1996. This programme was directed by Miller and transmitted as part of the history documentary strand *Timewatch* (1982–).

319   Henry Mayhew, *Voices of Victorian London: In Sickness and In Health* (London: Hesperus Press, 2011). Miller's text appears on pp. vii–xv.

320   Mayhew, *London Labour and the London Poor*, v.1, p. iii.

321   "Plays and players" (pp. 359–372) in Robert A. Hinde (ed.), *Non-Verbal Communication* (London: Cambridge University Press, 1972).

322   Ibid, p. vii.

323   Chekhov, *Chekhov Plays*, p. 119.

324   P. F. Strawson, "On referring", *Mind: A Quarterly Review of Psychology and Philosophy*, New Series v.59 n.235 (July 1950), pp. 320–344. Later reprinted in G. H. R. Parkinson (ed.), *The Theory of Meaning* (London: Oxford University Press, 1968), pp. 61–85. The relevant passage appears on p. 328 and p. 69 respectively.

325   Michael Hordern in the 1969 production at Nottingham Playhouse. See note 81 on p. 385.

326   Erving Goffman, "On face-work: an analysis of ritual elements in social interaction", *Psychiatry: Journal for the Study of Interpersonal Processes*, v.18 n.3 (August 1955), p. 226. This paper was later reprinted in Erving Goffman, *Interaction Ritual: Essays on Face-to-*

Face Behaviour (Harmondsworth: Penguin, 1972), pp. 5–45, with the quoted text on p. 35. The collection had previously been published in the US in 1967.

327   Bertolt Brecht, "Alienation effects in Chinese acting" (pp. 91–99) in John Willett (ed.), *Brecht on Theatre: The Development of an Aesthetic* (London: Methuen, 1964). The section quoted by Miller appears on p. 93. This 1936 essay previously appeared as "Verfremdungseffekte in der chinesischen Schauspielkunst" in *Schriften zum Theater* (Berlin: Frankfurt am Main, 1957). It was translated from this source text for *Brecht on Theatre*.

328   Leo Tolstoy, *Anna Karenina*. Trans. Constance Garnett. (London: William Heinemann, 1966), p. 215.

329   Communications theorist Marshall McLuhan (1911–80) was a leading figure in the emergent 'media studies' of the 1960s. Miller came to question the Canadian's ideas, and this resulted in a book-length critique, *McLuhan* (London: Fontana/Collins, 1971). In response to reviews which had bemoaned the lack of material in his book concerning the 'appeal' and 'substance' of McLuhan's theories about media, Miller wrote a supplementary radio talk which clarified their differences of opinion concerning television. This was transmitted as *Jonathan Miller on the Television Picture*, BBC Radio 3, 15 July 1971. It was also published as "Views", *Listener*, 15 July 1971, pp. 71–72.

The talk provoked a lengthy rebuttal from the professor. Describing the experience of reading *McLuhan*, he wrote that Miller 'peers at me uneasily as an undercover agent for Rome.' McLuhan dismissed his critic, first as someone who 'cannot but project me through his nineteenth-century mechanism of sensibility' and secondly for being a mere comedian. – "Letters: Marshall McLuhan responds to criticism", 26 August 1971, pp. 272–273.

Miller retorted in the letters page two weeks later, noting that in the ten years since *Beyond the Fringe*, 'I have dirtied my hands with nearly all the twentieth-century media that McLuhan claims to have understood,' proceeding to argue that he was in as good a position as McLuhan to comment on television and film. Of McLuhan's science-based arguments, he added, 'I am not saying that Professor McLuhan is wrong but, more direly, that he is not, in this context, actually saying anything at all.' – "Letters: Marshall McLuhan", 9 September 1971, p. 339.

Despite such contretemps, McLuhan was Miller's chosen subject on *Great Lives*, BBC Radio 4, 5 October 2001.

330   In *The Living World of Shakespeare: A Playgoer's Guide* (London: Macmillan, 1964), pp. 13–14, Wain wrote:

> Twentieth-century attempts to revive the 'poetic drama' have very seldom succeeded. They have tended to start from the assumption that verse, and figurative language, will do the job by themselves. Actually the chief enemy of 'poetic drama' is not prose but the proscenium arch. Sitting in darkness, with an orchestra pit between ourselves and the stage, we feel so much cut off from the action that participation becomes impossible. We are still moved by the drama we witness, but we are not involved in its minute-to-minute shifts of tone: and poetic drama depends essentially on this involvement.
>
> That this is so is borne out by stage history. When the theatres opened in 1660, after the Puritan interregnum, the proscenium arch was established. But not in its fully developed modern form. Restoration theatres used a small proscenium arch,

with folding doors that opened to reveal painted scenery, so that the scene could be changed without lowering a curtain. And much of the action took place on the space – reduced, it is true, but still significant – in front of the arch. In other words, the contact between actor and audience was diminished but not quite abolished. And the theatre in this period still used verse a good deal, still considered the use of verse as normal, at any rate for high subjects. What kind of verse? Significantly, the rhymed heroic couplet: the rhythmically regular, end-stopped couplet that comes down heavily on its rhymes. Such verse lacks the conversational fluidity of Elizabethan blank verse just as the Restoration stage lacks the freedom and intimacy of the Elizabethan. The heroic couplet, in fact, is a public-address system. It chimes or booms at the audience, throwing its meaning well out over the footlights. That such an idiom should have developed at the same times as the proscenium arch began to creep forward, shows clearly the relation between a 'poetic' drama and an audience-to-actor *rapport*.

331   José Ortega y Gasset, *The Dehumanization of Art* (Princeton: Princeton University Press, 1968). The essay of the title appears on pp. 3–54, in a translation by Helene Weyl.

332   "Onwards and upwards" appeared in the London edition only, on pp. 160–161.

333   The John Birch Society is an American conservative fringe group, founded in 1958 by Robert Welch. For further reading see D. J. Mulloy, *The World of the John Birch Society: Conspiracy, Conservatism and the Cold War* (Nashville: Vanderbilt University Press, 2014).

334   Paraphrased from Ernest Hemingway, *The Sun Also Rises* (New York: Charles Scribner's Sons, 1926), p. 259.

335   *Parkinson*, BBC1, 12 January 1980. The other studio guests this week were Janet Suzman and Max Wall.

336   A reference to Miller's tenure as producer of BBC2's *Television Shakespeare*. See "Directing Shakespeare" on pp. 129–158 of this volume, and its accompanying notes, for more information.

337   *Three Wishes*, BBC World Service, 7 July 1988. Miller's choices were *1.* to possess better mathematical skills *2.* the ability to play a musical instrument *3.* to be physically brave.

338   *Agenda*, BBC World Service, 26 January 2001.

339   Miller's 'Mafia' *Rigoletto* for the ENO, set in 1950s America, opened at the Coliseum on 22 September 1982.

340   *Parkinson*, ITV1, 23 June 2007. The other studio guests this week were Meera Syal and Ken Dodd. Music was provided by Travis.

341   *The Dick Cavett Show*, PBS, 15 May 1980.

342   Stage interview at San Diego State University, 7 December 1987, published as "Colloquium" (pp. 1–22) in *The Afterlife of Plays* (San Diego: San Diego State University Press, 1992). The quoted section appears on pp. 2–3.

343   *Writers and Company*, CBC Radio, July 2000. This was transcribed as "Jonathan Miller" (pp. 7–46) in Wachtel, with the quoted section appearing on pp. 37–39.

344   *Parkinson*, BBC1, 29 January 1977. In this programme Miller was the sole studio guest. Extracts later appeared as "The director's *not* for blocking" in *Listener*, 10 February 1977, p. 175.

345   John Osborne's *Plays for England* – comprising *The Blood of the Bambergs* and *Under Plain Cover* – opened at the Royal Court on 19 July 1962. Miller directed the second play.

346   *Desert Island Discs*, BBC Radio 4, 23 January 2005. See note 350 on p. 405. for details of his choices.

347   See Jonathan Miller, *Nowhere in Particular* (London: Mitchell Beazley, 1999). Exhibitions devoted to Miller's art include *Paper and Metal Works* (Flowers East, 2001), *Jonathan Miller* (Boundary Gallery, 2003), *Wood Work* (Daniel Katz, 2005), *One Thing and Another* (NT, 2010), *Collages and Constructions* (Cross Street, 2013) and *Jonathan Miller* (Cross Street, 2015).

348   *The Lebrecht Interview*, BBC Radio 3, 31 August 2009.

349   *When I Get to Heaven*, BBC1, 10 May 1987.

350   Miller has appeared twice as a castaway on BBC Radio's *Desert Island Discs* (1942–).

On the 24 April 1971 edition (recorded 19 February), when interviewed by Roy Plomley, Miller's musical choices were: "Sambre et Meuse" performed by Batteries et Musique de la Garde République; Franz Schubert's "Der Hirt auf dem Felsen" (Opus 129) performed by Margaret Ritchie, Gervase de Peyer and George Malcolm; Henry Purcell's "Sound the Trumpet" from *Come Ye Sons of Art Away*, performed by Alfred Deller and John Whitworth with the St Anthony Singers and L'Ensemble Orchestra de l'Oiseau-Lyre and Ruggero Gerlin; "Immortal, Invisible, God Only Wise" performed by the Choir of St John College, Cambridge; Domenico Scarlatti's "Harpsichord Sonata in E major", performed by Wanda Landowska; Johann Sebastian Bach's *Goldberg Variations* (BWV 988) performed by Charles Rosen; Ludwig van Beethoven's "String Quartet No. 13 in B flat major" (Opus 130) performed by the Amadeus String Quartet (Miller's eventual favourite); and "Goodnight Irene" by Lead Belly. His choice of book was *The Road to Xanadu* by John Livingstone Lowe, and a razor served as his luxury item.

For Miller's 23 January 2005 appearance, when interviewed by Sue Lawley, his musical choices were: Bobbie Gentry's "Ode to Billie Joe"; Eric Coates' "Calling All Workers"; Anton Karas' "The Harry Lime Theme" from the soundtrack to *The Third Man*; Dinah Shaw's "Yes, My Darling Daughter"; the Comedian Harmonists with "Wochenend und Sonnenschein"; Ravi Shankar's theme for Miller's *Alice in Wonderland*; The Beach Boys' "Surfin' USA"; and Glenn Gould's recording of Johann Sebastian Bach's "Aria" from the *Goldberg Variations*. This latter track was Miller's eventual favourite. His choice of book on this occasion was *The Invertebrates* by Libbie Henrietta Hyman, and his luxury item a canvas roll containing a dissecting set.

351   *Front Row*, BBC Radio 4, 16 March 2007.

352   *The Dick Cavett Show*, PBS, 16 May 1980.

353   Ibid.

354   *Kirsty Wark Talks to Jonathan Miller*, BBC4, 11 October 2004.

355   Ibid.

356   *In the Psychiatrist's Chair*, BBC Radio 4, 12 September 1999. A Michael Ember Associates production.

357   *In Confidence*, Sky Arts, 11 May 2010. An Associated-Rediffusion production.

Bibliography

Print sources

Adamson, John William, *Pioneers of Modern Education, 1600–1700* (Cambridge: Cambridge University Press, 1921).

Anstie, Francis E., *Stimulants and Narcotics, Their Mutual Relations: With Special Researches on the Action of Alcohol, Æther, and Choloroform, on the Vital Organism* (London: Macmillan and Co., 1864).

Arendt, Hannah, *Eichmann in Jerusalem: A Report on the Banality of Evil* (London: Faber and Faber, 1963).

Aristophanes, *A Metrical Version of The Archanians, The Knights and The Birds with Occasional Comment*. Trans. John Hookham Frere. Second edition. (London: George Routledge and Sons, 1887).

Aristotle, *The Complete Works of Aristotle: The Revised Oxford Translation, Volume 2*. Ed. Jonathan Barnes. (Princeton: Princeton University Press, 1984).

Armstrong, David Malet, *Bodily Sensations* (London: Routledge and Kegan Paul, 1962).

Austin, J. L., "A plea for excuses", *Proceedings of the Aristotelian Society*, New Series v.57 (1956–57), pp. 1–30.
 – "Pretending", *Proceedings of the Aristotelian Society*, v.32 (1958), pp. 261–278.
 – *The Philosophical Papers*. Eds J. O. Urmson and G. J. Warnock. (London: Clarendon Press, 1961).
 – *How to do Things with Words: The William James Lectures delivered at Harvard University in 1955*. Ed. J. O. Urmson. (London: Clarendon Press, 1962).
 – *The Philosophical Papers*. Eds J. O. Urmson and G. J. Warnock. Revised second edition. (London: Clarendon Press, 1970).
 – *The Philosophical Papers*. Eds J. O. Urmson and G. J. Warnock. Third edition. (Oxford: Oxford University Press, 1979).

Bagehot, Walter, "Physics and Politics No. IV – Nation-making", *Fortnightly Review*, New Series v.10 n.60 (1 December 1871), pp. 696–717.
 – *Physics and Politics, or Thoughts on the Application of the Principles of 'Natural Selection' and 'Inheritance' to Political Society* (London: Henry S. King and Co., 1872).

Bailey, J., *A Theatre for All Seasons: Nottingham Playhouse, the First Thirty Years, 1948–1978* (Stroud: Alan Sutton in association with Nottingham Playhouse, 1994).

Barber, H. S., "North American fireflies of the genus Photuris", *Smithsonian Miscellaneous Collections*, v.117 (1953), pp. 1–58.

Bargreen, Melinda, "'End of the Affair' will kick off Seattle Opera's 2005–06 season", *Seattle Times*, 1 February 2005. Accessed 2 March 2016.

Barzun, Jacques, *The House of Intellect* (London: Secker and Warburg, 1959).

Bassett, Kate, *Jonathan Miller: In Two Minds* (London: Oberon Books, 2012).

Beccaria, Cesare, *On Crimes and Punishments and Other Writings*. Ed. Aaron Thomas. Trans. Aaron Thomas and Jeremy Parzen. (Toronto: University of Toronto Press, 2008).

Benedict, David, "Review: The Cherry Orchard", *Variety.com*, 26 March 2007. Accessed 28 February 2016.

Bennett, Alan and Peter Cook, Jonathan Miller, Dudley Moore, *Beyond the Fringe* (London: Methuen, 1987).

Bergan, Ronald, *Beyond the Fringe...and Beyond: a Critical Biography of Alan Bennett, Peter Cook, Jonathan Miller and Dudley Moore* (London: Virgin, 1989).

Bergson, Henri, *Laughter: An Essay on the Meaning of the Comic*. Trans. Cloudesley Brereton and Fred Rothwell. (London: Macmillan and Co., 1911).

Bernheimer, Richard, *Wild Men in the Middle Ages: A Study in Art, Sentiment, and Demonology* (Cambridge, Mass.: Harvard University Press, 1952).

Bettelheim, Bruno, *The Empty Fortress: Infantile Autism and the Birth of the Self* (New York: The Free Press, 1967).

Billington, Michael, "Doctor's dilemma", *Guardian*, 17 April 1974, p. 12.
– "Duel by metaphor", *Guardian*, 25 August 1988, p. 15.
– "Lost soul of Lear", *Guardian*, 30 March 1989, p. 28.

Blakemore, Michael, *Stage Blood* (London: Faber and Faber, 2013).

Blumenbach, Johann Friedrich, *The Institutions of Physiology*. Trans. John Elliotson. Second Edition. (London: E. Cox and Son, 1817).
– *The Institutions of Physiology*. Trans. John Elliotson. Third Edition. (London: Longman, Hurst, Rees, Orme, and Brown, 1820).
– *The Institutions of Physiology*. Trans. John Elliotson. Fourth Edition. (London: Longman, Hurst, Rees, Orme, and Brown, 1828).

Brecht, Bertolt, *Schriften zum Theater* (Berlin: Frankfurt am Main, 1957).

Brewster, David, "Connexion of intellectual operations", *Quarterly Review*, v.45 (1831), pp. 341–358.

Briggs, Asa, *The History of Broadcasting in the United Kingdom, Volume III: The War of Words* (Oxford: Oxford University Press, 1970).

Brissaud, Édouard, *Leçons sur les Maladies du Système Nerveux* (Paris: Masson, 1895).

Butler, Samuel, *Erewhon, or Over the Range* (London: Trübner and Co., 1872).

Capote, Truman, *In Cold Blood: A True Account of a Multiple Murder and Its Consequences* (Harmondsworth: Penguin Books, 1966).

Carpenter, Humphrey, *That Was Satire That Was: The Satire Boom of the 1960s* (London: Victor Gollancz, 2000).

Carroll, Lewis, *Alice's Adventures in Wonderland* (London: Macmillan and Co., 1867).
– *Through the Looking-Glass, and What Alice Found There* (London: Macmillan and Co., 1872).

Chalmers, David, *The Conscious Mind: In Search of a Fundamental Theory* (New York: Oxford University Press, 1996).

Chaucer, Geoffrey, *The Canterbury Tales of Chaucer, Volume 2*. Ed. Thomas Tyrwhitt. Second edition. (Oxford: Clarendon Press, 1798).

Chekhov, Anton, *Chekhov Plays*. Trans. Elisaveta Fen (Harmondsworth: Penguin Classics, 1960).

Chenevix, Richard, "Animal magnetism: on mesmerism, improperly denominated animal magnetism", *London Medical and Physical Journal*, New Series v.6 n.33 (March 1829), pp. 219–230.

– "Mesmerism: observations and experiments on mesmerism", *London Medical and Physical Journal*, New Series v.6 n.36 (June 1829), pp. 491–501.

– "Mesmerism: experiments and observations on mesmerism", *London Medical and Physical Journal*, New Series v.7 n.38 (August 1829), pp. 114–125.

– "Mesmerism: experiments and observations on mesmerism", *London Medical and Physical Journal*, New Series v.7 n.39 (September 1829), pp. 210–220.

– "Mesmerism: experiments and observations on mesmerism", *London Medical and Physical Journal*, New Series v.7 n.40 (October 1829), pp. 315–324.

Chesterton, Gilbert K., *The Napoleon of Notting Hill* (London and New York: John Lane, 1904).

Churchland, Paul M. and Patricia S. Churchland, "Recent work on consciousness: philosophical, theoretical, and emperical", *Seminars in Neurology*, v.17 n.2 (June 1997), pp. 179–186.

– *On the Contrary: Critical Essays, 1987–1997* (Cambridge, Mass.: The MIT Press, 1998).

Cicero, Marcus Tullius, *The Nature of the Gods*. Trans. Horace C. P. McGregor. (Harmandsworth: Penguin Books, 1972).

Coe, Jonathan, *Like a Fiery Elephant: The Story of B. S. Johnson* (London: Picador, 2004).

Cohn, Norman, *The Pursuit of the Millennium* (London: Secker and Warburg, 1957).

Cole, Peter (ed.), *Syntax and Semantics, Volume 9: Pragmatics* (New York: Academic Press, 1978).

– *Radical Pragmatics* (New York: Academic Press, 1981).

Coleridge, Samuel Taylor, "The Rime of the Ancyent Marinere, in Seven Parts" in Wordsworth and Coleridge, *Lyrical Ballads*, pp. 1–51.

– *Biographia Literaria; or Biographical Sketches of My Literary Life and Opinions* (London: Rest Fenner, 1817).

– *Letters of Samuel Taylor Coleridge, In Two Volumes*. Ed. Ernest Hartley Coleridge. (London: William Heinemann, 1895).

Colquhoun, J. C., *Isis Revelata: An Inquiry into the Origin, Progress, and Present State of Animal Magnetism, Volume 2* (Edinburgh: Maclachlan and Stewart, 1836).

Comte, Auguste, *The Positive Philosophy of Auguste Comte*. Trans. Harriet Martineau. (London: John Chapman, 1853). Two volumes.

Condee, William F., "Breaking out of the box: An interview with Jonathan Miller", *Theatre Design and Technology*, v.27 n.1 (Winter 1991), pp. 41–49.

Coward, Simon, Richard Down and Christopher Perry (eds), *The Kaleidoscope British Independent Television Drama Research Guide 1955–2005* (Dudley: Kaleidoscope Publishing, 2005). Five volumes.

Crawford, Marion, *The Little Princesses* (London: Cassell and Co., 1950).

Critchley, Macdonald (ed.), *James Parkinson (1755–1824)* (London: Macmillan and Co., 1955).

Curtis, George William (ed.), *Modern Ghosts* (New York: Harper and Brothers, 1890).

Darwin, Charles, *On the Origin of the Species, By Means of a Natural Selection, or the Preservation of Favoured Races in the Struggle for Life*. Third Edition. (London: John Murray, 1861).

– *The Expression of the Emotions in Man and Animals* (London: John Murray, 1872).

Davidson, Donald and Gilbert Harman (eds), *The Logic of Grammar* (Encino: Dickenson Publishing, 1975).

Dawson, Helen, "Briefing", *Observer*, 9 May 1971, p. 25.

de Maupassant, Guy, *Le Horla* (Paris: 1887). See English trans. Jonathan Sturges in Curtis (ed.), *Modern Ghosts*, pp.1–55.

Dickens, Charles, *Barnaby Rudge: A Tale of the Riots of 'Eighty* (London: Chapman and Hall, 1841).

– *Dealings with the Firm of Dombey and Son: Wholesale, Retail and for Exportation* (London: Bradbury and Evans, 1848).

– *The Personal History of David Copperfield* (London: Bradbury and Evans, 1850).

– *Bleak House* (London: Bradbury and Evans, 1853).

– *Great Expectations* (London: Chapman and Hall, 1861). Three volumes.

– *Little Dorrit* (London: Bradbury and Evans, 1870).

Diderot, Denis, '*Rameau's Nephew' and 'D'Alembert's Dream'*. Trans. L. W. Tancock. (Harmondsworth: Penguin, 1966).

– *Jacques the Fatalist and his Master*. Trans. David Coward. (Oxford: Oxford University Press, 1999).

Donne, John, *The Songs and Sonets of John Donne* (London: Methuen and Co., 1956).

Dougary, Ginny, "Inspiring talent", *Observer*, 20 August 1989, p. B4.

Douglas, Mary, *Purity and Danger: An Analysis of Concepts of Pollution and Taboo* (London: Routledge and Kegan Paul, 1966).

– *Evans-Pritchard* (Glasgow: Fontana, 1980).

Dreiser, Theodore, *An American Tragedy* (New York: Boni and Liveright, 1926). Two volumes.

Dwyer, Daisy Hilse (ed.), *Law and Islam in the Middle East* (New York: Bergin and Garvey Publishers, 1990).

Edwards, Betty, *Drawing on the Right Side of the Brain* (London: Souvenir Press, 1981).

Eliot, George, *Middlemarch: A Study of Provincial Life* (Edinburgh and London: William Blackwood and Sons, 1871–2). Eight volumes.

Eliot, T. S., "Tradition and the individual talent" [Part 1], *Egoist*, September 1919, pp. 54–55.

– "Tradition and the individual talent" [Part 2], *Egoist*, December 1919, pp. 72–73.

– *The Sacred Wood: Essays on Poetry and Criticism* (London: Methuen and Co., 1920).

Ellenberger, Henri F., *The Discovery of the Unconscious: The History and Evolution of Dynamic Psychiatry* (New York: Basic Books, 1970).

Elliotson, John, "Prospectus", *Zoist*, v.1 (March 1843), pp. 1–4.

Ellis, Havelock, *Impressions & Comments*. New Edition. (London: Constable and Co., 1930).

Empson, William, *The Structure of Complex Words* (London: Chatto and Windus, 1951).

Epicurus, *The Art of Happiness*. Trans. George K. Strodach (New York: Penguin, 2012).

Erasmus, Desiderius, '*Praise of Folly' and 'Pope Julius Barred from Heaven'*. Trans. Roger Clarke. (Richmond: Oneword Classics, 2008).

Evans-Pritchard, E. E., *Witchcraft Oracles and Magic Among the Azande*. Abridged. (Oxford: Clarendon Press, 1976).

Eyre, Richard, *National Service: Diary of a Decade* (London: Bloomsbury, 2003).

Falconer, William, *A Brief Account of the Qualities of the Newly-Discovered Mineral Water at Middle-Hill, near Box, in Wiltshire*. Second Edition. (Bath: 1789).

– *A Dissertation on the Influence of the Passions Upon Disorders of the Body*. Third Edition. (London: 1796).

Ficino, Marsilio, *Opera Omnia* (Basileae: 1576).

Foucault, Michel, *The Order of Things: An Archaeology of the Human Sciences* (London: Tavistock Publications, 1970).

Gallup Jr, Gordon G., "Chimpanzees: Self-recognition", *Science*, v.167 n.3194 (2 January 1970), pp. 86–87.

– "Self-recognition: research strategies and experimental design" in Parker, Sue Taylor with Robert W. Mitchell and Maria L. Boccia (eds), *Self-awareness in Animals and Humans: Developmental Perspectives*, pp. 35–50.

Gershoni, Israel and James P. Jankowski, *Egypt, Islam, and the Arabs: The Search for Egyptian Nationhood, 1900–1930* (New York: Oxford University Press, 1986).

Gilliatt, Penelope, "In praise of Carrying On", *Observer*, 9 August 1964, p. 20.

– "Doctor in spite of himself", *New Yorker*, 17 April 1989, pp. 52–56, 79–84, 86–89.

Gillispie, Charles Coulston, *The Edge of Objectivity: An Essay in the History of Scientific Ideas* (Princeton: Princeton University Press, 1960).

Ginzburg, Carlo, *The Cheese and the Worms: The Cosmos of a Sixteenth-Century Miller*. Trans. John and Anne Tedeschi. (London and Henley: Routledge and Kegan Paul, 1980).

Goffman, Erving, "On face-work: an analysis of ritual elements in social interaction", *Psychiatry: Journal for the Study of Interpersonal Processes*, v.18 n.3 (August 1955), pp. 213–231.
– *Behavior in Public Places: Notes on the Social Organization of Gatherings* (New York: Free Press of Glencoe, 1963).
– *Relations in Public: Microstudies of the Public Order* (London: Allen Lane, 1971).
– *Interaction Ritual: Essays on Face-to-Face Behaviour* (Harmondsworth: Penguin, 1972).
– "Replies and responses", *Language in Society*, v.5 n.3 (1976), pp. 257–313.
– *Forms of Talk* (Oxford: Basil Blackwell, 1981).

Gold, R. J. M., "Fallopians – 1957", *UCH Magazine*, v.42 n.2 (December 1957), pp. 51–52.

Golding, William, *Lord of the Flies* (London: Faber and Faber, 1954).

Gombrich, E. H., *Art and Illusion: A Study in the Psychology of Pictorial Representation* (New York: Pantheon Books, 1960).

Goodman, Nelson, *The Languages of Art: An Approach to a Theory of Symbols* (London: Oxford University Press, 1969).

Grice, H. Paul, "Logic and conversation" in Davidson and Harman (eds), *The Logic of Grammar*, pp. 64–73.
– "Further notes on logic and conversation" in Cole (ed.), *Syntax and Semantics*, pp. 113–127.
– "Presupposition and conversational implicature" in Cole (ed.), *Radical Pragmatics*, pp. 183–198.

Handke, Peter, *Kaspar*. Trans. Michael Roloff (London: Eyre Methuen, 1972).

Harvey, Deryck, "Caesar according to Miller", *Cambridge Evening News*, 1 October 1971, p. 6.

Haygarth, John, *Of the Imagination, as a Cause and as a Cure of Disorders of the Body; Exemplified by Fictitious Tractors, and Epidemical Convulsions* (Bath: Cadell and Davies, 1800).

Hazlitt, William, *The Spirit of the Age, or Contemporary Portraits* (London: Henry Colburn, 1825).

Hemingway, Ernest, *The Sun Also Rises* (New York: Charles Scribner's Sons, 1926).

Henahan, Donal, "Opera: 'Così fan Tutte'", *New York Times*, 18 June 1982, p. C26.

Higgins, John, "Jonathan Miller: after Beaumarchais, Mozart", *Times*, 22 November 1978, p. 14.

Hill, Christopher, *The World Turned Upside Down: Radical Ideas During the English Revolution* (London: Maurice Temple Smith, 1972).

Hinde, Robert A. (ed.), *Non-Verbal Communication* (London: Cambridge University Press, 1972).

Hirst, David, "Off with their hands – Colonel Gadafy", *Guardian*, 13 October 1972, p. 1.

Hollander, Anne, *Seeing Through Clothes* (New York: Viking Press, 1978).

Hopkins, David and Charles Martindale (eds), *The Oxford History of Classical Reception in English Literature, Volume 3 (1660–1790)* (Oxford: Oxford University Press, 2012).

Houghton, Walter E., *The Wellesley Index to Victorian Periodicals, 1824–1900, Volume 1* (London: Routledge, 1988).
– *The Wellesley Index to Victorian Periodicals, 1824–1900, Volume 2* (London: Routledge and Kegan Paul, 1972).

Hughes, Thomas [uncredited], *Tom Brown's School-days, By an Old Boy* (London: Macmillan and Co., 1896).

Hugh-Jones, Stephen and James Laidlaw (eds), *The Essential Edmund Leach, Volume 2: Culture and Human Nature* (New Haven and London: Yale University Press, 2000).

Huxley, Aldous, *Brave New World* (London: Chatto and Windus, 1932).

Jackson, John Hughlings, "A study of convulsions", *Transactions of the St Andrews Medical Graduates*, v.3 (1870), pp. 162–204.

  – "On epilepsies and on the after effects of epileptic discharges (Todd and Robertson's hypothesis)", *West Riding Asylum Medical Reports*, v.6 (1876), pp. 266–309.

  – "Evolution and Dissolution of the Nervous System: Lecture II", *Lancet*, n.3163 (12 April 1884), pp. 649–652.

  – *Selected Writings of John Hughlings Jackson, Volume 1: On Epilepsy and Epileptiform Convulsions*. Ed. James Taylor. (London: Hodder and Stoughton, 1931).

  – *Selected Writings of John Hughlings Jackson, Volume 2: Evolution and Dissolution of the Nervous System, Speech, Various Papers, Addresses and Lectures*. Ed. James Taylor. (London: Hodder and Stoughton, 1932).

James, M. R., "Lost Hearts", *Pall Mall Magazine*, v.7 n.32 (December 1895), pp. 639–647.

  – *Ghost-Stories of an Antiquary* (London: Edward Arnold, 1904).

Johannsen, Wilhelm, *Elemente der exakten Erblichkeitslehre* (Jena: Gustav Fischer, 1909).

Johnson, B. S. (ed.), *The Evacuees* (London: Victor Gollancz, 1968).

Kafka, Franz, *America*. Definitive Edition. Trans. Willa and Edwin Muir. (London: Secker and Warburg, 1949).

Kantorowicz, Ernst H., *The King's Two Bodies: A Study in Mediaeval Political Theology* (Princeton: Princeton University Press, 1957).

Kapuściński, Ryszard, *Cesarz* (Warsaw: Czytelnik, 1978).

  – *The Emperor: Downfall of an Autocrat*. Trans. William R. Brand and Katarzyna Mroczkowska-Brand. (London: Quartet, 1983).

Lane, Harlan, *The Wild Boy of Aveyron* (Cambridge, Mass.: Harvard University Press, 1976).

Larkin, Philip, *The Complete Poems*. Ed. Archie Burnett. (London: Faber and Faber, 2012).

Leach, Edmund, "Sermons from a man on a ladder", *New York Review of Books*, 20 October 1966, pp. 28–31.

Leitch, David, "Atticus: Miller in Wonderland", *Sunday Times*, 27 February 1966, p. 11.

Levi, Primo, *If This Is A Man*. Trans. Stuart Woolf. (London: The Orion Press, 1960).

Lewis, I. M., *Ecstatic Religion: An Anthropological Study of Spirit Possession and Shamanism* (Harmondsworth: Penguin, 1971).

Lewis, Sinclair, *Elmer Gantry* (New York: Harcourt, Brace and Co., 1927).

Linné, Charles, *A System of Nature, Through the Three Grand Kingdoms of Animals, Vegetables, and Minerals, Systematically Divided Into their Several Classes, Orders, Genera, Species, and Varieties, with their Habitations, Manners, Economy, Structure, and Peculiarities*. Trans. William Turton (London: Lackington, Allen and Co., 1806). Seven volumes.

Lovejoy, Arthur, *The Great Chain of Being: A Study of the History of an Idea* (New York: Harper Torchbooks, 1960).

Lowes Dickinson, G., *A Modern Symposium* (London: Brimley Johnson and Ince, 1905).

Lucretius Carus, Titus, *Of the Nature of Things*. Trans. Thomas Creech. (London: G. Sawbridge, 1714). Two volumes.

Lynton, Norbert, "How far through the orchard?: Four generations of modern sculpture reviewed", *Guardian*, 29 June 1967, p. 7.

Maclaurin, Colin, *A Treatise of Fluxions, in Two Books* (Edinburgh: 1742).

  – *An Account of Sir Isaac Newton's Philosophical Discoveries, in Four Books* (London: Patrick Murdoch, 1748).

Macpherson, C. B., *The Political Theory of Possessive Individualism: Hobbes to Locke* (Oxford: Clarendon Press, 1962).

Mahmood, Tahir, "Legal system of modern Libya: Enforcement of Islamic Penal Laws" in
Mahmood et al, *Criminal Law in Islam and the Modern World*, pp. 375–388.
– (et al), *Criminal Law in Islam and the Muslim World: A Comparative Perspective* (Delhi:
Institute of Objective Studies, 1996).

Mallock, W. H., *The New Republic: Culture, Faith and Philosophy in an English Country House*
(Leicester: Leicester University Press, 1975).

Mann, William, "Stylish 'Rigoletto'", *Times*, 5 November 1975, p. 11.

Marchand, Leslie A. (ed.), *Byron's Letters and Journals, Volume 3: 1813–1814 – 'Alas! The love of
women!'* (London: John Murray, 1974).

Marcus, Steven, *The Other Victorians: A Study of Sexuality and Pornography in Mid-Nineteenth
Century England* (London: Weidenfeld and Nicolson, 1966).

Marsden, C. David and Stanley Fahn (eds), *Movement Disorders* (London: Butterworth Scientific,
1982).

Martineau, Harriet, "Miss Martineau on mesmerism", *Athenaeum*, 23 November 1844, pp.
1070–1072.
– "Miss Martineau on mesmerism", *Athenaeum*, 30 November 1844, pp. 1093–1094.
– "Miss Martineau on mesmerism", *Athenaeum*, 7 December 1844, pp. 1117–1118.
– "Miss Martineau on mesmerism", *Athenaeum*, 14 December 1844, pp. 1144–1145.
– "Miss Martineau on mesmerism", *Athenaeum*, 21 December 1844, pp. 1173–1174.
– *Letters on Mesmerism* (London: Edward Moxon, 1845).

Mayer, Ann Elizabeth, "Reinstating Islamic criminal law in Libya" in Dwyer, *Law and Islam in the
Middle East*, pp. 99–114.

Mayhew, Henry, *London Labour and the London Poor, Volume 1* (London: 1851).
– *London Labour and the London Poor, Volume 2* (London: 1851).
– *London Labour and the London Poor, Volume 3* (London: 1851).
– *London Labour and the London Poor, Volume 4* (London: Charles Griffin and Co.,
1862).
– *Voices of Victorian London: In Sickness and In Health* (London: Hesperus Press, 2011).

Mayr, Ernst, *Populations, Species and Evolution: An Abridgment of 'Animal Species and Evolution'*
(Cambridge, Mass.: The Belknap Press, 1970).

McDougall, William, *The Group Mind: A Sketch of the Principles of Collective Psychology with Some
Attempt to Apply Them to the Interpretation of National Life and Character* (Cambridge:
Cambridge University Press, 1920).

McGreevy, John (ed.), *Cities* (London: Angus and Robertson, 1981).

McLuhan, Marshall, "Letters: Marshall McLuhan responds to criticism", *Listener*, 26 August
1971, pp. 272–273.

McNeil, Alex, *Total Television*. Fourth revised edition. (New York: Penguin Books, 1996).

Mellor, D. H. (ed.), *Ways of Communicating* (Cambridge: Cambridge University, Press, 1990).

Meltzoff, A. N. and M. K. Moore, "Imitation of facial and manual gestures by human neonates",
Science, New Series v.198 n.4312 (7 October 1977), pp. 75–78.

Merryn, Anthony, "Opera: Kent Opera", *Stage and Television Today*, 17 October 1974, p. 10.

Miles, Patrick (ed.), *Chekhov on the British Stage* (Cambridge: Cambridge University Press, 1993).

Mill, John Stuart, *A System of Logic, Ratiocinative and Inductive, Being a Connected View of the
Principles of Evidence and the Methods of Scientific Investigation* (London: John W. Parker,
1843). Two volumes.
– *Autobiography* (London: Longmans, Green, Reader, and Dyer, 1873).

Miller, Betty, *On the Side of the Angels* (London: Capuchin Classics, 2012).

Miller, Jonathan, "Cambridge diary", *Varsity*, 6 November 1954, p. 6.

– "The heat-death of the universe" in Bennett, Alan and Peter Cook, Jonathan Miller, Dudley Moore, *Beyond the Fringe*, pp. 31–32.

– (as John Lydgate) "Intestinal ethics", *Spectator*, 20 January 1961, p. 88.

– (as John Lydgate) "Where is thy sting?", *Spectator*, 3 March 1961, p. 308.

– (as John Lydgate) "It's all in the Mind, y'know", *Spectator*, 17 March 1961, p. 381.

– "A bit of a giggle", *Twentieth Century*, July 1961, pp. 39–45.

– "Can English satire draw blood?", *Observer*, 1 October 1961, p. 21.

– "West side stories", *New Statesman*, 8 February 1963, pp. 213–214.

– "The sick white negro", *Partisan Review*, Spring 1963, pp. 149–155.

– "Trailing clouds of glory?", *New Yorker*, 31 August 1963, pp. 56, 59–60.

– "Black-mailer", *Partisan Review*, Winter 1964, pp. 103–107.

– "3 ½", *New York Review of Books*, 20 February 1964, pp. 11–12.

– "Jokers in the pack", *Times Literary Supplement*, 6 August 1964, p. 703.

– "In cold print", *Listener*, 17 March 1966, p. 395.

– "On Lenny Bruce (1926–1966)", *New York Review of Books*, 6 October 1966, pp. 10, 12.

– "Tiny Alice", *Vogue* [London], 15 October 1966, pp. 144–145, 171.

– "Onwards and upwards", *Vogue* [London], 15 October 1966, pp. 160–161.

– "Alice in wonderland", *Vogue* [New York], December 1966, pp. 240–247, 261.

– "Chit chat", *Stage and Television Today*, 25 May 1967, p. 8.

– "Beyond dispute", *Times Literary Supplement*, 27 July 1967, p. 652.

– "Views and reviews", *Vogue* (London edition), August 1967, p. 10.

– "I won't pay for the trip: no chemical routes to paradise", *Vogue* [New York], 1 September 1967, pp. 286, 287, 350.

– "I won't pay for the trip: no chemical routes to paradise", *Vogue* [London], 15 October 1967, pp. 98–99.

– "Evacuee" in Johnson, B. S. (ed.), *The Evacuees*, pp. 199–204.

– "Death and destruction", *Listener*, 16 May 1968, pp. 635–636.

– "Views", *Listener*, 19 December 1968, p. 814.

– "In praise of fear: Jonathan Miller on Dickens", *Listener*, 28 May 1970, pp. 704–705.

– *McLuhan* (London: Fontana/Collins, 1971).

– "Views", *Listener*, 15 July 1971, pp. 71–72.

– "Letters: Marshall McLuhan", *Listener*, 9 September 1971, p. 339.

– "My day", *Vogue* [London], 1 October 1971, pp. 25, 43, 44.

– (ed.), *Freud: The Man, His World, His Influence* (London: Weidenfeld and Nicolson, 1972).

– "Plays and players" in Hinde (ed.), *Non-Verbal Communication*, pp. 359–372.

– "The dog beneath the skin", *Listener*, 20 July 1972, pp. 74–76.

– "Mesmerism", *Listener*, 22 November 1973, pp. 685–690.

– *The Uses of Pain* (London: South Place Ethical Society, 1974).

– "Before the Fringe", *Listener*, 17 July 1975, pp. 80–81.

– "The call of the wild", *New York Review of Books*, 16 September 1976, pp. 10, 12, 13.

– *The Body in Question* (London: Jonathan Cape, 1978).

– "Native medicine", *Listener*, 18 January 1979, pp. 74–75.

– "Jonathan Miller's London" in McGreevy, John (ed.), *Cities*, pp. 108–127.

– "Valete" in *The Edinburgh International Television Festival*, n.9 (1984), pp. 84–87.

– "Foreword to Ivan" – published as "Introduction" in Vaughan, Ivan, *Ivan: Living with Parkinson's Disease*, pp. xiii–xvi.

– *Subsequent Performances* (London: Faber and Faber, 1986). Includes "On Chekhov" (pp. 164–171) and "On rehearsing" (pp. 96–102).

–"Aboard the Victory O" in O'Connor, Garry (ed.), *Olivier: In Celebration*, pp. 125–129.

– (with Alan Parkin and Richard Vincent), "Multiple neuropsychological deficits due to anoxic encephalopathy: A case study", *Cortex*, v.23 n.4 (December 1987), pp. 655–665.

– (with John Durant (eds)), *Laughing Matters: A Serious Look at Humour* (Harlow: Longman Scientific and Technical, 1988). Includes "Jokes and joking: a serious laughing matter" (pp. 5–16).

– Communications without words" in Mellor, D. H. (ed.), *Ways of Communicating*, pp. 113–124.

– *The Afterlife of Plays* (San Diego: San Diego State University Press, 1992).

– *"King Lear* in rehearsal: a talk" in Sokol, B. J. (ed.), *The Undiscover'd Country*, pp. 17–38.

– "Satire's brightest star: Peter Cook", *Guardian*, 10 January 1995, p. 14.

– *On Reflection* (London: National Gallery Publications, 1998). Includes "Self-recognition" (pp. 134–150).

– *Nowhere in Particular* (London: Mitchell Beazley, 1999).

– "Reflections" – published as "Jonathan Miller Reflects (on damaged brains, acting, the afterlife of artworks, etc.)", *Engineering and Science*, v.62 n.3 (1999), pp. 28–37.

– "Foreword" in Mayhew, Henry, *Voices of Victorian London*, pp. vii–xv.

– "Foreword" in Miller, Betty, *On the Side of the Angels*, pp. 9–10.

– *On Further Reflection: 60 Years of Writing* (Newbold on Stour: Skyscraper Publications, 2014).

Montessori, Maria, *The Montessori Method: Scientific Pedagogy as Applied to Child Education in 'The Children's Houses' with Additions and Revisions by the Author*. Trans. Anne E. George. (London: William Heinemann, 1915).

Morley, Marguerite Anne, "Greenwich 'All's Well That Ends Well'", *Stage and Television Today*, 17 July 1975, p. 9.

Morrison-Low, A. D. and J. R. R. Christie, *'Martyr of Science': Sir David Brewster 1781–1863* (Edinburgh: Royal Scottish Museum, 1984).

Mulloy, D. J., *The World of the John Birch Society: Conspiracy, Conservatism and the Cold War* (Nashville: Vanderbilt University Press, 2014).

Musil, Robert, *Young Törless*. Trans. Eithne Wilkins and Ernst Kaiser. (London: Secker and Warburg, 1955).

Nagel, Thomas, "What is it like to be a bat?", *Philosophical Review*, v.83 (October 1974), pp. 435–450.

– *Mortal Questions* (Cambridge: Cambridge University Press, 1979).

Neve, Michael, "Freud's theory of humour, wit and jokes" in Miller and Durant (eds), *Laughing Matters*, pp. 35–43.

Newton, Isaac, *Opticks: or, a Treatise of the Reflexions, Refractions, Inflexions and Colours of Light. Also Two Treatises of the Species and Magnitude of Curvilinear Figures* (London: Sam. Smith and Benj. Walford, 1704).

Nicholson, Steve, *The Censorship of British Drama 1900–1968* (Exeter: University of Exeter Press, 2003–15). Four volumes.

O'Connor, Garry (ed.), *Olivier: In Celebration* (London: Hodder and Stoughton, 1987).

Ortega y Gasset, José, *The Dehumanization of Art* (Princeton: Princeton University Press, 1968).

Osborne, John, *The Entertainer* (London: Faber and Faber 1957).

– *Plays for England* (London: Faber and Faber, 1963).

415

Palmer, George Herbert (ed.), *The English Works of George Herbert, Volume 1: Essays* (Boston and New York: Houghton Mifflin and Company, 1905).

Palmer, James F. (ed.), *The Works of John Hunter with Notes, Volume 1* (London: Longman, Rees, Orme, Brown, Green, and Longman, 1835).

Parker, Sue Taylor with Robert W. Mitchell and Maria L. Boccia (eds), *Self-awareness in Animals and Humans: Developmental Perspectives* (Cambridge: Cambridge University Press, 1994).

Parkinson, G. H. R. (ed.), *The Theory of Meaning* (London: Oxford University Press, 1968).

Parkinson, James, *An Essay on the Shaking Palsy* (London: Sherwood, Neely and Jones, 1817).

Parkinson, Michael, "The director's *not* for blocking", *Listener*, 10 February 1977, p. 175.

Petty, William, *The Advice of W. P. to Mr Samuel Hartlib for the Advancement of Some Particular Parts of Learning* (London: 1647).

Pixley, Andrew, "Flashback: Alice in Wonderland – A dream of childhood", *TV Zone Special*, n.54 (2003), pp. 40–46.

Plomley, Roy with Derek Drescher, *Desert Island Lists* (London: Hutchinson, 1984).

Premack, David and Guy Woodruff, "Does the chimpanzee have a theory of mind?", *Behavioral and Brain Sciences*, v.1 n.4 (December 1978), pp. 515–526.

Proust, Marcel, *Time Regained*. Trans. Stephen Hudson. (London: Chatto and Windus, 1931).

Racine, Jean, *Jean Racine's Andromache*. Trans. Eric Korn. (London: Applause, 1988).

Raine, Craig, *'1953': A Version of Racine's Andromaque* (London: Faber and Faber, 1990).

Raphael, Frederic, *The Glittering Prizes* (London: Allen Lane, 1976).

Reed, Talbot Baines, *The Fifth Form at St Dominic's* (London: Thames Publishing, 1951).

Rennie, Bryan (ed.), *Mircea Eliade: A Critical Reader* (London: Equinox, 2006).

Rivers, W. H. R., *Instinct and the Unconscious: A Contribution to a Biological Theory of the Psycho-Neuroses*. Second Edition. (London: Cambridge University Press, 1922).

– (with Henry Head), "A human experiment in nerve division", *Brain: A Journal of Neurology*, v.31 n.3 (November 1908), pp. 323–450.

Roberts, Peter, "Theatregoers' chance to spot the winners", *Times*, 11 September 1968, p. 8.

Robertson, Donald (ed.), *The Discovery of Hypnosis: The Complete Writings of James Braid, the Father of Hypnotherapy* (Studley: National Council for Hypnotherapy, 2008).

Romain, Michael, *A Profile of Jonathan Miller* (Cambridge: Cambridge University Press, 1992).

Rosenthal, Daniel, *The National Theatre Story* (London: Oberon Books, 2013).

Rosenthal, Harold, "Miller on producing opera: extracts from a conversation between Jonathan Miller and the Editor", *Opera*, October 1977, pp. 932–938.

– "Miller on producing opera: Part 2 – Extracts from a conversation between Jonathan Miller and the Editor", *Opera*, November 1977, pp. 1030–1034.

Rutt, John Towill (ed.), *Life and Correspondence of Joseph Priestley, Volume 2* (London: R. Hunter, M. Eaton and C. Fox, 1832).

Ryle, Gilbert, *The Concept of Mind* (London: Hutchinson's University Library, 1949).

Schilder, Paul, *The Image and Appearance of the Human Body: Studies in the Constructive Energies of the Psyche* (New York: International Universities Press, 1950).

Schofield, Robert E., *Mechanism and Materialism: British Natural Philosophy in An Age of Reason* (Princeton: Princeton University Press, 1969).

Searle, John R., *The Rediscovery of the Mind* (Cambridge, Mass.: The MIT Press, 1992).

Shakespeare, William, *King Lear*. Arden Shakespeare. Second Series. Ed. Kenneth Muir. (London: Methuen, 1955).

– *Antony and Cleopatra*. Arden Shakespeare. Third Series. Ed. John Wilders. (London: Methuen, 1995).

– *King Lear*. Arden Shakespeare. Third Series. Ed. R. A. Foakes. (London: Methuen, 1997).

– *Othello*. Arden Shakespeare. Third Series. Ed. E. A. J. Honigmann. (London: Methuen, 1997).

– *Hamlet*. Arden Shakespeare. Third Series. Eds Ann Thompson and Neil Taylor. (London: Methuen, 2006).

– *The Taming of the Shrew*. Arden Shakespeare. Third Series. Ed. Barbara Hodgdon. (London: Methuen, 2010).

Shaw, Bernard, *Back to Methuselah: A Metabiological Pentateuch* (London: Constable and Co., 1922).

Shellard, Dominic and Steve Nicholson with Miriam Handley (eds), *The Lord Chamberlain Regrets: A History of British Theatre Censorship* (London: British Library, 2004).

Simpson, N. F., *Collected Plays* (London: Faber and Faber, 2013).

Slater, Ann Pasternak, "Jonathan Miller: An Interview", *Quarto*, n.10 (September 1980), pp. 9–12.

Sokol, B. J. (ed.), *The Undiscover'd Country: New Essays on Psychoanalysis and Shakespeare* (London: Free Association Books, 1993).

Θυος Μαθος [Mary Anne South], *Early Magnetism in its Higher Relations to Humanity, as Veiled in the Poets and Prophets* (London: H. Bailliere, 1846).

Spencer, Herbert, "Progress: Its Law and Cause", *Westminster Review*, New Series n.22 (April 1857), pp. 445–485.

Stanislavsky, Constantin, *My Life in Art*. Trans. J. J. Robbins. (London: Geoffrey Bles, 1962).

Stendhal [Marie-Henri Beyle], *Le Rouge et le Noir: Chronique du XIX Siècle* (Paris: René Hilsum, 1831).

Stenger, Victor J., *Physics and Psychics: The Search for a World Beyond the Senses* (Buffalo: Prometheus Books, 1990).

Stokes, Patrick and Adam Buben, *Kierkegaard and Death* (Bloomington and Indianapolis: Indiana University Press, 2011).

Strawson, P. F., "On referring", *Mind: A Quarterly Review of Psychology and Philosophy*, New Series v.59 n.235 (July 1950), pp. 320–344.

– "On referring" in Parkinson (ed.), *The Theory of Meaning*, pp. 61–85.

Stringer, Robin, "£1.5m pledge may save the Old Vic for the nation", *Evening Standard*, 29 June 1998, p. 14.

Sutcliffe, Tom, "A summer storm", *Guardian*, 17 May 1988, p. 37.

Svevo, Italo, *Confessions of Zeno*. Trans. Beryl De Zoete. (London and New York: Putnam, 1930).

Tennyson, Alfred, Lord, *In Memoriam*. Fifth edition. (London: Edward Moxon, 1851).

– "Tithonus", *Cornhill Magazine*, v.1 n.2 (February 1860), pp. 175–176.

Thackeray, William Makepeace, *The History of Pendennis; His Fortunes and Misfortunes, His Friends and His Greatest Enemy* (London: Bardbury and Evans, 1850). Two volumes.

– *The Adventures of Philip on His Way Through the World; Shewing Who Robbed Him, Who Helped Him, and Who Passed Him By* (London: Smith, Elder and Co., 1862). Three volumes.

Tolstoy, Leo, *Anna Karenina*. Trans. Constance Garnett. (London: William Heinemann, 1966).

Tommasini, Anthony, "A modern 'Così,' with spike heels and leather", *New York Times*, 12 August 2004, p. E1.

Townshend, Chauncy Hare, *Facts in Mesmerism, with Reasons for a Dispassionate Inquiry Into It* (London: Longman, Orme, Brown, Green, and Longmans, 1840).

Trotter, Wilfred and H. Morriston Davies, "Experimental studies in the innervation of the skin",

Journal of Physiology, v.38 n.2/3 (9 February 1909), pp. 134–246.

Trotter, Wilfred and J. Davies, "The peculiarities of sensibility founds in cutaneous areas supplied by regenerating nerves", *Journal of Psychology and Neurology*, v.20 (1913), pp. 102–150.

Turner, Victor W., *Schism and Continuity in an African Society: A Study of Ndembu Village Life* (Manchester: Manchester University Press, 1957).

– *The Ritual Process: Structure and Anti-Structure* (London: Routledge and Kegan Paul, 1969).

– *Dramas, Fields, and Metaphors: Symbolic Action in Human Society* (London: Cornell University Press, 1974).

Unsigned, "'Animal magnetism'; or, 'Mesmerism' – Experiments performed on Elizabeth and Jane O'Key at the House of Mr Wakley, Bedford Square, in August 1838", *Lancet*, v.2 (1 September 1838), pp. 805–814.

– "The faculties of Elizabeth O'Key", *Lancet*, v.2 (15 September 1838), pp. 873–877.

– "University College and Hospital: Expulsion of Elizabeth O'Key – Resignation of Dr Elliotson – Meeting of Students", *Lancet*, v.1 (5 January 1839), pp. 561–562.

– "University College and Hospital: Meetings of students to discuss the resignation of Dr Elliotson", *Lancet*, v.1 (12 January 1839), pp. 590–597.

– "The 'Opportunity State'", *Times*, 5 January 1952, p. 3.

– "Theatres", *Times*, 19 December 1960, p. 2.

– "Ballot for last night of Crazy Gang", *Times*, 15 March 1962, p. 8.

– "Farewell to the Crazy Gang", *Times*, 21 May 1962, p. 5.

– "Court Circular", *Times*, 8 June 1967, p. 12.

– "Cues", *Plays and Players*, October 1968, p. 8.

– "New plays at Nottingham", *Times*, 14 August 1969, p. 11.

– "Miller to direct 'Becket'", *Stage and Television Today*, 2 September 1971, p. 1.

– "Cues", *Plays and Players*, October 1971, p. 10.

– [advert for Arts Theatre and Cinema], *Cambridge Evening News*, 1 October 1971, p. 2.

– "Legit bits", *Variety*, 16 February 1972, p. 70.

– [advert for New Theatre], *Observer*, 20 February 1972, p. 22.

– [advert for Nottingham Playhouse], *Guardian*, 11 April 1973, p. 18.

– [advert for Chichester Festival Theatre], *Guardian*, 23 May 1973, p. 15.

– "Measure for Measure on tour", *Times*, 24 September 1973, p. 8.

– [advert for Greenwich Theatre], *Guardian*, 11 January 1974, p. 6.

– [advert for Sadler's Wells], *Guardian*, 23 March 1974, p. 8.

– "Kent Opera", *Times*, 18 October 1974, p. 14.

– "On the way", *Stage and Television Today*, 22 April 1976, p. 1.

– "'Three Sisters' at the Cambridge Theatre", *Times*, 18 June 1976, p. 9.

– "Entertainments", *Times*, 18 September 1976, p. 8.

– "Television this week", *New York Times*, 11 May 1980, p. D35.

– [advert for Donmar Warehouse], *Observer*, 19 September 1982, p. 35.

– "Currently running", *London Theatre Record*, v.7 n.6 (1987), p. 300.

– "Currently running", *London Theatre Record*, v.7 n.18 (1987), p. 1092.

– "Classical", *Guardian*, 17 May 1988, p. 37.

– [advert for Old Vic], *Observer*, 19 June 1988, p. 40.

– [advert for Old Vic], *Guardian*, 17 August 1988, p. 34.

– *Cambridge Evening News* (What's On supplement), 10 February 1989, p. 7.

– "Listings", *Guardian*, 10 July 1989, p. 5.

Vaughan, Ivan, *Ivan: Living with Parkinson's Disease* (London: Macmillan, 1986).

Vickers, Brian (ed.), *Occult and Scientific Mentalities in the Renaissance* (Cambridge: Cambridge University Press, 1984).

Wachtel, Eleanor, *Original Minds: Conversations with CBC Radio's Eleanor Wachtel* (Toronto: HarperFlamingoCanada 2003).

Wagner, Richard, *Kunstwerk der Zukunft* (Leipzig: 1850).

Wain, John, *The Living World of Shakespeare: A Playgoer's Guide* (London: Macmillan, 1964).

Wakley, Thomas [uncredited], *Undeniable Facts Concerning the Strange Practices of Dr. Elliotson, with his Female Patients; and his Medical Experiments Upon the Bodies of E. & J. Okey, etc.* (London: 1842).

Walker, D. P., *Spiritual and Demonic Magic From Ficino to Campanella* (London: Warburg Institute, 1958).

Walker, Martin, "A prince caught in a bottleneck", *Guardian*, 13 August 1982, p. 11.

Walshe, F. M. R., "The anatomy and physiology of cutaneous sensibility: a critical view", *Brain: A Journal of Neurology*, v.65 (1942), pp. 48–112.

– *Critical Studies in Neurology* (Edinburgh: E. and S. Livingstone, 1948).

Wardle, Irving, "The uniqueness of Chekhov", *Times*, 30 November 1968, p. 21.

– "Julius Caesar", *Times*, 5 October 1971, p. 17.

– "The School for Scandal", *Times*, 12 May 1972, p. 10.

– "Shakespeare's moral doublethink", *Times*, 11 July 1975, p. 8.

– "New view of the Duke", *Times,* 14 August 1975, p. 12.

Wells, H. G., *The Time Machine: An Invention* (London: William Heinemann, 1895).

– *The War of the Worlds* (London: William Heinemann, 1898).

– *The Shape of Things to Come* (London: Hutchinson and Co., 1933).

Whewell, William, *The Philosophy of the Inductive Sciences, Founded Upon Their History* (London: John W. Parker, 1840). Two volumes.

White, Gilbert, *The Natural History and Antiquities of Selborne, in the Country of Southampton* (London: B. White and Son, 1789).

Willett, John (ed.), *Brecht on Theatre: The Development of an Aesthetic* (London: Methuen, 1964).

Willis, Susan, *The BBC Shakespeare Plays: Making the Televised Canon* (Chapel Hill: University of North Carolina Press, 1991).

Wood, Alan, *Bertrand Russell: The Passionate Sceptic* (London: Allen and Unwin, 1957).

Wordsworth, William and Samuel Taylor Coleridge, *Lyrical Ballads, with A Few Other Poems* (London: J. and A. Arch, 1798).

Young, Thomas, *A Course of Lectures on Natural Philosophy and the Mechanical Arts, Volume 1* (London: Joseph Johnson, 1807).

Zolotow, Sam, "Lowell finishes drama trilogy", *New York Times*, 9 October 1963, p. 46.

– "Church theater to be renovated", *New York Times*, 12 February 1964, p. 30.

– "Lowell's 'Old Glory' to open American Palace Theatre", *New York Times*, 5 October 1964, p. 42.

Broadcast sources

Agenda (BBC World Service, 26 January 2001).

Alice in Wonderland (BBC1, 28 December 1966).

All's Well That Ends Well (*Television Shakespeare*, BBC2, 4 January 1981).

"Alternative worlds" (*Writers in Society*, BBC1, 11 November 1971).

Antony and Cleopatra (WNET/PBS, 20 April 1981; *Television Shakespeare*, BBC2, 8 May 1981).

The Anxieties of Growing Up (BBC Network Three, 20 December 1966).

Arden Must Die (BBC Radio 3, 19 April 1974).

Boxing Night at the Mill (BBC1, 26 December 1979).

Bring on the Albanians! (*Kaleidoscope*, BBC Radio 4, 20 July 1991).

Clive Anderson Talks Back (Hat Trick for Channel 4, 17 December 1993).

"A conversation with Richard Dawkins" (*The Atheism Tapes*, 116 Films for BBC4, 8 November 2004).

"A conversation with Susan Sontag" (*Monitor*, BBC1, 17 November 1964).

Così fan Tutte (BBC2, 31 March 1986).

The Death of Socrates (*Sunday Night*, BBC1, 3 July 1966).

Desert Island Discs (BBC Radio 4, 24 April 1971).

Desert Island Discs (BBC Radio 4, 23 January 2005).

The Dick Cavett Show (PBS, 15 May 1980).

The Dick Cavett Show (PBS, 16 May 1980).

Dickens (BBC Radio 3, 31 May 1970).

Did You See..? (BBC2, 16 October 1983).

The Drinking Party (*Sunday Night*, BBC1, 14 November 1965).

The Emperor (*Arena*, BBC2, 5 February 1988).

The Evacuees (*Release*, BBC2, 24 October 1968).

Front Row (BBC Radio 4, 16 March 2007).

The Glittering Prizes (BBC2, 21 January–25 February 1976).

Great Lives (BBC Radio 4, 5 October 2001).

Henry VI (*Television Shakespeare*, BBC2, 2–16 January 1983).

The Horror Story: "Ghosts" (*Study on 3*, BBC Radio 3, 23 December 1971).

In Confidence (Associated-Rediffusion for Sky Arts, 11 May 2010).

In the Psychiatrist's Chair (Michael Ember Associates for BBC Radio 4, 12 September 1999).

Ivan (*Horizon*, BBC2, 3 December 1984).

Jonathan Miller Directs (BBC2, 7 May 1981).

Jonathan Miller on Reflection (BBC2, 16 September–7 October 1998).

Jonathan Miller on the Television Picture (BBC Radio 3, 15 July 1971).

Jonathan Miller's London (1979; *Cities*, ITV, 3 September 1981).

King Lear (*Play of the Month*, BBC1, 23 March 1975).

King Lear (*Television Shakespeare*, BBC2, 19 September 1982).

Kirsty Wark Talks to Jonathan Miller (BBC4, 11 October 2004).

The Lebrecht Interview (BBC Radio 3, 31 August 2009).

Life File (BBC2, 5 April 1988).

Lifeline (BBC1, 15 April 1990).

Long Day's Journey into Night (ABC, 10 March 1973; *Sunday Night Theatre*, ITV, 22 April 1973).

Macbeth (Thames/ITV, 4 January 1979).

Man: The Double Animal (*Are Hierarchies Necessary?*, BBC Radio 3, 3 July 1972).

The Merchant of Venice (ATV/ITV, 10 February 1974).

The Merchant of Venice (*Television Shakespeare*, BBC2, 17 December 1980).

Mesmerism in Nineteenth-Century England (BBC Radio 3, 24 October 1973).

A Midsummer Night's Dream (*Television Shakespeare*, BBC2, 13 December 1981).

Miller on Mozart (BBC2, 27 March 1986).

"Native medicine" (*The Body in Question*, BBC2, 15 January 1979).

The Opera Island: Bornholm (DR (Denmark), 2002).

Orfeo (BBC Radio 3, 5 June 1976).

Orfeo (BBC2, 13 January 1979).

Othello (*Television Shakespeare*, BBC2, 4 October 1981).

Parkinson (BBC1, 29 January 1977).

Parkinson (BBC1, 12 January 1980).

Parkinson (ITV1, 23 June 2007).

Prisoners of Consciousness (*Equinox*, Uden Associates for Channel 4, 14 August 1986).

Prometheus Bound (BBC Radio 3, 3 January 1971).

"Shadows of doubt" (*Atheism: A Rough History of Disbelief*, 116 Films for BBC4, 11 October 2004).

The South Bank Show (LWT/ITV, 12 February 1995).

The Stalls of Barchester (*A Ghost Story for Christmas*, BBC1, 24 December 1971).

The Strongest Influence in my Life (BBC Radio 4, 27 May 1975).

The Taming of the Shrew (*Television Shakespeare*, BBC2, 23 October 1980).

Third Ear (BBC Radio 3, 29 January 1988).

Three Wishes (BBC World Service, 7 July 1988).

Timon of Athens (*Television Shakespeare*, BBC2, 16 April 1981).

The Tragedy of Coriolanus (WNET/PBS, 26 March 1984; *Television Shakespeare*, BBC2, 21 April 1984).

Troilus and Cressida (*Television Shakespeare*, BBC2, 7 November 1981).

Voices of Victorian London (*Timewatch*, BBC2, 11 February 1996).

When I Get to Heaven (BBC1, 10 May 1987).

Whistle and I'll Come To You (*Omnibus*, BBC1, 7 May 1968).

Who Cares? (BBC2, 11 May 1989).

The Winter's Tale (*Television Shakespeare*, BBC2, 8 February 1981).

Writers & Company (CBC, July 2000).

Miscellaneous sources

BBC Written Archives Centre

Sally Harvey to Marie Deans, 18 April 1966, WAC T51/9/1 Alice in Wonderland
   – File I.

J. P. Mallik to Jonathan Miller, 8 June 1966, WAC T51/9/1 Alice in Wonderland
   – File I.

The National Archives

Extracts from a draft for a speech to be given by new Prime Minister Harold Macmillan at Leicester on 18 March 1957 (CAB 21/4767).

Index